PRENTICE-HALL, INC.
Englewood Cliffs, New Jersey 07632

Stephen P. Robbins
San Diego State University

SECOND EDITION
THE ADMINISTRATIVE PROCESS

Library of Congress Cataloging in Publication Data

Robbins, Stephen P   (date)
   The administrative process.

   Includes bibliographies and index.
   1. Management. I. Title.
HD31.R564 1980   658.4   79-23564
ISBN 0-13-007385-7

Editorial/production supervision by Kim Gueterman
Interior design by Suzanne Behnke
Cover design by Suzanne Behnke
Manufacturing buyer: Harry P. Baisley

Printed in the United States of America
10 9 8 7 6 5 4 3

PRENTICE-HALL INTERNATIONAL. INC., *London*
PRENTICE-HALL OF AUSTRALIA PTY. LIMITED, *Sydney*
PRENTICE-HALL OF CANADA, LTD., *Toronto*
PRENTICE-HALL OF INDIA PRIVATE LIMITED, *New Delhi*
PRENTICE-HALL OF JAPAN, INC., *Tokyo*
PRENTICE-HALL OF SOUTHEAST ASIA PTE. LTD., *Singapore*
WHITEHALL BOOKS LIMITED, *Wellington, New Zealand*

To Alix—
   For reasons that should be obvious but aren't

Contents

v

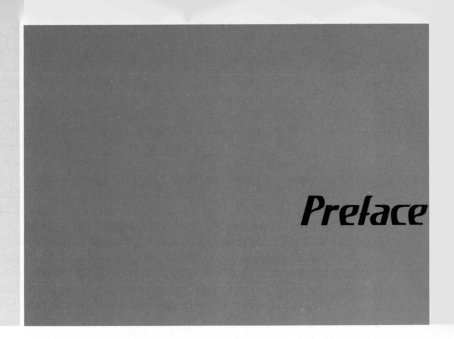

Preface

The primary objectives of this second edition are unchanged from the first—to produce a textbook on management and administration that is pragmatic in nature and generic in scope. The book is based on two current trends within the management discipline.

The first is the movement toward relevance. Students are increasingly looking for texts and courses with direct practical applications; and instructors are looking for an approach which can explain why administrative theory and practice are frequently different. In addition to knowing how one *ought* to manage, it is now of equal importance to know how practitioners *actually* manage. This book, then, elevates the research on administrative practices to the same level as the normative theory.

How is this integration achieved? In chapters 4 and 5, I present the theory and realities of administrative decision making. In chapters 6 through 17, I review the four functions in the administrative process; interspersing within each chapter research findings and observations on actual administrative practices. These inserts—highlighted in brown type—review administrative practice, compare it with the prior theory, and attempt to explain any differences using the descriptive decision-making concepts presented in chapter 5. Using this format, *The Administrative Process* presents theory and practice, and proposes to explain differences between them when they arise.

The second trend is the movement toward synthesizing business and public administration curriculums. Educators have come to realize that many students are interested in administration but are uncertain as to whether they will practice it in the private or public sector. Additionally, it is becoming increasingly popular for administrators to move between sectors during their careers. This suggests a need for a book that fully integrates the administrative process into a framework that applies to both profit and non-profit organizations. *The Administrative Process* treats administration as a generic process applicable to business (manufacturing and service), educational, medical, governmental, religious, charitable, and athletic organizations. Of course, there are some important differences between public and private organizations, but they are far more alike than not. Where differences surface, you will find them discussed in this book.

While the objectives of this second edition remain the same, the means of attaining them have been substantially revised. I have updated and expanded the book's research base and given greater depth to the topic coverage. The new emphasis on decision-making; resequencing of chapters; new material on staffing, quantitative techniques, and organizational change; and the introduction of short original cases, all have been made in the belief that this "new and improved" second edition offers a clearer and more logical structure in which to study what administration is about. You will also find that each of the major sections now concludes with an action-oriented chapter. Though *The Administrative Process* is far from a "how-to" book, I have sought to increase the proportion of material directly related to application. The section on planning ends with a chapter on management by objectives. The section on organizing finishes with a chapter on organizing for maximum performance. I've integrated the literature on change, communication, and conflict in chapter 15, to show its relevance to the leading function. Finally, the section on controlling concludes with a chapter discussing such techniques as cost-benefit analysis, zero-base budgeting, and human-resource accounting.

One feature that has remained untouched from the first edition is the writing style. I've continued the conversational approach, extensive use of examples, and logical organizational format that instructors and students commented so positively upon the first time around.

I am hopeful that the overall result from these changes is one of the most teachable, readable, and relevant textbooks currently available in the field of management and administration.

Acknowledge-ments   Every author has a long list of individuals to whom he is indebted. I am no exception. The writings of Herbert Simon continue as a major influence on my thinking—particularly his views on the central role of decision making in the administrative process and his concern with descriptive, as well as normative, approaches to administration. The comments of previous and current reviewers have added considerably to the finished product. These include Professors John R. Anstey (University of Nebraska at Omaha), H. Randolph Bobbitt, Jr. (Ohio State University), Richard H. Hall (State

University of New York, Albany), Karl Price (Temple University), Thomas A. Natiello (University of Miami), David A. Tansik (University of Arizona), Lawrence Ettkin (University of Tennessee, Chattanooga), John P. Alexander (Burlington County College), Curtis Clarke (Eastfield College), Ray Curtis (Lorain County Community College), Paul Harmon (University of Utah), Dewey E. Johnson (California State University, Fresno), Gerald L. Rose (University of Iowa), Joan C. Tonn (University of Massachusetts, Boston), and Gary Johns (Concordia University, Montreal).

I want to thank my former departmental colleagues at Concordia University in Montreal for their ideas and suggestions. I am particularly indebted to Gunther Brink, for having provided the administrative support for my writing efforts.

At Prentice-Hall, I want to single out and thank Mike Melody, Ted Jursek, Barbara Piercecchi; Barbara's assistant, Linda Albelli; my production editor, Kim Gueterman; and designer Suzanne Behnke.

Last, and possibly most importantly, I want to acknowledge my dependence on Sandy Pritchard. She typed the entire book and, as near as I can figure, she has done over 3500 manuscript pages for me during the past six years. Needless to say, she has made the task of writing a lot easier. Thanks Sandy!

Stephen P. Robbins
San Diego, California

PART

INTRODUCTION

Chapter

1

Administration: An Overview

AFTER STUDYING THIS CHAPTER, YOU SHOULD BE ABLE TO—

Define and explain the following key terms and concepts:

Organizational society   Planning
Administrator   Organizing
Administration   Leading
Administrative process   Controlling

Describe:

The impact of administrators on society
The misconception about what administrators do
The three commonalities for any comprehensive definition of administration
The role of decision making in the administrative process
The four functions making up the administrative process
Why top administrators in organizations often receive very high compensation

Have you ever considered that the future of modern civilization rests with administrators? That may sound like a pretty bold statement, but it reflects that we live in a world dominated not by individuals but by organizations. And administrators determine what organizations do.

Think about it for a moment. We are born in hospitals and buried by mortuaries. Both are organizations. The schools that educate us are organizations, and so are the stores where we buy our food, the companies that make our automobiles, and the people who take our income tax, collect our garbage, provide for our military defense, and print our daily newspapers.

We exist in an organizational society, and administrators are the individuals who direct organizations. The decisions made by administrators make the difference between war and peace, inflation and stability, prosperity and depression; their decisions directly affect such crucial issues as the quality of health care, the implementation of technological advances, the availability of desired goods and services, and the quality of the environment. Administrators in government agencies, hospitals, prisons, schools, small businesses, and billion-dollar corporations make decisions which touch most of our lives. Individually, these decisions reach only small segments of the population—with the exception of actions taken by the federal government and some of the largest corporate giants. However, in aggregate, these individual decisions shape our lives and our future.

One may or may not describe this influence as desirable, but that is not the issue here. What is relevant is the active control administrators have over our lives. That is a fact in a modern, technological society. Therefore, what administrators believe and how they act may be one of the most important areas for academic investigation. Whether or not you desire to pursue administration as a career, you should find this book of interest. If you think that you may want to be an administrator, this book will give you a reasonable overview of what you will do. If you plan to work in an organization in a nonadministrative capacity, it will be useful to have some insight into what administrators do and why, if for no other reason than that their actions will affect you personally. Finally, even if you are independently wealthy or otherwise see no reason to be a member of an organization in a work-related context, your life will still be affected by decisions that administrators make. A glance at Figure 1-1 should dramatize the breadth of organization and administrative influence.

Who are administrators?

In this book, the term *administrator* is used to describe a number of different jobs. The term applies to those with formal decision-making authority—from the person at the top of the organization down to the lowest

FIGURE 1-1   Various types of organizations that require administrators

General classification*	Some examples
Business–Manufacturing	General Motors Corporation U.S. Steel Corporation Xerox Corporation
Business–Service	Johnny's One-Hour Dry Cleaning McDonald's Tucson Gas & Electric
Government–Federal	Bureau of Indian Affairs Internal Revenue Service Social Security Administration
Government–State/Provincial	California Highway Patrol Kansas State Penitentiary Toronto International Airport
Government–Local	Atlanta Police Department City of Dallas Department of Sanitation City of Waterloo
Health & Medical	Four-Seasons Nursing Home Mount St. Mary's Hospital Syracuse Health Care Clinic
Education	New York P.S. 107 San Francisco Unified School District Slippery Rock State College
Social Services	American National Red Cross Lil Punkin Nursery School Y.M.C.A.
Arts & Culture	Boston Symphony Orchestra Omaha City Library Royal Ontario Museum
Athletic	Chicago Bears Montreal Canadiens Portland Trailblazers
Cooperatives	State Farm Insurance Utah Savings Bank
Other	Boy Scouts of America National Organization of Women United Lutheran Church

* Note: These categories are not fully independent. Some organizations overlap into two or more classifications.

level supervisor. At each administrative level, a variety of titles exist. At the highest levels, administrators carry designations like chairman of the board, president, chief executive officer and managing director. In the middle and lower ranks, they may be called project administrators, deans, district or division managers, unit chiefs, department heads, and foremen. In a small business, there may be only one administrator, called the owner or proprietor. But what do these individuals have in common? What unique functions do administrators perform that differentiate them from those people in organizations who are not administrators? And is *administration* different from *management?*

What is administration?

The terms *administration* and *management* are considered interchangeable in this book. Although distinctions have been made between them, the perceived differences are far from consistent; indeed, if there are any differences, they are insignificant. So, to alleviate confusion, we shall view the terms as synonymous. However, to many the term *management* is reserved for profit-making organizations alone. Therefore, we have emphasized the term *administration* because it is more readily acceptable in both profit and nonprofit sectors. In addition, since neither term is more accurate than the other and since there are academic programs in business administration, public administration, health administration, educational administration, and so on, it appears logical and consistent to use *administration* rather than management.

Still, administration means different things to different people. A popular belief is that administration refers to certain individuals with indistinct powers who are involved in making our lives difficult. Administration means the people who are to blame for raising our prices, packing our goods cockeyed, producing shoddy products, giving poor service, increasing taxes, never listening to our complaints, and generally disturbing our lives.[1] Another view, usually restricted to the upper echelons of administration, sees administrators as individuals who occupy luxuriously carpeted offices the size of basketball courts, who are whizzed about in limousines and Lear jets, and who, when not wining, dining or holding press conferences, spend their time behind large walnut desks barking orders into a telephone or instructing their subordinates on the decisions they wish carried out. Unfortunately, even for the top level decision makers, administration is far less glamorous than the above Hollywood characterization. Nevertheless, administrators do accomplish things through other people, and they do make decisions.

A more accurate definition of administration is *the universal process of efficiently getting activities completed with and through other people*. Its concepts are transferable between organizations, and as applicable to nonprofit organizations as they are to the profit sector. The "process" refers to the planning, organizing, leading, and controlling that take place to accomplish objectives, and this process can take place in any type of organization.

A review of the administrative literature lends support to three commonalities for any comprehensive definition of administration. These are goals, limited resources, and people. In reference to the definition above, goals are the "completed activities"; limited resources are implied in "efficiently"; and people are those in "other people."

First, goals are necessary because activity must be directed toward some end. Considerable truth lies in the observation that "if you do not know where you are going, any road will take you there." The established

Walter A. Kleinschrod, "The Public's Dim View of 'Administration'," *Administrative Management*, March 1972, p. 20.

goals may not be explicit, but where there are no goals, there is no need for administrators.

2) Second, there must be limited resources. Economic resources, by definition, are scarce; therefore, the administrator is responsible for their allocation. This requires not only that administrators be *effective*—that is, in achieving the goal or goals that are established—but additionally, that they be *efficient*—that is, in relating resources utilized to output produced. They must seek a given output with less input than is now being utilized, or , for a given input, strive for a greater output. Administrators, then, are concerned with the attainment of goals (effectiveness) and with the best allocation of scarce resources (efficiency).

3) The need for two or more people is the third and last requisite for administration. It is with and through people that administrators perform their work. The legendary Robinson Crusoe could not become an administrator until the man Friday's arrival.

In summary, administrators are those who work through people, allocating scarce resources, to achieve goals. If any one of these criteria is missing, there is no need for administration.

Coming attractions: the administrative process

Our definition of administration described it as a process comprised of planning, organizing, leading, and controlling. Our goals are determined in the planning function. Allocation of limited resources is the principal factor in both planning and organizing. Leading is achieving the goals through people. And finally, the controlling function compares performance with the established goals and, if necessary, initiates corrective action. Each of these functions requires decisions, so any study of administration must include a look at decision-making. These components, then, make up the major segments of this book: Part 2 discusses the theory and practical realities of decision making, and Parts 3–6 review the functions of planning, organizing, leading, and controlling, respectively. However, in order to give you an overview of the administrative process, the next few pages present some "coming attractions."

Planning

Planning is determining in advance the objectives to be accomplished and the means by which these objectives are to be attained. It is deciding what to do, how to do it, and who is to do it. Because it bridges the gap from where we are to where we want to be, it is the most basic of the four functions.

Successful planning seeks to reduce the impact of change upon the organization. Short-term changes are easier to anticipate than changes five, ten or twenty years down the road. Therefore, we will find that organizations develop relatively complete short-term plans and more flexible long-term plans.

Planning begins with the establishment of objectives—"where you are going." Hence, objectives should cover economic, service, and social dimensions of the organization, and set the parameters by which administrators can determine if the ongoing activities of members are making positive contributions to the organization.

The multifarious objectives are illustrated by those of a moderate-sized midwestern insurance company. The author's discussions with the management indicated that, in addition to an adequate profit, the firm was concerned with improving its market position, generating new and innovative policies, developing a strong and consistent upward trend in revenues, and upgrading the company image with the public and within the insurance industry. Additionally, numerous subobjectives evolved from these major ones.

Once the reason for the organization's existence is made clear through the statement of major objectives, administrators will establish subobjectives and formulate forecasts.

Forecasting is the process of gathering data and developing assumptions about the future. Information must be gathered and assumptions made regarding external and internal variables. External variables include such considerations as government fiscal and monetary policies, growth in the gross national product, and changes in price levels, population trends, and technology. Internal variables relate to demand for the organization's product or service expressed in revenue terms, the expenses incurred in generating the revenue, and capital and manpower needs.

After objectives have been formulated and forecasts made, administrators can develop an organizational strategy—a comprehensive plan which encompasses the objectives and subplans of the organization, and includes a plan of action for their attainment.

Organizing Organizing is the establishment of relationships between the activities to be performed, the personnel to perform them, and the physical factors that are needed. To coordinate the available resources, the administrator designs a formal structure of relationships that will foster the effective and efficient attainment of goals. The major concerns in organizing consist of dividing up the jobs to be done, determining the grouping of work, staffing positions, forming authority grades, and equalizing authority and responsibility.

As far back as 2,300 years ago, the potential to increase productivity dramatically through the division of work was recognized. Plato, in his *Republic*, wrote, "Each thing becomes more plentiful, finer, and easier, when one man, exempt from other tasks, does one thing according to nature and at the crucial moment."[2] By having people specialize in very few tasks, getready and put-away time is reduced, greater skills are developed, and high work speeds attained. The automobile assembly line illustrates the value of specialization in manufacturing, as does the surgeon, gynecologist, or ear,

[2] *The Republic of Plato,* trans. Allan Bloom (New York: Basic Books, 1968), p. 47.

nose, and throat specialist in the provision of medical services. The maturation of organizations has historically depended upon developing increasingly higher degrees of skill in people who perform more and more specialized activities. Recently, however, considerable concern has been expressed that the pendulum may have swung too far, creating some extremely dehumanizing work environments. That is, even though highly specialized jobs are efficient, the benefits of specialization are more than offset by the boredom and fatigue that workers are forced to endure. An increasing amount of recent evidence supports job expansion, rather than contraction, as a means to improve productivity.[3]

As organizational members developed greater specialization, it became necessary to determine the number of people who should report to an immediate superior. An administrator's potential to successfully coordinate the activities of others ranges from some number greater than one to something obviously less than infinity. The span of administration defines the number of subordinates an administrator can effectively direct. Depending on the activities performed, the skills of the subordinates, their educational level, experience, and other variables, some administrators can effectively direct forty, whereas others are fully employed supervising only three. The decision regarding this span will directly influence the number of levels in the organizational hierarchy and, hence, its complexity.

Recognition that no one person can manage an unlimited number of subordinates makes it necessary to break work activities into governable segments. The objectives outlined in the planning function determine the tasks that must be performed. These tasks are combined into activities and the activities joined together to create departments. The ways that are determined for defining methods of departmentation are key determinants in organization design and the potential interaction between members. And, of course, based on the activities that have to be done, positions will have to be staffed with individuals capable of performing them effectively.

Finally, we find a graduation of authority in all organizations. Authority flows through a chain of command and results in the vertical growth of the structure. Through delegation of this authority, top management empowers middle- and lower-level executives with the capability to achieve their objectives. Designing our organizations so that an equality exists between authority and responsibility ensures that the rights to enact compliance are balanced with the expectations of performance.

Leading

In the leading function, we guide and supervise subordinates. This function carries out the objectives established in planning. Basically, leading consists

[3] See, for example, W.J. Paul, Jr., K.B. Robertson, and F. Herzberg, "Job Enrichment Pays Off," *Harvard Business Review*, March-April 1969, pp. 61–78; R.N. Ford, *Motivation Through the Work Itself* (New York: American Management Association, 1969); and W.J. Roche and N.L. MacKinnon, "Motivating People with Meaningful Work," *Harvard Business Review*, May-June 1970, pp. 97–110.

of supervision, motivation, communication, bringing about change, and managing conflict.

All employees need and expect to be supervised. This supervision may take a strict form, or it may be loose, low-awareness direction. Some jobs necessitate that employees be under constant surveillance; others are structured to allow the bare minimum of supervision, such as weekly reports sent to the boss 500 miles away. In between these two extremes are an infinite number of superior-subordinate supervisory relations. Supervision requires observation of the work, workers, and working conditions to ensure that the unit's objectives are achieved.

The leading function also includes the responsibility for motivating personnel. No matter how fine the plans or efficient the organization, nothing happens until the people who make up the organization are stimulated to perform. This impetus may be totally internal to the employee, but most frequently it requires the leader to exert an external stimulus. Early studies of management and human behavior stressed the motivating power of money. We now recognize that what motivated effectively in 1900 may have little relevance to our current affluent society. Today, the 100 million members of the North American work force are better educated and more financially secure than any previous generation was. Basic physiological, security, and social needs have been substantially met through high pay, liberal fringe benefits, and satisfactory working conditions. Although these extrinsic variables are important, many workers seek more from their jobs. They desire to satisfy esteem and self-fulfillment needs in the workplace and, therefore, they seek in their work the intrinsic qualities of recognition, achievement, growth, and advancement.

Those who lead must be able to communicate effectively, bring about necessary changes, and manage conflict within their unit and between their unit and other units. Change, conflict, and communication are three highly interwoven concepts. Many employees resist change, yet it is necessary if the organization is to be adaptable. Resistance to change can create conflict; at the same time, conflict can bring about change. Effective communication can facilitate the acceptance of change and help to minimize destructive conflict. The administrator should seek to understand change, conflict, and communication in order to more effectively lead his or her constituency.

Controlling

The final function of the administrator is controlling. In this function he or she reviews, regulates, and controls performance to ensure that it conforms to certain standards. In control, we assume that performance standards have previously been established in the planning function. The control process is then as follows: Performance is measured, it is compared to the standards, and, should there be significant deviations, corrective actions are instituted. As with leading, control may be strict or loose; however, where it is lax, we increase the probability of our failing to note and correct aberrant activities.

with the planning, organizing, and leading functions when action is initiated to correct deviant performance. If performance is found to be unsatisfactory, one option is to alter the plans—that is, to adjust the objectives or the plans—since deviations may be not so much a result of inadequate performance as they are of inadequate or incorrect plans. A second option is to reorganize; altering the relationships between the activities to be performed, the personnel to perform them, and the physical assets necessary may correct the deviation. Finally, correction can be achieved through an adjustment in the leading function; by increasing or decreasing the depth of supervision, altering motivators, changing communication patterns, or altering conflict levels, performance that is out of tolerance may be brought into line.

The making of choices—*decision making*— and the activities of *planning, organizing, leading,* and *controlling* are what differentiate administrators from nonadministrators. Chapters 4 through 18 will review these topics in detail.

Are administrators really important?

It is our position that administrators are the single most important ingredient in determining an organization's success or failure. Whether in business, government, education, medicine, or religion, the quality of an organization's administrators determines the quality of the organization itself. Successful administrators anticipate change, vigorously exploit opportunities, correct poor performance, and lead the organization toward its objectives. In contrast to other groups within the organization, administrators have the greatest opportunities to turn straw to gold—or the reverse.

This belief in the omnipotence of administrators, while held by most administrative theorists, is not without its critics. For example, Pfeffer and Salancik argue that the evidence does not support the view that administrators have a profound impact on an organization's performance.[4] Specifically, Pfeffer and Salancik suggest that the economic cycle, competitors' actions, manpower availability, and other external factors diminish the effect of administrators. However, one need not look too far to find examples of the influence administrators have on their organizations, especially when, in retrospect, their decisions have proved faulty.

In the profit sector during the last decade, several major corporations verged on bankruptcy as a result of questionable administrative decisions. The Penn Central operated a number of extremely unprofitable ventures and averted bankruptcy only with the help of federal financial assistance.

[4] Jeffrey Pfeffer and Gerald R. Salancik, *The External Control of Organizations: A Resource Dependence Perspective* (New York: Harper & Row, 1978).

ADMINISTRATION:
AN OVERVIEW

Similarly, the federal government's agreement to guarantee a $250 million loan to Lockheed prevented its departure from the corporate scene in 1970—a financial crisis generally attributed to decisions by company administrators to develop the L-1011 jumbo jet in spite of being several years behind the competition's offerings: Boeing's 747 and McDonnell-Douglas' DC-10. Do you remember W. T. Grant and Railway Express? These are two companies that disappeared in the mid-1970s as a result of their administrators failing to react to changes in consumer preferences. Recently, Westinghouse Electric Corporation's future has been threatened by its administrators' high-growth–high-risk philosophy.[5] In the 1960s, decisions were made to supply power utilities with uranium through the 1990s. Westinghouse wrote contracts to sell 80 million pounds of uranium at under $9 a pound, but had only 15 million pounds to cover the contracts. These decisions were made on the belief that uranium prices would not rise above $10 a pound. In 1978, with the price of uranium at $43 a pound and 1980 futures quoted at nearly $54, the company's potential liability was *in excess of $2 billion.*

It is not difficult to cite public sector examples in which the actions of administrators have had a dramatic effect on the populace: The decision to commit hundreds of billions of U.S. dollars to an undeclared war in southeast Asia, and the resultant need to impose wage and price controls as inflation spread; the go-ahead for an office break-in and subsequent conspiracy that destroyed a president and seriously wounded a political party; the decisions—or lack of them—that have led to the gradual deterioration of the U.S. mail service; and, more recently, the financial dilemma of New York City.

Each of these examples of major organizational or societal problems could have been prevented by astute administrators. Unfortunately, it is easier to describe ineptitude than it is to find instances of significant administrative success. But some of the more recognized outstanding administrative accomplishments would be those of Alfred Sloan, the organizational genius behind General Motors; Robert Hutchins, who, as president of the University of Chicago, led it into the ranks of the finest universities in the world; the late coach of the Green Bay Packers football team, Vince Lombardi; or John Wooden, the genius who lead U.C.L.A. to continual basketball victories in the 1960s and early 1970s.

We can conclude this chapter by citing several illustrations of what some business firms have been willing to pay in order to keep or acquire the services of a "super-star" administrator.

Harold S. Geneen took over as chief executive of International Telephone and Telegraph in 1959. Its yearly sales were then $766 million. When he retired in 1977, the company's sales were $13.1 billion. Profits rose even

[5] "The Opposites: GE Grows While Westinghouse Shrinks," *Business Week*, January 31, 1977, pp. 60–66; "Westinghouse: A Blow in the Uranium Wars," *Business Week*, November 13, 1978, p. 40.

more impressively—from $29 million to $562 million. Geneen's personal annual compensation during this period grew from $173,546 to $934,000. In spite of an income of nearly a million dollars a year, Geneen recognized his value to I.T.T. and the fact that the company's success was due directly to his astute administrative talents when he said in the early 1970s, "I still feel underpaid."[6]

In September 1976, Volkswagen of America hired James W. McLernon away from General Motors to run VW's auto manufacturing plant in Pennsylvania. The price to woo McLernon to the VW camp was a reported $2 million, guaranteed over a five-year period.[7]

One of the most sumptuous compensation packages put together in order to obtain a senior executive took place in 1974 to attract Michel C. Bergerac to the presidency of Revlon.[8] Bergerac was the 42-year-old president of I.T.T.–Europe. To entice him to leave his job in Brussels and head up the second largest cosmetic company in the U.S., Revlon settled on a lump sum payment of $1.5 million just for Bergerac's reporting to work on September 16, 1974; options on 70,000 shares of Revlon stock which in less than a year gave Bergerac a paper profit of over $2 million; a base salary of $325,000 a year; a five year contract, with an added provision of two years at full salary if his contract was not renewed at its expiration; moving expenses from Brussels to New York; and to protect himself against a declining real estate market, the right to sell to Revlon for $400,000 a cooperative apartment in New York that Bergerac had bought for $425,000. This package inspired one consultant to describe Bergerac as "the first big corporate bonus baby."[9] More recently, Archie McCardell received a $1.5 million bonus in 1977 from International Harvester when he was recruited from Xerox. A similar recruitment sum was paid in 1978 to Lee Iacocca in order for Chrysler to secure his services.

The point of these million dollar deals is not to suggest that all administrators are rich. Such is far from the case. While the chief executives of Fortune 500 firms in 1975 averaged $209,000 a year in income,[10] lower- and middle-level administrators in business, government, and education generally earn annual salaries in the $25,000 to $50,000 range. The reason we have mentioned these million dollar examples is to provide specific evidence of the value that organizations place on administrators. The purpose of this chapter has not only been to define administration and to survey what administrators do, but to propose that administrators are *the* single most important ingredient in determining an organization's success or failure.

---

[6] "What Price Geneen?," *Fortune*, March 13, 1978, p. 16.

[7] Reported in the *New York Times*, January 16, 1977, p. Fl.

[8] Marylin Bender, "Bonus Baby in the Executive Suite," *New York Times*, May 11, 1975, p. Fl.

[9] Ibid.

[10] Charles G. Burck, "A Group Profile of the Fortune 500 Chief Executive," *Fortune*, May 1976, p. 173.

summary of major points

1. We live in a world dominated by organizations, and administrators determine what organizations do.
2. The term *administrator* applies to those with formal decision-making authority—from the person at the top of the organization to the lowest-level supervisor.
3. *Administration* and *management* can be viewed as synonymous terms.
4. Administration is *the universal process of efficiently getting activities completed with and through other people.*
5. Any comprehensive definition of administration must include three components:
   a. Goals
   b. Limited resources
   c. People
6. The administrative process is composed of four activities:
   a. Planning
   b. Organizing
   c. Leading
   d. Controlling
7. Administrators have been presented as the single most important ingredient in determining an organization's success or failure.

FOR DISCUSSION

1. How do administrative decisions influence our lives?
2. "Elected government officials, not administrators, have the most profound effect on our lives?" Do you agree or disagree with this statement? Discuss.
3. Which, if any, of the following positions would not be considered an administrator? Explain. (a) District manager; (b) Department head; (c) Foreman; (d) Director of Research and Development.
4. Why do you think many people use the term "manager" to describe decision makers in business, and "administrator" to describe decision makers in government?
5. Is any one of the four functions that an administrator performs more important than the others? Discuss.
6. Is a college instructor an administrator? Explain.
7. "What is good for the country is good for General Motors, and what's good for General Motors is good for the country." Do you agree or disagree? Discuss.

8. The President of the United States is undoubtedly an administrator who makes important decisions. He is paid approximately $200,000 annually. How do you explain the fact that some senior executives in industry, whose decisions have far less impact, receive compensation that is two or more times what the President of the U.S. earns?

case exercise

Welcome to the wonderful world of administration

Betty Traynor graduated from State College with her B.S. in 1976. She took a job as a caseworker in the State of Illinois' Department of Social Services. Her basic responsibilities were to interview and evaluate couples who had applied for a child through the Department's adoption service.

After nearly three years as a caseworker, Betty has been offered a promotion to a supervisory position within the adoption services group. The promotion carries with it a significant raise, but more importantly it would give her valuable administrative experience and allow her the opportunity to influence a number of the decisions that were made regarding who could or could not adopt a baby.

As Betty ponders whether to accept the promotion, she has reflected back on a course in Fundamentals of Administration that she took during her junior year at college. She remembered how the course had really perked her interest in administration as a career. About the only dilemma she experienced during the course was dealing with the guilt she felt from wanting the power that goes with an administrative position. At the time, she had resolved the guilt by arguing, at least to herself, that she would never abuse the power of an administrative position. Rather, she would use it to make things run better.

Three years have passed and now opportunity was knocking. If she accepted the promotion, she would supervise the activities of eight caseworkers and four secretaries. If she turned it down, she knew it might be several years before the opportunity came around again.

Questions

1. How valuable do you think the three years' experience as a caseworker will be in helping Betty to be an effective supervisor?
2. Might Betty's past guilt about the power that goes with an administrative position have any justification?
3. How might the activities of planning, organizing, leading, and controlling, which she learned about in her college course in administration, be relevant to being a supervisor in a social service agency?

FOR FURTHER READING

Barnard, C.I., *The Functions of the Executive.* Cambridge, Mass.: Harvard University Press, 1938. Classic book that presents executives as interconnecting centers in a communication system who seek to secure the coordination essential to cooperative effort.

Drucker, P.F., *Management: Tasks, Responsibilities and Practices.* New York: Harper & Row, 1973. The world's most well-known management guru presents a practical and results-oriented review of the manager's job.

Galbraith, J.K., *The New Industrial State.* New York: Houghton-Mifflin Co., 1967. The creation of large organizations, and their professional managers, has altered many of the important assumptions underlying economic decision-making.

Miner, J.B., "The Real Crunch in Managerial Manpower," *Harvard Business Review,* November-December 1973, pp. 146–58. Argues that, in the future, there may be a significant shortage of individuals with the attitudes, motives, and values to assume managerial roles.

Mintzberg, H., "The Manager's Job: Folklore and Fact," *Harvard Business Review,* July–August 1975, pp. 49–61. Offers another perspective to the traditional view that managers plan, organize, lead, and control.

Reich, A., *The Greening of America.* New York: Random House, 1970. Administrators control not only society at large but also the smallest aspects of one's personal life.

Chapter

2

A Point
of Departure

**AFTER
STUDYING
THIS CHAPTER,
YOU SHOULD
BE ABLE TO—**

Theory   Science
Practice   Philosophy
Generic   Values
Organizational behavior   Training
Art   Education

Why we need to know both theory and practice
Whether administration is a universal process in all organized activity
The differences between administration and organizational behavior
Whether administration is an art or a science
Why administration should be viewed as a philosophy
Determinants of administrative behavior
Why it is difficult to train administrators

The first chapter made assumptions, some explicit and others implicit, about administration. The purpose of this chapter is to clarify these assumptions. Specifically, we will briefly compare administrative theory and administrative practice, consider whether administration is universal in all organized activities, contrast the field of administration with organizational behavior, address the "art versus science" issue, and conclude the chapter by demonstrating the role of values in the study of administration.

Theory vs. practice

A number of years ago, I taught my introductory course in administration from a purely theoretical perspective. I believed, at the time, that the best way to teach was to show students what administrators were supposed to do. I thought that by presenting an ideal picture, the students would have something to strive toward. But one year, about halfway through the term, a student interrupted my lecture to challenge my prescriptive approach. "Come on, Professor Robbins," he said, "what you've been saying all semester is nice in theory, but I've worked in four different places, and from my vantage point, administrators sure don't act the way you describe." My first response was defensive: "This is not a training school! You're here to learn, to be educated. You should be introduced to how best to function as an administrator. Most administrators do practice in the way our textbook says. Sure, there are some exceptions, but they just haven't been exposed to the wealth of books and articles on how to be a good administrator. Did it occur to you that there may be something wrong with your vantage point?"

To make a long story short, that interaction challenged me to question my position. I knew, in reality, that the student was right! The textbook we were using in class completely failed to explain that, although the theory correctly prescribed how an administrator should function, finding an administrator who fit the prescription was more difficult than Diogenes' search, lantern in hand, for the man of virtue. What I was exposing the student to was how an *ideal* administrator, in an *ideal* organization, should act. More importantly, I realized that it was a disservice to students to propose that my normative "fairy tales" were, in fact, reality. This book is a response to those textbooks which fail to acknowledge the realities of organizational life.

Theory is important. There is no question about that. One social scientist summed it up by saying "there is nothing so practical as a good theory."

But what is *good theory?* It seems it should be able to pass the only meaningful test: to accurately explain and predict actual administrative practices. But current administrative theory, for the most part, only explains and predicts how administrators *should* practice.

My conclusions are threefold. First, a student of administration should have a sound theoretical base in order to know what good practices ought to be. In that way, one has a standard to strive toward. Second, theory and practice are frequently divergent, and the student should be aware of this reality. A textbook in administration, therefore, should present theory and, when practice differs, present it as such. Third, the textbook should attempt to explain to the reader *why* theory and practice differ when they do.

The above conclusions have influenced the direction and content of this book. It includes both the normative (theory) and the descriptive (practice) and explores why administrative behavior frequently contradicts traditional administrative theory.

The generic controversy

This book proposes that administration is *generic;* that is, it is a universal process in all organized activities. Every administrator, from a top-level executive to a supervisor, is a decision maker and performs the functions of planning, organizing, leading, and controlling. Similarly, the process cuts across organizations, indicating that administrative skills are transferable between, say, private and public organizations.

Of course, there are factors that are unique to certain positions and certain organizations. These factors make it impossible for us to lay down universal principles which would be applicable in all situations. Yet, there is a common body of activities that are generic—they are performed by all administrators, regardless of the size of their organization or their level in the hierarchy.

There is a significant minority of academics and practitioners who disagree with our position that administration is generic. Some believe that public administration, for example, should be a separate and unique area of study from business administration or that a supervisor's job is uniquely different from the chief executive officer's job.

Are administrators transferable across organizations? Can Veronica Miller, the successful director of public relations at General Foods, be equally successful doing the same job at Xerox? Could W. Michael Blumenthal successfully transfer the administrative talents he showed as the chief executive officer of Bendix Corporation to head of the U.S. Treasury? Let us look specifically at the comparison between public and private organizations.

A POINT OF
DEPARTURE

Comparing public and private organizations

The argument against transferability states that profit-making organizations are faced with more marketplace competition, fewer legal and formal constraints, fewer practical influences, less public scrutiny, clearer objectives, and greater incentive structures than public organizations.[1] These differences contribute to a view of the private sector as rational, economically efficient, and profit-oriented, in contrast to the public sector which is characterized by consensus seeking and compromise.

The argument favoring transferability questions the notion that profits are the sole reason for the existence of private business, argues that political factors are relevant to decisions in both public and private organizations, and states that there are common activities in *any* complex organization: "defining purpose and objectives, planning, organizing, selecting managers, managing and motivating people, controlling and measuring results, and using a variety of analytical, problem solving and managerial techniques."[2]

After reviewing the logic of both positions, we believe the evidence weighs in favor of accepting that administration has universal applications whether it be in the profit or business sector or in the nonprofit public sector. Although there are important distinctions to be made, administration in the private sector and in the public sector are more similar than different.[3]

The public-private debate is only one of the dialogues concerning transferability. Two other prominent issues concern cross-cultural transferability and whether horizontal transfers are more likely to be successful at different levels of an organization.

Cross-cultural transferability

The field of comparative administration has evolved out of an interest in transferring knowledge between different nations and cultures. Because cultures differ in terms of their economic, technological, social, and political systems, a practice which is successful in North America may fail miserably in India or France. As a result, while we can find similarities across cultures, we do not make the claim that the contents of this book are applicable worldwide. They are appropriate for organizations in the United States and Canada and are reasonably applicable to countries such as England and Australia. However, this generalizability does not necessarily carry over to non-English speaking countries or nations of the third world. We are not saying that the administrative process, as described in this book, may not be applicable outside North America, only that there may be important cultural differences that modify the process.[4]

[1] Hal G. Rainey, Robert W. Backoff, and Charles H. Levine, "Comparing Public and Private Organizations," *Public Administration Review*, March-April 1976, pp. 233–44.

[2] Fredric H. Genck, "Public Management in America," *AACSB Bulletin*, April 1973, p. 6.

[3] Michael A. Murray, "Comparing Public and Private Management: An Exploratory Essay," *Public Administration Review*, July-August 1975, pp. 364–71.

[4] For the reader interested in comparative administration, see: R. Farmer and B. Richman, *Comparative Management and Economic Progress* (Homewood, Ill.: Richard D. Irwin, 1965); J. Massie and J. Luytjes, *Management in an International Context* (New York: Harper & Row, 1972); and R. Webber, *Culture and Management* (Homewood, Ill.: Richard D. Irwin, 1969).

Effect of hierarchical position

It is easier for a top executive to make a successful move from one organization to another than it is for a middle or lower-level administrator.

Figure 2-1 dramatizes the fact that, although all administrators plan, organize, lead, and control, their position in the organization influences the amount of time they spend on each function. Even though no specific breakdowns are widely accepted, we do recognize that as one rises in the organizational hierarchy, one spends more time on planning efforts and less on leading. Additionally, this fact indirectly demonstrates that specific expertise in an area (such as purchasing, production, finance, or engineering) is most necessary at low-level administrative jobs, whereas top administrators have little direct contact with day-to-day operations and therefore require a general perspective. Accounting supervisors must be knowledgeable in accounting tasks if they are to perform effectively. However, the accountant who rises to become the chief executive of Price, Waterhouse or the city manager of Phoenix, Arizona, spends little of his time directing the daily activities of his organization, but much in planning the future direction of the organization and preparing the best road map to achieve that end.

It appears easiest for an administrator to make successful moves when

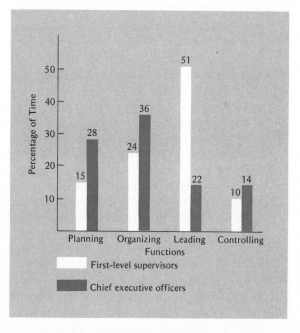

Source: Adapted with minor modifications from T. A. Mahoney, T. H. Jerdee, and S. J. Carroll, "The Job(s) of Management," *Industrial Relations*, Vol. 4, No. 2 (1965), 109.

FIGURE 2-1   Time spent per function

he or she holds the top position in the organization. At that level, specific job knowledge is least necessary, and administrative skills dominate. Supervisors of punch-press operators, bricklayers, cost accountants, or nurses must know the jobs they supervise. However, the mayor of Cincinnati need know little about the specifics of law enforcement, tax appraising, or the functioning of school systems in order to perform successfully. The president of the Ford Motor Company need not know how to build cars or the specifics of marketing them. These individuals have subordinate executives with expertise in these areas. Similarly, the amount of knowledge the president of Prentice-Hall needs about printing presses can be learned in hours, whereas the knowledge a printing-press foreman requires is extensive.

We find numerous practical examples of the transferability of administrative skills. Every day, people move from one organization to a totally different kind of organization. A few of the more visible include Dwight D. Eisenhower, who moved from being a U.S. Army general to the presidency of Columbia University, then to the presidency of the United States; Robert McNamara, who was president of the Ford Motor Company and then Secretary of Defense before becoming president of the World Bank; Franklin Murphy, who left his position as chancellor of the University of California at Los Angeles to become chairman of the board of the Times-Mirror publishing empire; and Arthur D. Lewis, who in a ten-year period, moved from the presidency of a small airline—Hawaiian Airlines—to the number two place at a big one—Eastern Airlines—to the helm of an old line investment banking house—F.S. Smithers & Co. Inc.—to the chairmanship of a government agency—the United States Railway Association.

Almost all of us know of people who have made changes across organizational lines. Although there is often a good deal of resistance to administrators' crossing diverse organizational lines at the lower or middle levels, it is more common at the senior-level positions in an organization. The higher one moves in an organization, the less is the demand for specific job skills and the more one engages in general administrative functions.

In summary, we propose that administration is a generic field of study. The concepts of planning, organizing, leading and controlling are equally valid whether applied to political, educational, military, religious, social, and athletic groups, or to profit-making firms. While we acknowledge that there are important differences between public and private organizations, we argue that there are more similarities than differences. A reality of the 1970s and 1980s is that it is no longer clear where the public sector ends and the private begins. For example, either directly or indirectly, the federal government now subsidizes state, provincial and city governments, agriculture, business, industry, universities, school districts, students, poor people, sick people, hungry people, and other special interest groups. To view private-sector organizations as clear and distinct from public-sector organizations is no longer consistent with reality.

We have qualified our generic label to emphasize organizations in

North America. Even though similarities exist in administrative activities between San Francisco and Hong Kong, we recognize that there are also significant differences. For the sake of simplicity, we have constrained our view of the administrative process to North America.

Finally, the evidence suggests that transferability of administrative skills is likely to be more successful the higher one moves in an organization. The administrative activities of top executives are highly similar, whereas lower-level administrators are increasingly required to engage in activities that require technical skills.

Administration versus organizational behavior

During the last decade, many academics and students have lost sight of the difference between the subject matter in organizational behavior and that in the field of administration, and have confused the two. But administration and organizational behavior are not the same!

Organizational behavior (O.B.) is concerned with the behavior of individuals in organizations. Administration is concerned with the optimum attainment of organizational goals. However, since these goals are unattainable without human input, O.B. is a significant subset or segment of administration.

We must note here that O.B. is not an end in itself. Patterns of leadership, motivation, communication networks, and other areas that have received substantial investigation by behavioral scientists are significant only in the contributions that studies of them have made to more efficient and effective organizations. These contributions are of importance to the student of administration only for what they can contribute toward goal attainment: achieving higher goals for a fixed input or attaining a given goal with less input. That may mean efficiency through savings in time, effort, or cost.

Behavioral scientists (psychologists, sociologists, anthropologists) have contributed significantly to the development of administrative thought. We cannot overemphasize the importance their findings have had in upgrading our knowledge of human behavior in organized settings. However, to ignore the contributions of other disciplines—specifically, engineering, economics, and mathematics—is to fail to recognize the full field of study, and to become interested in understanding behavior as an end rather than as a means to an end.

Art or science?

Another area of contention is the state of the field: Is administration an art or a science? To a large degree, it is both.

It has been suggested that the goal of administrative scholars has been the development of a science that could replace the confusion of an administrative philosophy.[5] However, a more realistic view recognizes that there is no science of administration in the same sense as the natural or physical sciences.[6] With the exception of some planning and controlling tools, we must candidly admit that the discipline of administration has not yet evolved to the point where we can explain and predict with the precision expected in the exact sciences. This position can best be expressed by considering whether there are any principles or laws in administration such as one finds in physics, biology, or chemistry.

A *principle* is defined as "a fundamental or universal truth." A *law* possesses stronger impact, for it is "an exact formulation of a principle, occurring with unvarying uniformity under repetition of the same conditions." So, in the purely definitional sense, there are clearly few such things as laws or principles in administration.

The key words that exclude administration from qualifying as a true science are "universal" and "unvarying uniformity." Although we have concepts that have application under certain qualifications, they are not universal. Koontz and O'Donnell have listed more than five dozen "principles,"[7] yet even though these may apply most of the time, in most organizations, they cannot be correctly classified as fundamental or universal truths because many of them fail the test of universality. For example, Koontz and O'Donnell's principle of direct supervision states, "The more direct personal contact with subordinates is, the more effective will their direction be."[8] This represents an excellent general guide to students of administration, but it is not universally applicable.

In the sense that the discipline can be "organized into an elaborate system of explicit primary and secondary theories, which have been or are being listed by logic and the realities of the universe, so that past and current changes in the system can be explained and future changes predicted or produced, we call that ball of knowledge a science."[9] A science can be viewed as an organized store of applicable knowledge. It becomes an operational science when it is organized so as to serve practice most effectively.[10] Administration can, however, be described as a science if the term is used loosely, as in the "social sciences." Economics, psychology, sociology, and

[5] John Miner, *The Management Process* (New York: Macmillan, 1973), pp. 98–99.
[6] Theo Haimann and William G. Scott, *Management in the Modern Organization* (Boston: Houghton-Mifflin, 1970), p. 14.
[7] Harold Koontz and Cyril O'Donnell, *Principles of Management*, 5th ed. (New York: McGraw-Hill, 1972).
[8] Ibid., p. 576.
[9] Luther Gulick, "Management Is a Science," *Journal of the Academy of Management*, March 1965, p. 10.
[10] Harold Koontz, "A Model for Analyzing the Universality and Transferability of Management," *Academy of Management Journal*, December 1969, p. 420.

the other social sciences must be called inexact sciences because they deal with the human element, and human behavior complicates immensely the task of explaining and predicting phenomena. However, the social sciences can define, analyze, and measure phenomena, using the same techniques as the exact sciences do. It is only their ability to control and explain intervening variables that is less precise. Additionally, administration can be studied through the scientific method: hypotheses or statements of expected results established; data gathered, tabulated, analyzed, and compared to hypotheses; and hypotheses supported or negated. Therefore, the scientific method can be applied as it is applied in the exact sciences, but the social sciences cannot withstand the vigorous experimentation of the exact or physical sciences.

In contrast, administration is also an art, a fact that need not reflect negatively on the discipline. In reality, there are few pure sciences. Koontz clearly delineates administration's position when he describes it as an art, "but so are engineering, medicine, accounting and baseball! For art is the application of knowledge to reality with compromise, blend or design to get the best total results."[11]

The approach to administration as an art recognizes that although there are specific skills one can learn—the on-the-job-training part of our discipline—knowledge, per se, does not ensure success. For example, if one student makes an A in his or her introductory administration course and another makes a C, this does not mean that the former would be any more effective as an administrator than the latter. Similarly, medical students specializing in surgery cannot effectively develop their skills in the classroom or in the laboratory—they need actual practice. This applies to administrators as well.

In summary, administration should be recognized as both a science and an art. It has a body of thought that can be systematized and from which phenomena can be predicted, but the field lacks the capability of making absolute predictions. The theory, or the "what," represents the science. The ability to apply it correctly, or the "how," is the art.

Administration as a philosophy

In their decision-making capacity, administrators are required to take unorganized masses of opinions and inspect, scrutinize, and organize these views into a meaningful, coherent, and consistent system. Now, it happens that philosophers perform the same activities: They seek to gather a body of related knowledge that supplies a logic of effective thinking for the

[11] Koontz, "A Model," p. 420.

A POINT OF
DEPARTURE

25

solution of certain kinds of problems. Given these similarities, it can be a valuable exercise to look at administration as a philosophy.

The term *philosophy* is universally acknowledged as extremely difficult to define. It can mean an attitude toward certain activities, as in a person's "philosophy of doing business." The term can take on the meaning of a long-range, detached view of certain immediate problems, as for example, when, after failing the final examination, the college student remarks that he "ought to be more philosophical." Finally, a philosophy can be an evaluation or interpretation of what is important or meaningful in life.

The last definition relates back to the comments we made in chapter 1: in the aggregate, the decisions that administrators make shape our destiny when they determine how our resources are to be utilized. However, we can only influence the aggregate by studying the individual. So, we turn to our first definition of philosophy: an attitude toward certain activities.

Values

All administrators have a philosophy; that is, a value system which prioritizes basic convictions. This value system guides the way that administrators deal with organizational problems by assessing what is a desirable or preferred action. In decision making, an administrator's philosophy shows itself both in the choice of desirable outcomes or goals and in the means chosen for their attainment.

For example, the belief that organizations should seek growth; efficiency; strong, forceful leaders; and distribute material rewards for hard work is value-laden. Contrasting values might advocate that organizations provide stability; interesting and challenging work for their employees, regardless of the implications on efficiency; promote democracy in decision making; and distribute material rewards on the basis of need. Clearly, neither of these sets of values is right or wrong. However, they *are* different, and that is what is important. The administrator who places humanistic considerations above economic returns will make different decisions than one whose values are reversed. Again, we cannot say that there is a single correct value system for an administrator, though textbooks in administrative theory have traditionally used cost minimization (efficiency) and goal attainment (effectiveness). We will also use efficiency and effectiveness as desirable outcomes, although we will make some modifications in chapters 4, 5 and 7.

A review of the literature concludes that an individual's value system is determined by cultural norms and the education and experience that he or she has been exposed to. This individual value system, when combined with the unique history of an organization, determines an administrator's behavior. Figure 2-2 describes this relationship.

No administrator functions within a vacuum. One is influenced heavily by the current cultural milieu—values, beliefs, and attitudes prevalent in society, as well as the culture unique to the organization. A fact often overlooked, however, is that the present has been determined by the past: The

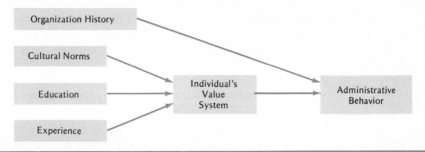

FIGURE 2-2   Determinants of administrative behavior

previous successes and failures that the organization has encountered, dominant administrative philosophies espoused by prior administrators, and precedents set by earlier administrative decisions are a few of the historical factors that influence the behavior of current administrators.

Of the four inputs shown in Figure 2-2, a textbook can influence only the education input. Although pseudoexperience can be gained through case and simulation work, experience is difficult to develop in a classroom. The other two inputs are also beyond our influence. Therefore, what we shall do in the following pages is assist the reader, through an understanding of the administrative process, toward building his or her own philosophy on how best to allocate and coordinate an organization's resources in order to attain the organization's goals.

Implications for educating administrators

The above discussion addressed *education* but made no mention of *training* administrators. This may seem to be of no consequence, for, after all, what is the difference between education and training? We believe there is an important difference.

Training is the process of learning a sequence of programmed behaviors. It enables a person to solve a repetitive problem. We train bricklayers, television repairmen, typists, and hospital admission clerks. The activities of these jobs can be precisely defined, broken down, analyzed, and a "one best way" determined. Training is the *application* of knowledge. It gives people an awareness of the rules and procedures to guide their behavior.

In contrast, education instills sound reasoning processes rather than merely imparting a body of serial facts. Education is the understanding and interpretation of knowledge. It does not provide definitive answers, but rather develops a logical and rational mind that can determine relationships among pertinent variables and thereby understand phenomena. The work of philosophers or researchers is too varied and complex for programmed training.

A POINT OF DEPARTURE

We suggest that administrators must, therefore, be educated rather than merely trained. True, there are some specific administrative abilities

27

that can be taught—for example, listening skills—but little of what administrators do lends itself to specific job training. Administration is a discipline that is situational, having few laws or principles, and hence the need for education.

> There is no such thing as *the* right way for a manager to operate or behave. There are only ways that are appropriate for specific tasks of specific enterprises under specific conditions, faced by managers of specific temperaments and styles.[12]

We can give people the so-called "tools to administer" in an undergraduate or graduate program, but can we state with assurance that these students will outperform, on the job, those that have not been exposed to these tools? The evidence is clouded. We do know, however, that many outstanding administrators have never had a formal course in administration, whereas many incompetents have a long list of impressive academic credentials. Finally, we know that grades in an administrative program are inadequate predictors of success in performing administrative functions. These findings can be interpreted to support our contention that administrators cannot be trained. In fact, we are undoubtedly guilty in many of our academic programs of overemphasizing facts at the expense of analytical appraisal.

We know also that many who are exposed to a short course in administration, management, or leadership return to their jobs unaffected by the experience. Such "instant administrators" are doomed to fail, for there are no instant solutions. As Harvard professor Theodore Levitt has stated, "We can teach *about* management, but we cannot teach management. We can teach what a manager does, but not by teaching enable someone to do it."[13] A summary of our position would be: *We cannot train people to administer; we can only educate them to think like administrators.* Therefore, a course or textbook in administration will develop your knowledge and understanding of the administrative process which will enable you to improve your potential for making organizations perform better.

We cannot certify administrative ability. No degree or certificate ensures competence. In some circles—for example, among elementary and secondary school officials—it has become appropriate to require administrative certificates. We should recognize, given our previous discussion, that this is an exercise most difficult to defend. We cannot measure administrative competence by years of experience, courses completed, or scores on an examination, factors that are the basis for most administrative certificates in education. The only valid evidence is performance in the arena of battle, and, of course, education and experience make up only two determinants of an administrator's success.

[12] Theodore Levitt, "The Managerial Merry-Go-Round," *Harvard Business Review*, July-August 1974, p. 121.
[13] Levitt, "The Management Merry-Go-Round," p. 124.

Successful administrators have analytical, human, conceptual, and specialized skills. They are able to think and understand. Courses in administrative theory, organizational behavior, financial analysis, accounting principles, or statistical methods cannot *make* an administrator. They cannot overcome the inability to understand cause-and-effect relations, to synthesize from experience, to visualize relationships, or to think logically.

However, training can fine-tune specific skills, and all administrators need to develop specialized functional expertise. That is, few people are general administrators; rather, they administer within a specific function—say, finance, accounting, personnel, research, engineering, marketing, transportation, medicine, or dentistry—and to their functional expertise, they add administrative responsibilities. Therefore, administrators must have particular expertise in the area within which they administer, but they must also possess an awareness of administrative concepts so that they are able to conceptualize, to question, and to understand the administrative process.

By merging specialized skills with knowledge of the administrative process, people prepare themselves for successful administrative careers. This book will contribute through assisting in the development of that knowledge. While we can make no claim that this knowledge will guarantee success, it can be enthusiastically stated that this knowledge will improve one's potential for success.

A qualifying note

Consistent with your author's personal "truth-in-advertising" policy, we should make explicit what this book does *not* attempt to do.

First, do not look for simple answers. If you were hoping to find in this book the ten easy steps to becoming a successful administrator, look elsewhere. While this book has been written to present the administrative process in a clear and logical format, this does not mean the information is simple to apply.

Second, there is still a lot more we need to know about the administrative process. In a number of areas, further research is required to clarify the mixed results that have been achieved to date. Therefore, when we are confronted with findings that are contradictory or that do not allow us to make reasonably valid conclusions, we will state that fact.

Finally, the purpose of this book is not to convince you that you should choose a career in administration. If you find this book interesting, you may want to take further courses and more fully consider the opportunities in administration. But this is not a propaganda document meant to entice you into an administrative career. Being an administrator can be a tough job, and it is not for everyone. The field does offer exciting challenges and opportunities, but not without costs. You may have to make decisions which are personally displeasing—for example, closing an office in a community which is already facing economic hardships or terminating an em-

A POINT OF
DEPARTURE

ployee who has tried hard but failed to perform adequately—but administrators frequently have to make these tough decisions. What this book can do is to help you begin to weigh the advantages and disadvantages of a career in administration.

summary of major points

1. This book presents a sound theoretical base so one will know what good administrative practices ought to be. However, since theory and practice are frequently divergent, the book also attempts to explain why theory and practice differ when they do.
2. Administration is generic; that is, a universal process in all organized activities.
   a. All administrators plan, organize, lead and control.
   b. Skills are transferable, with certain qualifications, between public and private organizations.
   c. There are cultural differences which limit generalizability between nations.
   d. Successful transferability increases at the upper levels of organizations.
3. Organizational behavior is a subfield within the discipline of administration.
4. Administration is both an art and a science.
5. All administrators have a philosophy; that is, a value system which prioritizes their basic convictions and guides the way they deal with organizational problems.
6. Administrators must be educated rather than merely trained.
7. This book depicts the administrative process, but it does *not*:
   a. Provide simple answers or guarantees of administrative success.
   b. Attempt to draw firm conclusions when the research evidence is mixed.
   c. Try to *convince* the reader that he or she should choose a career in administration.

FOR DISCUSSION

1. Why should a student of administration know both theory and practice?
2. Build an argument to defend the statement: "Administration in the private and public sectors is more similar than different."
3. What are the predominant values advocated by administrative theory?
4. "Training and a philosophical approach to administration are incom-

patible." Do you agree or disagree with this statement? Explain your position.

5. "Administration is a subfield within organizational behavior." Do you agree or disagree with this statement? Explain your position.

6. "Administration can be viewed as a science." Build an argument to support this statement. Then build an argument against this statement.

7. "A good administrator will be a good administrator anywhere." Do you agree or disagree with this statement? Explain your position.

8. Would you describe your current academic program as education or training? Why?

case exercise

The new job with a 90 percent pay-cut

Arjay Miller joined the Ford Motor Company in 1947 as an assistant treasurer. He was thirty-one years old, and he came to his job from three years of post-graduate work at the University of California, a stint in the Army during World War II, and several years' experience as an economist with the Federal Reserve Bank in San Francisco.

Miller's career progress at Ford was certainly impressive. In 1953, he was promoted to corporate controller, achieved a vice-presidency in 1957, and in 1963 was made president of the corporation. At the age of 47, he was second in command (to Henry Ford II, chairman of the board) at one of the world's largest corporations. But in February 1968, Mr. Ford decided that a change in the presidency was needed to bolster sagging sales performance. Miller was given the title of vice chairman, and a top General Motors executive was hired to fill the presidency. In his new position, Miller was to be responsible for external and financial affairs and long-range planning.

Soon after this change in responsibilities at Ford, Miller received an offer to take on a new challenge. He was asked to become Dean of the Graduate School of Business at Stanford University. The opportunity had its appeal. Stanford represented one of the top two graduate schools of business in the U.S. It would offer Miller the chance to influence the direction of management education. It also would allow him to alter the business school at Stanford to reflect an area he found particularly important—turning out managers that could apply their talents to government and educational organizations, as well as business.

If Miller accepted the Stanford post, he would not be breaking new ground. Other executives had preceded him in moving from the corporate world to leadership roles at quality business schools. For example, John Barr went from president and chairman of Montgomery Ward to head the business school at Northwestern University. George James went from a senior vice-president at Mobil Oil to become dean of Columbia's Graduate School of Busi-

A POINT OF DEPARTURE

ness. But accepting Stanford's offer meant ending a twenty-three-year career at Ford and taking an estimated 90 percent cut in pay from his 1968 earnings of $470,000.

Miller decided to accept the Stanford offer. It took him nearly a year to clean-up things at Ford, but in July 1969 he was in California beginning his new job at Stanford's Graduate School of Business.

Questions

1. What similarities are there between the presidency of the Ford Motor Company and dean at Stanford?
2. What differences are there between the two positions?
3. What would motivate Miller to take a job that results in a 90 percent reduction in compensation?

FOR FURTHER READING

Cassell, F.H., "The Politics of Public—Private Management," *MSU Business Topics*, Summer 1972, pp. 7–18. The author argues that the distinction between public and business administrators is blurred and that there are common denominators between the two; nevertheless, there are important differences in the decision-making process for the setting of priorities.

Collins, R.C., "Training and Education: Trends, Differences, and Issues," *Public Administration Review,* November-December 1973, pp. 508–15. Discusses the growth in government efforts to increase managerial and executive effectiveness through training and emphasizes that we must go beyond training to education.

Duncan, W.J., "Management Theory and the Practice of Management," *Business Horizons,* October 1974, pp. 48–52. Survey of management teachers and practicing managers found that although their perceptions are different, both have similar ideas about the nature of the schism between management theory and management practice.

Gribbins, R.E., "Is Management a Science?" *Academy of Management Review,* January 1978, pp. 139–44. Management is a science because it satisfies each of the three critical criteria: there exists a distinct subject matter, it presumes underlying regularities, and utilizes the scientific method.

Muse, W.V., "The Universality of Management," *Academy of Management Journal,* June 1967, pp. 179–84. Based on a study of social fraternities, the author found that success was related to following selected management concepts. The author concluded that management concepts have universal application.

Siffin, W.J., "Business Administration—Public Administration," *Business Horizons,* Winter 1963, pp. 69–76. An early position paper articulating the perceived differences between business and public administration.

Chapter

The Evolution of Administrative Thought

**AFTER
STUDYING
THIS CHAPTER,
YOU SHOULD BE
ABLE TO—**

Industrial revolution	Contingency movement
Scientific management	Psychology
Bureaucracy	Sociology
Human-relations movement	Social psychology
Decision-science movement	Anthropology
Behavioral movement	Political science
Task approach	Engineering
Organizational-humanist	Economics
movement	Mathematics and
Systems movement	statistics
Power dynamics movement	Physiology

Contributions of the church and military to administrative thought
Frederick Taylor's four principles of management
Henri Fayol's contribution to administrative thought
The Hawthorne studies and their impact on administrative thought
The arguments against "principles of administration"
The conflict between diversity and integration
Why diversity created what has been called "a management theory jungle"

Oliver Wendell Holmes, Jr. said it so well: "When I want to understand what is happening today or try to decide what will happen tomorrow, I look back." The message in this phrase has important relevance for students of administration.

If we are to appreciate the current state of administrative thought, we need to retravel the road that brought us to where we are. We will find that the practice of administration goes back thousands of years, but only in recent history has this experience been accumulated and synthesized into a body of knowledge or a discipline.

Historical background

We find evidence that the Egyptians practiced decentralization and the use of staff advice, 2,000 years before Christ. The mere physical presence of the pyramids forces us to accept that there had to exist formal plans, organization, leadership, and control systems. How else would it have been possible to build a structure covering as much as 13 acres, with nearly 2½ million stone blocks, each weighing an average of 2½ tons? "Construction is estimated to have taken the labor of over one hundred thousand men for twenty years."[1] To put this into perspective, this achievement is equivalent to administering an organization three times the size of the Shell Oil Company. Clearly, such an undertaking indicates the effective practice of administrative functions.

We also have evidence that in approximately 1100 B.C., the Chinese recognized the need for planning, organizing, leading, and controlling. And by the time of Christ, we find evidence that the unity of command, management by exception, and delegation to subordinate administrators were practiced.

In the Bible, for example, Moses' father-in-law said to Moses:

The thing thou doest is not good. Thou wilt surely wear away, both thou, and this people that is with thee: for this thing is too heavy for thee; thou art not able to perform it thyself alone. Hearken now unto my voice, I will give thee counsel .... Moreover thou shalt provide out of all the people able men ... and place such over them, to be rulers of thousands, and rulers of hundreds, rulers of fifties, and rulers of tens: And let them judge the people at all seasons: and it shall be, that every great matter they shall bring unto thee, but every small matter they shall judge: so shall it be easier for thyself, and they shall bear the burden with thee. If thou shalt do this thing, and God command thee so, then thou shalt be able to endure, and all this people shall also go to their place in peace.[2]

[1] Claude S. George, Jr., *The History of Management Thought*, 2nd ed. (Englewood Cliffs, N.J.: Prentice-Hall, 1972), p. 4.
[2] Exod. 18:17–23.

This reference brilliantly dramatizes the need to delegate authority in a large organization and to review only the unusual or exceptional cases that cannot be resolved by subordinate administrators. This brief quotation explains simplistically why organization charts have been historically pyramid-shaped!

Two other institutions that contributed significantly to the development of organization design and administrative theory were the church and the military. The former is best exemplified by the Roman Catholic church. It has endured for nearly 2,000 years with a simple, five-level hierarchy.

In the Catholic church, the chain of authority moves from the pope to cardinals, to archbishops, to bishops, and finally to parish priests. This simple structure has proved viable for an organization with over 430,000 clergymen. It has remarkably few authority layers, in comparison to those of a giant corporation. General Motors, for example, has 30,000 people in administrative posts, and requires approximately thirteen levels in the hierarchy, from the chairman of the board to the foreman on the assembly line. At General Motors, it is indeed rare for an administrator to have more than fifteen subordinates reporting to him; however, it is not unusual for a bishop to have more than 500 priests responsible to him.

Military organizations were also singled out as contributors to our field. The use of staff support advice, uniform methods for performing tasks, and discipline were practiced by Alexander the Great, Hannibal, Caesar, and Napoleon.[3] More recently, the armed forces have acted as a major source for studies in leadership, authority, and conflict.

The most important, pretwentieth century influence on administration was the industrial revolution. In the eighteenth and nineteenth centuries, a technological "revolution" took place in England. Machine power was rapidly substituted for human power. Additionally, the steam engine provided more efficient and cheaper power. As the market for products increased, it became more efficient to bring people together to produce goods in factories rather than in their private homes. For example, where previously the weaving of cloth was done by hundreds of women working separately in their homes, these women were brought together under one roof in order to take advantage of the economies made possible by the new technology. Suddenly, there was a need for administration to organize the factories, determine who would do what, direct daily activities, and insure that output quantities and standards were maintained.

In the 1830s, Charles Babbage wrote about the need for the systematic study and standardization of work operations to improve productivity. He argued for dividing up work and assigning work to individuals on the basis of skill. Babbage also examined the feasibility of replacing manual operations with automatic machinery. His work laid the groundwork for what has become known as "scientific management."

[3] George, *History of Management Thought*, pp. 20–23

If one were required to specifically pinpoint the time when the field of modern management or administrative theory was born, the date would have to be 1911, because of the publication then, and subsequent acceptance, of Frederick Winslow Taylor's *Principles of Scientific Management*. This work, along with the studies conducted prior to and following its publication, established Taylor as the father of scientific management.

Taylor's ideas developed out of his engineering work at the Midvale and Bethlehem Steel companies during the late nineteenth and early twentieth centuries. He spent more than two decades employing the scientific method on the shop floor, seeking the "one best way" for each job.

Taylor had become increasingly aware of shortcomings in factory operations of his day. There were no clear concepts of worker and management responsibilities. Virtually no effective work standards were applied. The potential of incentives to improve labor's performance was untapped. Workers purposely worked at a slow pace. Management decisions were of the "seat-of-the-pants" nature, based on hunch, intuition, or past experience. Workers were placed at tasks for which they had little or no ability or aptitude. Most important, management and workers viewed themselves as at odds with each other, rather than cooperating to their mutual benefit.

As a result of these perceptions, Taylor sought to create a mental revolution by defining clear guides for improving production efficiency. He defined four principles of management: (1) the replacement of rule-of-thumb methods for determining each element of a worker's job with scientific determination; (2) the scientific selection and training of workmen; (3) the cooperation of management and labor to accomplish work objectives, in accordance with the scientific method; and (4) a more equal division of responsibility between managers and workers, with the former doing the planning and supervising, and the latter doing the execution.

The most frequently cited example of Taylor's method, his classic pig-iron experiment, illustrates his approach. The average output of 92-pound pigs loaded onto rail cars was 12½ tons per man per day. Taylor's analysis indicated that the figure should be between 47 and 48 tons per day. After studying the most minute details of this job, he instructed the workers in how to lift, how fast to walk, and when to rest. By putting the right man on the job, with the correct tools or equipment, by having the worker follow his supervisor's instructions exactly, and by motivating the worker through economic incentives (promising $1.85 a day wages, in contrast to the going rate of $1.15), he was able to reach his 48-ton objective.

Overall, Taylor was able to achieve improvements in productivity in the range of 200 percent or more. He reaffirmed the role of managers to plan and control, and of workers to perform as they were instructed. Although today we find this systematizing and proceduring of jobs as rather a codification of the obvious, it was a dramatic, even revolutionary approach in its day. The social benefits resulting from a productivity increase in excess of 200 percent were translated into lower costs, and ultimately into a high standard of living for all of society. If we acknowledge that acceptance of an idea is strongly dependent on the environment and needs of society at the time, Taylor's contribution can be better understood. At this point in industry's development, concern was with increasing productivity. The populace was receptive to efficiency suggestions. A claim, made in 1910 by an efficiency expert, that the railroads could save a million dollars a day (equivalent to about 30 million dollars a day in 1980 dollars) through the application of scientific management, had great appeal to both manufacturers and the general public. It should not surprise us to find, therefore, that Taylor's scientific management was accepted by managers and adopted not only in the United States, but in France, Germany, Russia, and Japan.

Taylor's efforts inspired others to study and develop methods of scientific management. Probably of greatest note was his impact on Frank and Lillian Gilbreth and Morris Cooke. The Gilbreths became known for their work in motion study,[4] and Cooke broadened the ideas of scientific management to include their application in universities and municipal organizations.[5]

Frank Gilbreth's background was as a construction contractor. Influenced by Taylor, he gave up his contracting career in 1912 to study scientific management. He directed his efforts to work arrangements, eliminating wasteful hand and body motions, and designing and using the right tools and equipment for optimizing work performance. For example, he reduced the number of motions in bricklaying from 18 to 4½ per brick laid—an improvement in productivity of over 300 percent.

As did Taylor, Gilbreth sought the one best way to perform jobs. Specifically, he emphasized hand and general body motions to optimize their efforts. He believed in and supported the idea that efficiency and speed did not have to be lost to gain quality. He advocated competition, in addition to pay, to achieve high performance. What Taylor contributed to scientific management through time study, Gilbreth contributed through motion study.

Of the other half dozen names usually included as significant contributors to scientific management, let us conclude our discussion by noting the contributions of Morris Cooke, who wrote between 1910 and 1920.

Cooke, who personally studied under Taylor for a year and a half, produced several reports which removed scientific management techniques and principles from the industrial sector and demonstrated their applicabil-

---

[4] See, for example, Frank B. Gilbreth, *Motion Study* (New York: D. Van Nostrand Co., 1911); and Frank B. and Lillian M. Gilbreth, *Fatigue Study* (New York: Sturgis and Walton Company, 1916).

[5] Morris Cooke, *Academic and Industrial Efficiency* (New York: Carnegie Foundation for the Advancement of Teaching, Bulletin No. 5, 1910); and Cooke, *Our Cities Awake* (New York: Doubleday, 1918).

ity to university administration and municipal management. He found that administrative practices in universities were even worse than Taylor was finding in industry. Although committee decision-making was slow and cumbersome, it was the predominant way decisions were made; coordination was hampered by allowing departments excessive autonomy; pay was allocated on the basis of seniority rather than merit; and high-priced professors' teaching and research suffered because they spent a great deal of time on work that assistants could do at a lower cost. In the City of Philadelphia, Cooke revamped budgeting procedures, introduced formal selection procedures in hiring, and sought to replace committees with individuals who could be held accountable for their decisions. Further, he fired 1000 workers who were inefficient, saved $1 million in garbage collection over a four-year period, and reduced utility rates by over $1 million.[6]

Cooke's contribution, therefore, was in realizing early on that scientific management could be transferred from the industrial to the educational and public sectors. He recognized that the concepts of efficiency, so valuable to the profit sector, could be equally valuable in nonprofit and service organizations.

General administrative theorists

Writing at the same time as Taylor, but on another continent, was Henri Fayol, of France. In contrast to Taylor, who was concerned with shop management, Fayol took a broader view. Fayol can be described as the first of the general administrative theorists—that is, those concerned with principles of organization and the functions of an administrator. His most relevant contributions, from our perspective, were the designation of administrative functions and his recognition that the discipline was universal in nature.

Fayol's primary work, *General and Industrial Administration,* viewed administration as a separate body of knowledge that had applicability to all forms of group activity. Foremost was Fayol's definition of administration: planning, organizing, commanding, coordinating, and controlling. Here was the first enunciation of the functions of an administrator. Six decades have passed since the publication of this work, yet our description of an administrator as one who plans, organizes, leads, and controls is almost unchanged. Commanding is only a more directive and formal view of what we today call leading. We consider that coordinating, which Fayol described as the unifying and harmonizing of all activity and effort, permeates the other four basic functions. We must coordinate our plans, our organization, human factors, and our controls if goals are to be accomplished.

Several other writers deserve to be recognized as major general administrative contributors—Max Weber, Oliver Sheldon, Leonard D. White,

[6] Daniel A. Wren, *The Evolution of Management Thought* (New York: Ronald Press, 1972), pp. 173–76.

Mary Parker Follett, James D. Mooney, Luther Gulick and Lyndall Urwick, and Chester Barnard.

Max Weber was a German sociologist. Writing in the early part of this century, although relatively unheard of in English-speaking countries until the 1940s, Weber developed a theory of authority structures and described organizational activity based on authority relations. The ideal type of organization which he described became the first fully developed theory of bureaucracy. Weber's ideal bureaucratic type can be briefly characterized by the following features:

1. Division of labor
2. A defined authority hierarchy of superior-subordinate relationships
3. Formal set of rules and procedures
4. Impersonal interactions
5. Selection and promotion based on merit

Bureaucracy, as described by Weber, is not unlike scientific management in its ideology. Both emphasize rationality, predictability, impersonality, technical competence, and authoritarianism. While Weber's writings were far less operational than Taylor's, they developed a sociological theory of organization that significantly influenced academics and practicing administrators following World War II.

Oliver Sheldon wrote his *Philosophy of Management* in 1923. It marked a departure from earlier writings by adding ethics and social responsibility to the scientific study of management. Administrators were recognized as having a responsibility to their community, and it was in Sheldon's normative approach to the subject that he was able to develop the first comprehensive attempt to view management as both a science and a philosophy.

The first full textbook devoted uniquely to the public sector was Leonard D. White's *Introduction to the Study of Public Administration,* published in 1926. In this book, White argued that administration should be separate from, and not intrude upon, politics; that the field of administration is a legitimate discipline, lending itself to scientific study; and that the mission of administration is economy and efficiency. White will be most remembered for his contribution toward giving the study of administration academic legitimacy and developing public administration as a discipline.

A quarter of a century ahead of her time, Mary Parker Follett made significant contributions in the areas of motivation, leadership, power, and authority during the first third of this century. Like Sheldon, she is best described as a managerial philosopher. Her recognition that organizations could be viewed from the perspective of individual and group behavior established her as an early advocate of what was to become the behavioral movement.

James D. Mooney, in 1931, coauthored a classic in the development of organization, entitled *Onward Industry.* His investigation demonstrated that military, religious, and industrial organizations have common attributes.

Specifically, he concluded that they all require coordination, have a system of hierarchically formed superior–subordinate relationships, and clearly define the duties and responsibilities for each job.

In 1937, Luther Gulick and Lyndall Urwick created a series of papers on the science of administration which brought together the major writings of the time. Six years later, Urwick published *The Elements of Administration,* which like his earlier co-edited series, is more notable for its synthesizing properties than for its originality. While many of the scientific management and general administrative theorists differed in their terminology, Urwick found numerous similarities in their thought. His work, crystallized these similar concepts that had been developed independently, integrating them into a relatively uniform body of knowledge.

It has been written that "Chester I. Barnard has probably had a more profound impact on the thinking about the complex subject matter of human organization than has any other contributor to the continuum of management thought."[7] As the president of the New Jersey Bell Telephone Company, he wrote from his experience as a practicing manager, as did Fayol. He demonstrated the importance of the informal organization and was an early advocate of viewing an organization as a system of coordinated activities. Barnard introduced social aspects into the analysis of managerial functions and processes. His book, *The Functions of the Executive,* written in 1938, is a landmark effort in portraying the administrator as the nucleus of a complex social system, the organization.

Human-relations movement

It is generally agreed that the human-relations movement began as a result of studies undertaken at Western Electric Company's Hawthorne Works in Chicago between 1927 and 1932. Conducted under the direction of Harvard psychologist Elton Mayo, they began as an examination of the relation between the physical environment and productivity. Illumination, temperature, and other working conditions were selected as symbolic of this physical environment. The researchers' initial findings contradicted their anticipated results.

In the first series of experiments, two work groups were established. An experimental group was presented with varying intensity of illumination, while the controlled unit worked under a constant illumination intensity. The researchers had expected individual output to be directly related to the intensity of light. However, there were contradictions in their findings. As the light level was increased in the experimental unit, output rose for each group. But to the surprise of the researchers, as the light level was dropped in the experimental group, productivity continued to increase in both. In fact, a productivity decrease was observed in the experimental group only when the light intensity had been reduced to that of moonlight.

[7] George, *History of Management Thought,* p. 140.

Mayo and his associates concluded that illumination intensity clearly was not directly related to group productivity, but they could not explain the behavior they had witnessed.

A second experiment took place in the relay-assembly test room at the plant. Its objective was to determine the effect that changes in various working conditions had on group productivity. Their conclusions were that there was little or no relationship between working conditions and productivity.

In a third experiment, the researchers sought to determine the effect of a group piecework incentive pay system on group productivity. The results indicated that the wage incentive plan was less of a determining factor on a worker's output than were group pressure and acceptance, and the concomitant security. Social norms of the group, therefore, were concluded to be the key determinants of individual work behavior.

It is generally agreed upon by scholars in administration that the Hawthorne studies had a dramatic impact on the direction of administrative thought. Mayo's conclusions were that behavior and sentiments were closely related, that group influences were significant in affecting individual behavior, that group standards were highly effective in establishing individual worker output, and that money was less a factor in determining output than group standards, sentiments, and security. These conclusions led to a new emphasis on the human factor in the functioning of organizations and the attainment of their goals. They also led to increased paternalism by administration, and the somewhat naive assumption that happy employees would be productive workers.

The Hawthorne studies have not been without critics. Attacks have been made on procedures, analysis of the findings, and the conclusions drawn.[8] However, from our standpoint, it really is of little importance whether the studies were academically sound or its conclusions justified. What is important is that they were significant in stimulating an interest in the human factors. From a historical perspective, the Hawthorne studies began a new direction—a recognition that human beings are a complex and influential input into organizational performance. Man is not a machine, and scientific management's "one best way" approach had to be tempered to recognize the effect of group behavior.

Decision-science movement

Decision making is the process of problem definition, alternative development, alternative appraisal, and solution selection. All administrators perform this process, and the decision-science movement has taken this process as the nucleus for its argument: Since administration is charac-

EVOLUTION OF ADMINISTRATIVE THOUGHT

[8] See, for example, Henry A. Landsberger, *Hawthorne Revisited* (Ithaca, N.Y.: New York State of Industrial Relations, Cornell University, 1958); and Alex Carey, "The Hawthorne Studies: A Radical Criticism," *American Sociological Review,* June 1967, pp. 403–16.

terized by decision making, decision making must be the central focus of administrative theory.

The works of Herbert Simon, James March, Russell Ackoff, Jay Forrester, Martin Starr, and Kenneth Boulding have made major contributions in this area. Areas of their concern include applications of statistics, optimization models, information models, and simulation. Specific contributions relate to linear programming, critical-path scheduling, inventory models, site-location models, and various forms of resource-allocation models. The rigorous approach of these decision scientists reactivated the logic of the scientific method, which had been subordinated by the human-relations movement in the latter 1930s and throughout the 1940s. They have aided in our ability to more effectively plan and control.

The decision-science movement is probably the most recent influential effort in upgrading the study of administration. Quantitative methods of decision appraisal, combined with the widespread use of computers, have added new complexity and sophistication to the field of study.

Behavioral movement

Paralleling the work of the decision scientists was a movement built upon ideas developed by Follett, Barnard, and Mayo. Its modern contributors have been behavioral scientists. This movement can be broken down further into two different sets: the "principles-blacklash" group and the behavioral-integrationist group.

The scientific management and general administration movements sought to develop principles of administration. Taylor, Fayol, Weber, White, Gulick, and Urwick all fall into this category. In the late 1940s, Herbert Simon and Dwight Waldo unleashed separate attacks on these previous approaches—both, in effect, arguing that there could be no such thing as a "principle" of administration.

Simon's *Administrative Behavior*[9] was probably the most important contribution of the 1940s. He demonstrated that for every "principle" of administration advocated in the literature there was a counter-principle, thus rendering the very idea of principles moot. He concluded that "principles of administration" were little more than ambiguous and mutually contradictory proverbs and that a new approach was needed to establish a consistent and useful administrative theory. He then predated the contingency movement by thirty years, saying:

> ... we see a steady shift of emphasis from the "principles of administration" themselves to a study of the *conditions* under which competing principles are respectively applicable. We no longer say that organization should be by purpose, but rather that under such and such conditions purpose organiza-

[9] Herbert A. Simon, *Administrative Behavior: A Study of Decision-Making Processes in Administrative Organizations* (New York: Macmillan, 1947).

tion is desirable, but under such and such other conditions, process organization is desirable.[10]

In 1948, Dwight Waldo also attacked the pseudoscience underlying principles.[11] He interpreted these so-called "principles" as being derived from common sense and the collection of facts, the assumption being that if enough data was accumulated, a science of administration would somehow emerge. He concluded, in spite of some encouraging research into informal organization, that the literature regarded people and the elements of an organization more or less as interchangeable parts in a modern machine.

The behavioral-integrationist group surfaced in the 1950s and 1960s and included Wilfred Brown, sociologist George Homans, and psychologists Victor Vroom, Lyman Porter, and Edward Lawler. In contrast to the human-relationist view which assumed that happy workers are productive workers, the behavioral-integrationists have been goal- and efficiency-oriented; yet they consider the understanding of human behavior to be the major means to that end. This direction, described by Wilfred Brown as a task approach, attempts to integrate our knowledge of people, structure, and processes.

Among the contributions of the behavioral scientists are the introduction of organizational change, motivation and leading of employees, conflict management, and integration of the goals of the individual and the organization. These people have increased significantly our knowledge about organizational behavior and added the rigorous research methodology of the social sciences to that used by the decision scientists. The result has been a quantum leap in the quality of organizational research and an accelerated increase in our understanding of the administrative process.

Organizational-humanist movement

The 1960s and 1970s also saw the human relations philosophy updated to create a new version of the "happiness movement." Popular names associated with this humanist orientation are Douglas McGregor, Rensis Likert, and Chris Argyris. Their unifying theme was that people are basically good and, in order to stimulate their performance, we should humanize work: Let people participate and take an active role in those decisions that affect them, have trust and confidence in people, reduce external control devices, and other such prescriptions characterize this movement.

The organizational-humanists are as much evangelist as scholar, maybe more so. They believe strongly in their cause and have appeared inflexible in their beliefs, even when faced with contradictory evidence.[12] An

[10] *Ibid.*, p. 240.

[11] Dwight Waldo, *The Administrative State* (New York: Ronald Press, 1948).

[12] One obvious exception has been Warren Bennis, a student of McGregor, who has moved away from his extreme humanistic position as a result of his experience as a senior administrator at SUNY-Buffalo and the University of Cincinnati.

example of this was the career of Douglas McGregor, whose book, *The Human Side of Enterprise*, made a strong argument for administrators to shift their assumptions about the nature of man and to seek an integration of individual and organizational goals. In his 1954 farewell address, after six years as president of Antioch College, McGregor recognized that his philosophy had failed to cope with the realities of organizational life.

> I believed, for example, that a leader could operate successfully as a kind of adviser to his organization. I thought I could avoid being a "boss." Unconsciously, I suspect, I hoped to duck the unpleasant necessity of making difficult decisions, of taking the responsibility for one course of action, among many uncertain alternatives, of making mistakes and taking the consequences. I thought that maybe I could operate so that everyone would like me—that "good human relations" would eliminate all discord and disagreement.
>
> I couldn't have been more wrong. It took a couple of years, but I finally began to realize that a leader cannot avoid the exercise of authority any more than he can avoid responsibility for what happens to his organization.[13]

Upon leaving Antioch, McGregor returned to his professorship at M.I.T. and, ironically, almost immediately began preaching his humanistic doctrine and continued doing so until his death in 1964.

In a similar vein, Chris Argyris has consistently argued for democracy in organizations. After studying two hundred American companies, however, he was disheartened to find them all authority conscious. Harvard colleague David McClelland candidly commented: "Chris, did it ever occur to you that the reason you didn't get a chance to study the organizations which are democratic is because they didn't stay in business long enough?"[14]

The point is that there are some individuals who so strongly believe in a certain philosophy that it can cloud their objectivity. This appears to be true of the organizational-humanists. Yet, in spite of this lack of objectivity, they have had a definite influence on administrative theory and practice.

Systems movement

The 1960s were the decade of the systems process. The advocates of the systems movement viewed this approach as the way to unify administrative theory.

The focus of the systems movement was on the organization. Organizations became increasingly described as input absorbers, processors, and output generators. The organizational system could be envisioned as made

---

[13] Douglas McGregor, "On Leadership," *Antioch Notes,* May 1954, pp. 2–3.
[14] "McClelland: An Advocate of Power." *International Management,* July 1975, p. 28.

up of "interdependent factors, including individuals, groups, attitudes, motives, formal structure, interactions, goals, status, and authority."[15]

This organizational system, however, is really a subsystem within the larger system of society, with its social, cultural, legal, physical, technical, and economic components—in the same way that the human heart is a subsystem within the body's physiological system. Understanding of organizational processes is advanced by viewing organizations as analogous to biological systems. The system must receive inputs to survive, these inputs must be processed, and output must be dispensed at a rate that maintains the viability of the organism.

Systems advocates have recognized that a change in any factor within the organization has impact on all other organizational or subsystem components. To better understand organizational processes, these advocates investigate the subsystems within the organization, the relationships between subsystems, and how subsystems interact to form a complete system. This approach has aided in the integration of administrative theory, and in the perception of organizations as dynamic and complex systems that must compatibly interact with a larger system or environment.

Power dynamics movement

In the 1970s there arose a theme, originally proposed by Weber, that power was the important element in understanding administration. Those who took this position acknowledged not only the role that decision making plays in the administrative process, but also the internal dynamics in decision making. Those who made the decisions and reaped the rewards were those with power. Prominent names in this movement include Abraham Zaleznik,[16] David McClelland,[17] David Kipnis,[18] Jeffrey Pfeffer, and Gerald Salancik.[19]

The power dynamics advocates could properly be included in the updated behavioral movement, yet their perspective is unique and important enough to justify separation. It would be correct to conclude that what the humanists are to idealism, these power-dynamists are to realism, and we should expect this movement to have a significant impact on administrative theory during the 1980s.

[15] Kenyon B. DeGreen, *Sociotechnical Systems* (Englewood Cliffs, N.J.: Prentice-Hall, Inc., 1973), p. 13.
[16] Abraham Zaleznik, "Politics and Power in Organizational Life," *Harvard Business Review,* May-June 1970, pp. 47–60.
[17] David McClelland, "The Two Faces of Power, *Journal of International Affairs,* vol. 24, no. 1, 1970.
[18] David Kipnis, *The Powerholders* (Chicago: University of Chicago Press, 1976).
[19] Jeffrey Pfeffer and Gerald R. Salancik, "Organization Design: The Case for a Coalitional Model of Organization," *Organizational Dynamics,* Autumn 1977, pp. 15–29.

The most recent direction taken by administrative theory can be described as a contingency or situational approach. Both the systems and contingency movements accept the dynamics and the complex interrelationships inherent in organizations and in the behavior of their members. As such, the contingency perspective is more an outgrowth of systems than an opposing philosophy.

It has become increasingly clear that it is difficult, if not impossible, to make broad-based generalizations about administrative practice that are applicable to all situations. The complexity of the subject and the distinctiveness of each situation have resulted in the expansion of the number of exceptional cases, to the point where there appears to be no universal law or principle that can be applied in every instance.

As a result, the contingency movement began by looking for some common characteristics that might exist in a number of situations, and that could make it possible to qualify the theory to the specifics of the situation. If we cannot say, "If X, then Y," possibly we can say, "If X, then Y, but only under conditions specified in Z." The efforts of contingency advocates have been directed predominantly at attempts to isolate "the Z variable," or situational determinants.

A contingency approach to the study of the administrative process is intuitively logical. Since organizations are diverse, it seems unlikely that there would be universally applicable "principles" that would work in all situations. But it is one thing to say that *it all depends* and another to say *what* it depends upon. Researchers in administration have been directing their efforts toward identifying these "what" variables.

From early work on organization design,[20] leadership,[21] and motivation,[22] separate contingency theories have more recently been advanced for determining how far ahead administrators should plan, the degree of specificity required in the establishment of objectives, and the degree of control that is necessary. While we have not yet developed a comprehensive and fully integrated theory, there are a group of variables that tend to frequently reappear. These are shown in Figure 3-1.

The variables identified in Figure 3-1 are not exhaustive. It would be possible to list more than a hundred factors that have been used as contingency variables. The purpose, however, of presenting the more popular ones is to provide you with some examples of what is meant by the term *contin-*

[20] See, for example: Tom Burns and G. M. Stalker, *The Management of Innovation* (London: Tavistock, 1960); James D. Thompson, *Organizations in Action* (New York: McGraw-Hill, 1967); Joan Woodward, *Industrial Organization: Theory and Practice* (New York: Oxford University Press, 1965); and Paul R. Lawrence and J.W. Lorsch, *Organization and Environment* (Boston: Harvard Business School, Division of Research, 1967).

[21] See, for example, Fred E. Fiedler, *A Theory of Leadership Effectiveness* (New York: McGraw-Hill, 1967).

[22] See, for example, Victor H. Vroom, *Work and Motivation* (New York: John Wiley, 1964).

Variable	Range		
Organization's size	Small	_____	Large
Ambiguity and complexity of task technology	Routine	_____	Nonroutine
Administrator's positional locale	Supervisor	_____	Chief Executive Officer
Administrator's position power	Low	_____	High
Individual differences among subordinates	?	_____	?*
Perceived clarity and equity of the reward system	Low	_____	High
Degree of environmental uncertainty	Stable and Certain	_____	Unstable and Uncertain

* Popular individual difference factors include the subordinate's growth need, dependency need, preference for structure, values, risk propensity, and aspiration level.

gency variable and to introduce you to those situational factors that will re-surface throughout chapters 6 through 17. Remember, though, that this list is not meant to present *every* contingency variable, only those that have been the most accurate in explaining why certain actions work sometimes and fail others. Nor should you assume that each of these variables is relevant to every activity in which an administrator engages. What we find is that in some situations, certain contingency variables will be active, while in other situations these same variables may be of little significance. The relevance of any variable will vary with the situation.

Organization's size   The number of people in an organization is a major in-fluence on what administrators do. As size increases, so do the problems of coordination. As an organization grows, it becomes necessary to develop more formal and sophisticated techniques to promote this coordination. For example, having a separate long-range planning department or devel-oping a thousand-page personnel policy manual would be necessary for I.B.M. with its more than 250,000 employees, but absurd for a county wel-fare agency that employs 15.

Ambiguity and complexity of task technology   In order for an organization to achieve its purpose, it uses technology; that is, it engages in the process of converting resource inputs into client-satisfying product or service outputs. Certain technologies are routine, such as an automobile assembly line at General Motors. Routine technologies require high regimentation and structure. On the other hand, the Rand Corporation, the renowned "think tank," solves unique problems for its clients. Each is a bit different. There-fore, Rand requires custom or nonprogrammed responses to satisfy the indi-

EVOLUTION OF
ADMINISTRATIVE
THOUGHT

vidual needs of a varying clientele. To illustrate, the organization design or leadership style that is successful with a routine technology may be a total failure with a nonroutine technology.

Administrator's positional locale   In chapter 2, we demonstrated that the level of an administrator within an organization influences his or her successful transfer between organizations. The positional locale of an administrator has even greater generalizability as a contingency variable. For instance, while all administrators plan, the type of planning changes at different levels in the organization. Similarly, there are differences in leading depending on whether one supervises operatives or directs the activities of other administrators.

Administrator's position power   Not all administrative positions entail the same degree of influence. Though we tend to see power increasing the higher up one goes in an organization, there are also significant differences between organizations. The director of purchasing for the City of Milwaukee and the director of purchasing for the City of Seattle do not necessarily have equivalent degrees of discretion. Their abilities to make commitments or to hire, fire, promote, and give raises to their staff will depend on the power they have in their position. This power varies widely among administrative jobs.

Individual differences among subordinates   We know people are different. Their education, background, personal attitudes, and expectations differ widely. It should not be surprising, therefore, that these differences would affect the actions of an administrator. We will find that these differences are particularly important when an administrator must select the best way to motivate and lead his or her subordinates. An approach that is successful with employees who want their work to be challenging and free from close supervision, for example, will be considerably different from the approach that is equally successful with employees who want to be told exactly what they are supposed to do each day and who want to avoid responsibility for any mistakes that they make.

Perceived clarity and equity of the reward system   Organizations differ in the degree to which they allocate rewards on the basis of performance. In addition, certain jobs can be clearly measured in terms of performance (i.e., individuals on piecework, baseball players, or sales personnel), while other jobs are much more difficult to appraise—teaching, for example. Some argue that students can accurately evaluate a teacher. Others argue that the value of a learning experience can be appraised only after leaving school. Still others would argue that it is impossible to objectively evaluate teaching performance. The result is that in spite of the fact that there are many poor teachers, it is rare that teachers are fired because they cannot teach. Documenting poor teaching is just too difficult. We will find, therefore, that administrators will need to alter their actions to reflect the clarity and objectivity of the organization's performance evaluation system and performance-reward linkage, and to the particular characteristics of each job they direct.

Degree of environmental uncertainty   Administrators are not immune from factors outside the organization. For instance, during the late 1970s, when Quebec seriously considered severing its ties with Canada, administrators in both the public and private sectors of Canada were forced to consider the implications of a separate Quebec in their decisions. The degree of uncertainty caused by political, technological, sociocultural, and economic changes does impact on the administrative process. What works best in a highly volatile or changing environment may be totally inappropriate in a stable and predictable environment.

Where are we in the 1980s?

Looking back, from today's vantage point, we begin to see that administrative thought has grown and suffered from the strain of two conflicting forces: diversity and integration. Let us use these two themes to examine where we are today.

The product of diverse inputs

A vast number of disciplines have made direct contributions to administrative theory. The physical sciences, social sciences, and humanities have all contributed to a better understanding of how man can best achieve his goals in organized activities.

It is difficult to conceive of any area of academic study that has not or could not contribute to our discipline. Although the topics that follow obviously do not constitute a comprehensive list, they are fields that have made major contributions. They are presented to demonstrate that administrative theory is the product of diverse inputs.

Psychology   Psychology is the science that seeks to measure, explain, and sometimes change the behavior of man and other animals.[23] Psychologists concern themselves with studying and attempting to understand *individual* behavior. Those who have contributed and continue to add to the field of administration are learning psychologists, personality theorists, counseling psychologists, linguistic psychologists, and certainly organizational psychologists.

Early organizational psychologists concerned themselves with problems of fatigue, boredom, and any other factors relevant to working conditions that could impede efficient work performance. More recently, their contributions have been expanded to include training, supervision, leadership styles, needs, motivational forces, performance reviews, attitude measurement, and general shaping of the behavior of organizational members to facilitate repetition of desirable behaviors.

[23] Robert E. Silverman, *Psychology* (New York: Appleton-Century-Crofts, 1971), p. 2.

Sociology   Whereas psychologists focus on the individual, sociologists study the social system in which individuals fill their roles; that is, sociology studies man in relation to his fellow human beings.[24] Specifically, sociologists have made their greatest contribution to administration through their study of group behavior in organizations, particularly formal and complex organizations.

Areas within administration that have received valuable input from sociologists include group dynamics, formal organization theory, bureaucracy, authority, communications, power, and conflict.

It is my own belief that one of the major failings in current administrative research has been an inadequate integrating of sociological contributions. Recent behavioral efforts have emphasized psychological dimensions, particularly in the areas of leadership and motivation. In contrast, we have made slower progress in advancing, from where we were fifteen years ago, our knowledge of communicative processes, conflict management, political processes, or power relationships.

Social psychology   A relatively new field in its own right, social psychology examines interpersonal behavior. Whereas psychology and sociology attempt to explain individual and group behavior respectively, social psychology seeks to explain how and why individuals behave as they do in group activities. One of the major areas receiving considerable investigation by social psychologists has been *change*—how to implement it, and how to reduce barriers to its acceptance. Additionally, we find social psychologists making significant contributions in measuring and understanding attitudes, the problem-solving process, communication patterns, and how group activities can satisfy individual needs (such as through affiliation and power).

Anthropology   Recognition that how we behave is a function of our culture dramatizes the contribution anthropologists have made to the study of administration. As we noted previously, cultural differences exist within nations as well as between nations. There are differences in fundamental values, attitudes, and norms of acceptable behavior. Our individual value systems—that is, our priorities on what is important—will affect our attitudes and, therefore, our behavior on the job. Additionally, the work that anthropologists have done with animals, especially in the ape family, has been valuable in drawing generalizations about individual and group behavior.

Political science   Political scientists have made contributions in areas of allocation of power and authority, as well as the structuring of conflict. Their most noteworthy concern is how people manipulate power for individual self-interest.

As we are increasingly learning, politics, power, and conflict are reali-

---

[24] Alvin L. Bertrand, *Basic Sociology,* 2nd ed. (New York: Appleton-Century-Crofts, 1973), p. 3.

ties in organizational activities. Although ignored in many administrative treatises, the contributions of political scientists are significant to the further understanding of behavior in organizations.

Engineering   The early work in management, particularly during the first quarter of this century, centered around efficiency, and the designing of jobs and work procedures that would optimize performance. Generally, the contributions made in this period were the result of using industrial engineering techniques.

Engineers have added significantly to our ability to integrate physical work conditions with human capabilities. They have effectively reduced job fatigue and increased per capita output through their efforts in job design, work flow and procedures, and location selection and layout.

Economics   Economists have contributed heavily to administration through their work in forecasting and decision making. Their effort to optimize the allocation of resources has shown itself in advising administrators of more effective ways to adjust to external conditions and through giving input to improve internal decision making.

Concepts such as fixed and variable costs, opportunity costs, marginalism, elasticity, discounted cash flows, breakeven analysis, planning–programming–budgeting systems, return on investment, and economic forecasting are tools of administrators, yet it has been largely the economists who have developed and perfected these techniques.

Mathematics and statistics   Mathematicians and statisticians have made contributions in the same areas as economists by providing aids to improve decision making. In fact, econometricians and mathematical economists can be described as economists who use quantitative methods to make optimum resource allocations.

Quantitative contributions to administrative theory come from work in making decisions under risk and uncertainty, control systems, and such specific decision techniques as economic order quantity, queuing theory, and linear programming.

Physiology   An area whose contribution to administrative knowledge is often overlooked is that of the biological sciences, particularly physiology. Research from this field has been used in designing jobs and in understanding better and correcting the problems of anxiety and stress.

An example of the potential in this area is work being conducted at the University of Washington in Seattle, which demonstrates the effect of life changes on a person's physical well-being and general health.[25] Another area of potential is indicated by some preliminary work in organizational psychopharmacology, the use of drugs to affect behavior in the work en-

[25] Thomas Holmes and M. Matsuda, "Psychomatic Syndrome," *Psychology Today,* April 1972, p. 71.

FIGURE 3-2

The Blind Men and the Elephant
By John G. Saxe

It was six men of Indostan,
    To learning much inclined,
Who went to see the elephant
    (Though each of them was blind,)
That each by observation
    Might satisfy his mind.

The first approached the elephant,
    And happening to fall
Against his broad and sturdy side,
    At once began to bawl:
''God bless me! but the elephant
    Is very much like a wall!''

The second, feeling of the tusk,
    Cried: ''Ho! what have we here
So round, and smooth, and sharp?
    To me 'tis very clear
This wonder of an elephant
    Is very like a spear!''

The third approached the animal,
    And happening to take
The squirming trunk within his hands,
    Thus boldly up he spake:
''I see,'' quoth he, ''the elephant
    Is very much like a snake!''

The fourth reached out his eager hand,
    And fell upon the knee:
''What most this wondrous beast is like,
    Is very plain,'' quoth he;
'''Tis clear enough the elephant
    Is very like a tree!''

The fifth who chanced to touch the ear
    Said: ''E'en the blindest man
Can tell what this resembles most:
    Deny the fact who can,
This marvel of an elephant
    Is very like a fan!''

The sixth no sooner had begun
    About the beast to grope,
Then, seizing on the swinging tail
    That fell within his scope,
''I see,'' quoth he, ''the elephant,
    Is very like a rope!''

And so these men of Indostan
    Disputed loud and long,
Each in his own opinion
    Exceeding stiff and strong,
Though each was partly in the right,
And all were in the wrong!

vironment.[26] The former research has implications for improving safety performance and reducing absenteeism, and the latter offers an approach to treating worker alienation.

On the road toward synthesis and integration

As one might perceive at this point, administration as a discipline is a large field, with people from vastly different backgrounds investigating the area and expanding the frontiers of knowledge. Additionally, as one might expect, these vast differences in background have brought about a situation that has been called a "management theory jungle."[27] Few can agree on definitions, or on content in the discipline. What one group believes is an ideal approach to the study of the subject is ridiculed by other groups. It becomes difficult to separate the wheat from the chaff, as vested interests cloud reality. "Selective perception," which is the screening of "facts" in a situation by people according to their backgrounds and experiences, aptly describes a major problem in the study of administration at the present time. Each researcher and author selectively perceives the "facts" from his or her point of view.

Figure 3-2 humorously illustrates our dilemma in administrative theory: It is where you are, and what perspective you take, that determines what you see. The result has been a number of approaches to the study of our discipline. But this evolution in administrative thought from scientific management to contingencies is theoretical. Ironically, little evidence has been offered to support the notion that such "movements" actually have or do exist in the real world. Practicing administrators have always sought integration; it has been the academicians and theorists who have created "the jungle."

Figure 3-3 presents four dichotomies (or crossroads) and is offered as a simplistic path out of the jungle and toward a unified theory. It begins by noting that few theorists suggest any longer that there are "principles" of administration. We have made progress in the 1970s—there is general agreement today that a contingency framework is necessary.

The generic vs. "separate but equal" dichotomy appears to have come full circle. Early general administrative theorists, like Fayol, viewed administration generically. However, the 1940s through 1960s were a period of growing separation. Business administration and public administration sought different roads. The 1970s regained a view of the similarities within the discipline. Most theorists now acknowledge, possibly with more "lip service" than action, that the administrative process is applicable to both public and private, nonprofit and profit organizations.

In the economic vs. humanistic debate, the evidence suggests that the-

[26] Stephen P. Robbins, "Another Alternative: Organizational Psychopharmacology," in Stephen P. Robbins, *Organizational Behavior: Concepts and Controversies* (Englewood Cliffs, N.J.: Prentice-Hall, Inc., 1979), pp. 394–95.

[27] Harold Koontz, "The Management Theory Jungle," *Journal of the Academy of Management,* December 1961, pp. 174–86.

FIGURE 3-3   Divergent perspectives on administration

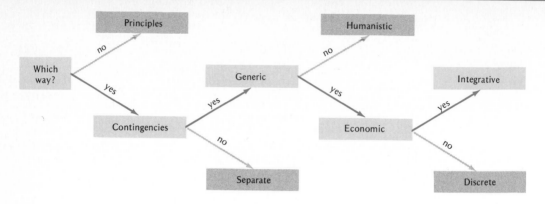

ory is aligning itself with practice. Humanistic concerns have been minimal among practitioners. Whether this is desirable, of course, is questionable, but the evidence suggests that economic criteria have been accepted by practitioners, and now theorists. This is most noticeable in the proposed new "socially responsible" role of business. In spite of the media attention and concern given the topic by academicians and practitioners, the evidence appears to overwhelmingly demonstrate that administrators in profit-making organizations continue to use profitability as a basis for their decisions.[28] When they make "socially responsible" decisions, they look for some positive and direct benefits for their organizations.

Finally, we arrive at the integrative vs. discrete dichotomy. The process approach, which is integrative, is the most popular organizational device for describing what administration is about; that is, administrators plan, organize, lead, and control. In contrast, one discrete approach used in some textbooks is to view administration from three schools of thought: the classical (which includes the contributions of scientific management and the general administrative theorists), the behavioral, and the quantitative. Another discrete approach has been to look at the individual, the group, and the organization as three separate elements. The process approach recognizes the contribution of the classical, behavioral and quantitative schools but does not separate them.

In conclusion, Figure 3-3 offers an optimistic picture. Certainly, not all administrative theorists would agree with my interpretation. Yet, the evidence indicates movement towards unification. This book will continue toward that end by utilizing a generic, contingency framework; measuring administrative performance in economic terms; and synthesizing the contributions of the various movements into the integrative process approach.

[28] Gerald D. Keim, "Managerial Behavior and the Social Responsibility Debate: Goals Versus Constraints," *Academy of Management Journal,* March 1978, pp. 57–68.

The plan of this book

It is our position that decision making is the central core of administration. In fact, we will demonstrate in the next two chapters how an understanding of decision making will allow us to substantially explain the frequent differences between administrative theory and practice.

In chapter 4, we will review decision theory; that is, we will present how administrators should make decisions. In chapter 5, we will modify this theory by introducing findings from behavioral research which demonstrate that there are human and organizational constraints that impinge upon the decision maker. After you have read chapters 4 and 5, you should understand how decisions *ought* to be made and how they are *actually* made in organizations. This, then, will become the foundation for the remainder of the book.

The four administrative functions of planning, organizing, leading, and controlling are presented in chapters 6 through 17. Each chapter is interspersed with research findings and observations on actual practices, as well as explanations whenever theory and practice diverge. These commentaries on practice (printed in brown ink) develop out of concepts presented in chapters 4 and 5. In the last chapter of the book, we will examine, point-by-point, what can be done to make organizations perform more effectively and efficiently and how to close the gap between administrative theory and the way it is practiced.

summary of major points

1. To understand the field of administration today, it is necessary to consider its history.

2. Evidence of administrative practice predates Christ by two thousand years.

3. The most important, pretwentieth century influence on administration was the industrial revolution.

4. The birth of modern administration or management occurred in 1911, through the work of Frederick Winslow Taylor, who has been called the father of scientific management. Other important contributors to the scientific management movement included:
   a. Frank Gilbreth, father of motion study
   b. Morris Cooke, first to recognize the universality of scientific management principles to nonindustrial activities

5. Henri Fayol was the first of the important general administrative theorists. He defined administration as being made up of five functions: planning, organizing, commanding, coordinating, and controlling. Other administrative theorists include:

EVOLUTION OF
ADMINISTRATIVE
THOUGHT

a. Max Weber, who presented the first fully developed theory of bureaucracy
b. Oliver Sheldon, who saw management as both a science and a philosophy
c. Leonard D. White, first to develop a full textbook in public administration
d. Mary Parker Follett, an early advocate of what was to become the behavioral movement
e. James D. Mooney, recognized the generic nature of organizations
f. Luther Gulick, an important synthesizer with Urwick
g. Lyndall Urwick, an important synthesizer
h. Chester Barnard, who viewed organizations as systems

6. The Hawthorne studies, which took place between 1927 and 1932, ushered in a new concern for the human factor, or what is referred to as the human-relations movement.

7. More recent movements in the field have centered around:
   a. Decision-science
   b. Behavior
   d. Organizational-humanism
   d. Systems
   e. Power dynamics
   f. Contingencies

8. Administration can be viewed as a synthesis of work from a number of disciplines, including:
   a. Psychology
   b. Sociology
   c. Social psychology
   d. Anthropology
   e. Political science
   f. Engineering
   g. Economics
   h. Mathematics and statistics
   i. Physiology

9. The road toward synthesis has had to treat divergent perspectives on administration. Four specific dichotomies are:
   a. Principles vs. contingencies
   b. Generic vs. separate-but-equal
   c. Humanistic vs. economic
   d. Integrative vs. discrete

FOR DISCUSSION

1. "Since administrative practice is discussed in the Bible, it is one of the first academic disciplines, preceding physics, biology, mathematics, or chemistry." Do you agree or disagree with this statement? Explain your position.

2. Who were Frederick Taylor and Frank Gilbreth? What were their contributions to the development of administrative thought?

3. What weaknesses in scientific management led to the emphasis on human relations?

4. What did Max Weber mean when he used the term "bureaucracy"?

5. Contrast process, systems, and contingency views of administration.

6. "Taylor gave us some specific principles of management. Contingency proponents now argue that 'it all depends.' It appears that we have gone backwards during the past 60 years in our search toward building a 'science' of administration." Do you agree or disagree with this statement? Explain your position.

7. It has been said that "those who cannot remember the past are condemned to relive it." Analyze this statement by tracing the major contributions to administrative thought and how these contributions could help you to be a better administrator.

8. "The development of administrative thought has been determined by times and conditions." Build an argument to support this statement. Can you identify any relevent deviations?

case exercise

The qualities of a good administrator

Executive Consultants (EC) is well known in the northeast for the quality of its executive and supervisory development courses. One of their more popular courses is a three-day seminar, restricted to twelve participants, which assists supervisors with high potential to think about the problems of middle-management positions and the abilities necessary to succeed in these jobs.

In March of 1980, four companies each sent three of their supervisors to the three-day EC course. The participants flew to EC's development headquarters in the New York Catskill Mountains on a Tuesday, prepared to begin their course on Wednesday morning.

Marc Stern and John Mather would both be in this three-day seminar. Marc and John were employed by a major Pittsburgh steel producer, and in the few years they had been with their company, both had displayed outstanding abilities and were expected to move quickly into the upper echelons of their firm. But the two had distinctly different backgrounds. Marc was an accountant, held a CPA certificate, and was currently a supervisor in the accounting office. John, on the other hand, had a degree in psychology and was a supervisor in the corporate relations group.

The seminar began promptly at 8:00 A.M. on Wednesday morning, and the participants showed no reluctance to talk, share experiences, or disagree with comments made by others. After lunch on the first day, the EC discussion leader asked the question: "What are the qualities of a good administrator?" While no one lacked for an opinion, it was rapidly evident that John and Marc were the most dogmatic and polarized.

John summed up his position curtly: "It's clear to me that a good administrator knows the behavioral sciences and can apply their findings. It's obvious that the factors that make or break an administrator are things like: Can he communicate effectively? Is he able to lead his employees? Does he know how to motivate employees? Does he know what to look for in selecting people to work for him? These are issues that the behavioral sciences can help answer. So, I'm convinced a good administrator understands behavior."

Marc's summary indicated that he couldn't have disagreed more: "You look at the good administrators and compare them against the poor ones. What I see is that the good ones know their numbers. They know how to allocate scarce resources. They understand economics. The difference between success and failure lies in the ability to develop a well-coordinated operating system. This means the administrator better be able to design jobs, identify efficient work methods, know what equipment is necessary, be able to layout and coordinate his unit's work flow, schedule his personnel and the work to be completed, and be capable of establishing and monitoring controls over things like the quality and quantity of output and costs."

Questions

1. Discuss the validity of both John and Marc's arguments.
2. Is one more right than the other?
3. Can you think of any ways that Marc can be encouraged to understand and accept John's view, and vice-versa?

FOR FURTHER READING

Bedeian, A.G., "A Historical Review of Efforts in the Area of Management Semantics," *Academy of Management Journal,* March 1974, pp.101–14. Reviews general management dictionaries and glossaries in an effort to alleviate conflicts within the management field.

Bradenburg, R.G., "The Usefulness of Management Thought for Management," in *Contemporary Management: Issues and Viewpoints,* ed. J. W. McGuire. Englewood Cliffs, N.J.: Prentice-Hall, Inc., 1974, pp. 99–113. Answers the questions: What is management thought good for? What are its limitations? How are the major schools of thought used, and by whom?

Henry, N., "Paradigms of Public Administration," *Public Administration Review,* July-August 1975, pp. 378–86. Reviews five paradigms of public administration and argues that public administration should assert its identity and establish itself as an autonomous field.

Luthans, F., "Contingency Theory of Management: A Path Out of the Jungle," *Business Horizons,* June 1973, pp. 67–72. The author reviews major schools of thought in management and argues that contingency theory can draw the disparate elements together.

Wrege, C.D., and A.G. Perroni, "Taylor's Pig-Tale: A Historical Analysis of Frederick W. Taylor's Pig-Iron Experiments," *Academy of Management Journal,* March 1974, pp. 6–27. Reviews and analyzes Taylor's famous pig-iron experiments and finds the facts do not necessarily align with current interpretations.

Wrege, C.D., and A.M. Stotka, "Cooke Creates a Classic: The Story Behind F.W. Taylor's Principles of Scientific Management," *Academy of Management Review,* October 1978, pp. 736–49. Analysis of an unpublished manuscript by Morris Cooke and correspondence between Cooke and Taylor reveals that Taylor used much of Cooke's manuscript to prepare the text of *The Principles of Scientific Management.*

PART

DECISION MAKING

4

Theory of Decision Making

**AFTER
STUDYING
THIS CHAPTER
YOU SHOULD
BE ABLE TO—**

Decision making	Lateral thinking
Problem solving	Brainstorming
Programmed decisions	Gordon technique
Objectives	Synectics
Standards	Quantitative skills
Procedures	Linear programming
Methods	Queuing theory
Rules	Probability theory
Policies	Inventory models
Nonprogrammed decisions	Marginal analysis
Programs	Breakeven models
Strategies	Network models
Budgets	Simulation
Judgment	Return on investment
Creativity	

The decision-making process
The difference between programmed and nonprogrammed decisions
Personal qualities required in decision making
Ways that we can increase creativity
When group decisions can be superior to individual decisions
Potential drawbacks of group decisions

Decisions, decisions, decisions! That is the crux of the administrative process. Decision making is the means by which administrators plan, organize, lead, and control. Administrators both *decide* upon courses of action and then *implement* their choice. The following two chapters will review what decision making is and how administrators decide.

What do we mean by decision making?

The essence of decision making is *choice*. When we talk about an administrator making a decision, he or she must have two or more alternatives from which to choose. However, this choice of a preferred alternative is only the culmination of a larger process which includes ascertaining the need for a decision and developing and evaluating alternatives. While some writers call this larger process "problem solving"[1] and may differentiate it from decision making, we will treat decision making as a multi-step process which culminates in the selection of one alternative over another.

Decision making can be active; that is, when a choice is made to do something different. Although this is what comes to mind when most of us think of decision making, our definition also encompasses passive decisions. When the president of the United States utilizes the "pocket veto," this is a "decision not to decide," or a passive decision. Similarly, when a public welfare agency determines to maintain the size of its counseling activities merely because the decision was never made to expand, a passive decision is illustrated. So, not only are we interested in considering those choices that result in change, we are also interested in those cases that result in a maintenance of the status quo—the decision to do nothing is, in actuality, a decision to keep doing what we have been.

Additionally, our perspective will focus on *administrative* decision making. We know, of course, that one does not have to be an administrator to make decisions in an organization. For example, a secretary decides to go through the mail before typing correspondence; an automobile mechanic, in performing a tune-up, chooses not to replace the spark plugs after checking their condition. Neither of these people are administrators, yet they make decisions. What we are concerned with are those decisions that go beyond a single person's specific job; we are looking at those decisions that are made by administrators in the pursuit of an organization's objectives.

[1] See, for example, the review provided in James R. Lang, John E. Dittrich and Sam E. White, "Managerial Problem Solving Models: A Review and a Proposal," *Academy of Management Review,* October 1978, pp. 854–66.

The decision-making process

Figure 4-1 outlines the six main steps in the decision-making process. These steps, of course, represent a simplification of the process. In actual decision situations, the orderly, step-by-step process depicted by Figure 4-1 is rare. For example, several steps may be going on simultaneously, some steps may be skipped or repeated, and so forth. Nevertheless, this approach should clarify what we mean by "the decision-making process."

FIGURE 4-1   Steps in the decision-making process

1. Ascertain the need for a decision
2. Establish decision criteria
3. Allocate weights to criteria
4. Develop alternatives
5. Evaluate alternatives
6. Select the best alternative

Step 1. Ascertain the need for a decision

The decision-making process begins by determining that a problem exists; that is, that there is an unsatisfactory condition. This is frequently expressed as a disparity between what is and what should be.

Whether a decision is necessary depends on the administrator's perception. What one person sees as a "problem," another may see as a perfectly acceptable state of affairs. So, the decision process begins with the administrator's recognition that there is a gap between what is desired and what actually is.

Step 2. Establish decision criteria

Once the need for a decision has been determined, the administrator must establish decision criteria. This requires identifying those characteristics that are important in making the decision. As an example, let us look at a decision most of us have made or will make soon—taking a job. You may recognize the need to make this decision in a number of ways: graduation from college is imminent, dissatisfaction with your current job, or being fired by your current employer, to name the more obvious. Now, you must select the relevant criteria. They are likely to include such factors as beginning salary, advancement potential, reputation of the organization, security, and geographical location (climate, cost of living, quality of schools, opportunities for spouse to find work, cultural amenities). These criteria reflect what you, as the decision maker, think is relevant. Note that the criteria omitted say as much as those that are listed. For instance, this list fails to include such factors as the organization's sense of social responsibility, the availability of urban transportation, and the amount of traveling or overtime required. This suggests that these latter criteria are not relevant to you!

THEORY OF
DECISION MAKING

65

<table>
<tr><td>Step 3.
Allocate
weights
to criteria</td><td>The list of criteria must now be prioritized. Since some are obviously more important than others, you need to weight each criterion to reflect its importance in the decision. Continuing our job selection illustration, suppose you chose the weights shown in Figure 4-2.</td></tr>
</table>

FIGURE 4-2   Criteria and weights in an individual's job selection decision

Criteria	Weights (1–10)
Advancement potential	10
Opportunities for spouse to work	7
Cultural amenities	4
Beginning salary	3
Reputation of the organization	3
Cost of living	2
Quality of schools	1
Climate	1
Security	1

Figure 4-2 indicates that you judge certain factors in your decision to be much more important than others. For example, you consider advancement potential more important than the entry salary or security offered by the job. This, of course, is a matter of personal preference. Because you do not place high importance on the beginning salary is not to imply that others agree with your value judgment.

**Step 4.
Develop
alternatives**

Now, we proceed to develop a list of the alternatives that may be viable in dealing with the stated problem. Since this step is only the enunciation of alternatives and avoids any evaluation of the choices, it draws on the administrator's ability to comprehend a wide number of possible alternatives. For our example, let us assume that you have unearthed six potential job opportunities through personal contacts, national advertisements, and your campus placement office. These are summarized in Figure 4-3.

**Step 5.
Evaluate
alternatives**

Once the alternatives have been enumerated, the administrator must critically evaluate each one. The strengths and weaknesses of each will become evident as they are compared against the criteria and weights established in steps 2 and 3.

If we assume that you have been fortunate enough to receive offers from each of the organizations you contacted, you now have to evaluate each of them. If you received only one offer, this step might result in returning to the development of alternatives stage—you may now want to consider the alternative, for example, of going on to graduate school.

Figure 4-4 shows the results when the six alternatives are appraised against the nine criteria identified in Figure 4-2. You have rated each crite-

DECISION MAKING

66

FIGURE 4-3   Job possibilities

Title	Organization	Location	About the job
Administrative Analyst	City of Omaha	Omaha, Nebraska	Supervise studies relating to urban affairs. Salary of $13,000 a year.
Assistant to the Vice President of Personnel	General Mills (milling & processing)	Minneapolis, Minnesota	Perform support service for vice president. Responsible for affirmative action programs. Salary of $16,000 a year.
Assistant Director of Admissions	San Francisco State University	San Francisco, California	Supervise admissions office at a large state university. Salary of $12,000 a year.
Sales Representative	Xerox Corporation (duplicating & information processing equipment)	Phoenix, Arizona	Contact commercial clients to sell them duplicating equipment. Salary of $14,000 a year plus car.
Director of Human Resource Development	Meridian Corporation (Sells and operates food franchises)	Jacksonville, Florida	Run program to prepare managers and operating personnel to run franchise units. Salary of $13,000 a year.
Assistant Plant Personnel Manager	Pabst Brewing	Milwaukee, Wisconsin	Responsible for hiring in a manufacturing plant employing 3000. Salary of $15,500 a year.

rion on a scale from 1 (low) to 10 (high) in terms of how successful it is in satisfying your requirements. The scores in Figure 4-4 were found by multiplying each individual criterion by its respective weight and then adding up these scores for each alternative.

Step 6. Select the best alternative

The final step in the decision-making process takes place when all the alternatives have been enumerated and evaluated against the decision criteria. This final step is the selection of the best alternative, which has quantitatively been determined in our job selection example to be the offer of Director of Human Resource Development from the Meridian Corporation.

Notice that you have chosen what we call the "best" alternative. But "best" is a subjective term. While we will discuss the implications of looking for the best alternative thoroughly in the next chapter, you should recognize that the criteria chosen as being important in your decision (step 2) and the weights assigned to each (step 3) reflect your priorities and the degree of importance you believe each carries. Another college graduate, confronted with identical employment alternatives but placing greater weight on such factors as a high starting salary and the status of being part of a large and well-known organization, would have calculated a different "best" choice.

THEORY OF DECISION MAKING

| Weight | 10 | 7 | 4 | 3 | 3 | 2 | 1 | 1 | 1 | |
Criteria / Alternative	Advancement Potential	Opportunities for Spouse	Cultural Amenities	Salary	Organization's Reputation	Cost of Living	Quality of Schools	Climate	Security	Total
City of Omaha	40	21	8	15	18	16	8	3	10	139
General Mills	60	35	16	30	27	10	10	1	5	194
San Francisco State University	10	70	40	6	12	2	2	7	7	156
Xerox Corp.	70	49	20	24	30	12	7	10	3	225
Meridian Corp.	100	56	28	12	15	20	8	10	4	253
Pabst Brewing	60	28	24	27	18	4	8	1	5	175

FIGURE 4-4   Evaluating the job alternatives

Types of decision-making problems

We now want to look at the types of problems you might encounter as a decision maker. The following discussion develops from the fact that problems are not all alike and, as a result, the way that a decision maker handles them will differ. This point can be made clearer if we take a look at the task of grading college examinations and assigning marks.

What types of examinations do you think are easier for a college instructor to grade—objective tests made up of true-false and multiple choice questions, or subjective tests requiring essay answers? Obviously, objective tests are easier to grade. Why? Because they are programmed; the answers are definite. Once the correct answers have been prepared by the instructor, a ten-year-old could mark the exam. But could that same ten-year-old grade an essay exam? Of course not. It is unlikely that even a graduate student could grade the examination accurately unless he or she was given considerable guidance by the instructor.

The above paragraph is meant to demonstrate, in rather simplistic terms, the difference between programmed and nonprogrammed decisions.[2] It should suggest to you that, in organizations, some decisions are easier to make because they are structured, are relatively unambiguous, and follow a long line of precedents. In this section we will show you that different types of problems require different types of decision approaches.

If a problem or situation occurs frequently, organizations will usually develop a routine or programmed approach for solving it. A university admissions office must constantly evaluate the applications of prospective students. The laboratory of a large hospital must test hundreds of blood samples. The production foreman knows that some of his workers will be absent on any given day, and he will have to make some adjustment to insure that the day's production requirement is still met. Each of these problems has a common element: it is, for the most part, a repetitive situation. As a result, the administrator will find it worthwhile to develop a routine approach for solving it. In other words, if a university admissions officer must choose from among three thousand applicants for the school's five hundred freshman vacancies, it makes sense to isolate certain admission criteria and to program the decision. By stating that all graduates of accredited high schools with a 3.0 grade point average and a minimum score of 1200 on the Scholastic Aptitude Tests will be granted admissions on a first-come, first-served basis, the admissions officer can efficiently process and allocate the five hundred openings.

At many universities, high school grades and scores on admission tests are only part of the final matriculation decision. Other factors may be relevant: class rank, rating of the candidate's high school, state of residence, quality of letters of recommendation, financial aid requirements, participa-

[2] Herbert A. Simon, *The New Science of Management Decision* (New York: Harper & Row, 1960), p. 5.

tion in extracurricular activities, or whether one of the applicant's parents attended the university. Now, as you can readily see, we have significantly complicated the decision. In the first case, we had a simple approach. The admission decision was repetitive, routine, and a definite procedure could be followed. We began to complicate the decision by adding a number of unweighted criteria. For example, what is more important, the fact that a candidate was chosen as high school All-American in gymnastics or that a candidate's grandparents and parents were graduates of the university to which application was being made? When problems are unique and unstructured, they require a different type of approach—one which we will call the nonprogrammed decision. The programmed-nonprogrammed dichotomy represents, in actuality, the two extremes of a continuum, one endpoint being highly programmed and the other highly nonprogrammed. While we will discuss the two as if decisions were either one or the other, most decisions tend to be relatively programmed or nonprogrammed rather than representative of the extreme.

Figure 4-5 depicts the relationship between programmed and nonprogrammed decisions. It also points out that the higher administrators are in the organization, the more nonprogrammed decision making in which they tend to be engaged. Conversely, lower-level administrators tend to be predominantly faced with programmed decisions.

At this point, it is important to note that the results shown in Figure

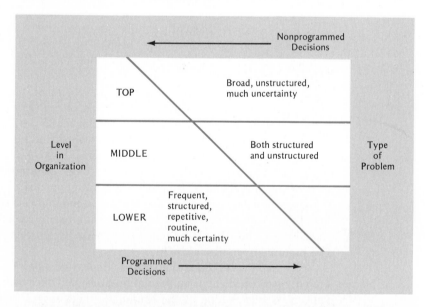

Source: James H. Donnelly, Jr., James L. Gibson, and John M. Ivancevich, *Fundamentals of Management: Functions, Behavior, Models*, 3rd edition (Dallas: Business Publications, Inc., 1978), p. 347.

FIGURE 4-5   Types of problems, types of decisions, and level in organization

4-5 are purposely sought by organizations and they go a long way toward explaining why, in general, the higher one moves in an organization, the greater income and fringe benefits he or she receives.

Programmed decisions minimize the need for the decision maker to exercise discretion. This is relevant because discretion costs money. Administrative positions which require extensive nonprogrammed decision making demand greater judgment. Since sound judgment is an uncommon quality, it costs more to acquire the services of administrators who possess this ability. (An administrative position that is highly programmed can perhaps be filled successfully for $15,000 a year. If the same job, however, has vaguely defined decision-making criteria, it may cost as much as $35,000 a year for a competent person.) As a result, organizations attempt to program as much of the decision making as possible, although it is recognized that successively higher levels of administrative responsibility become less structured and routine, more ambiguous, and generally less amenable to programmed decisions.

Programmed decisions

Decisions are programmed to the extent that they are repetitive and routine and to the extent that a definite approach has been worked out for handling them so that they do not have to be treated as new or unusual each time they occur. Given a certain known situation, the administrator need only evoke a learned and appropriate response. The "search for alternative" step in the decision process is minimal or nonexistent. Once the problem is defined, its solution is either self-evident or at least reduced to a very few alternatives which have proven successful over time. In many cases, it becomes decision making by precedent; that is, the administrator simply does what he or others have done in the same situation. Examples include the pricing of an ordinary customer's orders or determining salary payments to employees who have been ill.

Job training seeks to give an administrator a repertoire of response programs: If this, do that! One of the purposes of providing students of administration with case studies is to allow them to gain problem-solving experience so that if they confront a similar situation, they will have an appropriate response.

Objectives, standards, procedures, methods, rules, and policies all represent examples of programmed decisions. Let us consider, specifically, how organizations use each of these to elicit effective and efficient administrative decisions.

Objectives   Objectives are the ends toward which activity in the organization is directed. Examples of objectives include: to earn a 20 percent return on investment; to obtain 10 percent of a given market; to reduce average daily hospital room rates to $60.00; to achieve an undefeated season.

71

The organization's objectives provide guidance for administrators, though admittedly they are broad guidelines. Objectives establish a common set of expectations and serve as criteria by which decisions can be made. If a business firm's objectives include earning a 20 percent return on investment, administrators will be directed away from proposals that offer returns in the 5–10 percent range and toward those that will be consistent with the objectives sought. As we will see, however, objectives probably are the weakest or the most unstructured mechanism for making decisions programmed.

Standards Criteria against which something can be compared are standards. For example, the criterion that every person in a given department must generate 500 units of output per day is a standard. It represents a benchmark by which performance can be measured. Organizations have implicit, if not explicit, standards by which work and behavior can be measured, and these also guide administrators in their decision making. We describe them as programmed guides because what they stipulate remains basically unchanged from day to day. Only when a major change in job-performance expectations is made would standards be altered. However, there are instances where standards are re-established for each individual task if the tasks are rapidly changing. When such a situation occurs, these would be nonprogrammed decision guides.

Procedures A procedure is a series of interrelated sequential steps established for the accomplishment of a task. We find in organizations a number of job activities, and jobs themselves, that have been "procedurized" to reduce their complexity and the degree of discretionary skills they require. If one were to ask an accounts payable clerk what his or her job involved, the answer would probably correspond closely with the procedurized description of his or her activities. In other words, rather than having the clerk, through trial and error, develop an individual way of handling the accounts payable, the administration has provided a procedure. For example, when invoices are received daily, they are stamped in, alphabetized, and merged with purchase orders, then tabulations are checked and vouchers are prepared. These steps follow a specific sequence that results in a desired end.

Methods A method is one step of a procedure. To use our accounts payable example above, the method for preparing a voucher can be stipulated as follows: Use preprinted voucher tags, place voucher number in top right corner, place date in top left corner, write in appropriate accounts to be charged, check to determine if total of accounts equals invoice amount, initial in bottom right corner. By taking complex tasks, breaking them down into specific procedures, and then developing comprehensive methods for each step in those procedures, it is possible for us to place people in jobs for which their skills are considerably lower than what would have been required otherwise.

DECISION MAKING

72

Rules Explicit statements that tell a person what he or she ought or ought not to do are rules. A classic statement is the phrase "No Smoking." It states a particular and specific behavior pattern. There is no room for judgment or discretion; one is either smoking or not smoking. Other examples of rules are, "We sell for cash only," and "We promote from within."

As with procedures and methods, rules allow organizations to place into positions of responsibility people who need not be capable of making a wide variety of judgments. A plant controller who is guided by a vast array of procedures, methods, and rules need not have the same qualifications, experiences, and abilities as one who must handle each case on its own particular merits. As we noted before, discretion costs money; and whenever a job can be made programmable through methods, procedures, and rules, we can place a less expensive worker in that position.

Policies Policies are vague guides to decision making, allowing the administrator to utilize judgment within specific constraints. In direct contrast to a rule, a policy must provide ambiguity to allow the administrator to utilize his judgment. We noted that the statement, "We promote from within," is a rule; however, it can become a policy by the addition of the words "whenever possible." The statement, "We promote from within, whenever possible," allows the administrator to utilize discretion and judgment in determining if, in a given situation, a satisfactory applicant exists within the organization. If, in the administrator's judgment, this is not the case, the policy allows him to look outside for a capable candidate. The phrase "whenever possible" is ambiguous and in need of interpretation. Policies, therefore, do not specify the decisions to be made, but rather set discretionary limits for the decision maker. Statements intentionally developed to include ambiguous terms (such as *best, satisfied, competitive*) leave interpretation to the decision maker.

The statement from the personnel manual at a major midwestern hospital that it will "pay competitive wages" illustrates a policy. This personnel policy does not tell the wage and salary administrator what he should pay, but it does give direction to the decision he will make. The term *competitive* is vague, yet it sets discretionary limits. If other local hospitals pay between $2.60 and $3.20 an hour for an inexperienced orderly, hourly rates of $2.10 or $4.60 would clearly not be within the guidelines set by hospital policy.

The most common form of policy is the one that is internally *originated* by top management for middle- and lower-level administrators. However, three other sources of policy should also be pointed out.

In addition to originating from above, policy can be established by a *precedent* set in an earlier decision. Although not purposely originated from above, this type of policy gives direction for future actions based on past actions.

Policies need not be explicitly stated. From their perceptions concerning the actions around them, those within the organization interpret *implied* policies. For example, an organization may never state that it gives hiring preference to relatives of middle- and top-level executives; however, nepotism may be an observable practice there.

Finally, policies can originate from *externally imposed* sources. Powerful influences from unions, government, trade associations, competition, the church, or community pressures can impose general guides that affect administrative action.

Nonprogrammed decisions

Occasionally, decisions must be made concerning a situation that is relatively novel and unstructured. No cut-and-dried solution exists for handling the problem because either it has never arisen before; its structure is vague, ambiguous, or complex; or it is so important that it deserves a custom-tailored treatment.[3]

Nonprogrammed decisions include the large and dramatic—such as Truman's decision to drop the atomic bomb at Hiroshima or Kodak's decision to manufacture and market a self-developing camera to compete against Polaroid. But this is not true for all nonprogrammed decisions. The rules, procedures and policies discussed under programmed decisions, for instance, did not materialize out of thin air. They, too, evolved out of a nonprogrammed task. For example, a company's employee grievance procedure may be used repeatedly by its foremen when confronted by a grievance. But when the need for a grievance procedure first came to the attention of the company's executives, it had all the characteristics of a nonprogrammed decision. It had not been confronted previously, and the company had no prior experience with decisions that had been used successfully before. So, we find that designing programmable decisions is a nonprogrammed task. We should also inject here that there *are* exceptions to Figure 4-5. While nonprogrammed decision making does tend to be the province of senior administrators, this does not mean that lower-level decision makers will not encounter nonprogrammed situations. A computer supervisor, maintenance foreman or similar level administrator may confront a new and novel problem which he or she can effectively resolve. In such cases, the decision should be made without passing it upward for attention.

Every organization, no matter how large or small, is confronted with its share of nonprogrammed decisions, but some considerably more often than others. Three frequently used nonprogrammed decision guides are programs, strategies, and budgets.

Non-prog. decision guides

Programs

A program is a complex of plans for achieving an objective. Social-service agencies work out programs to deal with floods, hurricanes, earthquakes, or other natural disasters. A large insurance company, planning to move its

[3] Ibid., p. 6.

74

head offices, formulates a program that considers office allocations, telephone hookups, movement of equipment, and other key elements in the move. A program should contain all the activities necessary for achieving the objective, and should clarify who should do what, and when.

Strategies   Strategies are plans in reaction to, or taking into consideration, the actions of others. In chapter 7, we will consider organizational strategies, but strategies can also exist for divisions, departments, and other sub-units. Within an organization, we find strategies in such areas as marketing, finance, research and development, personnel, and procurement. For example, if the purchasing administrator for a school district anticipates a shortage of paper later in the year, he might prepare a strategy: Place orders with a number of suppliers; rent additional warehousing facilities for storage; encourage lower usage of paper by teachers and pupils.

Budgets   Probably the most familiar nonprogrammed decision guide is the numerical budget. Budgets are typically prepared for revenues, expenses, and capital-expenditure needs such as machinery and equipment. Additionally, however, budgets can be used for improving time, space, and material-resource utilization. These latter forms of budgets substitute nondollar numbers for dollar terms. Items like man-hours, capacity utilization, and units of production can be planned for daily, weekly, or monthly appraisal.

Each of these types of nonprogrammable decision guides meets the needs of a specific objective. In contrast to programmable decisions, they are not routine, nor do they exist for continual reuse. They are responses to novel and uncertain circumstances.

Personal qualities for effective decision making

Are there qualities that differentiate good decision makers from poor ones? If there are certain qualities that are important, are these qualities used in making all types of decisions? For instance, are the qualities that go into making good programmed decisions the same as those for making good nonprogrammed decisions? This section will attempt to answer these questions.

Four qualities appear to be important to effective decision making: experience, good judgment, creativity, and quantitative skills. We do not propose that other qualities may not be helpful, but rather that these four appear to be the most critical requirements. We will look at what each of these qualities means and how each contributes to better decisions; in addition, we will demonstrate how different problem situations require different qualities in the decision maker.

① Experience   It is intuitively logical to assume that experience increases one's ability to perform on a job. The concept of seniority, with those individuals who have

75

worked a job longest being the highest paid, is built on the value of experience. Similarly, personnel selection traditionally places a premium on an individual's experience. Past successes and failures form a basis for future action. Having learned from past mistakes, it is believed that the potential for future mistakes is reduced. Furthermore, it is hoped that the intelligent individual can assess why certain actions in the past succeeded and then attempt to repeat them. Therefore, ten years of experience implies a wider breadth of responses than does five years of experience, assuming that learning has continued throughout the period. It is possible that ten year's experience is nothing other than one year's experience repeated ten times.

Experience plays an important role in decision making. When confronted with a situation, the administrator draws from his or her past experiences to solve the problem in a way that has worked previously. Experience leads to the development of specific responses which are demonstrated by habit—without hesitation—in a particular situation. For situations requiring a programmed response, the advantage of experience is obvious. Because Sheila Thomas has supervised a group of claim agents at Mutual of Omaha for seven years, she is able to solve most of the day-to-day problems that her agents bring to her. From experience she has a fairly good idea of what has and has not worked in the past. Not only does her experience increase the probability that her decision will prove effective, her seven years on the job also shows itself through the speed in which she can make her decision. In seconds she may be able to resolve a problem that might take an equally talented, but less experienced, claims supervisor, much longer.

When a situation requires a nonprogrammed response, experience can provide both disadvantages and advantages. Its major disadvantage, as implied previously, is the danger that the lessons of experience may be entirely unsuited to the new problem, resulting in a poor decision. However, experience can be a positive force when it provides insight into differing situations; for instance, when it helps the decision maker to recognize that a situation requires a nonprogrammed rather than programmed response.

Judgment

By judgment we mean the ability to evaluate information wisely. It is made up of one's common sense, maturity, ability to reason, and experience. As a result, we often think of judgment improving with age and experience. But one can gain experience without improving his or her judgment. We have, therefore, separated judgment from experience.

Those who have good judgment demonstrate it by their ability to perceive critical information, weigh its importance, and evaluate it. In a decision-making context, we can say that judgment allows you to draw a conclusion based on past experiences and the information that is available.

Basically, a judgment develops in the following way:[4] based on the in-

---

[4] The section is adapted from Martin F. Kaplan's "Judgment by Juries," in *Human Judgment and Decision Processes in Applied Settings*, ed. Martin F. Kaplan and Steven Schwartz. (New York: Academic Press, Inc., 1977), pp. 32–43.

formation at hand and past experience, the decision maker forms beliefs made up of facts, opinions, and general knowledge. For instance, an administrator, in evaluating her subordinates, may believe that college graduates make more productive employees. This belief will affect judgments she will make about her subordinates' productivity. These beliefs, and every decision maker will have a large number of them, will then be valued along some judgment dimension (such as "productivity") and given a weight to reflect their relative importance. In this way, the decision maker can take diverse or even conflicting information, integrate it with the different beliefs he or she holds, and form judgments. As you might expect, the judgments arrived at are not always objective or error-free. We will discuss some problems in human information processing that have implications for making good judgments in the next chapter.

The above should not be construed to mean that judgment is relevant only to steps 5 and 6 in the decision-making process, evaluating alternatives and selecting the best one. Although the previous example emphasized judgment's role in evaluation, it is also important in determining the need for a decision, what criteria are relevant in the decision, the weights assigned to the criteria, and in identifying what alternatives may be available.

③ Creativity

I believe that one quality that significantly differentiates good decision makers from poor is creativity. Why is creativity important in decision making? Why do successful administrators need this skill? The answer is: to formulate adequate problem definition, develop alternatives, enrich possibilities, and imagine consequences.

The creative individual is able to more fully appraise and understand the problem, including seeing problems others cannot see. However, creativity's most obvious value is in the development of alternatives. When administrators seek alternative solutions to a given problem, they can call upon their past experience, their knowledge of what others have done in similar circumstances, or their creativity in seeking alternative solutions. In most cases, past experience will "make do"; since the majority of problems are routine, or at least have been confronted before. What has worked in the past may be an effective indication of what will work in the future, and if one's experience is limited or the problem unique, imitating what others have done in the same circumstances represents a common approach. However, a problem becomes difficult when its solution demands responses that deviate from common ones or those previously learned. These are the nonroutine problems—the problems requiring creative alternatives. Additionally, there are problems we continue to handle according to our past experience or what others have done, only because the innovative solution has not been considered. These, too, require creativity.

It is easy to select the obvious alternatives, but over the long run, the administrator who can bring about unique alternatives will, all other things being equal, make better decisions. In a number of cases, even after the innovative alternatives have been generated, one of the "obvious" choices will be selected. But there are instances when traditional solutions are inappropriate for the problem, or when better results can be achieved by attempting a different approach to a familiar problem.

Defining creativity   Assuming that creativity is an important aspect of effective decision making, can we agree on what creativity is? In general usage, creativity means a talent for unique combination or unusual association of ideas. But these ideas must not only be novel, they must be useful, too.

> Just because an idea is unusual or different does not indicate that it is creative or superior, since it might indicate abnormality as well. Confusion over this differentiation might explain why the genius is often regarded as insane. For unusual solutions to be classified as superior, they must work, which means they must respect reality. [5]

An excellent example of creativity was introduced by Adelphi University in New York. Adelphi desired to expand its graduate program in business administration, yet recognized the time constraints on those who were most interested in the school's educational offering—businessmen who receive subsidies for their education from their companies. The solution: Adelphi brought the classroom to the students. Classes are given four days a week on commuter trains into and out of New York. "We took a concept of a service like higher education. We studied the needs of our customers— prospective students—and we came up with a delivery system," said the program's director. Where before, people may not have had the time to further their education, the "Classroom on Wheels" opened up a whole new area for Adelphi's graduate program in business. As summed up by its creator, "It's such a ridiculously simple and obvious idea that I'm amazed it's never been done before."[6]

Can we increase creativity?   It is not easy to be creative—to see things that others do not see. As soon as you conceive of something different, you become a minority of one. Organizations frequently make it difficult for individuals to maintain their unique perspective on things. It is not easy to be different in environments that support and encourage homogeneity.

But are those people who are creative different? Are they born with their ability, or is it learned? The evidence indicates that both heredity and environmental factors influence the development of creativity.[7]

Creativity should be viewed as an attribute that, to some degree, all people possess. What is necessary is to stimulate this potential within members of the organization, especially administrators. Creativity cannot be

[5] Norman R. F. Maier, *Problem Solving and Creativity* (Belmont, Calif.: Wadsworth, 1970), p. 83.
[6] "Commuter M.B.A. Program Rolls On," *New York Times,* May 25, 1975, p. F.5.
[7] William E. Scott, Jr., "The Creative Individual," *Academy of Management Journal,* September 1965, pp. 212.

viewed as a dichotomy—as something you either have or haven't. On the other hand, although everyone possesses some creative potential, certain people have inherent abilities that make them more successful than others in utilizing this potential.

A number of characteristics are attributed to creative people: dissatisfaction with the status quo, an enriched childhood environment, possible lack of logic and order in thought, less anxiety, more autonomy and dynamism, less authoritarianism, more achievement orientation, more acceptance of their inner impulses, and responsiveness to moderate levels of conflict.[8]

These traits seem to contradict our statement that all people possess some creativity. However, they are meant to describe the *highly* creative person. Research supports the theory that people with outstanding creative abilities are different from those with moderate or marginal capabilities.

> The creative thinker is, above all, flexible and adaptable in his intellectual functioning. He is not committed to the preservation of an existing *status quo,* and is prepared to rearrange his thinking. On the other hand, the rigid individual is convinced of the logic and rightness of his existing view of the world. He is unwilling to make rapid or drastic changes in intellectual orientation, perhaps even incapable, and he clings firmly to what he "knows" is right. In this latter kind of person, the intellectual flexibility which characterizes the creative individual is missing, and he functions in a highly convergent manner.[9]

As mentioned above, organizations themselves have been found to influence the degree to which people demonstrate creativity. For example, organizations with the following characteristics have been found to stifle creative thought: narrowly defined jobs, clearly defined authority relationships, formal sets of rules and procedures to guide behavior, and impersonal relationships.[10] They stifle diversity of opinions and opposing positions; require secrecy, which hinders the dispersion of information; reinforce a high degree of specialization; have control systems built around stability, predictability, and routinization; and rely more on extrinsic rewards, such as salary and benefits, than on intrinsic qualities like interesting, challenging, flexible, and self-directed work activities. The evidence suggests that "it is unlikely that organizations that are overburdened with written rules, regulations, policies and controls can hope for much creativity."[11]

Given that everyone has some potential for creativity if the organiza-

---

[8] See Joe Kelly, *Organizational Behavior,* rev. ed. (Homewood, Ill.: Richard D. Irwin, 1974), pp. 472–75; and Scott, "The Creative Individual," pp. 211–19.

[9] A. J. Cropley, "S-R Psychology and Cognitive Psychology," in *Creativity,* ed. P. E. Vernon. (London: Penguin Books Ltd., 1970), p. 124.

[10] Larry Cummings, "Organizational Climates for Creativity," *Academy of Management Journal,* September 1965, pp. 220–27.

[11] E. J. Koprowski, "Creativity, Man and Organizations," *Journal of Creative Behavior,* vol. 1, 1972, p. 53.

tional environment is supportive, what specifically can be done to stimulate a decision maker's creativity?[12]

Individual methods for stimulating creativity   It is possible for creativity to be increased by the mere action of instructing someone to "be creative" and to avoid obvious approaches to a problem.[13] This *direct instruction* method is based on the assumption that people tend to accept obvious solutions and that this tendency prevents them from performing up to their capabilities; so the mere statement that unique and creative solutions are sought acts to encourage such ideas.

Another individual technique is *attribute listing.* In attribute listing, the decision maker isolates the major characteristics of traditional alternatives. Each major attribute of the alternative is then considered in turn and is changed in every conceivable way. No ideas are rejected, no matter how ridiculous they may sound. Once this extensive list is completed, the constraints of the problem are imposed in order to eliminate all but the viable alternatives.

Creativity can also be stimulated by teaching individuals to replace traditional vertical thinking with *lateral* or zig-zag thinking.[14] Vertical thinking is highly rational. It is a stepwise process, with each step following the previous step in an unbroken sequence. It must be correct at every step. Further, vertical thinking selects and deals only with what is relevant. In contrast, lateral thinking is thinking sideways: not developing a pattern but restructuring a pattern. It is not sequential. For example, one might tackle a problem from the solution end rather than the starting end, and back into various beginning states. Lateral thinking does not have to be correct at each step. It may be necessary to pass through a "wrong" area in order to reach a position from which the correct path may be visible. Finally, lateral thinking is not restricted to relevant information. It deliberately uses random or irrelevant information to bring about a new way of looking at the problem.

Group methods for stimulating creativity   Most work in fostering creativity revolves around the use of groups. Most notable of the group methods are brainstorming, the Gordon technique, and synectics. Both *brainstorming* and the *Gordon technique* are similar in that a half dozen to a dozen people sit around a table and "freewheel" for a given length of time, attempting to generate as many alternatives as possible. No criticism is allowed, and all the alternatives are recorded for later discussion and analysis. The difference between the two methods is that in brainstorming, the members of the group are aware of the problem. The group leader states the problem in a

[12] For a comprehensive review for techniques for stimulating creativity, see Morris Stein, *Stimulating Creativity,* vol. 1 on individual procedures (1974) and vol. 2 on group procedures (1975). Both published in New York by Academic Press.

[13] Melba A. Colgrove, "Stimulating Creative Problem Solving: Innovative Set," *Psychological Reports,* vol. 22 (1968), pp. 1205–11.

[14] Edward deBono, *Lateral Thinking: Creativity Step by Step* (New York: Harper & Row, 1970).

clear manner so that it is understood by all participants, then it is up to the group members to generate as many ideas as possible.

The Gordon technique, on the other hand, offers greater opportunities for truly original alternatives because only the group leader is aware of the exact nature of the problem. Rather than stating the problem explicitly to the group, in this latter method he only indirectly points to it. For example, where the leader in a brainstorming session would state the problem as, "In our school district, we just do not have enough classroom space to handle next year's estimated enrollments," the leader in the Gordon technique approach might say only the word "space," or "overpopulation." Although this latter method is considerably more time-consuming and less goal-directed, it offers the opportunity for the participants to develop alternatives unencumbered by traditional solutions to the problem. Rather than limiting the mind by its interpretation of realistic solutions, the method allows the mind to wander completely free, constrained only by the connotations of the word or phrase that the Gordon-technique leader has given his group.

One of the most fruitful areas for the development of creative abilities is *synectics*, a method for fitting together different and irrelevant elements to form new solutions to problems. It recognizes that "most problems are not new. The challenge is to view the problem in a new way. This viewpoint in turn embodies the potential for a new basic solution."[15] Its goal, therefore, is to make the strange familiar and the familiar strange.

In order to find new approaches to old problems, it is necessary to abandon familiar ways of viewing things. For instance, most of us think of hens laying eggs. But how many of us have considered that "a hen is only an egg's way of making another egg"? Obviously, this represents another way of looking at the situation.

Synectics makes extensive use of analogies to look for similarities between relationships or functions. As a case in point, the direct analogy can disclose new alternatives by comparing parallel facts, knowledge, or technology. Alexander Graham Bell saw a potential in taking concepts that operate in the ear and applying them in his "talking box." After noticing that the massive bones in the ear are operated by a delicate membrane, he wondered why, then, a thicker and stronger piece of membrane should not move a piece of steel. Out of that analogy the telephone was conceived.

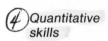 **Quantitative skills**

The final quality required of decision makers is the development of quantitative skills. These techniques should be viewed as tools to assist administrators in making more effective decisions. By no means can they replace sound judgment in the decision-making process. In this section, we will only describe popular quantitative techniques, thus making the reader aware of their availability. The Appendix following this chapter presents some of the techniques in greater detail and demonstrates procedures for their use.

[15] William J. J. Gordon, *Synectics* (New York: Harper & Row, 1961), p. 34.

Linear programming   Linear programming uses graphic, algebraic, or simplistic techniques to optimally allocate scarce resources. The technique requires competition between two or more activities for limited resources and assumes a linear relationship in the problem and the objective. For example, assuming that spending depends on income, then a linear relationship exists when we say that if income goes up 10 percent, spending also increases by a commensurate 10 percent. Linear programming is especially useful when input data can be quantified and objectives are subject to definite measurement. It is well suited for problems surrounding the logistics of operating facilities, such as warehousing and transportation.

Let us assume that an automobile manufacturer, which makes both automobiles and trucks, seeks to maximize its profits. Let us also assume that we know the profit generated by each truck or car produced. If we have scarce resources—for example, a given production space and a given number of available man-hours—and if resources expended to manufacture trucks are at the expense of resources to manufacture automobiles, we could utilize linear-programming techniques to determine how many cars and how many trucks should be produced to maximize profit.

Queuing theory   How many tollbooths should the San Francisco Bay Bridge Toll Authority provide at the entrance to the bridge? Queuing theory, or what is frequently referred to as waiting-line theory, can assist in answering this question. Wherever a decision's objective is to balance the cost of having a waiting line against the cost of service to maintain that line, queuing theory can be of value. The objective is to minimize employee idle time while servicing clients adequately. It is obvious that our toll-bridge authority could erect thirty or more toll booths and keep waiting time to a minimum. On the other hand, it would be possible to have only one tollbooth and minimize cost. Somewhere between these two extremes is a number of booths that will balance the cost incurred by travelers in waiting to pay their tolls and the cost to the toll authority of erecting and staffing booths.

Probability theory   Probability theory is the use of statistics to assist the decision maker in reducing risk. Based on past predictable patterns, an administrator can improve current and future decisions. It makes for a higher quality of decisions when, for example, the marketing manager knows that the mean age of his customers is 35.5 years, with a standard deviation of 3.5. Assuming that the ages of the customers are normally distributed, through probability theory the manager can calculate that 95 out of 100 of his customers are between 28.6 and 42.4 years of age. If he were developing a new marketing program, this information about customers' ages could help the organization to spend its marketing dollars more effectively.

Inventory models   Organizations that maintain inventories must be concerned with minimizing the costs of carrying them. Inventory models attempt to balance the ordering costs against the carrying costs. At one extreme, carrying costs can be minimized by making frequent orders. At the other extreme, if large average inventories are carried, the chance for stockouts is reduced. By estimating overall demand for a given period, the cost of placing each order, carrying costs, and the value of each item in inventory, it is possible to determine an optimum size for efficient order quantities.

Marginal analysis   The concept of marginal or incremental analysis is helpful to the decision maker in optimizing returns or minimizing costs. Marginal analysis deals with the additional cost in a particular decision, rather than the average cost. For example, the dry cleaner who wonders whether he should take on a new customer would consider not the total revenue and the total cost that would result after the order was taken, but rather, what additional revenue would be generated by this particular order, and what additional costs. If the incremental revenues exceeded the incremental costs, total profits would be increased by accepting the order.

Breakeven analysis   Breakeven analysis is concerned with determining the relationship between total costs and total revenues. That point where revenues cover all variable costs, and the increment left over is exactly equal to fixed costs, is defined as the breakeven point. The model considers fixed costs, those that do not change regardless of revenues; variable costs, those that change in direct relation to output; total revenue, which is computed as quantity times price; and the marginal concepts of incremental costs and incremental revenues. For example, given that total fixed costs are known, as well as price and variable costs, it is possible to determine the number of units an organization would have to sell in order to break even financially.

Network analysis   Methods such as the Critical Path Method (CPM) and Program Evaluation and Review Technique (PERT) can assist administrators in determining how activities may be scheduled in order that specific deadlines may be met. Activities to be performed are defined, time estimates are established for completing activities, and consideration is given to activities that can be performed simultaneously. Network flow charts can then be constructed to assist administrators in making planning and control decisions and to highlight areas where resources may need to be reallocated to ensure that deadlines are met.

Simulation   Entire operations of a unit or an organization can be simulated in a model when the variables, components, and a relationship within a system are known. Inputs can be varied to determine the effects on both the system and its outputs.

Not infrequently, in compex social and commercial situations, the model created by the decision scientist does not provide an easy or direct solution. Typically, this is the case when the variables in the model are complex and interrelated, or when important decisions in a dynamic situation are both subjective and beyond the control of the decision model. In such cases, the technique of computer simulation has proved effective.

**THEORY OF
DECISION MAKING**

83

In computer simulation, we structure a computer to behave in precisely the same fashion that an individual or organization would *when faced by the same stimuli.* Establishing such a structure is a delicate art, requiring intimate knowledge of computer programming, detailed information about the actual system being modeled, and a flair for embodying the subjective, and even whimsical, actions that might occur in a developing dynamic situation.

Any proposed change (as in organizational structure, personnel, services, pricing, or location) can be implemented on the computer, and the result measured. If repeated simulations indicate that the proposed modification is beneficial, one can proceed to implement that change in the actual situation. If the proposed modification leads to (simulated) disaster, we have obtained important information and paid only for the use of the computer and its electricity, not for the disaster.

Return on investment   The final decision-making tool we will discuss is return on investment (ROI). Among profit-making organizations, ROI is a highly popular single criterion by which to measure productivity of assets. By computing profits as a percentage of capital invested in an organization, it is possible to determine how well the investment is being utilized to generate profits, and thus, to compare organizations within industries and between industries. Given that all profit-making firms compete for capital dollars, one measure of administrative efficiency is a high ROI.

The above techniques offer objective methods for analyzing and evaluating problems. However, the outcome that a technique generates can be only as good as the assumptions that underlie that technique. Therefore, it is important that one understand the limitations of each before applying it to a problem.

In a modern economy, where computerization is widespread, we should not overlook the use of these techniques to improve the quality of decision analysis. Again, however, we must caution against viewing quantitative techniques as decision makers. They are not. These decision tools can assist administrators, but they can never replace the decision maker's individual judgment.

Are these four qualities always of equal importance?   We cannot say that judgment, experience, creativity and quantitative skills are of equal importance to every decision maker. The importance of each quality can vary according to the step in the decision process and the type of decision situation.

The need for experience and good judgment appears to permeate the entire decision-making process, beginning with the determination of what is a desirable or undesirable state of affairs and concluding with the selection of a choice that reflects the decision maker's experiences and qualitative judgments, as well as quantitative facts. Creativity is most likely to prove critical in the "development of alternatives" stage where the ability to develop new approaches should be most significant. Similarly, quantitative skills should be most valuable when evaluating alternatives.

Though there is an absence of research relating the four decision qualities to the type of decision situation, we can propose two hypotheses. First, since routine situations require relatively programmed decisions, experience should be highly correlated to successful decision making. Second, unique situations require nonprogrammed decisions, which place increased importance on creativity.

It is possible that an overreliance on either experience or creativity, in the wrong type of decision situation, could have a significant adverse effect on the outcome. Creativity in a situation requiring a programmed decision may be an unwelcomed influence that results in reduced decision efficiency. Similarly, extensive experience could actually handicap an administrator making a nonprogrammed decision if that experience resulted in automatically searching for a past "tried-and-true" solution. When confronted with a unique situation, the decision maker with extensive experience may seek an old solution to a new problem.

But what about group decisions?

Until now we have treated *individual* decision making as synonymous with decision making. But what about group decisions? Is there a theory of group decision making equivalent to that for individual decision making?

A review of the group decision-making literature finds that it is almost entirely of a descriptive nature. That is, concern has been on describing how groups make decisions rather than how they *should* make decisions. What little theory there is has concentrated on determining when groups should be used in place of the individual.

In certain types of situations, it appears that decisions made by groups can be superior to those made by individuals. In fact, we can begin by saying that, on the average, groups make better decisions than individuals. However, this must be moderated by several important facts. First, while group decisions are better than those which would be reached by the average individual in the group, group decisions are rarely as good as the performance of the best individual. Second, groups consume more resources so their improved effectiveness must be compared against their poorer efficiency. It is possible that the benefits of a better decision are more than offset by the costs of reaching that decision. Finally, the superiority of group decision making varies according to the type of decision situation and the interpersonal relationships within the group.[16] This last point requires further elaboration.

[16] Gerald L. Rose, "Assessing the State of Decision-Making," in *Contemporary Management,* ed. Joseph W. McGuire. (Englewood Cliffs, N.J.: Prentice-Hall, Inc., 1974), p. 503.

Nonprogrammed decisions appear to be more effectively made by groups, providing group members have heterogeneous backgrounds and experiences.[17] Diverse views can provide the questioning and challenging needed to uncover weak or erroneous assumptions, as well as increase opportunities for the development of creative alternatives. On nonprogrammed decisions, errors frequently have a greater impact; therefore, these types of decisions can often most benefit from the collective judgment of a group.

If the acceptance of a decision by a number of individuals is critical to its effectiveness, having these individuals participate in the decision is a logical conclusion.[18] Participation in the process increases the commitment and motivation of those who will have to carry out the decision. Since individuals are more reluctant to fight or undermine a decision which they helped to develop, group decisions increase acceptance of the final solution and facilitate its implementation.

The effectiveness of group decision making is also influenced by the size of the group. The larger the group, the greater the opportunity for heterogeneous representation. Of course, increased size also requires more coordination and increased time to allow all members to contribute. What this means is that groups probably should not be too large—a minimum of five or six members, a maximum of fifteen or sixteen.[19] Evidence indicates that committees of five are highly effective when the five members possess adequate skills and knowledge.[20]

The above comments about group decision making are necessarily sketchy. As noted previously, this is due to the descriptive nature of group decision-making research. In the next chapter, you will find that we know considerably more about the practice of group decision making.

[17] E. Frank Harrison, *The Managerial Decision-Making Process* (Boston: Houghton Mifflin Co., 1975), p. 211.

[18] N. R. F. Maier, *Problem-Solving Discussions and Conferences* (New York: John Wiley, 1963).

[19] Ernest Dale, *Planning and Developing the Company Organization Structure,* Research Report No. 20 (New York: American Management Association, 1952), p. 90.

[20] Alan C. Filley, "Committee Management: Guidelines from Social Science Research," *California Management Review,* Fall 1970, pp. 13–21.

summary of major points

1. Decision making is the crux of the administrative process.
2. Decision making is defined as the selection of a preferred course of action from two or more alternatives.

3. The decision-making process is made up of six main steps:
   a. Ascertain the need for a decision.
   b. Establish decision criteria.
   c. Allocate weights to criteria.
   d. Develop alternatives.
   e. Evaluate alternatives.
   f. Select the best alternative.

4. Programmed decisions are standardized responses. They are applicable in structured, repetitive, and routine situations. Examples of programmed decision guides are:
   a. Objectives
   b. Standards
   c. Procedures
   d. Methods
   e. Rules
   f. Policies

5. Nonprogrammed decisions are unique responses to problems that are novel; vague, ambiguous, or complex; or important enough to deserve special custom-tailored treatment. Examples of nonprogrammed decision guides are:
   a. Programs
   b. Strategies
   c. Budgets

6. Four personal qualities can contribute to better decisions:
   a. Experience
   b. Good judgment
   c. Creativity
   d. Quantitative skills

7. Experience leads to the development of specific responses which are demonstrated by habit—without hesitation—in a particular situation.

8. Judgment is the ability to evaluate information wisely. It is made up of one's common sense, maturity, ability to reason, and experience.

9. Creativity is the conceiving of original and unique ideas. All individuals have some creative ability which can be stimulated by the organizational environment and through specific individual and group methods.

10. Quantitative tools can assist administrators in making better decisions but cannot replace decision makers and their judgment. Well-known quantitative techniques include:
    a. Linear programming
    b. Queuing theory
    c. Probability theory
    d. Inventory models
    e. Marginal analysis
    f. Breakeven analysis
    g. Network analysis
    h. Simulation
    i. Return on investment

11. The work in group decision making has been almost entirely of a descriptive nature. What little theory there is has concentrated on determining when groups should be used in place of the individual.

THEORY OF
DECISION MAKING

FOR DISCUSSION

1. Describe the decision-making process.
2. Why is it that, generally speaking, the higher up in an organization an administrator moves, the more nonprogrammed decision making he or she is likely to engage in?
3. Contrast *rules* and *policies*.
4. "There is no substitute for experience." Analyze this statement as it relates to decision making.
5. What is the value of quantitative tools to decision making?
6. "A good quantitative model can replace the need for a decision maker to utilize judgment." Do you agree or disagree with this statement? Explain your position.
7. When is creativity important in decision making?
8. "Groups always make better decisions than individuals acting alone." Do you agree or disagree with this statement? Support your position.

case exercise

An office-space decision

The Canadian Immigration Department (C.I.D.) has offices in all major metropolitan areas within Canada and in many smaller communities. One of its largest offices is in Montreal. The Montreal office employs several hundred personnel and occupies 35,000 square feet of space in a downtown office building. The Department is currently paying an annual rent of $7.20 per square foot. This rate has been in effect for four years, but a decision by the Department's administration needs to be made because this lease will expire next year.

The current facilities have been evaluated by the Montreal director who believes that they would be adequate for at least another five-year period. The only drawback is that the building has aged, and many new buildings have recently been erected that offer greater prestige and finer amenities. For example, in the current building, parking facilities are severely limited, only three elevators are available to service the twenty-four-story building, and there is no underground link between the building and the city's Metro subway.

The leasing agent for the building has recently contacted the Montreal director and proposed a ten-year renewal at $8.60 a square foot. Included in the price, as previously, were all taxes and utilities, plus a full repainting and recarpeting of all the Department's office space.

Of course, other options are available. Several new buildings have a surplus of space and are anxious to attract a tenant such as the C.I.D. The McMahon group has proposed the C.I.D. consider 35,000 square feet in their new building. They offered the space at $7.15 a square foot but did not include utilities which the C.I.D. estimated at between $1.30 and $1.50 per square foot. Their building is 40 stories tall, has eight elevators, ample parking space, and is within a block of the nearest Metro station. Place Ville Marie, the city's largest office and shopping complex, has also offered C.I.D. 35,000 square feet of space. One of the most prestigious addresses in Montreal, the P.V.M. offer is at $9.00 a square foot, including all utilities and taxes. With this price comes a Metro station in the building, nearly four full floors in the sixty-five-story office structure, and the prestige of the P.V.M. address.

As the C.I.D.'s Montreal director reviewed the choices, he recognized that a move would be costly. At a minimum, he figured it would cost $200,000, but of course, if the new lease were for ten years, that was only $20,000 a year. Then, too, there was the disruption inherent in any move and the problems it would cause employees and the department's clientele.

As he pondered the costs and benefits of each alternative, he got a phone call from a real estate group inquiring as to his interest in moving his operation into a new building going up next to the airport. Although the airport was ten miles out of downtown, an inconvenience for many employees and clients, the rental price seemed incredibly attractive—$6.50 a square foot, including all expenses.

Questions

1. What is the best dollars-and-cents choice?
2. What are the key qualitative criteria that must also be considered?
3. Can you think of other alternatives that the administrator might want to consider?

FOR FURTHER READING

"B-School Buzzword: Creativity," *Business Week,* August 8, 1977, p. 66. Some graduate schools of business are introducing courses in generating creative ideas so as to get potential administrators to analyze problems in unconventional ways.

Elbing, A., *Behavioral Decisions in Organizations,* 2nd ed. Glenview, Ill.: Scott, Foresman & Co., 1978, chaps. 3–7. Presents a five-step framework for decision making.

Harrison, E. F., *The Managerial Decision-Making Process.* Boston: Houghton Mifflin, 1975. Sophisticated review of the major theories and research studies of the decision-making process.

Levin, R. I., and C. A. Kirkpatrick, *Quantitative Approaches to Management,* 3rd ed. New York: McGraw-Hill, 1975. Excellent source for straightforward presentation of quantitative tools useful for decision making.

Miller, D. W., and M. K. Starr, *The Structure of Human Decisions.* Englewood Cliffs, N.J.: Prentice-Hall, Inc., 1967. A short book that tells how to recognize the appropriate classification for a decision problem and how to approach the problems of each class in accord with the theory.

Soelberg, P., "Unprogrammed Decision Making," *Industrial Management Review,* Spring 1967, pp. 19–29. Presents a model and suggests how managers' unprogrammed decision making may be improved.

Appendix to Chapter 4: Using quantitative tools

Students of administration frequently encounter the quantitative side of decision making in courses concerning quantitative methods, production management, or operations research. For those who may not have exposure to such courses or who desire a brief treatment of their application, this section discusses decision-making conditions and illustrates how a few of the more well-known techniques can be utilized for special kinds of decision problems.

When an administrator is faced with a decision, we can say that one of three conditions prevail. The ideal situation is one of *certainty;* that is, the administrator is able to make perfectly accurate decisions because the outcome of any action is known. As you might expect, this is *not* the environment under which most decisions are made. It is more idealistic than pragmatic.

A far more relevant situation is one of *risk.* By risk, we mean those conditions where the decision maker is able to estimate the likelihood of certain outcomes. This ability to assign probabilities to outcomes may be the result of personal experience or secondary information. However, the point is that under the conditions of risk, the administrator has historical data that can allow him or her to assign probabilities to different alternatives. Let's look at an example.

Suppose that you manage a ski resort in the Colorado Rockies. You are contemplating whether to add another lift to your current facility. Obviously, your decision will be significantly influenced by the amount of additional revenue that the new lift would generate, and this will depend on the level of snowfall. The decision is made somewhat clearer when you are reminded that you have reasonably reliable past data on snowfall levels in your area. The data indicates that during the past ten years, you received three years of heavy snowfall, five years of normal, and two years of light snow. Can you use this information to determine the expected future annual revenue if the new lift is added? If you have good information as to how much the revenues would be for each level of snow, the answer is yes.

You can create an expected value formulation; that is, you can compute the conditional return from each possible outcome times its probability. The result is the average revenue that can be expected over time if the given probabilities hold. So, as Figure 4-6 shows, the expected revenue from adding a new ski lift is $687,500. Of course, whether that justifies a positive or negative decision would depend on the costs involved in generating this revenue; factors such as the cost of erecting the lift, the additional annual maintenance expenses as a result of having another lift, the interest rate for borrowing money, and so forth.

What happens if we have to make a decision when neither certainty nor reasonable probability estimates are available? We call such a condition *uncertainty,* and choice will be influenced by the psychological orientation

Event	Revenues	×	Probability	=	Expected value of each alternative
Heavy Snowfall	$850,000		0.3		$255,000
Normal Snowfall	$725,000		0.5		$362,500
Light Snowfall	$350,000		0.2		$ 70,000
Expected Revenues					$687,500

of the decision maker. The optimistic administrator will follow a *maximax* choice (maximizing of the maximum possible payoff), the pessimist will pursue a *maximin* choice (maximizing the minimum possible payoff), while the administrator who desires to minimize his maximum "regret" will opt for a *minimax* choice.

Consider the case of the marketing manager at Citibank in New York. He has determined four possible strategies for promoting Citibank's Mastercharge cards throughout the Northeast. But the marketing manager is also aware that his major competitor, Chase Manhattan, has three competitive actions of its own for promoting its Visa card in the same region. In this case, we will assume that the Citibank executive has no previous knowledge that would allow him to place probabilities on the success of any of his four strategies. With these facts, the Citibank manager has formulated the matrix in Figure 4-7 to show the various Citibank strategies and the resulting profit to Citibank depending on the competitive action chosen by Chase Manhattan.

In this example, if our Citibank manager is an optimist, he will choose S_4 because that will produce the largest possible gain—$28 million. Note that this choice maximizes the maximum possible gain.

But if our manager is a pessimist, he will assume that only the worst can occur. The worst outcome for each strategy is as follows: $S_1 = 11$; $S_2 = 9$; $S_3 = 15$; $S_4 = 14$. These are the most pessimistic outcomes from each strat-

FIGURE 4-7 Payoff matrix (in millions of dollars)

Citibank marketing strategies	Chase Manhattan's response		
	CA$_1$	CA$_2$	CA$_3$
S_1	13	14	11
S_2	9	15	18
S_3	24	21	15
S_4	18	14	28

THEORY OF
DECISION MAKING

egy. Following the maximin choice, he would maximize the minimum payoff; that is, he would select S_3.

The third approach recognizes that once a decision is made, it will not necessarily result in the most favorable payoff. This implies regret of profits foregone on the part of the manager; regret being defined as the payoff for each strategy under every competitive action subtracted from the most favorable payoff that is possible with the occurrence of the particular event. For our Citibank manager, the highest payoff, given that Chase engages in CA_1, CA_2, CA_3, is $24 million, $21 million, and $28 million respectively (the highest number in each column). Subtracting the payoffs in Figure 4-7 from these figures produces the results shown in Figure 4-8.

FIGURE 4-8   Regret matrix

Citibank marketing strategies	Chase Manhattan's response		
	CA_1	CA_2	CA_3
S_1	11	7	17
S_2	15	6	10
S_3	0	0	13
S_4	6	7	0

The maximum regrets are: $S_1 = 17$; $S_2 = 15$; $S_3 = 13$; and $S_4 = 7$. Since the minimax choice minimizes the maximum regret, our Citibank manager would choose S_4. By making this choice, he will never have a regret of profits foregone of more than $7 million. This contrasts, for example, with a regret of $15 million had he chosen S_2 and Chase Manhattan taken CA_1. In such a case, he would regret that he had not taken S_3, for then he would have made $24 million.

Breakeven analysis

How many units of product does a firm have to sell in order to just break even, where there is neither profit nor loss? A decision maker may want to know how low sales can go before he or she will lose money or, especially relevant for a new company, how much must be sold before the company stops losing money? The answer to these questions can be found through breakeven analysis.

Breakeven analysis is a simplistic formulation, yet it can be valuable to a decision maker by pointing out the relationship between revenues, costs, and profit, which can be used for decisions concerning pricing, renting, or buying of equipment, and whether a product should be added or discontinued.

Certain information is needed to compute the breakeven point (BE). We need to know the unit price of the product being sold (P), the variable cost per unit (VC), and total fixed costs (TFC). Some of these terms may be new to you, so we will define them briefly.

A company breaks even when its total revenue is just enough to equal its total costs. Total revenues is a fairly straightforward concept. Assuming the price does not fluctuate, it is merely "price times quantity." But total cost has two parts—a fixed component and a variable component.

Fixed costs are those expenses that do not change, regardless of the volume. Examples include insurance premiums and property taxes. This concept is only relative in the short-term because, in the long-run, commitments terminate and thus are subject to variation. Variable costs, as the name implies, change in proportion to output. In a manufacturing organization, the amount of raw materials purchased, labor costs, and energy costs are examples of variable costs.

To compute the breakeven point in units, we can use the following formula: $BE = \dfrac{TFC}{P-VC}$. This formula tells us that total revenue will equal total cost when we sell enough units at a price that covers all variable unit costs, and the difference between price and variable costs, when multiplied by the number of units sold, equals the fixed costs.

The above relationships can be visualized when we look at the following data provided by Dave's Photocopying Service:

Selling Price: 10 cents per copy
Fixed Costs: $27,000 a year
Variable Costs: 4 cents per copy

Using our formula, we compute Dave's breakeven point as: $\dfrac{\$27,000}{\$.10 - .04}$ = 450,000 copies, or when annual revenues are $45,000. This same concept can be portrayed graphically, as shown in Figure 4-9.

Inventory models

For those organizations that are required to maintain inventories, administrators are confronted with a dilemma: how much inventory should be carried for a particular item? Holding inventory both incurs warehousing costs and ties up part of the organization's capital. So the decision maker wants to keep inventory levels as low as possible. However, it can often be costly to the organization if it runs out of an item. It can lose sales and goodwill. The issue, therefore, is to balance the cost of carrying the inventory against the cost of running out. The economic order quantity (EOQ) model has been proposed to assist the administrator with this decision.

The objective of the EOQ model is to minimize the total costs in carrying and ordering inventory, as depicted in Figure 4-10. Notice how carrying costs and ordering costs vary. As orders get larger, so do carrying costs. But larger orders mean decreased ordering costs. The lowest total cost and the most economic order quantity are reached at the same point.

The EOQ formula requires that we have the following data: demand

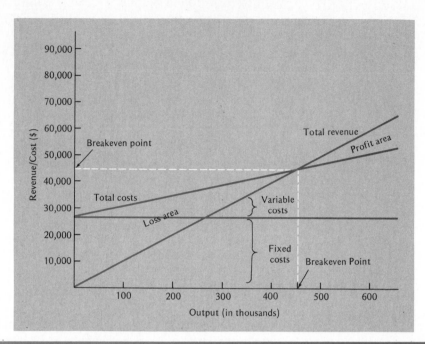

FIGURE 4-9   Dave's photocopying service

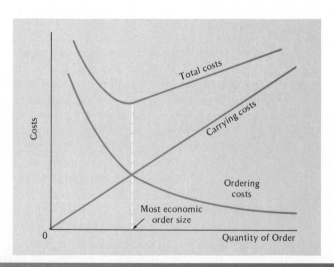

FIGURE 4-10   Determining the most economic order quantity

for the item during the period (D); the cost of placing each order (OC); the value of the item (V); and the cost of maintaining the total inventory—taxes, insurance, etc.—expressed as a percentage (IM). We can now present the formula and demonstrate its use with an example.

$$EOQ = \sqrt{\frac{2 \times D \times OC}{V \times IM}}$$

Zenco Electronics annually uses 100,000 fine-tuning devices in manufacturing their Century videotape replay recorder. Each of these fine-tuning devices is worth $10, to place an order for the tuners costs $45, and annual insurance and taxes are computed at 10 percent. If the Texas Tuner Corporation offers Zenco a 5 percent discount on their purchases, if they buy in minimum lots of 5,000, what is the quantity that Zenco should purchase?

First, we can compute the least cost order quantity. The formula tells us that:

$$EOQ = \sqrt{\frac{2 \times 100,000 \times \$45}{\$1.00}}$$

$$EOQ = \sqrt{9,000,000}$$

$$EOQ = \quad 3,000$$

Without any cost savings from a discount, Zenco should order in quantities of 3,000; that is, they should order about 33 times a year. At this order quantity, the value of Zenco orders would be $30,000. We can now compute Zenco's yearly costs:

Value of tuners ($10 × 100,000)	=	$1,000,000
Carrying costs (10% × average inventory value: $30,000/2)	=	1,500
Ordering Costs (33 × $45)	=	1,485
Approximate costs	=	$1,002,985

With the 5 percent discount and 5,000 unit minimum order, yearly costs become:

Value of tuners ($9.50 × 100,000)	=	$ 950,000
Carrying costs (10% × $\frac{\$47,500}{2}$)	=	2,375
Ordering costs (20 × $45)	=	900
Approximate costs	=	$ 953,275

The above computations demonstrate that by ordering in the larger quantities, fewer times per year, and obtaining the discount, we can generate an annual savings of over $49,000. In response to our original question, Zenco should purchase 5,000 units per order.

The final quantitative decision technique we will present is network analysis. The most popular network approach, which can be used in planning and controlling projects, is the Program Evaluation and Review Technique (PERT). For brevity, we will limit our discussion to this technique alone.

PERT requires the decision maker to identify the key activities in a project, their order of dependence, and to estimate the time to complete each. When complete, PERT can be used to assess the implications of interruptions or delays on achieving the target completion date of the project. Because of its capabilities, PERT is a popular tool in construction projects and other major programs that have not been done before and are unlikely to be done again in the same way.

The steps in a PERT process are as follows:

1. Identify every significant event that must be achieved for a project to be completed.
2. Ascertain the order in which these events must be completed.
3. Calculate the time required to complete each activity.
4. Diagram the flow of activities from the project's start to its finish, identifying each event and its relationship to all other events.

Most PERT projects are quite complicated, with hundreds or thousands of events, so we will illustrate the concept with an extremely simplified example from building construction. We will assume that we are interested in seeing how long it will take to put up an office building and turn it over to the building management group. In Figure 4-11, we have identified the major events in the construction project and the estimated time to complete each activity. In Figure 4-12, we have diagrammed our PERT network.

Our PERT network tells us that if everything goes as planned, it will take fifty weeks to complete the building. This is calculated by tracing the longest path of the network: A-B-C-D-G-H-J-K. This longest sequence of events is also called the *critical path*, because any delay in completing the

---

FIGURE 4-11   Simple PERT network for erecting an office building

Event	Description	Expected time (in weeks)	Preceding event
A	Approve design and get permits	10	None
B	Dig subterranean garage	6	A
C	Erect frame and siding	14	B
D	Construct floors	6	C
E	Install windows	3	C
F	Put on roof	3	C
G	Install internal wiring	5	D,E,F
H	Install elevators	5	G
I	Put in floor covering and paneling	4	D
J	Put in doors and interior decorative trim	3	I,H
K	Turn over to building management group	1	J

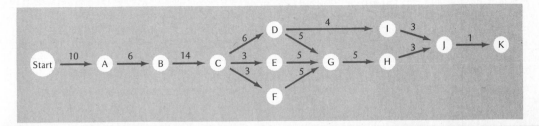

FIGURE 4-12 PERT network diagram

events along this path will delay the completion of the entire project. So, for example, if it took six weeks instead of four to put in the floor covering and paneling (event I), there would be no effect on the final completion date. Why? Because C − D + D − I + I − J equals only thirteen weeks, while C − E + E − G + G − H + H − J equals sixteen weeks. If we wanted, however, to cut the fifty-week time frame, we would give attention to activities along the critical path that might be sped up. Similarly, if there were a penalty incurred by the contractor if the building were not completed in fifty weeks, the administrators on the construction project would want to pay close attention to the activities on the critical path. A delay in these activities, in contrast to others, would automatically translate into a delay in the final completion schedule.

5

Decision Making in Practice

**AFTER
STUDYING
THIS CHAPTER,
YOU SHOULD
BE ABLE TO—**

Peter Principle	Risk avoidance
Economic man	Decision confirmation
Administrative man	Norms
Satisficing	Conformity
Bounded rationality	Compromise
Modern administrative man	Groupthink
Hedonism	Risky-shift phenomenon
Successive limited comparisons	

The difference between how best-selling books in administration and textbooks present decision making

Herbert Simon's contribution to administrative decision making

The influence that self-interest plays in the practice of decision making

Why administrators do not rely heavily on creativity and quantitative tools in decision making

The type of consistent errors decision makers tend to make

The impact that organizationally imposed limitations have on decision makers

Why power is sought by administrators

The difference between individuals and groups in their propensity to assume risk

Why visible problems may get more attention than important problems

The previous chapter presented the theory of decision making. It would be accurate to state that it was a normative view, presenting how decisions *should* be made. Yet, there is a large body of descriptive literature on decision making which paints a dramatically different picture. Though much of this material represents a single individual's experiences in organizations, rather than tightly controlled research designs based on broad samples, these "war" stories should not be totally disregarded. The success of such books as *The Peter Principle* and *Up The Organization* suggests that a significant segment of the book-buying public believes that actual decision making in organizations is not nearly as objective and straightforward as the normative picture presented previously. In order to provide some insights into how several practitioners envision the decision-making process in organizations, we have selected a few excerpts from their best-selling books.

In 1969, Laurence J. Peter and Raymond Hull collaborated on a book that questioned the decision process as it applies to the selection of competent personnel:

> When I was a boy I was taught that the men upstairs knew what they were doing. I was told, "Peter, the more you know, the further you go." So I stayed in school until I graduated from college and then went forth into the world clutching firmly these ideas and my new teaching certificate. During the first year of teaching I was upset to find that a number of teachers, school principals, supervisors and superintendents appeared to be unaware of their professional responsibilities and incompetent in executing their duties. For example, my principal's main concerns were that all window shades be at the same level, that classrooms should be quiet and that no one step on or near the rose beds. The superintendent's main concerns were that no minority group, no matter how fanatical, should ever be offended and that all official forms be submitted on time. The children's education appeared farthest from the administrator's mind. . . .
>
> I began to suspect that the local school system did not have a monopoly on incompetence.
>
> As I looked further afield, I saw that every organization contained a number of persons who could not do their jobs. . . .
>
> So my analysis of hundreds of cases of occupational incompetence led me on to formulate *The Peter Principle:*
>
> In a Hierarchy Every Employee Tends
to Rise to His Level of Incompetence[1]

The former chairman of Avis-Rent-A-Car, Robert A. Townsend, opined in his *Up the Organization* that the decision process at a board of

---

[1] Excerpts abridged from pp. 19, 20, 25 of *The Peter Principle* by Dr. Laurence J. Peter and Raymond Hull. Copyright © 1969 by William Morrow and Company, Inc. By permission of the publisher. The copyright holder in the British Commonwealth is Souvenir Press Ltd., London.

directors' meeting bears little resemblance to the theory and that effective administrators may need to avoid openness:

> ...In the years that I've spent on various boards I've never heard a single suggestion from a director (made *as* a director *at* a board meeting) that produced any result at all.
>
> While ostensibly the seat of all power and responsibility, directors are usually the friends of the chief executive put there to keep him safely in the office. They meet once a month, gaze at the financial window dressing (never at the operating figures by which managers run the business), listen to the chief and his team talk superficially about the state of the operation, ask a couple of dutiful questions, make token suggestions (courteously recorded and subsequently ignored), and adjourn until next month. . . .
>
> To get something done involving several departments, divisions or organizations, keep quiet about it. Get the available facts, marshal your allies, think through the opponents' defenses, and then go.
>
> A premature announcement of what you're going to do unsettles potential supporters, gives opponents time to construct real and imaginary defenses, and tends to ensure failure.
>
> It's a poor bureaucrat who can't stall a good idea until even its sponsor is relieved to see it dead and officially buried.[2]

More recently, two books rose to the top of the best-sellers' list: Michael Korda's *Power* and Robert Ringer's *Winning Through Intimidation*. Along with the others we have excerpted, they argue that organizations and their decision makers are not necessarily fair and objective, nor are those who work the hardest most likely to get ahead.

Korda sees success in terms of getting and using power. In support of his thesis, he offers a description of how one person built a dynasty. The story is told by a fellow named Mark about an acquaintance who works for a major television network in New York City.

> "When I first came here, we had a guy who was making merchandising tie-ups with the network's shows, you know, toys, games, cocktail napkins, stuff like that. He was doing it out of one small office, and he saw what everyone else was doing, and decided to grow. I was working for him then, and what he did was to fill up his office with so much junk that he needed a display area. At that time, we were in an old building on Lexington Avenue, and space was tight, but the network had leased part of an old hotel off Third Avenue, and since everybody was embarrassed at making money off floating rubber ducks and Indian chief make-up kits for kids, they moved us over there. It was a weird place. There was a health club on the roof, two floors full of hookers and most of the rest were network offices in hotel rooms. Some guys who were divorced or separated actually moved in there. I mean

[2] Robert Townsend, *Up the Organization* (New York: Alfred A. Knopf, 1970), pp. 49, 55.

why not—with the hookers and the health club and the coffee shop downstairs, it was a perfect life. Everybody had to go over to the corporate headquarters once a week to sign for their pay check, and the secretaries had to go over to get pencils and typewriter ribbons, but apart from that, we were pretty much on our own. My boss knew just what he was doing. He took over room after room, suite after suite, until he had a whole floor. We had merchandising racks, display rooms, strange guys developing new toys and games, we built up files, an international licensing department, we got ourselves our own screening room. I thought he was crazy—he was expanding so fast that we didn't even know what we were doing half the time, but he told me not to worry. 'Listen, Mark,' he said to me, 'right now this corporation is building a big new building over on Sixth Avenue. When we left the old one, we had a couple of rooms, right? When we move back in, they're going to have to give us half a floor. Just remember that every senior executive with kids gets one of everything we do, compliments of this department.' Of course, he was right. When the new building was ready, we had a whole department to move in, with display rooms, conference rooms, big offices, everything you could want. It was beautiful. The only trouble was that they'd installed a central computer system, and when they got it working, they discovered we'd been losing money for two years. Even then, we were okay. Nobody was going to wind up a department that had half a floor of office space, and people had gotten used to receiving the toys and things. I mean, they weren't about to start going out and paying money for birthday presents and Christmas gifts after two years of getting them by the gross on the cuff. All they did was give my boss a title and put a financial guy in under him, with authority to straighten things out. After all, you don't fire a guy for expanding too fast—that's optimism. Today, he's got the audio-visual cassette department as well, and he's making a hundred thousand dollars a year, and the only thing he really knows is how to grab for space, and to have everything under his control painted the same color, so people can see just how big his area is. It's always primrose yellow—even the men's rooms. I think he has his own painters in the closet, ready to go out at a moment's notice and paint up another office yellow so people will know it belongs to him. By now, I think he could just have the painters in at night to paint an office yellow, and people would assume it was his and whoever was in it was working for him. If he ever gets to be the chief executive officer, I guess he'll have the building painted yellow."[3]

Ringer presents his "Uncle George Theory" as a response to the myth of hard work:

> The simplest way I know to explain this theory is to tell you, . . . all other things being equal—that if you keep your nose to the grindstone and work hard, long hours, you're guaranteed to get only one thing in return: OLD![4]

Ringer sums up the common thread running throughout these four books when he says that "reality isn't the way you wish things to be, nor the

[3] Michael Korda, *Power! How to Get It, How to Use It* (New York: Random House, 1975), pp. 75–77.
[4] Robert J. Ringer, *Winning Through Intimidation* (Greenwich, Conn.: Fawcett Publications, Inc., 1973), p. 26.

way they appear to be, but the way they actually are. . . . You either acknowledge reality and use it to your benefit or it will automatically work
against you."[5] If we are to understand what administrators actually do,
which to most readers is probably of more value than the normative "ought
to do," we should not ignore the message these practitioners are sending
us—actual decision making does not necessarily mirror theory. Yet, we must
treat this message as a counterpoint to chapter 4. Many of the points made
by these best-selling authors are exaggerations. To accept their appraisals of
administrative decision making to the exclusion of all others can lead us as
astray as accepting exclusively the normative position of chapter 4. Who
then are we to believe? Do we have an accurate descriptive model of administrative decision making? The answer to the former question is that neither holds the ultimate truth; while the answer to the latter question is that
the academic community has made extensive progress in recent years toward demonstrating how decision makers actually behave.

Herbert Simon received the Nobel Prize largely for his explanations
on how administrators make decisions. We can use his monumental work as
a foundation upon which to build.[6]

The economic-man model

Decision theory originally grew out of a view of the decision
maker as a purely economic being. As such, he is completely rational, making "optimal" choices in a highly specified and clearly defined environment.[7]
His frame of reference for defining "optimal" would normally be the equivalent of organizational goal attainment. So when confronted with a problem, economic man should:

1. Clearly define the decision criteria.
2. Be knowledgeable of all relevant alternatives.
3. Be aware of all possible consequences of each alternative.
4. Evaluate the consequences against the decision criteria.
5. Rank alternatives in a preferred order of economic impact.
6. Select the alternative which rates highest (*most* preferred) in economic terms.

In actuality, economic man is a normative theory. It is concerned with
what a decision maker *should* do rather than what he actually does in making choices. For instance, rarely is anyone ever knowledgeable about *all* the
relevant alternatives in a decision or about *all* the possible consequences of
each. As a result, Simon rejected this model in favor of one that he believed

---

[5] Ibid, p. 31.
[6] The following discussion of economic-man and administrative-man models is
based on Herbert A. Simon, *Administrative Behavior,* 2nd ed. (New York: Macmillan,
1957).
[7] James March and Herbert Simon, *Organizations* (New York: Wiley, 1958), p. 137.

more accurately reflected reality. He called his replacement administrative man.

The administrative-man model

Replaced

Simon attacked the economic-man model on a number of points. It is not feasible for a person to search for each and every alternative. The sole motive in making decisions is not the economic incentive. Further, decisions are not made in an environment of certainty, where all alternatives are known to the decision maker. Finally, individuals cannot always objectively state their decision criteria, nor list their preferences from most preferred choices to least preferred. Simon acknowledged that human beings have a limited capacity for comprehending the inherent complexity in decision making. They cannot be perfectly rational; rather, they function within the constraints of bounded rationality. His administrative-man model, therefore, proposed that the decision maker will:

1. Recognize only a limited number of decision criteria.
2. Propose only a limited number of alternatives.
3. Be aware of only a few of the consequences of each alternative.
4. Formulate a simplified and limited model of the real situation.
5. Select the alternative which presents a satisfactory solution.

Administrative man assumes that decision makers cannot optimize. Such could only be attained if the decision maker had either a single objective or fully compatible multiple objectives. Unfortunately, this is often not the case (i.e., a production manager attempts to minimize costs while at the same time achieve high reliability). In most cases, decision makers confront multiple, competing objectives. In addition, the decision criteria would have to be stable over time if optimizing were to be achieved. This, too, we recognize is not possible. Even if the criteria in a decision could be clearly identified, their importance is likely to fluctuate widely. Utilizing our job selection illustration from chapter 4, although climate may seem unimportant on one day, on another day it may be of greater consequence. Climate, for instance, may not seem to be a high priority in choosing between jobs in Minneapolis and San Diego in July but may take on increased importance if the decision is made in February (especially if the decision maker is in Minneapolis).

Decision situations, rarely, if ever, meet the economic-man assumption of certainty. Decision makers just do not have full knowledge of all alternatives and their consequences. Administrative man's assumptions state that the typical approach is for the decision maker to construct a simplified model of the real situation. Complexity is, therefore, reduced to the level at which a human being can make a decision within the limitations imposed by his or her thinking capabilities and knowledge. Rather than dealing with the totality of the real world, which is impossible for the decision maker to comprehend, decisions are made in terms of personal abstractions. The values and personality characteristics of the decision maker strongly influence these abstractions, and therefore, an administrator, in reaching a decision, typically views only a selected sample of possible alternatives.

This limitation might also suggest that decisions are rarely made in a way that is fully consistent with the demands of rationality. Rather than considering *all* alternatives, and listing them from most-preferred to least-preferred, an administrator begins by searching for probable courses of action. This search continues until he finds an alternative that meets some personally determined minimum acceptable level. Once this level is attained, he rarely goes beyond to find a maximizing decision. Rather, he satisfices (meaning satisfactory and sufficient) or looks for a course of action that is "good enough" for the intended purpose. Since a decision maker searches for alternatives only as long as he is dissatisfied with the best choice he has, there is no attempt to find alternatives or to order them according to a hierarchy of preferred order, as economic-man assumptions would suggest.

> The decision maker is constrained in the acquisition and assimilation of the informational inputs by three primary limitations. The first of these, and the one closest to him, is his own intellectual capacity for dealing with only a few of the many complex variables bearing on the decision. The second is the very real and practical constraint associated with the amounts of time and money that can be spent in the quest for relevant alternatives and the comparison, evaluation and eventual choice of the most desirable alternative. And, of course, the third limitation is the virtual impossibility of obtaining anything close to perfect information even if one had limitless time and money.[8]

Is the administrative-man model valid? Does it accurately depict how administrators behave? These are complex questions to answer since we cannot expect *any* model to explain all behavior. When the decision maker is confronted with a simple problem, with few alternative courses of action, and where the cost to search out and evaluate alternatives is low, the original economic-man model may well accurately describe practice.[9] But in the more typical type of administrative decisions, the evidence indicates that administrative man more accurately describes how decisions are made.[10]

Nearly four decades have passed since Simon originally proposed the administrative-man model. During this time, research has provided information that allows us to extend this original model and make explicit some of the implicit statements made by Simon. Let us now take a look at modern administrative man as a decision maker.

[8] E. Frank Harrison, *The Managerial Decision-Making Process* (Boston: Houghton Mifflin, 1975), pp. 75–76.

[9] D.L. Rados, "Selection and Evaluation of Alternatives in Repetitive Decision Making," *Administrative Science Quarterly,* June 1972, pp. 196–206.

[10] For a review of the research, see Alan C. Filley, Robert J. House, and Steven Kerr, *Managerial Process and Organizational Behavior,* 2nd ed. (Glenview, Ill.: Scott, Foresman & Co., 1976), pp. 113–29.

Modern administrative man

Simon's original administrative man was characterized as constrained by human limitations. Decision makers sought solutions that were "good enough" because they face multiple and competing objectives. In addition, they are limited in their ability to acquire and absorb information, as well as structure and evaluate alternatives. Nothing in the recent research in decision making suggests these conclusions were in error. When we accept the human limitations thesis, however, several important predictions which were implied by Simon can be elaborated upon. In this section we want to show how the administrative-man model leads us to view decision makers as acting hedonistically, making limited use of their creative abilities or quantitative skills, and making consistent errors in judgment.

Additionally, other evidence has evolved that may not be obvious from administrative-man assumptions. If there is a common thread to these findings, it is that in addition to inherent human limitations, the organization itself imposes certain constraints and pressures on decision makers. We will demonstrate how the organization's performance evaluation and reward procedures; goals, policies, and historical precedents; and system-imposed time constraints tend to encourage power seeking, risk avoidance, a short-term frame of reference, style over substance, and an early choice of an implicit favorite alternative by decision makers. By merging our knowledge of human and organizationally imposed limitations, we develop a politically oriented view of the decision maker. We call this view the modern administrative-man model.

Some elaboration on administrative man

Hedonistic   Decision makers are motivated by what they believe is in their personal self-interest, which goes beyond strict economic considerations. They seek to maximize pleasure from their actions and minimize pain. Whether it is called hedonism or self-serving behavior, whatever the label, the underlying concept is the same—administrators act so as to maximize what they perceive to be in their self-interest.

Acceptance of the hedonistic concept entails viewing decision makers as acting politically; that is, acknowledging that decision makers "play politics." When they act to enhance their own position, regardless of costs to the organization or to others, they are acting politically. The implications of this reality should be obvious: "We can assume that where alternatives are perceived to have equal consequences for the organization, the individual will select that alternative which favors his sphere of action—enlarging it if possible, or defending it."[11] But since the consequences of a decision are rarely so evident as to make it clear what is in the organization's best interest, we can expand our prediction to state that "in any complex decision where per-

[11] James D. Thompson, *Organizations in Action* (New York: McGraw-Hill, 1967), p. 123.

sonal . . . factors apply [which includes all nonprogrammed decisions], the individual's preference will dominate the results."[12]

Limited use of creativity Since administrators rarely seek an optimum solution, but rather a satisfactory one, we should expect to find a minimal use of creativity in practice.

Efforts will be made to try to keep the search process simple. It will tend to be confined to the neighborhood of the problem symptom and to the neighborhood of the current alternative.[13] More complex search behavior, which includes the development of creative alternatives, will only be resorted to when a simple search fails to uncover a satisfactory alternative.

Rather than formulating new and unique problem definitions and alternatives, with frequent journeys into unfamiliar territory, the evidence indicates that decision making is incremental rather than comprehensive. This means that administrators avoid the difficult task of considering all the important factors and weighing their relative merits and drawbacks. Instead, they make successive limited comparisons.[14] This branch approach simplifies decision choices by comparing only those alternatives that differ in relatively small degree from the choice currently in effect; this approach also makes it unnecessary for the decision maker to thoroughly examine an alternative and its consequences: one need investigate only those aspects in which the proposed alternative and its consequences differ from the status quo.

What emerges from the above is a decision maker who takes small steps toward his or her objective. It acknowledges the noncomprehensive nature of choice selection; in other words, administrators make successive comparisons because decisions are never made forever and written in stone, but rather made and remade endlessly in small comparisons between narrow choices. This, of course, is consistent with the satisficing assumptions of the administrative-man model, yet offers a solution to how decision makers actually operationalize the satisficing process.

Limited use of quantitative tools The rapid expansion of courses in quantitative analysis in college programs in administration and management might lead one to conclude that practicing administrators are increasingly using these tools to improve the quality of their decisions. The evidence does not confirm this conclusion. Quantitative tools *can* improve the quality of decision making—on that there is little doubt—but it appears fair to state that the use of these tools in practice is quite limited. When they are used, it

[12] Alan J. Rowe, "The Myth of the Rational Decision Maker," *International Management*, August 1974, p. 38.
[13] Richard M. Cyert and James G. March, *A Behavioral Theory of the Firm* (Englewood Cliffs, N.J.: Prentice-Hall, Inc., 1963), p. 121.
[14] Charles E. Lindholm, "The Science of 'Muddling Through,'" *Public Administration Review*, Spring 1959, pp. 79–88.

is generally to objectively support choices that were made subjectively. This is a strong statement, so let us review some of the evidence.

A survey of firms in the New York City area that employed members of the Planning Executives Institute found that more than one-half of the respondents used less than three quantitative-decision techniques.[15] For example, only 44 percent used simulation, 33 percent used linear programming, 11 percent used queuing theory, and 2 percent used game theory.

A survey of 275 manufacturing firms in seven southwestern states, all with 250 or more employees, was not encouraging. More than half did not use *any* of the fourteen quantitative techniques the researchers asked about.[16]

Results from a study of twenty managers in three major aerospace companies are of particular interest because, as the researcher noted, one would expect the aerospace industry to be sophisticated in quantitative tools, since its decision makers are almost all engineers who possess mathematical backgrounds and who have been trained in the scientific method. Additionally, accurate decisions are especially critical in this industry. When the managers were asked to indicate the guides they felt were most important to their decisions—including both quantitative guides such as network analysis and linear programming, and qualitative guides such as judgment and experience—the researcher found that subjective factors were mentioned over three times as frequently as sophisticated methods of analysis.[17] Nine of the twenty managers did not mention even one of the sophisticated techniques as being valuable to them for making any of their important decisions.

The above findings appear to be generalizable to government, too. C. Jackson Grayson, former dean of the business school at Southern Methodist University and well trained in the use of quantitative techniques, admits that when he was putting together the Price Commission during Phase II of the U.S. Economic Stabilization Program in 1973 and 1974, absolutely no quantitative tools were explicitly used in decisions he had to make.[18] Grayson defended his actions on the grounds of limited time, inaccessibility of data, resistance to change, long response time, and invalidating simplifications inherent in quantitative techniques.

The most comprehensive and possibly damning evidence indicating the limited use of quantitative tools in decision making were responses from vice-presidents for production, or their equivalent, at seventy-eight Fortune

[15] Richard J. Coppinger and E. Stewart Epley, "The Non-use of Advanced Mathematical Techniques," *Managerial Planning* (May-June 1972), pp. 12–15.

[16] Norman Gaither, "The Adoption of Operations Research Techniques By Manufacturing Organizations," *Decision Sciences,* October 1975, pp. 797–813.

[17] Clayton Reeser, "The Use of Sophisticated Analytical Methods for Decision Making in the Aerospace Industry," *MSU Business Topics* (Autumn 1971), pp. 63–69.

[18] C. Jackson Grayson, "Management Science and Business Practice," *Harvard Business Review* (July–August 1973), pp. 41–48.

**DECISION MAKING
IN PRACTICE**

500 manufacturing firms. The executives were asked to what extent they used nineteen different quantitative techniques.[19] In looking at responses to all nineteen techniques, the researchers noted that:

> Nine of the techniques were not being used at all by 60 percent or more of the responding organizations. At the other extreme, only seven of the 19 techniques were of frequent use or extensive use by 25 percent or more of the respondents. A definite lack of utilization of quantitative techniques in production/operations management is reflected in these data.[20]

Many of the nineteen techniques selected were of limited value to production executives, so the researchers identified seven techniques that had definite applicability to production operations. The results are shown in Figure 5-1.

Again, the results are not encouraging. Better than 60 percent of the respondents were unfamiliar with three of the techniques or, if they knew of it, did not use it. Only three of these "relevant" techniques were described as frequently or extensively used by more than 20 percent of the executives. One can only surmise that, if these results accurately reflect the practice in production operations of the largest corporations in the United States, usage of quantitative tools in the bulk of North American organizations is indeed very limited. Of course, this would be consistent with the administrative-man model. The appeal of quantitative techniques declines when one seeks only to find a solution that is "good enough."

Consistent errors in judgment Decision makers are not infallible; they make errors in judgment. A consistent pattern emerges from these errors. One summary of these consistencies found:

1. Decision makers will use irrelevant information in forming a judgment. Even after repeated episodes where information has been linked to some specific outcome, decision makers will still use this irrelevant information.
2. Information that is nonlinear tends to be unidentified.
3. Information reflecting a negative relationship between the information and a given outcome is underutilized.
4. Once a set of weights is learned and has demonstrated success, it is more difficult to learn changes in these weights than it was to learn the original weights.[21]

Decision makers also tend to make their judgments hastily, particularly as the complexity of the decision increases. Additional information is often not sought even though it could greatly increase the quality of the de-

[19] Thad B. Green, Walter B. Newsom, and S. Roland Jones, "A Survey of the Application of Quantitative Techniques to Production/Operation Management in Large Corporations," *Academy of Management Journal* (December 1977), pp. 669–76.

[20] Ibid., p. 670.

[21] Ronald J. Ebert and Terence R. Mitchell, *Organizational Decision Processes: Concepts & Analysis* (New York: Crane, Russak & Co., 1975), p. 131.

Quantitative technique	Unfamiliar with technique	Percentage of Responses				
		No use	Little use	Moderate use	Frequent use	Extensive use
Simulation	10	22	29	22	14	3
Queuing theory	19	42	27	5	3	4
Network analysis	3	14	28	23	17	15
Inventory models	11	11	11	22	12	33
Linear programming	4	13	27	20	19	17
Nonlinear programming	14	49	21	14	1	1
Goal programming	41	30	7	13	4	5

cision and could be acquired at low or reasonable costs.[22] Further, the order in which information is received tends to influence one's judgment. There is considerable evidence that information received early tends to be given greatest weight, though at other times the last information carries the greatest weight. Overall, the former case—called the primacy effect—is probably more prevalent.

Some extensions of administrative man

We now want to consider how the organization itself limits the decision maker; that is, how the "system" imposes constraints through factors such as its performance evaluation and reward procedures; and goals, policies, and historical precedents which apply standards of acceptable behavior (social sanctions) on members. This system, which certainly has its benefits, also has its drawbacks, one of which is that it places constraints on decision makers. Let's look at how these factors constrain decision makers and then at how they contribute toward extending the administrative-man model.

The evaluation or appraisal system and the reward structure within an organization influences decision makers by suggesting to them what choices are preferable in terms of their personal payoff. We believe behavior to be a function of its consequences and, therefore, expect that decision makers will constantly be "looking over their shoulder" to assess the consequences of their actions.

Administrators will be strongly influenced in their decision making by the criteria by which they are evaluated. If a division manager believes that the manufacturing plants under his responsibility are operating best when he hears nothing negative, it should not surprise us to find that his plant managers spend a good part of their time ensuring that negative information does not reach the division boss. Similarly, if a college dean believes that an

[22] G.F. Pitz, H. Reinhold, and E.S. Geller, "Strategies of Information Seeking in Deferred Decision Making," *Organizational Behavior and Human Performance,* Vol. 4, 1969, pp. 1–19.

instructor should never fail more than 10 percent of his students—to fail more reflects on the instructor's ability to teach—we should expect that new instructors, who are most influenced by the dean's evaluation, will be reluctant to fail too many students.

Rewards condition behavior by directing decision makers in ways to maximize their reward payoff. Regardless of what the organization says it rewards, decision makers will be constantly looking to what is actually rewarded. For instance, the administrator who constantly assures her supervisor that she welcomes suggestions on how she can do her job better, yet ridicules any and all suggestions, impresses upon these supervisors by her behavior that she does not reward suggestions. In another company, senior executives were known for articulating sincere displeasure with those middle-level managers who "apple polished," yet it was perceived by the midmanagers that this behavior was rewarded, so they had their "polishing rags" always close at hand. In summary, the criteria chosen to evaluate an administrator's performance and this administrator's perception of what "pays off" in the organization will significantly influence his or her decision choices.

Goals exist in an organization to give direction. If an organization expects to achieve something, that "something" has to be articulated and communicated to the personnel within the organization. The organization's goals, therefore, constrain decision makers in the sense that they clarify preferred ends.

Policies act in the same way. As broad guidelines that establish parameters for decision-making, they are organizationally imposed constraints on the administrator's decision-making freedom.

Decisions can never be made in a vacuum. Decisions made in the past are ghosts which continually haunt current choices. Therefore, administrators find that historical decisions establish a pattern. This can be seen in the commitments made by various presidents to South Vietnam. Beginning in the early 1950s under Truman, the U.S. began committing resources for the protection of freedom in South Vietnam. Eisenhower and Kennedy inherited these minimal commitments, and the Johnson administration chose to further accelerate funds and personnel. By the time Nixon reached the presidency, the decisions made by four prior administrations formed a set of historical precedents which, in a number of ways, limited his options. Even if one had wanted to stop funding the war immediately, such a course was nearly impossible. Prior commitments constrained his options.

Governmental budget decisions also offer an illustration. It is common knowledge that the largest determining factor of the size of any given year's budget is last year's budget.[23] Choices made today, therefore, are largely a result of choices made over the years. Historical precedents apply to constrain decision choices for business executives too. For example, take the

[23] A. Wildavsky, *The Politics of the Budgetary Process* (Boston: Little, Brown & Co., 1964).

case of Montgomery Ward. As World War II was coming to an end, its president, Sewell Avery, was adamant in his belief that a major recession would follow, just as had happened following World War I and other wars. So while Montgomery Ward's main competitor, Sears, Roebuck, was rapidly expanding its inventories and adding new stores, Ward was consolidating and building up large cash reserves. In retrospect, we know Sears was right. But Ward executives have spent a third of a century living with the results of Avery's decision and attempting to recoup their position in the marketplace.

The above factors, when combined with our earlier discussion of human limitations, leads us to a further description of decision makers. First, they are desirous of power so as to be able to control the decisions that affect them personally. Second, they are concerned with avoiding risks because they perceive the penalties attached to failure to be greater than the rewards associated with risk taking and success. Third, decision makers look to the short-term because that is the basis upon which rewards are conditioned. Fourth, style tends to overwhelm substance since visible decisions tend to be rewarded more than important decisions. Fifth, decision makers frequently establish an implicit favorite alternative and then are inclined to rationalize this choice by searching not for a better solution, but data to support this favored alternative. We will now briefly expand on each of these statements.

Importance of gaining power   Power is measured in terms of the degree of influence an individual or group has in decision making. It additionally includes one's capability of "limiting the scope of actual decision making to safe issues by manipulating the dominant . . . values, myths, and political institutions and procedures."[24] This view recognizes that the ability to deter a decision from being made, or to effect nondecisions, is as significant as influencing actual decisions.

Power is coveted by decision makers because it is the primary means by which they can gratify their desires. It provides the opportunity to control and allocate those things that provide satisfaction.[25] Consistent with the self-interest motive, we should expect administrators to attempt to gain and hold power.

The importance of gaining power was well publicized at the Ford Motor Company in the late 1960s.[26] Henry Ford II, chairman of the board at Ford, chose to hire a president from outside Ford, deciding upon Semon Knudsen, who at the time was a vice-president at General Motors. This decision hit the ambitions of Lee Iacocca particularly hard.

Iacocca had risen to a vice-presidency at Ford on a string of successes,

[24] Peter Bachrach and Morton A. Baratz, *Power and Poverty* (New York: Oxford University Press, 1970), p. 18.
[25] David Kipnis, *The Powerholders* (Chicago: University of Chicago Press, 1970), pp. 171–72.
[26] Abraham Zaleznik, "Politics and Power in Organizational Life," *Harvard Business Review*, May-June 1970, pp. 47–60.

most notably the creation of the Mustang. In his rise at Ford, Iacocca had developed a group of strong supporters who, because of their competence and loyalty, had been moved up rapidly in the organization on Iacocca's coat tails. No novice to the importance of power in an organization, Iacocca believed that employees were either "with me or against me." There was no middle ground.

Upon the announcement that Knudsen was to be the new president at Ford, Iacocca began immediately to muster the support to ensure Knudsen would be powerless. As president, Knudsen found himself consistently undermined on decisions by Iacocca and his associates. Iacocca, through the power base he had established, made it impossible for Knudsen to function effectively. It did not take Henry Ford long to assess what was happening. His decision to fire Knudsen within eighteen months of his appointment and promote Iacocca to the presidency was a classic example of the importance that power plays in effecting decisions in an organization.

As an epilogue, we should note that "he who lives by the sword, dies by the sword." The coveting of power ironically proved to be a major factor in Mr. Ford's decision to subsequently fire Iacocca in the summer of 1978.[27] Although Iacocca had thirty-two years with the company, Henry Ford concluded that "the body chemistry wasn't right" between him and Iacocca. Their personalities had clashed frequently after Iacocca assumed the presidency in 1970. Iacocca had apparently made the mistake of encouraging subordinates to regard him as the heir-apparent to Mr. Ford's chairmanship position. This antagonized Mr. Ford who ultimately chose to sack Iacocca. Interestingly, Iacocca was aware in the weeks prior to being fired that his position was in jeopardy. In a last ditch maneuver to save his job, he launched a fevered campaign to gather support from the company's outside directors. Although some backed him, the effort proved fruitless, "since the chairman has the power to pick whomever he wishes as president."[28]

② **Risk avoidance**   Few behaviors are more evident, particularly in large organizations staffed by career administrators, than the reality that decision makers seek to avoid taking unnecessary risks.[29] This tendency toward conservatism is particularly true as the complexity of the decision increases.[30] The more serious an administrator believes the consequences of error to be, the more he will seek to evade discretion.[31]

Two reasons may account for this behavior. First, research indicates that an intolerance for ambiguity is associated with an administrative bias

[27] "Upheaval in the House of Ford," *Time,* July 24, 1978, pp. 60–61.
[28] Ibid., p. 60.
[29] The statement may also be valid for independent entrepreneurs, who traditionally were thought to be risk takers. See Frederick A. Webster, "A Model for New Venture Initiation: A Discourse on Rapacity and the Independent Entrepreneur," *Academy of Management Review,* January 1976, pp. 26–37.
[30] J.C. Myers and E. Sadler, "Effects of Range of Payoffs As a Variable in Risk Taking," *Journal of Experimental Psychology,* vol. 60, 1960, pp. 306–09.
[31] James D. Thompson, *Organizations in Action,* p. 120.

DECISION MAKING

toward certainty. Individuals who are uncomfortable with ambiguity and hold administrative positions will tend to be oriented toward certainty.[32] The second reason, which appears to be far more overwhelming, is the reality that organizations, in general, do not reward risk taking. On the contrary, the system tends to reward conservatism. "If one does little or nothing new, there will be no criticism, but if one tries wild ideas and they don't work, censure is certain . . . The system is structured to reward inaction and minor, expected gains, and to punish radical change."[33] This is exemplified by a publishing executive's comment to your author: "I never lost money on a book I didn't publish."

It has been shown, for example, that risk avoidance creates a tendency to underestimate revenues and overstate costs when administrators are required to develop budgets for their units.[34] Administrators recognize that the negative sanctions for missing a tight budget are likely to have more impact than the rewards for making a tight budget.[35]

An observer of several business firms' investment decisions confirmed this tendency toward safe choices:

> In estimating the value to their company of a potential investment, the managers in the organization studied are preoccupied with searching for a comparable prior investment rather than identifying the relevant variables and forecasting the underlying uncertainty. Uncertainty is avoided like the plague, while the certainty of historical information is accorded such a premium that it dominates the managers' mental processes completely.[36]

This tendency has been suggested as an explanation of why the Federal Drug Administration is so cautious in licensing new drugs. Thousands can suffer and die because a little known drug is buried under an avalanche of FDA regulations, yet this agency can generally be assured that their risk-avoiding behavior will generate no public outcry.

> This regulatory agency is not protecting the consumer or the industry it regulates; it is protecting itself. The FDA knows that if it lets one drug out that deforms or kills, the public, the press, and a whole host of congressmen will be on their back. But the FDA also knows that it can tie a lifesaving drug up for years in bureaucratic red tape and get little or no adverse reaction. The blame for those that die and suffer needlessly will not be placed on the FDA.[37]

[32] Ibid., p. 152.

[33] Richard N. Farmer, "The Age of Reaction," *Business Horizons,* February 1978, p. 14.

[34] M. Schiff and A.Y. Lewin, "The Impact of People on Budgets," *The Accounting Review,* vol. 45, 1970, pp. 259–68.

[35] M. Onsi, "Behavioral Variables Affecting Budgetary Slack," *The Accounting Review,* vol. 48, 1973, pp. 535–48.

[36] D.H. Woods, "Improving Estimates that Involve Uncertainty," *Harvard Business Review,* vol. 44, 1966, p. 95.

[37] Dwight R. Lee and Robert F. McNown, *Economics in Our Time: Micro Issues* (Chicago: Science Research Associates, 1975), p. 82.

Similarly, it should not surprise us that physicians faced with inconclusive diagnoses tend to err on the safe side or that personnel selection decisions tend to favor safe choices. For example, on this latter point, we see a heavy reliance on formal education and prior relevant experience in selecting a "preferred" candidate. You may be able to perform a job effectively, but that is often irrelevant if you do not have the appropriate credentials. Why? If you fail, the decision maker can always protect himself by arguing that "you looked qualified on paper." It is less risky to support the obvious than to do the unusual or different. This, too, is consistent with our previous conclusions relating to the use of creativity in decision making.

So, what can we conclude? "Examination of business decisions and governmental policy making suggests that, whenever possible, decision makers avoid uncertainty."[38] But a recent review of the decision-making literature has obtained some interesting and more specific conclusions on risk taking.[39]

1. If the risks involved in continuing to do whatever you have been doing in the past appear low, you are likely to go on doing it.
2. If the risks of continuing to do whatever you have been doing appear high, and if the risks of an obvious alternative appear low, you are likely to choose this low-risk alternative.
3. If all the obvious alternatives look risky, and if you also feel that you have little chance of coming up with a better one, you are likely to engage in "defensive avoidance," by trying to deny that a problem exists, exaggerating the advantages of a particular alternative you have chosen, or trying to get someone else to make the decision.
4. Only if you feel that all the obvious choices are risky, that there may be a better choice that is not obvious, and that there is sufficient time to look for this better choice, will you collect new information and engage in a comprehensive and thorough analysis.

③ **Short-term frame of reference** Consistent with our previous discussion of risk aversion, it is also in a decision maker's self-interest to be oriented to the short run. The farther the time horizon on a given decision, the greater the uncertainty and, hence, the greater the risk. Additionally, organizational rewards emphasize short-term performance. Salary increases, promotions, and other desirable rewards are contingent on favorable performance evaluations. But are these evaluations made at five- or ten-year intervals? Of course not! Performance evaluations take place weekly, monthly, quarterly, semi-annually, or at the extreme, once a year. A district sales manager may be indirectly appraised every week when she submits her sales report. At the

[38] Paul Slovic, "From Shakespeare to Simon: Speculations—and Some Evidence—About Man's Ability to Process Information," Oregon Research Institute, Research Monograph, vol. 12, no. 12, April 1972.

[39] Irving L. Janis and Leon Mann, *Decision Making: A Psychological Analysis of Conflict, Choice and Commitment* (New York: Free Press, 1977).

other extreme, a division manager's evaluation may come when the accountants produce her division's yearly income statement. The point is: while organizations may seek to survive and perform effectively over a very long period of time, they evaluate their personnel on the basis of immediate or recent activity. Most administrators quickly recognize that rewards go to those who show results in the short term and emphasize this dimension when they make decisions.

④ **Style over substance** The evaluation of a decision maker's performance is not as clear-cut or objective as an employee doing piecework. It is not nearly so tangible, and what he produces is difficult to measure. This is true of many white-collar jobs and almost all administrative positions. How do we know if a hospital administrator, government official, or corporate executive is making "good" decisions? Unfortunately, it is not an easy task to evaluate a decision maker's performance. Because of this reality, we find that administrators emphasize style over substance. They seek to look good. Ours is an age when the appearance of results can be better than solid accomplishments. This means decision makers must choose problems that are visible. The difficulty is that what is visible is not necessarily important. The system, however, pays off for making decisions on visible problems and ensuring that one "looks good." This desire to look good leads to efforts to dramatize one's accomplishments and withhold information from superiors about such negative issues as fights with other units, unforeseen costs, rapid changes in production, insufficient equipment, and so on.[40]

⑤ **Early alternative selection** Studies of how postgraduate decisions were made suggest decision makers may establish an implicit favorite alternative long before a formal decision is reached and that, contrary to the administrative-man model, search is continued even after an acceptable alternative has been found. The decision maker continues to search not to find a better solution but to rationalize and support his favored alternative.[41]

The search process might be described as follows. The decision maker considers more than one alternative at a time. A favorite is implicitly established early among the first acceptable alternatives, but the decision maker continues in what may be called a "decision confirmation" activity. Rather than objectively appraising alternatives after this favorite has been implicitly selected, the decision maker attempts to justify his favored alternative. This effort becomes self-fulfilling in that it ensures that the implicit favorite turns out to be the "best" choice.

[40] W. Read, *Factors Affecting Upward Communication at Middle Management Levels in Industrial Organizations,* Unpublished doctoral dissertation, Ann Arbor: University of Michigan, 1959.
[41] P. Soelberg, "Unprogrammed Decision Making," *Proceedings of the 26th Annual Academy of Management Meeting,* 1966, pp. 3–16.

DECISION MAKING IN PRACTICE

Group decision making in practice

As the final topic of discussion in this chapter, let us look at how group decisions are actually made in organizations. Not surprisingly, they acquire many of the same characteristics we attributed to modern administrative man in the making of individual decisions. They act in their self-interest, seek satisficing solutions, strive for power, have a short-term frame of reference, and emphasize style over substance. On the other hand, in contrast to the individual's aversion to risk, group decisions may lead to greater risk. However, before we discuss this propensity to accept greater risk, let us look at the more well-known problem with groups—they create pressures toward conformity and compromise in decision making.

Conformity and compromise

Research finds that groups establish norms which dictate acceptable standards of behavior for members. Group members then are influenced—in what may be either very subtle or blatantly overt ways—to modify and align their behavior in the direction of these norms. The result is that individuals in groups move toward conformity. The classic studies by Asch indicate how group pressures can influence individual members.[42]

Asch made up groups of seven or eight people, who sat in a classroom and were asked to compare two cards held by the experimenter. One card had one line, the other had three lines of varying length, but one was identical to the length of the line on the first. Importantly, the fact that one line on the second card was identical to the line on the first was quite obvious; in ordinary conditions, subjects made fewer than 1 percent errors. The object was to announce aloud which of the three lines matched the single line. But what happens if all the members in the group, except one, begin to give incorrect answers? Will the pressures to conform result in the unsuspecting subject (USS) altering his or her answer to align with the others? That was what Asch wanted to know. So he arranged the group so only the USS was unaware that the experiment was "fixed." The seating arrangement was prearranged: The USS was placed so as to be the last to announce his or her decision.

The experiment began with several sets of matching exercises. All the subjects gave the right answers. On the third set, however, the first subject would give an obviously wrong answer. The next subject gave the same wrong answer, and so did the others until it got to the unknowing subject. He knew which lines matched, yet everyone had chosen another. The decision confronting the USS is: Do you state a perception publicly that differs from the preannounced position of the others? Or, do you give an answer that you strongly believe is incorrect in order to have your response agree with the other group members?

---

[42] Solomon E. Asch, "Effects of Group Pressure Upon the Modification and Distortion of Judgments," in *Groups, Leadership and Men,* ed. Harold Guetzkow (Pittsburgh: Carnegie Press, 1951), pp. 177–90.

The results obtained by Asch demonstrated that over many experiments and many trials, subjects conformed in about 35 percent of the trials; that is, the subjects gave answers that they knew were wrong but that were consistent with the replies of other group members.

The above leads us to conclude that group decision makers are under pressure to conform to the group's norms. When those norms reinforce outward agreement and the withholding of deviant, minority, or unpopular views, we have "groupthink"; that is, there is a deterioration in the individual member's mental efficiency, reality testing, and moral judgments as a result of group pressures.[43]

We have all seen the symptoms of the groupthink phenomenon:

1. Group members rationalize any resistance to the assumptions they have made. No matter how strong the evidence may contradict their basic assumptions, members behave so as to continually reinforce those assumptions.

2. Members directly pressure those who momentarily express doubts about any of the group's shared views or who question the validity of arguments supporting the alternative favored by the majority.

3. Those members who have doubts or hold differing points of view seek to avoid deviating from what appears to be group consensus by keeping silent about misgivings and even minimizing to themselves the importance of their doubts.

4. There appears to be an illusion of unanimity. If someone does not speak, it is assumed that he or she is in full accord. In other words, abstention becomes viewed as a "yes" vote.[44]

All groups, to some degree, suffer from groupthink. As members of a decision-making group, we find it is more pleasant to be in agreement—to be a positive part of the group—rather than to be a disruptive force, even if disruption is necessary to improve the effectiveness of the group's decisions. But groupthink can have a destructive effect upon the quality of a group's decisions.

The above comments on conformity, when combined with the reality that decision-making groups frequently are composed of individuals with heterogeneous backgrounds, experience, and skills, leads us to the conclusion that groups move toward compromise. The task of identifying a problem is complicated because not all group members are likely to agree on the need for a decision. When this need is accepted, problems arise in reaching an agreement on the criteria and weights to be used in assessing the various alternatives. Differences of opinion will exist as to what is important, what is fact and what is conjecture, and what outcome is "best"—for what may be "best" for Department X, represented in the group by Mr. Simpson, may not be viewed as "best" by Ms. Crandall and her Department Y. The result is that group decisions tend to be characterized by compromise—in every step of the decision-making process.

[43] Irving L. Janis, *Victims of Groupthink* (Boston: Houghton Mifflin, 1972).
[44] Ibid.

The other hazard arises when comparing group decisions which have a clear dimension of risk with the individual decisions of members within the group. Evidence suggests that there are differences. Although in some cases the group decisions may be more conservative than the individual decision,[45] it is more likely that the shift will be toward greater risk taking. This latter phenomenon is called risky shift.

What might cause the risky shift phenomenon to occur? Four explanations have been proposed: the familiarization hypothesis, the leadership hypothesis, the risk-as-value hypothesis, and the diffusion-of-responsibility hypothesis.[46]

What causes

① The *familiarization* argument is that group discussion allows individuals to become more familiar with the situations being discussed, and this increased familiarity is responsible for the observed shift toward risk. Initially, there is a "feeling out" or go-slow period, but once individuals feel generally comfortable, they become bolder. If one accepts this view, then any procedure that will increase familiarity with an issue involving risk will cause persons to assume more risk on that issue. The *leadership* hypothesis suggests that risk takers are perceived as group leaders and are more dominant and influential in the group discussion; as a result, the risky shift can be explained in terms of the influence of risky leaders. The most popular and best supported argument is the *risk-as-value* hypothesis. It assumes that moderate risk has a stronger cultural value than caution in our society, that we generally admire persons who are willing to take risks, and that group discussion motivates individuals to show that they are at least as willing as their peers to take risks. Those whose initial private positions were less risky than the group average will recognize their relative cautiousness and recommend greater risk in order to restore their self-perceptions as being a relatively risky person. The final explanation, which seems intuitively most palatable, is the *diffusion-of-responsibility* position. It proposes that group decisions free the individual. If the decision fails, no one individual can be held wholly responsible.

②

③

④

No one of the four hypotheses can fully account for the shift toward risk. Nor can the hypothesis explain why sometimes the shift is toward more conservative choices. However, we should be aware of this risk tendency and its possible implications on group decision making.

Summary

The above findings lead us to several conclusions. First, when a single individual is required to make a decision, he or she will seek a satisficing outcome, an adequate solution that meets the needs of both the individual and the organizational unit. This often results in a compromise. However, when we have two or more individuals making the choice, more interests are in-

[45] D. C. Barnlund, "A Comparative Study of Individual, Majority and Group Judgment," *Journal of Abnormal and Social Psychology*, 58 (1959), pp. 55–60.
[46] Russell D. Clark III, "Group-Induced Shift Toward Risk: A Critical Appraisal," *Psychological Bulletin*, 76, no. 4 (1971), pp. 251–70.

volved, and hence more negotiation and compromise is likely to take place. The solution must satisfy the groups and individuals charged with the decision. It may be unfair to resurrect the old saw that "a camel is a race horse designed by a committee," but it does suggest the potential negative outcomes from the give-and-take environment of group decision making.

Secondly, a group's willingness to take greater risks in some situations may be a positive or negative factor. But when this increased propensity to assume risks is combined with greater difficulty in identifying responsibility, the potential for poor decisions is increased. For example, when a committee or task force makes decisions, who is responsible? Its chairman? Each member? Only those who voted in favor of the final choice? The answer is not simple, and because it is not, groups have a greater potential for irresponsible decision making than do individuals.

The above should not be construed to mean that groups always make poorer decisions than individuals. Such is not the case.[47] What it should point out is the *potential* for members to abrogate responsibility for their actions should they believe that they will not be held accountable in the same way they would if it were an individual decision.

Where to from here?

These last two chapters have presented you with both the normative theory of how decisions ought to be made and a description of how decisions are made in most organizations. Chapter 4 was generally built on economic-man assumptions. It assumed that decision makers have a single stable objective that can be maximized. It further assumed that, in pursuit of that objective, the decision maker will be fully knowledgeable of all the means by which that objective can be attained, the consequences of each alternative, and will choose that alternative which comes closest to achieving the objective.

In this chapter, we introduce administrative man as a descriptive model of decision making, then elaborated and expanded this framework to reach what we called modern administrative man. The modern administrative man/decision maker is depicted as constrained by the organization as well as by his own human limitations. The result is a picture of actual decision makers which is considerably different from that presented in chapter 4.

As we presented evidence in this chapter on how decisions are actually made, you may have noted findings that fail to align with your own experience. This is to be expected, since our modern administrative-man model is *only* a model, and cannot explain how *all* decision makers behave. There will be exceptions, but this should provide a framework to conceptualize how *most* decisions are made.

[47] I. Lorge, D. Fox, J. Davitz, and M. Brenner, "A Survey of Studies Contrasting the Quality of Group Performance and Individual Performance, 1920–1957," *Psychological Bulletin,* vol. 55 (1958), pp. 104–11.

We are now ready to go from "choice" to "action." With the foundation of decision making laid, we can move to the action phase of the administrative process—to planning, organizing, leading, and controlling. And as we proceed through these four functions, we will consistently look back to this chapter, and its politically oriented view of decision making, as the explanation of why, in many cases, theory and practice deviate.

summary of major points

1. Best-selling books on administration recognize that decision making in organizations is political. Textbooks tend to be composed of normative doctrines on how administrators should make decisions.

2. The economic-man model states that a decision maker should:
   a. Clearly define the decision criteria.
   b. Be knowledgeable of all relevant alternatives.
   c. Be aware of all possible consequences of each alternative.
   d. Evaluate the consequences against the decision criteria.
   e. Rank alternatives in a preferred order of economic impact.
   f. Select the alternative which rates highest in economic terms.

3. Herbert Simon proposed administrative man as a descriptive model. In this model, administrators:
   a. Recognize only a limited number of decision criteria.
   b. Propose only a limited number of alternatives.
   c. Are aware of only a few of the consequences of each alternative.
   d. Formulate a simplified and limited model of the real situation.
   e. Select the alternative which presents a satisfactory solution.

4. Administrative man implies:
   a. Hedonism
   b. Limited use of creativity
   c. Limited use of quantitative tools
   d. Consistent errors in judgment

5. A modern administrative-man model must consider organizationally imposed, as well as human, limitations. Adding these constraints, administrators can be further described as:
   a. Desiring power
   b. Avoiding risk
   c. Using a short-term frame of reference
   d. Placing style before substance
   e. Selecting an implicit favorite alternative early in the decision process.

6. Group decisions, in practice, tend to be influenced by many of the same characteristics attributed to modern administrative man. But group decisions are more susceptible to compromised solutions and may be riskier than decisions made by the individual.

FOR DISCUSSION

1. What are the major differences between the economic-man and administrative-man models?
2. What is the difference between satisficing and optimizing?
3. What does the modern administrative-man view add to the original administrative-man model?
4. "Decision making in organizations is a political process." Build an argument to support this statement. Then build an argument taking the opposite position.
5. "Quantitative tools are a waste of time for administrators who want to make better decisions." Do you agree or disagree with this statement? Support your answer.
6. How do decision makers tend to react to increased complexity?
7. Show how the way decision makers are evaluated and rewarded will influence the choices they make.
8. Do decision makers react differently to risk as individuals than they do as members of a group? Discuss.

case exercise

Looking back at the first year on the job

It has been a year since Sally Pritchard joined Big Time Foods, a large consumer products company with sales of over a billion dollars a year. After graduating with her masters in administration, she took a job at Big Time as a market researcher. As she reflected back over her first year, she couldn't help but think about how different things were at Big Time from the theories she had read in her college textbooks and heard from her instructors. Even the cases she had analyzed which were supposed to give her a feel for the real world had not prepared her for what she saw at Big Time. A few of the more unusual occurrences stood out in her mind.

Administrative theory always emphasized the importance of developing esprit de corps. Teamwork and cooperation were goals that administrators should pursue. But Sally saw a considerable amount of interdepartmental hostility. For instance, the market research group seemed to be continually trying to "one-up" the product design group. What she couldn't figure out was why people higher up in the organization didn't do something to eliminate these interdepartmental fights.

Sally was also aware of the loss in departmental morale as a result of recent personnel changes. Big Time had a long-standing reputation for promoting people from within the company when vacancies developed. In fact, this point was emphasized during her employment interviews a year earlier. Yet, during the past twelve months, three key positions opened up in the marketing area—vice president of marketing, assistant to the vice-president, and a regional sales executive slot—and all were filled from outside the organization. Sally wondered if ambitious people wouldn't begin to look for other jobs in other companies if opportunities looked limited at Big Time.

And then there was her salary adjustment. Sally was pleasantly surprised with her excellent performance appraisal and substantial pay raise; but her good friend, Bonnie, who had also joined Big Time a year ago and who appeared to be performing at least as well as Sally, received a terrible appraisal and a minimal salary adjustment. It was true that Bonnie was outspoken and preferred full-length "gypsy" dresses to three-piece suits, but she was certainly bright, hard working and highly productive. Why wasn't Bonnie being judged solely on her performance, or was she?

Finally, there was last month's encounter with her boss. Sally had come up with an idea that she figured would save the company about $100,000 a year. Sally's boss didn't share her enthusiasm. In fact, he told her to forget the idea. "Listen, Sally," she recounted him saying, "this company made fifty million dollars last year; it will make 50 million this year; and we'll make 50 million next year—with or without your ideas. We don't need suggestions from kids fresh out of college. Take some advice from me, Sally. Do your job, don't make waves, and in three or four years you'll have a soft job like mine, earning double your current salary."

Questions

1. Should Sally have expected her college course work to explain what she had seen during her first year?
2. What actions did Sally see that can be fully or partially explained by the modern-administrative-man view of decision makers?
3. How should Sally have responded to her boss's recommendation that she not make waves?

FOR FURTHER READING

Allison, G.T., *Essence of Decision*. New York: Little, Brown, 1971. Presents three models of complex strategic decision making: the rational actor model, the organizational process model, and the bureaucratic political model. The book's emphasis is on the political model.

Janis, I., and L. Mann, *Decision Making*. New York: Free Press, 1977. Describes how executives actually behave when confronted with major decision-making conflicts.

Pettigrew, A. M., *The Politics of Organizational Decision-Making*. London: Tavistock, 1973. Traces the case history of a complex computer equipment decision, noting the political factors in the decision process.

Pfeffer, J., and G.R. Salancik, "Organizational Decision Making as a Political Process: The Case of a University Budget," *Administrative Science Quarterly*, June 1974, pp. 135–51. Measures of departmental power in a university were found to be significantly related to the proportion of the budget received, even after controlling for such traditional bases of allocation as departmental work load, national rank, and number of faculty.

MacMillan, I.C., *Strategy Formulation: Political Concepts.* St. Paul, Minn.: West Publishing, 1978. Argues that administrators must take into account the behavioral and political components of human action when they formulate their organization's strategies.

Zaleznik, A., "Power and Politics in Organizational Life," *Harvard Business Review,* May-June 1970, pp. 47–60. How the limitations of businessmen, in their cognitive and emotional capacities, play a major role in decision making.

PART

III

PLANNING

6

An Overview of Planning

**AFTER
STUDYING
THIS CHAPTER,
YOU SHOULD
BE ABLE TO—**

Formal planning	Directional plans
Strategic plans	Objectives
Operating plans	Goals
Cascading of plans	Real objectives
Short-term plans	Stated objectives
Intermediate-term plans	Forecasting
Long-term plans	Structural change
Specific plans	Cyclical change

The value of formal planning
The similarities and differences between various types of plans
Types of objectives
Who sets an organization's objectives
The difference between stated and real objectives
The external and internal factors on which forecasts can be based

Planning is determining in advance *what* is to be done, *how* it is to be done, *when* it is to be done, and *who* is to do it. It encompasses setting objectives as well as making day-to-day decisions on how these objectives can best be achieved. Hence, planning involves the determination of both ends and means.

It is a cliché to suggest that administrators should "plan ahead." To plan "behind" is absurd; to prepare for the future certainly sounds good. Recommending that one engage in formal planning is akin to the little old lady who, upon hearing of the death of David Ben Gurion, the Israeli statesman, suggested he be given some chicken soup. A friend said, "The man is dead! What good will chicken soup do?" To which the little old lady replied, "It couldn't hurt!" The same reply is often used in advocating formal and organized rather than intuitive planning: "It couldn't hurt!" But formal planning (we will use the term planning to mean formal planning throughout this chapter unless it is otherwise noted) is not cost free. It is possible for the costs of planning to exceed its benefits. So before we review the planning process, let us review why planning makes sense in theory and then consider the actual evidence when organizations that plan are compared against those that don't.

Why plan?

Before we discuss the specific contributions of planning, it is important to note that the accuracy of plans is not as critical as it may first appear. On the surface, it might seem a bit ridiculous to argue that planning can be of considerable value, even if the plans made prove to be incredibly off the mark. How can this be? Because the value of planning is as much in the process of creating plans as in the plans themselves. This will become more evident when we discuss the planning process in detail but, at this time, suffice it to say that the discussion, clarification, and interaction that takes place when administrators engage in planning has significant value in and of itself. But back to our lead-in: Why plan?

Planning is a way to anticipate and offset change. Organizations are continually faced with changes—in client needs, government regulation, availability and prices of inputs, and new products or services introduced by competitors, to name just a few. Planning forces the administrator to look ahead and anticipate future deviations based on data from the past and present, to consider the impact of these changes on the organization, and to develop appropriate responses.

Planning gives direction to administrators and nonadministrators alike. It focuses attention on the organization's objectives. When everyone knows where the organization is going and what they are expected to contribute to achieving these ends, there should be increased coordination, co-operation, and more teamwork.

An organization's efficiency can be severely hindered if its goals are inconsistent or contradictory. For example, the chief executive of one organization emphasized cost-cutting to increase profitability during his tenure between 1965 and 1972. When he retired, his replacement sought to increase profitability by expanding the firm's product lines. Because there were no formal plans, inefficiencies resulted. A lack of plans can foster "zigzagging" and thus prevent an organization from moving smoothly toward its objectives.

Planning also can reduce overlapping and wasteful activities. When people know clearly what they are to do, which good planning should provide, inefficiencies become more obvious.

Finally, planning establishes the objectives and standards which will be used for facilitating control. If we are unsure of what we are trying to achieve, how can we determine if we have achieved it? In the planning process we develop the standards against which our actual performance can be compared. Evaluation and control will tell us if we have achieved that which we planned and provide the information needed to correct significant deviations.

Does planning justify the effort?

We are concerned with assessing the value of formal planning. As such, we want to review those studies that have compared the performance of organizations that formally plan with those that either do no planning or do it intuitively. While the studies we will look at use differing definitions of formal planning, a reasonable generalization is that formal planning exists if the organization has written, documented plans that cover a multiyear period and include specifications of objectives and strategies.

The overall evidence as to the value of formal planning is positive. For example, one study found that business organizations with formal planners significantly outperformed those that informally planned on criteria such as earnings per share, earnings on a common equity, and earnings on total capital employed.[1] These formal planners also outperformed their own records, based on an equal period of time prior to the beginning of formal planning. A follow-up study to replicate these findings clearly supported that during a seven-year period, organizations that formally planned outperformed, in terms of sales and profits, those that planned informally.[2]

Other studies have achieved similar results. One, covering ninety-three companies, showed that planners outperformed nonplanners on virtually

[1] Stanley S. Thune and Robert J. House, "Where Long-Range Planning Pays Off," *Business Horizons,* August 1970, pp. 81–87.
[2] David M. Herold, "Long-Range Planning and Organizational Performance: A Cross-Validation Study," *Academy of Management Journal,* March 1972, pp. 91–102.

every financial measure that the researchers utilized.[3] Another analyzed thirty-eight companies and again found that organizations that planned significantly outperformed nonplanners.[4]

The only study that questions this simple across-the-board relationship between formal planning and improved organizational performance found differences between industries.[5] In the durable industries, the planners outperformed the nonplanners. However, the nonplanners outperformed the planners in the service industries. The researchers concluded that it was impossible to determine whether formal planning was of benefit or not, but suggested that "such variables as timing, luck, and the immeasurable quality of 'overall managerial competence' have a more direct relationship on a firm's performance success than the formality of its long-range planning activity."[6]

The above evidence, although restricted to business firms and measures of performance defined in financial terms, is generally supportive. Yet, we should add an important qualifier. All of these studies used data that predated the 1974–75 recession. If this recession had any specific characteristic, it was the inability of planners to predict it. As we will see in our discussion of forecasting, plans rely on forecasts, and when the latter is significantly off target, so will the plans be. Major discontinuities, such as the 1974 oil embargo or the 1979 overthrow of the Shah's monarchy in Iran and resultant reduction in oil exports, play havoc on many organizations, having dire impact on planning effectiveness. Therefore, if we have entered an era, which some experts have proposed, where we will experience greater discontinuities with the past, then the results of these historical studies may not be generalizable to the future. Again, of course, this does not offset the value that the planning process provides over and above the accuracy of the plans.

The above does not imply that all administrators should devote an equal amount of time to planning. In general, the higher one moves in an organization, the more time he or she should allocate to planning activity.

Why is this the case? Because much of planning, particularly the establishing of the organization's objectives and major strategies, is of an organization-wide nature. Additionally, as noted in chapter 2, lower-level administrators spend more time, relatively speaking, in the leadership function. Top administrators are responsible for setting the overall direction of where the organization is going, so we should expect effective top administrators to expend more time on the planning function than lower administrators.

[3] H. Igor Ansoff, et al. "Does Planning Pay? The Effects of Planning on Success of Acquisitions in American Firms," *Long Range Planning,* December 1970.
[4] Zafar A. Malik and Delmar W. Karger, "Does Long-Range Planning Improve Company Performance?" *Management Review,* September 1975, pp. 27–31.
[5] Robert M. Fulmer and Leslie W. Rue, "The Practice and Profitability of Long-Range Planning," *Managerial Planning,* May–June 1974, pp. 1–7.
[6] Ibid., p. 7.

The planning process

The process of planning in an organization should be made up of five steps. It begins with identifying the objectives of the organization. 1 This first step seeks an answer to the question: What are we here to do? Once the purpose of the organization is clear, the second step begins: a search for 2 opportunities. Given the organization's objectives and resources, what advantages does it have? What events can be identified that can be used by the organization to satisfy the needs of its potential clients or customers? When these opportunities have been identified, they need to be translated into specific 3 courses of action. In this third step, administrators attempt to outline the specifics necessary to turn opportunities into accomplished objectives. 4 The fourth step further translates the specific courses of action into even more specific standards of performance. Finally, in the fifth step, administrators engage in a review to determine if the specific standards established 5 in step four have been accomplished. If not, then the plans are revised.

These five steps can be summarized into general topic areas. Identifying the objectives of the organization is *objective-setting*. The search for opportunities is *forecasting*. Translation of these opportunities into specific courses of action is called *strategy formation*. The setting of specific standards and the subsequent review and evaluation to ensure that these standards have been achieved fall within the topic area known as *management by objectives* (MBO).

In the remainder of this chapter, as well as in the next two chapters, we will follow the process that we have described. After we briefly identify various types of plans, we will discuss objective-setting and forecasting. In chapter 9, we will emphasize the important role that top executives should play in the planning function when we review strategy formation. Chapter 10 will demonstrate how planning can be operationalized and infused throughout the organization—from top executives down to lower-level operating administrators—by implementing MBO.

Types of plans

The term "plan" is often prefaced by an adjective, the most popular being strategic or operating; short-, intermediate-, or long-term, and specific or directional. Because of their heavy usage by practitioners, let us take a closer look at this terminology.

Strategic vs. operating plans

Those plans that tend to dominate at the highest levels of an organization are often called strategic. Ones that are the province of lower-level unit administrators are frequently referred to as operating or tactical plans. While the type of plan is not always based on the level in the organization, this is a reasonably valid generalization.

131

It has been suggested that the differences between strategic and operating plans relate to their time frame, scope, and whether or not they include a known set of organizational objectives.[7] The shorter the time frame that the plan covers, the more it tends to be concerned with day-to-day activities and, hence, it is more of an operating plan. Strategic plans tend to include an extensive time period, cover a broader area, and deal less with specifics. The second distinction relates to the number of organizational functions affected by the plan. The more functions involved, the more strategic the plan. The final distinction addresses the organization's objectives. Strategic plans include the formulation of objectives, while operating plans assume these objectives are already known and instead offer ways for attaining these objectives.

The differences cited above support our contention that the higher an administrator moves in an organization, the more he or she should be engaged in strategic planning. That is, top administrative planning focuses on a longer time frame, is broader in scope, and includes greater input from organizational units than lower-level administrative planning; in addition, strategic planning is responsible for the formulation of the organization's objectives.

Few plans fall neatly into one of these two categories. The distinctions are relative rather than absolute. The importance in distinguishing between the two, however, relates to the reality that the type of planning in which one engages depends largely upon the level within the organization that one occupies. Senior-level administrators will be more involved in strategy formation as we will present it in the next chapter than, say, a first-level supervisor would be. MBO, on the other hand, encompasses all levels of administration.

Figure 6-1 depicts the cascading of plans, from strategic concerns at the top to operating matters at the lower levels. This flow of plans from the top to the bottom of the organization will be a central theme when we discuss MBO thoroughly in chapter 8.

Short-, intermediate-, and long-term plans

Plans are frequently classified by their time frame, and the three most often mentioned types are short-, intermediate-, and long-term. What a plan is called, in terms of time, depends upon its impact on the organization and whether or not decisions in the plan can be modified.

In common financial parlance, short-term plans are ones that cover a period of less than one year; intermediate-term plans range from one to five years; and any plan that exceeds five years in length is classified as long-term. The problem with these definitions is that they fail to recognize important differences between organizations. A more appropriate approach, from an administrative standpoint, is to alter the definition to reflect the de-

[7] Russell Ackoff, "A Concept of Corporate Planning," *Long Range Planning,* September 1970, p. 3.

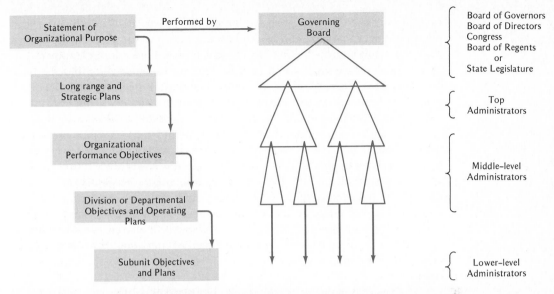

Adapted from Anthony P. Raia, *Managing By Objectives*, (Glenview, Ill.: Scott Foresman, 1974), p. 30.

FIGURE 6-1   Cascading of organizational plans

gree of flexibility that the plan provides administrators. Long-term plans involve a fundamental redirection of the organization's ends and means. As such, everything is viewed as variable; that is, it operates under the assumption that there are no fixed commitments. In intermediate-term plans, administrators must accept the general structure and strategy of the organization, but can influence the quantity of inputs, outputs, people, material, and capital. The greatest inflexibility lies in short-term plans, for they treat structure, strategy, and quantities as fixed. Administrators can only influence the application of resources and technology to scheduling specific activities in short-term planning.

The importance of the above distinction becomes clear if we contrast planning in a large public utility with that undertaken by a small dress manufacturer. Long-term plans by a public utility might extend twenty, fifty, or more years. When Hydro-Quebec decided to spend upwards of $16 billion to build the James Bay Hydro-Electric facility in northern Quebec, Hydro-Quebec executives had to forecast demand for electric power well into the twenty-first century. A project of this magnitude cannot simply be closed down if demand estimates prove incorrect since the commitment in funds is too large, requiring many decades to earn the expenditure back. Hydro-Quebec's intermediate-term plans might be somewhere between three and ten years, while short-term plans might cover two to four weeks. In contrast, a small dress manufacturer operating out of a rented facility might have short-term plans covering only the next several days, intermediate plans running through the current season of sixty to ninety days, and long-term plans no longer than six months. Should this manufacturer incorrectly estimate the fashion tastes for the coming season, there may not be another.

The above example also dramatizes the role of uncertainty in defining the time frame of an organization's plans. The greater the uncertainty an organization faces, the more changes that are likely to take place that will impact on the organization; and the greater the change, the less likely the plans are to be accurate. For example, one study found that one-year revenue plans tended to achieve 99 percent accuracy against 84 percent for five-year plans.[8] Therefore, organizations that face rapidly changing environments will seek greater flexibility. This translates into greater emphasis on short-term plans. Since the farther ahead our time horizon is, the greater the error, we should expect public utilities (who face relatively stable environments) to have relatively sophisticated and complex plans for many years into the future, while the orientation of marginally financed dress manufacturers (who face relatively dynamic environments) will be almost exclusively to the near term.

Can we say how far ahead one should plan? We find that the further today's plans impinge on future commitments, the longer the time frame for which one should plan.[9]

An organization should not plan for a longer period than is economically justifiable; yet to plan for too short a period may not ultimately be in the best interests of the organization. Therefore, we should plan just far enough to see through those commitments that are made today.

This implies that we are not really planning for future decisions but rather planning for the future impact of those decisions that we make today. Decisions made today become a commitment to some future action or expenditure. So, reflecting back on our comparison of planning by Hydro-Quebec and a small dress manufacturer, organizations that commit themselves to projects that will not be fully consumed or paid back for fifty years will need plans extending that far into the future, while organizations whose commitments extend no more than a year or two need not plan beyond those commitments.

Do organizations actually engage in strategic and long-term planning? Studies on planning practices tend to be restricted to large profit-making firms (annual sales of $50 million or more). Additionally, these studies probably understate the amount of planning going on because they concentrate on formal planning activities to the exclusion of informal planning efforts. Even though these constraints limit our ability to generalize, the studies are certainly still informative.

[8] Richard F. Vancil, "The Accuracy of Long-Range Planning," *Harvard Business Review,* September–October 1970, p. 99.

[9] Harold Koontz and Cyril O'Donnell, *Management: A Systems and Contingency Analysis of Managerial Functions,* 6th ed. (New York: McGraw-Hill, 1976), p. 151.

A survey of thirty-four companies sought to determine if the firms prepared an annual organization-wide plan. Seventy-one percent of those with revenues below $150 million had such a plan, while all of those with revenues above $350 million prepared an annual corporate plan.[10] The researcher concluded that only the smaller firms had not totally accepted the value of planning, yet he still found some resistance to planning beyond the short term. "Over 20 percent of the group with revenues of between $350 million and $1 billion and one with revenues of $2 billion have only a one-year planning period for strategic planning."[11]

A study of five very large and successful companies found that none engaged in long-term strategic planning. After talking with corporate executives to find out why, the researchers concluded that (1) these firms were not under competitive stress—conditions did not demand the comprehensive planning consistent with optimizing behavior, and (2) administrators perceived little environmental uncertainty.[12] In short, the executives in these firms could see no pay-off from long-term strategic planning.

A study of 400 firms found 19 percent had no long-range plans. Of those that did, 86 percent used a time horizon of three to five years while only 1 percent planned for longer than ten years.[13] Other studies confirm the popularity of five years as the normal long-term time horizon.[14]

An inquiry into planning practices at thirty U.S. firms achieved results similar to the larger study noted above: 15 percent of the companies had no long-term plans.[15]

Practice also reflects that when short-term and long-term objectives conflict, administrators will emphasize the short term. This recognizes that individual rewards in an organization are based on performance as measured in the short or near-intermediate term.

> If one tells a manager to develop a five year business plan, but evaluates him on variances against a quarterly budget, there is little doubt that his real plan will be to sacrifice the long run for the short run. . . . And if one develops a system of organizational success-patterns where managers with 'high batting' averages are promoted over those who encourage long term change, then there is little doubt that managers will develop projects which are likely to be approved, even if they don't reflect the degree of risk or profitability desired by the firm.[16]

[10] William E. Lucado, "Corporate Planning—A Current Status Report," *Managerial Planning,* November–December 1974, pp. 27–34.

[11] Ibid., p. 29.

[12] Charles B. Saunders and Francis D. Tuggle, "Why Planners Don't," *Long Range Planning,* June 1977, pp. 19–24.

[13] Robert M. Fulmer and L.W. Rue, *The Practice and Profitability of Long-Range Planning* (Oxford, Ohio: The Planning Executives Institute, 1973), p. 18.

[14] Lucado, *op. cit.;* and Parmanand Kumar, "Long-Range Planning Practices by U.S. Companies," *Managerial Planning,* January–February 1978, pp. 31–38.

[15] Toyohiro Kono, "Long Range Planning—Japan–USA—A Comparative Study," *Long Range Planning,* October 1976, pp. 61–71.

[16] William K. Hall, "The Impact of Managerial Behavior on Planning Effectiveness," *Managerial Planning,* September–October 1977, p. 22.

Rarely do organizations reward long-term performance. It sometimes appears that an individual is paid off for long-term contributions, but this usually reflects merely the summation of many short-term performances. The exception to this practice is the organization that is run by an owner-manager. An owner-manager can take a longer frame of reference, while the professional manager is forced to look for short-term performance. This explains, incidentally, why managers frequently emphasize one- to three-year turn-around situations. When was the last time you heard a business or government official state that it would take ten or twenty years to get things straightened out? Such administrators would not be around to see the fruits of their efforts.

> The planning process in large organizations is governed by limited search for alternatives, biased evaluation of alternatives, purposeful delay of risky alternatives, and the intentional selection of alternatives which compromise organizational goals for the goals of individual managers, as modified by the way they are controlled and rewarded within the organization.[17]

Specific vs. directional plans

It seems intuitively right that specific plans would always be preferable to directional or loosely guided plans.[18] Specific plans have clearly defined goals and strategies. Objectives are spelled out so that everyone in the organization can understand them. Specific plans focus the efforts of everyone in the organization. Because they avoid ambiguity, they help individuals to structure their work, to decide what activities should be undertaken, and to use their time efficiently.

Specific plans are not without their drawbacks, however. They often assume clarity and agreement where it does not actually exist. They reduce opportunities for innovation. Most importantly, specific plans limit flexibility. When changes occur because of technological, social, economic, legal, or other factors, which require concurrent changes in plans, it might be preferable to have directional plans.

Directional plans identify general guidelines. They formulate the direction of an organization's thrust but do not lock the administrators into hard and fast objectives. Instead of an administrator following the specific plan "to locate a new office in Miami next year," a directional plan might state that we "expand our services in the near future, particularly in the southeast." The flexibility inherent in directional plans in contrast to the more traditional specific plans is obvious. Yet, one is not always more desirable than the other. In certain circumstances, directional plans are preferable, while in other circumstances specific plans are best. What circumstances favor directional planning?

First, administrators should rely more heavily on directional plans when the organization is in its infancy. In the early years of an organiza-

[17] Ibid., p. 23.
[18] See, for example, M. Gene Newport, *The Tools of Managing* (Reading, Mass.: Addison-Wesley, 1972), p. 50.

tion's development, greater flexibility is desired. Objectives are still tentative, resource availability is more uncertain, the identification of clients or customers is also more uncertain, and directional plans offer administrators more flexibility to make changes as necessary. As objectives become more definite, resources more committed, and loyalty developed with clients or customers, specific plans may become more appropriate.

②   Second, the greater the environmental uncertainty, the more that plans should be directional in nature. If rapid or important technological, social, economic, legal, or other changes are taking place, well-defined and precisely charted routes are more likely to hinder the organization's performance than aid it. Great uncertainty can frequently result in significant deviations from patterns observed in the past. Specific plans will have to be altered to accommodate these changes—often at high costs and decreased efficiency. For example, the rapid legislative changes in the 1970s concerning minimum pollution levels and mileage standards for automobiles should have resulted in the automobile manufacturers developing more directional plans relative to the size of cars produced, their weight, and engine displacement.

We can conclude that most organizations have short-term plans, while many medium-sized and most large organizations have long-range plans that are probably directional in nature. This would reflect the reality that forecasts beyond the very near term are highly error-prone. Therefore, in cost-benefit terms, many organizations find that plans beyond the short term have a high probability of being inaccurate. Those organizations that do long-term planning tend to be larger and may even have formal planning groups or departments. Again, however, because accuracy declines rapidly as the time horizon expands, these long-range plans tend to be directional in nature. The environmental discontinuities experienced in the 1970s have further diminished some organizations' enthusiasm for long-term plans.

Now that we have some background concerning the types of plans that administrators frequently confront, let's take a look at the first step in the planning process—objective setting.

Objective setting

You might recollect the following dialogue from Lewis Carroll's *Alice in Wonderland:* Alice asked the Cheshire Cat, "Would you tell me, please, which way I ought to go from here?" "That depends a good deal on where you want to get to," said the Cat. Alice replied, "I don't much care where . . ." Concluded the Cat, "Then it doesn't matter which way you go."

Administrators need to know "which way to go." It is goals or objectives that provide that direction. It is the setting of these, therefore, that is the first step in planning.

Let us begin by clearing the air as to the alleged difference between "goals" and "objectives." Actually, the two terms should be viewed as interchangeable; there is no need to differentiate them. Administration, as a discipline, is complex enough. There is no need to create complexity for complexity's sake.

Some scholars have sought to separate objectives from goals by describing the former as applicable organizationwide, and goals as relating to units within the organization. This is similar to the differentiation some have tried to make between administration and management; however, if there are any differences, they are academic and insignificant for a working knowledge.

We define objectives to be the ends toward which all activity is directed. They suggest aspirations: desired ends that the organization attempts to realize. All functional organizational activity should be directed toward objectives, and the organization's performance should be determined by the degree to which it achieves these objectives.

For example, a *business* might state its objective as earning a satisfactory return on investment; the *church* exists to provide a road to Heaven through absolution; the *state* seeks to promote the general welfare of its constituents; and a *university* may define its objective as the transference of knowledge, or the preparation of people for the earning of a livelihood.

As one scans the paragraph above, it becomes immediately clear that each of these organizational forms has other objectives besides the ones mentioned. For example, businesses strive to meet other ends besides profit earning, and the church, in addition to providing absolution, has social objectives. Therefore, we must expand our view of organizational objectives to represent the multiplicity of goals.

Types of
objectives

Since organizations have more than a singular objective, it is valuable to consider areas from which goals can emanate. The following coverage is comprehensive; it recognizes that goals may be either internal or external— that is, relating to the direct needs of the organization or to the clients and society that it serves. Profit-oriented organizations may select goals from each of the following areas; nonprofit organizations, from all but the first. Also, it is important to realize that all organizations must have as one of their goals that of survival. Some of the following objectives contribute directly toward survival, but it is obvious that all organizations must survive if other objectives are to be achieved. The internal goals—the first five listed—are concerned with human, physical, and financial inputs and their transformation into desirable outputs. The external goals of client satisfaction and social awareness must be met as part of the organization's satisfying the needs of those groups that possess the power to curtail its life.

Profitability Profit-making organizations are, of course, concerned with the objective of earning a profit. This seldom, however, means a fixed dollar amount, but rather, a certain percentage return on the capital invested. All business firms need a reasonable return in order to justify their existence. If this reasonable return cannot be achieved, the survival of the firm becomes doubtful.

This objective not only differentiates business organizations from public or nonprofit organizations, but it gives business firms a common denominator for comparing performance. Profit is the primary objective of the business firm, and all subobjectives are compatible with it. No such common denominator exists in the public sector. For example, though public organizations often define their primary purpose in terms of service, what does service mean? Further, how does one measure it? The point is: profit organizations, in contrast to nonprofit ones, have a common and generally accepted standard by which one of their most important objectives can be measured.

Growth   It has been said that in business, you go either forward or backward—there is no middle ground. If not in real terms, then in relative terms, this is true. If your organization is stable while other, similar organizations are expanding, in relative terms you are going backward.

Administrators can establish growth objectives for total revenue, budgeted expenses, profits, number of employees, and expansion of physical plant, to name a few criteria. But although it may be valuable to grow in some of these areas, such growth may be dysfunctional.

For example, an administrator's prestige is somewhat reflected in the number of people he has working for him. To manage a unit of 200 people can be viewed as more impressive than managing only 20. In environments where size is correlated with status, given our knowledge of the realities in decision making, we should not be surprised to find administrators engaging in "empire building"—that is, expanding staff to meet the administrator's rather than the organization's needs. Experience shows that administrators are sensitive to their status position and will behave in a most self-serving way in order to maintain or expand their image in the eyes of others.

An interesting recent change in society's values is the apparently altering importance of growth as an objective. The quality of life appears to have attained equal status with the quantity of life. In an environment where there are declining reserves of natural resources, and where more is not necessarily better, the goal of stability, or of the deterring of contraction and decay, may be more realistic than that of growth.

Market penetration   The position an organization holds in its industry is closely linked with growth. Administrators seek to maintain and expand their relative market share in those situations where a monopoly does not exist. American Motors tries to expand its share of the automobile market at the expense of General Motors, Ford, and Chrysler; the city of Akron tries to increase its share of the new industries locating in Ohio. Similarly, New York University seeks to hold or expand its share of the college market in New York City, while at the same time the City University of New York,

Fordham University, and Manhattan College do the same. Some universities, such as the University of Washington in Seattle and the University of Minnesota in Minneapolis, have reached enrollment levels that their administrations believe are optimum for their institutions. As a result, they no longer attempt to expand. They accept the reality that if total enrollment in higher education increases in their state, their percentage of the market will decline. However, such behavior is obviously more likely to occur in a public institution than in financially squeezed private schools.

Leadership   Like the objective of growth, the objective of being the leader in one's market can be either healthy or unhealthy. When it culminates in a more viable, responsive, and effective organization, it is healthy. However, when such an objective serves only the needs of an executive group that seeks to be associated with an organization that is "the leader in its field," then it is dysfunctional and not in the best interests of the organization.

Leadership can result from innovation or changes in new products or services, or processes for creating these products or services. It may be a new banking service; an innovative academic curriculum; a low-cost, high-utility recreation facility; or a model correctional institution without barricades, where inmates are on the honor system. The bank, school, public parks agency, or prison that initiates one of these innovations differentiates itself from organizations that follow and adapt rather than lead through innovation. However, no one view is preferable over the other. Some organizations define their objectives in terms of leadership, with its consequential risks; some pursue more conservative goals of doing what others do, only better, more quickly, or at a lower cost; and some merely attempt to copy others.

Productivity   An organization's ability to transfer inputs to outputs at the lowest cost is the measure of its productivity. All organizations must have objectives in this area: generating a given output for the least input, or generating a maximum output for a given input. We should be concerned with this efficiency ratio in converting human material and financial resources into desirable outputs. No matter how successful we are in attaining our purpose (effectiveness), we cannot survive in the long term without attempting to minimize the relationship of input to output (efficiency).

Although productivity is usually viewed as a term in manufacturing or the profit segments of the economy, the term has value in nonprofit institutions as well. The concern for the relationship between inputs and outputs can be expressed by the following examples: A hospital manages to achieve higher output from the present staff by a reduction in the average number of days a patient is confined to a bed, or an increased number of contacts per patient per day; a school increases the quality of its output by producing higher average scores on standardized achievement tests, or improving the quality of teaching from the present staff; lower overhead costs are incurred by a fund-raising organization; a law-enforcement agency reduces the number of major crimes per law-enforcement official. Each of these examples demonstrates an attempt to gain productive efficiency—achieving greater output for a given input or lower input for a given output.

Client satisfaction No organization can survive in the long run if it does not meet the needs of some constituency. Government exists to serve the people; business firms serve their customers; charitable institutions serve the needy. When an organization no longer satisfies its clientele, it finds its charter rescinded, its revenues shrinking, or a lack of public support for its objectives. Therefore, all organizations must serve a constituency and satisfy some need of these clients.

Social awareness Our final objective is absolutely necessary, at least in theory, if the organization is to survive. All organizations operate with the approval of society. The society that establishes government institutions, or allows an organization to incorporate, can decide to withdraw its approval if it believes that the organization is no longer properly carrying out its function.

A union that fails to meet the needs of its membership will lose members and eventually dissolve. Additionally, however, if a union fails to respond to the needs of society, it can find its survival threatened. For example, in the mid-1970s, the union representing mechanics for all Montreal buses and subway cars supported an unauthorized walkout by its members and ignored a court order that they return to work. The result was elimination of all bus and subway service in the city. The government reacted by initiating action to revoke the union's charter. This union, like all organizations, has a responsibility to the society from which it receives its authority to function, and will not survive if this responsibility is ignored.

Social objectives place constraints on the organization, in that they must not conflict with the goals of society. The difficulty is that society's goals are not unchanging. For instance, in the first half of this century, numerous manufacturing organizations from Toledo to Buffalo openly pumped millions of tons of by-products into Lake Erie. The costs of this pollution were considered and appraised to be only a fraction of the price of other alternatives for handling the wastes. However, by the late 1960s, society was less willing to accept polluted water bodies as the price of, for example, greater steel production. The goals of society were changing. Increased manufacturing output, with the creation of greater job opportunities and a higher standard of living, brought with it costs that society considered greater than the benefits. In 1950, it would have been unheard of for a municipal or state government to threaten to close down a major manufacturing plant for polluting the environment. Society considered jobs and production too valuable. By 1970, however, times had changed. Members of society were valuing the quality of life as well as the quantity. All organizations have responsibilities to the society in which they operate, and therefore, their objectives must be acceptable and compatible with those of society.

In spite of the attention given to social awareness, there is little evidence to suggest that administrators, especially in profit-making organizations, consider social responsibility as an important objective.[19] For instance, a study asked 150 chief executives and chief financial officers in corporations with sales over $1 million to whom they owed their allegiance. The ranking was (1) stockholders, (2) employees, (3) customers, (4) creditors, and (5) society. Society was a dismal and consistent last-place finisher.[20] A more recent investigation asked executives at 220 companies to identify their firm's objectives. Social responsibility was not a dominant objective in any of them.[21] Instead, the major objectives involved financial success and company growth.

The obvious conclusion is that all organizations should have a multiple set of objectives, all of which should be compatible.

The importance of multiple objectives becomes increasingly clear when one recognizes the difficulty of finding a single, accurate measure of organizational performance. Qualitative as well as quantitative objectives are necessary. The organization that would use only "profit as a percent of sales" or "percentage reduction in direct costs" as the sole measure of performance risks having all activity directed toward "looking good" on this one criterion. Is a business firm willing to accept a 20 percent reduction in sales, by reducing sales of marginally profitable items, to increase profits as a percentage of sales from 6 to 8 percent? Obviously, no single measure of performance is adequate. Objectives must be set in a number of areas, utilizing a number of criteria.

Before we leave the subject of types of objectives, it should be pointed out that I have purposely omitted naming employee attitudes and morale as a separate category. I believe they belong in the realm of either productivity or social goals. If high employee morale leads to a reduction in turnover and absenteeism, it may belong in the former category. However, in a number of organizations, administrators seek favorable attitudes among the employees as an end in itself, irrespective of its effect on productivity. In such cases, these objectives are social goals, sought for the betterment of the external society, not for the internal benefits of the organization.

Whose objectives?

Up to this point, we have talked about objectives as if everyone within the organization participated and fully accepted the goals of the organization. Such a situation is rare, if it occurs anywhere. Organizational objectives are not the same as individual objectives, nor are they necessarily the sum of in-

---

[19] Gerald D. Keim, "Managerial Behavior and the Social Responsibility Debate: Goals Versus Constraints," *Academy of Management Journal*, March, 1978, pp. 57–68.
[20] Arthur W. Lorig, "Where Do Corporate Responsibilities Really Lie?," *Business Horizons,* Spring 1967, p. 53.
[21] Kamal M. Abouzeid and Charles N. Weaver, "Social Responsibility in the Corporate Goal Hierarchy," *Business Horizons,* June 1978, pp. 28–35.

dividual objectives. Two plus 2 plus 2 equals 6; however, it may also equal 3, or 50!

When we speak of organizational objectives, of whose objectives are we speaking? Are they found within an individual? a group of individuals? or are they inherent in the organization?

Some would assert that organizational objectives are found in, or as a product of, the motives and purposes of the members. Others would claim that they are much more clearly an organizational phenomenon, citing as supportive evidence the continuity through time of the same order and directions in activities despite changes in personnel.[22]

There is no easy answer to the question of who sets the organization's objectives but, in large organizations, they are clearly established by coalition and negotiation. Organizations are comprised of participants with widely varying preference orders. The participants include various internal constituencies within the organization and frequently external constituencies as well (such as regulatory agencies, consumer groups, or labor unions). These diverse participants, then, air their conflicting preference orders, which can be a positive mechanism for identifying differences and increasing the organization's adaptability. The result of this bargaining is that the participants enter into a coalition agreement for the purpose of ordering priorities and establishing objectives. Yet this "agreement" has been shown to exist around highly ambiguous goals. There is no clear preference ordering shared by all participants. And behind this agreement on rather vague objectives is considerable disagreement and uncertainty about subgoals. This explains why it often appears that various parts of an organization are pursuing different and partially inconsistent goals.[23]

In very small organizations, the members can influence the organization's goals; but in the vast majority of organizations, the decision coalition is made up predominantly of top administrators. "Organizational goals are established by individuals—but interdependent individuals who collectively have sufficient control of organizational resources to commit them in certain directions and to withhold them from others."[24] To forge effective coalitions, these top administrators will engage in explicit political activity.

> It is nearly certain that all managers involved in the planning process will disagree as to what the objectives of the enterprise should be. Conflict between corporate goals, divisional goals, and departmental goals are legend, as are conflicts between individual goals and the goals shared by a coalition of individuals within the enterprise.

[22] Charles K. Warriner, "The Problem of Organizational Purpose," *The Sociological Quarterly*, Spring 1965, p. 139.

[23] Richard M. Cyert and James G. March, "A Behavioral Theory of Organizational Objectives," in *Modern Organization Theory*, ed. Mason Haire (New York: John Wiley and Sons, 1959), p. 78.

[24] James D. Thompson, *Organizations In Action* (New York: McGraw-Hill, 1967), p. 128.

Thus it is not surprising that individuals and groups of individuals will bias their analyses to favor those alternatives which are in their self-interest.[25]

The above indicates that an organization's objectives evolve through coalition and negotiation. The final objectives represent the views of senior administrators but rarely reflect or perfectly mesh with the goals of any specific individual administrator. The objectives that are finally arrived at, because of compromise and the desire of participants to avoid subordinating their personal interests and those of the units they represent, tend to be stated in vague terms. This vagueness allows the appearance of agreement on overall objectives but can create operating problems when unit administrators attempt to develop subgoals for their divisions and departments.

Real vs. stated objectives

Formal objectives, the ones the organization states as its purpose, may mean little if one is concerned with the effect goals have on behavior, for there are, in fact, two distinct types of goals—stated and real. The stated goals are official statements. They are found in charters, annual reports, public-relations announcements, and the public statements made by administrators. Unfortunately, they merely mirror societal expectations. A study of goal statements among associations found that the statements issued in basic documents and articulated by members were "often quite irrelevant to what goes on in the organization or to the consequence of organizational actions. Furthermore, they seldom reflect changes through time in the direction of effort and activity...."[26] Stated goals are normative and reflect idealistic views of organizational purpose, emphasizing objectives such as employee welfare, public service, and quality products. The contradiction first becomes obvious from the different statements given to different audiences.

A corporation issues one statement of purpose to its stockholders or prospective stockholders. It addresses another to its customers, particularly if they are ultimate consumers. A third statement of purpose is directed to its employees, and another to the public; and finally, the management, which presumably has approved each of these other statements, will issue another to itself.[27]

However, the most obvious sign of contradiction is the inconsistencies between the stated objectives and what members of the organization actually do. If we want to know what the organization's stated goals are, then we should look to formal statements of purpose. If we want to know what its real purpose is, we need to look at what people are doing.

The contradiction between stated and real goals is clearly seen in the area of social goals. Society expects its organizations to profess social objec-

[25] Hall, "The Impact of Managerial Behavior," p. 22.
[26] Warrimer, "The Problem of Organizational Purpose," p. 140.
[27] Ibid., p. 140.

tives: hiring the handicapped and members of minorities, providing pleasant working conditions for employees, and ensuring that its productive efforts do nothing to damage the environment. As a result, our organization's statements of purpose reaffirm what the public wants to hear. Closer examination suggests, however, that actual behavior of organizational members frequently deviates from these stated goals.

We must conclude, as did Warriner, that formal statements of objectives should be treated "as fiction produced by an organization to account for, explain, or rationalize its existence to particular audiences rather than as valid and reliable indications of purpose."[28]

Why is there this deviation between real and stated goals? Why must organizations continue this fiction? It is partly due to the fact that the individuals who make up the organization do not align with the stated goals, and partly due to their realization that organizations do not necessarily reward behavior that leads to the attainment of stated goals. Let us briefly discuss each of these points.

It has been said that there is an inherent conflict between the objectives of the organization and those of its individual members, owing to a lack of congruence between the needs of healthy employees and those of bureaucratic organizations.[29] Whereas individuals seek independence, organizations want to create employee dependence. Individuals seek freedom, equality, and a wide range of interesting activities; organizations offer control, subordination, and narrowly defined, specialized tasks. The result is a situation of conflict and frustration that develops as divergent goal patterns interact. Stated organizational objectives are, therefore, rarely perceived as the means by which individual members of the organization can attain and satisfy personal objectives.

Additionally, organizations do not necessarily reward the attainment of stated objectives. Real objectives reflect the realities of the organization, the politics involved, and the desire to look good against the criteria that the administrative elite value most highly. There is no need for an administrator to spend several hundred hours a year representing his organization on the executive board of a local charity if the organization formally encourages community involvement but actually rewards only cost reduction or increased revenues. So one of the problems in setting objectives, particularly at the unit level, is the desire of individuals to protect themselves.

Self-protective and self-serving behavior is most evident when the difficulty of objectives is discussed. They should be challenging, yet not beyond the reach of the member. Do they represent the maximum or optimum allocation of member and organizational resources? Rarely! Administrators never have enough information to make optimum objective statements. And

---

[28] Ibid.

[29] Chris Argyris, "Personality and Organization Revisited," *Administrative Science Quarterly,* vol. 18, no. 2 (1973), 141–56.

more important, even if they had, what would encourage them to set such objectives?

As noted in Chapter 5, the result is satisficing behavior. Rather than establishing maximum objectives, administrators seek satisfactory levels of performance. Complex organizations represent social and political systems, rather than merely economic institutions.[30] In such an environment, maximizing behavior cannot be expected.

Forecasting

Forecasting is looking toward the future through the eyes of today. It forms the basis for planning by establishing assumptions about what will happen in the future. It identifies external events that will impact on the organization. Further, forecasting identifies the internal strengths and weaknesses of the organization. Based on predictions of what changes can reasonably be expected to occur outside the organization and an assessment of the organization's capability of responding to this external environment, administrators are able to determine what opportunities the organization is in a position to take advantage of.

External conditions

We will begin by considering the most significant external factors on which forecasts can be based. We have classified them under the headings of political, social, economic, technological, and market conditions.

Political Organizations in North America have generally operated within a stable political environment. In contrast to our South American neighbors, we expect changes in government to come about through democratic processes. We fall back upon a system of checks and balances in determining the direction in which our society will go. However, even in a genuinely stable environment, there are political issues that an organization may consider important to its future and that hence require the use of forecasting. Although it is easier for an organization to operate in an environment of political stability and certainty, it can still function effectively if the changing political environment can be predicted and understood. When a political government keeps altering the "rules of the game," then the direction and degree of change become difficult to forecast.

If we expect a change from a Republican to a Democratic presidency in the United States to affect attitudes toward our organization and eventually its revenues, then attempts to forecast changes in the presidency should be made. Changes in incumbents of public office are particularly important to public agencies. Municipal or state agencies are clearly affected

---

[30] John Kenneth Galbraith, "Economics and the Quality of Life," *Science,* July 10, 1964, pp. 117–32.

by a change in mayors, governors, or even elected positions at the national level.

For many organizations, to have been able to anticipate the wage and price freezes imposed by the U.S. government in 1971 could have been extremely beneficial. It has been suggested, in fact, that several large corporations did have inside information that controls would be imposed and raised their prices prior to implementation.

It should be evident that those involved in the provision of health facilities are concerned with political actions taken on Medicare. Aircraft and missile manufacturers are concerned about the political climate for defense expenditures. The election, in November 1976, of the Parti Quebeçois as the ruling party in Quebec has had a significant impact on Quebec and all of Canada. With the party's objectives including breaking Quebec off from Canada and the creation of a separate nation, as well as promoting French as the official language within the province, administrators in Quebec find themselves expending considerable energy and resources to forecasting the effect separation might have on their organizations' future.

Social No administrator can avoid forecasting social trends and changes. Changes in marriage rates and attitudes toward large families have affected birthrate trends and hence population trends. If an organization manufactures baby products or is attempting to estimate future elementary school needs, it is mandatory that it consider the changes in birthrates and population.The drop in the birthrate, for example, prompted Gerber, the baby-food manufacturer, to drop its advertising slogan, "Babies are our business—our *only* business," to carry its baby food to other parts of the world where the birthrate is still high, and to look for new business opportunities beyond the infant market. Similarly, Johnson & Johnson has been trying to interest grown-ups in using their baby powder and baby shampoo. Changes in population, as well as a leveling off in the percentage of high school students choosing to go on to higher education, had a major effect on the growth plans of state-supported higher education in California. Estimates of the eventual enrollments at the University of California's campuses at Santa Cruz and San Diego were scaled down in 1971 to less than half their original projections, and plans for the development of new campuses have, at least temporarily, been shelved.

Social forecasting must also consider changes in morality, values, ethics, and tastes. Changing tastes regarding men's hair length, for example, have increased the importance of hot combs, hair spray, and blow dryers, while practically eliminating the demand for Butch Wax. The increase in divorce rates and concern over inflation have rapidly increased the demand for homes by single individuals.

What society regarded as socially acceptable behavior ten years ago, for example, may not be accepted today. Many business executives still have not awakened to this reality, as they fail to recognize the importance of visibly demonstrating their concern for, and action in support of, socially responsible behavior by their firms. Further, the tastes that indicated preferences for Packards, Desotos, and Ipana, changed over time.

Economic Forecasting of economic indicators is easier than forecasting social trends and changes, in that a number of agencies are actively involved in this process, including the University of Michigan, the Wharton School of Finance at the University of Pennsylvania, and the Brookings Institution. The problem is that their estimates are rarely consistent. The range of their forecasts depends on the assumptions that the forecasters have included in their models.

Depending on an organization's mission, the type of estimated information available—which may or may not be important to the administrator—includes gross national product, disposable income, changes in price levels, percentage of the work force unemployed, interest rates, and new housing starts.

Changes in economic conditions can be seen by looking at what the 1974 oil embargo did to the home insulation market. As energy prices shot upward, so did the demand for insulation. Insulation manufacturers, such as Johns-Mansville, found that, in spite of running multiple shifts, they were still unable to meet the increased market for their product.

Technological Although clearly of greater importance to profit-making organizations, the forecasting of changes in technology is important even in the nonprofit sector. The March of Dimes, a nonprofit organization, was forced to totally revamp its objectives, and hence all activity within its organization, as a result of the discovery of the polio vaccine. Checkless banking, Teflon, radial tires, throwaway diapers, penicillin, open-heart surgery, freeze-dried coffee, and "the pill" have all had significant effects on particular industries and organizations. Some of these changes, particularly the pill, have significantly altered the social environment in which we live—not to mention the pharmaceutical companies that manufacture the product.

Market The estimating of market demand and revenues, which includes forecasting the actions of competitors, is a necessary part of any forecasting activity. In the nonprofit sector, Central Connecticut State College is concerned about the amount of money that will be spent on higher education in Connecticut during the upcoming years; the demand for hospital beds in the greater Portland, Oregon, area is of concern to the Portland General Hospital; and administrators in Providence, Rhode Island, are concerned with the amount of federal tax-sharing dollars that will be returned to their state and city. In profit-making organizations, such concern is obvious; as only one example, the Goodyear Tire and Rubber Company spends a considerable sum of money each year attempting to estimate future demands for original equipment and replacement tires.

PLANNING

All these forecasting activities are made in an environment of the recognition that revenues are dependent upon external clients. Further, in most cases, the organizations recognize that there is competition for these revenues, and hence, estimates are made of total market revenues and of the activities that competitors may take in order to increase their own percentages of the market.

The forecasting categories cited above view the organization as trying to adapt to a changing environment. However, they did not include internal forecasts, which allow the organization to determine its capabilities for responding to the environment; and so it is also necessary for an organization to forecast internal factors—revenues, expenses, capital, and manpower.

Revenues Revenue forecasts are computed by multiplying the average number of sales by the average price of each sale—although, in some organizations, they may be merely the yearly allotment allocated to the organization, and some, such as private hospitals and universities, depend on both the sale of their product and gifts from donors in order to establish their total-revenue forecast. For example, a school district may get a fixed-dollar allocation from the city budget, in addition to which, state or federal funds may supplement this allocation by grants of a stipend based on the number of students and class days attended.

Expenses The forecasting of expenses is easier than of revenue, in that, generally speaking, expenses are more controllable than revenue. Fixed expenses—those that remain unaltered regardless of revenue—are tabulated. Then, those expenses that vary with income are estimated, based on the previously established revenue forecast. Once both revenue and expense forecasts are made, the organization is in a position to estimate whether it will be operating in the black or the red. Although it is not absolutely necessary for an organization to have revenue equal to or greater than expenses every year, in the long run no organization can survive with expenses that considerably exceed revenue, with the possible exception of federal governments, which can prolong deficits by borrowing from themselves.

Capital Based on the estimated revenue, a capital forecast is made. It is basically twofold: (1) estimation of working-capital or cash needs in the operating period, and (2) projected longer-term financial needs for investment in new equipment, physical plant, or other major projects. The former compares cash inflows and outgoes to determine shortages, and the latter appraises investment proposals, estimation of cash flows for the proposals, and evaluation of cash flows. In addition to capital needs, these forecasts also consider prices or interest rates that will have to be paid to acquire capital, and the determination of the sources from which capital may be raised.

Manpower The final area requiring the development of an internal forecast is human resources. This is the estimating of the quantity and quality of manpower needed for present and future operations. Based on the revenue forecast, employee productivity data, and estimates of resignations and retirements, manpower forecasts can be developed for the number of unskilled, clerical, skilled, technical, and professional personnel that will be needed. Effective manpower forecasting contributes to both the attainment of short-term objectives and continuity among organizational personnel.

In total, the forecasts above form the assumptions on which other plans are made. Not all organizations require the same depth of forecasting, nor do they expend their forecasting resources in the same areas. Semiconductor manufacturers may be extremely sensitive to technological changes, but administrators in the Pentagon pay greater attention to political and economic factors. City governments, which historically have paid little attention to competitive factors, are in direct contrast to large retail chains, such as J. C. Penney or Sears, Roebuck, which are highly attuned to market demands and actions of their competitors.

Interestingly, though, a number of organizations that previously gave little attention to competition are now changing their perspective. For example, private colleges and universities, which historically viewed their products as unique and having little competition from state institutions, recognize that today's students are very sensitive to the price of higher education and look for significant differences in benefits to offset the significant differences in costs. As a result, administrators in higher education have become extremely alert to market changes and the actions of their publicly supported and private competitors.

Structural vs. cyclical change

All changes are not alike. Before an organization determines how it is going to react to change, the administrator must determine whether the change is of a structural or a cyclical nature.

Structural changes are substantive, in that they represent permanent changes in attitudes, beliefs, or values. Following World War II, the large increase in home ownership in the United States could be classified as a structural change. The increasing desire by families to own their own homes could be interpreted as a permanent change in attitudes and desires.

On the other hand, a cyclical change is of a temporary nature. A dress manufacturer forecasts a high demand for calf-length dresses and views this as cyclical, to be followed at a later date by a change in style. Technical changes tend to be of a more structural nature, whereas many political, social, economic, and market changes are merely short-term alterations and do not reflect permanence.

Could the movement to smaller cars in the mid-1970s be viewed as structural or cyclical? Experts within the industry had differing views, even though they all had extensive forecasting facilities at their disposal.

A General Motors vice-president believed that the small-car push was only temporary: "The car purchase and buying up to bigger cars in the market are the fundamental concept of American life. You've earned your way, so you can enjoy the fruits of your labor."[31] In direct contrast, Ford Motor Company's president believed tastes have changed: "A guy will no longer buy a car because it has a long hood."[32] The chairman of American Motors Corporation agreed: "People are looking on cars today in a more utilitarian way."[33]

Based on these different assessments, Chrysler, for example, made decisions based on the assumption that the movement was cyclical. It did not even offer a domestic subcompact until 1978, several years after its U.S. competitors. To date, the evidence indicates that Chrysler and the G.M. vice-president were wrong in their forecasts.

If, in the early 1930s, you had been an administrator with an organization that catered to the needs of the elderly, would you have interpreted the U.S. Social Security Act as cyclical or as structural? In retrospect, the answer is clear. The act represented the beginning of a structural change within society whereby the federal government assumed certain responsibilities in providing for the welfare of the aged.

We currently see changing views on morality. If you are a movie producer, do you commit resources to "R" or "X" movies, or do you consider them merely a passing fancy that the public will have had their fill of in a year or two? These are the kind of issues that administrators must consider regarding the nature of their forecasts.

Observations of practice suggest that administrators do not, in contrast to theory, *anticipate* change. Rather, they *react* to it. Anticipative behavior implies both reasonable knowledge of the future and willingness to take risks. The evidence indicates that administrators cannot predict the future very accurately nor are they inclined to accept risks. The results are that most administrators react to changes that occur but do not attempt to anticipate them. This, of course, is consistent with our description of modern administrative man as having inadequate information, desiring to minimize risks, and seeking satisficing objectives.

Time dimension

Our final consideration in forecasting concerns itself with how far we should forecast into the future, and the reality that forecasts extending beyond the very near term are likely to be grossly misleading.

As stated earlier in this chapter, we should plan far enough in advance to foresee the fulfillment of commitments involved in decisions that are currently made.

There is no question that commitments should influence the extent of future planning, but realities dictate that one can plan little beyond the immediate future. "If anyone still suffers from the delusion that man is able to

---

[31] "Has Detroit Learned Its Lesson?" *Business Week,* October 5, 1974, pp. 68–69.
[32] Ibid.
[33] Ibid.

forecast beyond a very short time span, let him look at the headlines in yesterday's paper, and ask which of them he could possibly have predicted a decade or so ago."[34] Therefore, in normative terms, the extent of one's forecasting and planning should be dictated by his commitments, However, the future is rarely an extension of the past, and attempts to forecast beyond the very near term are fraught with dangers.

Attempts to forecast political, social, economic, technical, or market shifts beyond the very short term become subjective guesswork. Who foresaw in 1960 the large commitment of American funds made to Southeast Asia merely five years later? Wage and price controls, which were established in August 1971, had been needed for nearly five years, yet in July 1971, how many administrators forecasted that those controls would be instituted a month later? Did the automobile manufacturers foresee the energy crisis of 1973? Did many organizations anticipate the shortage of supplies in 1973 and 1974 of critical products such as oil, paper, copper, steel, plastic, or food products? How many government officials foresaw that the June 1978 election in California would result in overwhelming support of Proposition 13, dramatically reducing the state's property tax revenue, and initiating moves throughout the U.S. to curtail the rapid growth in spending by local and state governments.

The National Research Council published a report in 1937 on technological trends and national policy that failed to foresee antibodies, atomic energy, jet propulsion, and radar. Yet all of these technologies were either in practical use or under development within five years of the report.[35] There is no reason to believe that the forecasting tools being used by today's decision makers are significantly better than those available in 1937.

The other side of the coin offers some interesting results. What trends *were* forecast but never came to fruition?

There were forecasts in the middle 1960s that electronic teaching machines would be dominating education within ten years. However, we find that audiovisual material and electronic teaching equipment have had little effect in replacing teachers in the classroom.

In 1972, economists were forecasting inflation for 1974 at a rate of approximately 4 percent. However, actual inflation rates were more nearly 12 percent. This high inflation, plus spiraling interest rates, caused a rapid decline in the stock market between mid-1973 and late 1974. With the market's decline, the Ford Foundation's assets, for example, shrank to $2 billion from $3 billion, forcing a 50 percent drop in grants awarded. How well would a major research organization that depended heavily on this foundation's support have done in estimating its 1975 grants based on 1972 assumptions? The answer appears to be clear—rather badly!

As a last point to ponder, consider the prediction made in 1958 that by

[34] Peter F. Drucker, *Management: Tasks, Responsibilities, Practices* (New York: Harper & Row, 1974), p. 123.
[35] Robert Ayre, *Technological Forecasting* (New York: McGraw-Hill, 1969), p. 12.

1980 there would be few such oddities as middle managers.[36] It was suggested that as a result of computer technology, some middle managers would be forced up into the top managerial echelon, while others would be forced downward into merely supervisory roles. It is now 1980, and there appears to be little evidence that this prediction came about. If anything, the advent of the computer has put increased pressure and demands upon middle managers.

The examples above are not meant to deter or denounce the value of forecasting in anticipating change. Rather, it has been an attempt to suggest that short-term forecasting can be quite effective, but that intermediate and long-term forecasts must, by definition, be vague. Specificity in these latter forecasts can rarely justify the cost involved.

[36] Harold J. Leavitt and Thomas Whisler, "Management in the 1980's," *Harvard Business Review,* November–December 1958, pp. 41–48.

summary of major points

1. Planning is determining in advance *what* is to be done, *how* it is to be done, *when* it is to be done, and *who* is to do it.
2. Planning is beneficial because
   a. The process itself provides clarification.
   b. Change can be anticipated and offset.
   c. It gives direction and focuses attention on objectives.
   d. It reduces overlapping and wasteful activities.
   e. Continuity of action is improved.
   f. Evaluation and control are facilitated.
3. The evidence generally supports the relationship between formal planning and improved organizational performance.
4. The planning process is composed of five steps:
   a. Identifying the objectives of the organization.
   b. Search for opportunities.
   c. Translation of opportunities into specific courses of action.
   d. Setting specific standards.
   e. Continual review and revision.
5. Strategic plans have a relatively long time frame, are broad in scope, have input from many organizational units, and include the formation of organizational objectives. Operative plans have a short time frame, a narrow scope, and assume that a set of organizational objectives exists.
6. Short-term plans treat structure, strategy, and quantities as fixed. Intermediate plans accept the general structure and strategy as given but interpret quantities as variable. In long-term plans, all factors are variable.
7. Specific plans have clearly defined goals and strategies; they provide well-defined and precisely charted routes. Directional plans identify general guidelines and provide flexibility by defining the direction of an organization's thrust.

8. Objectives are the end toward which all activity is directed.

9. Organizations require a multiple set of objectives. Areas in which objectives can be set include:
    a. Profitability
    b. Growth
    c. Market penetration
    d. Leadership
    e. Productivity
    f. Client satisfaction
    g. Social awareness

10. An organization's objectives evolve through coalition and negotiation.

11. Formally stated objectives may deviate considerably from an organization's real objectives. Stated objectives are the ones the organization states as it purpose; real objectives are determined by what organizational members actually do.

12. Forecasting establishes assumptions about what will happen in the future.

13. The external conditions about which it is necessary for an administrator to make assumptions are:
    a. Political
    b. Social
    c. Economic
    d. Technological
    e. Market

14. The internal factors that also need to be forecasted are:
    a. Revenues
    b. Expenses
    c. Capital
    d. Manpower

15. Forecasts assist administrators in anticipating change. However, it is important to differentiate structural or permanent changes from cyclical or temporary changes.

FOR DISCUSSION

1. Why should administrators engage in formal planning?

2. Review the planning process from the perspective of (a) economic man and (b) modern administrative man.

3. "There are objectives that are common to all organizations." Do you agree or disagree with this statement? Explain your position.

4. "An accurate description of an organization's objectives can be obtained from the organization manual and from organizational spokesmen." Discuss this statement.

5. "An organization should always have clear, definite objectives." Do you agree or disagree with this statement? Explain your position.

6. Discuss the advantages and disadvantages of comprehensive long-term forecasting.

7. Contrast the various areas that external forecasting should appraise.

8. Give examples of both structural and cyclical changes and consider their implications for planning.

We don't do no planning around here!

Few people in South Bend, Indiana, have ever heard of Doug Evans or his company, Medical Ties. And it shouldn't be too surprising, for Doug makes a product that most people never think much about—self-dissolving thread used by surgeons in doing sutures. He sells his product to large medical suppliers who then distribute it to hospitals and doctors.

But Doug's firm was described to this case writer by a purchasing agent at one medical supply house as "a money-making machine." With only ten employees and operating out of a plant not much bigger than an average size house, Doug confirmed that sales last year were nearly $8 million and that his after-tax profit was an astounding $2.6 million. The case writer's first impression was: Doug Evans must be some type of effective administrator! Not necessarily.

Doug bought the patent to his product in 1957 for $35,000. As a result, he effectively has no competition. His product is well made, performs a valuable function (relieving the surgeon from having to take out stitches), and no one has yet come up with a viable alternative to his chemical formula. "Even if they did," noted Evans, "medical suppliers would have no reason to drop my product. They know my reputation and my quality. And no one could produce a superior product. At best, someday, someone might develop a formula that makes a product as good as mine."

This case writer was particularly interested in learning the kind of plans that Doug Evans had developed over the years.

"I don't do any planning. Never have. I react to crises. Only got one product. Sales just keep going up every year. There are no cycles in this business. People always are being operated on. And I don't have to pay any attention to my supplies inventory. The salesmen who I buy my supplies from come by every couple of weeks, look at my inventory, and then order what is necessary to ensure I don't run out of things like chemicals and shipping containers. You ask me if I have objectives? Sure, I want to personally be worth $50 million by 1990. How do my employees know what to do? Simple—they merely ask the other people on the production floor what needs to be done."

Questions

1. Is it correct to say Doug Evans does no planning?
2. How can his firm be so profitable with such sloppy administrative practices?
3. Might Medical Ties be a more successful firm if Doug Evans did formal planning?

FOR FURTHER READING

Higgins, R.B., "Reunite Management and Planning," *Long Range Planning,* August 1976, pp. 40–45. Argues that planning has been isolated from the locus of decision-making power and insulated from information vital to the planning process; proposes a reunion of planning and decision-making processes.

Mockler, R.J., "Theory and Practice of Planning," *Harvard Business Review,* March–April 1970, pp. 153–59. Reviews more than 30 studies which the author believes are of relevance to practicing administrators.

Rue, L.W., "The How and Who of Long-Range Planning," *Business Horizons,* December 1973, pp. 23–30. A specific, practical model for long-range planning; plus data gathered in a survey of U.S. industry, compares the practice of long-range planning with an ideal model.

Spainhower, J.I., "Managerial Planning in State Government," *Managerial Planning,* March–April 1978, pp. 36–37ff. Obstacles to managerial planning in state government including patronage, bureaucratic inertia, immunity from political control, legislative control of budgets, electoral victories and losses, and personal or departmental political influence.

Steiner, G.A., *Top Management Planning.* New York: Macmillan, 1969. An encyclopedia on corporate planning, covering nearly 800 pages.

Turner, R.C., "Should You Take Business Forecasts Seriously?," *Business Horizons,* April 1978, pp. 64–72. Business forecasts over the past 20 years have been quite respectable, except when an unpredictable event outside the economy occurred.

Chapter

7

Strategy Formation

**AFTER
STUDYING
THIS CHAPTER,
YOU SHOULD
BE ABLE TO—**

**Define and
explain the
following
key terms
and
concepts:**

Strategy	Retrenchment strategies
Synergy	Combination strategies
General strategies	Product/service strategies
Specific strategies	Process strategies
Stability strategies	Marketing strategies
Growth strategies	Financial strategies

Describe: The characteristics of an effective strategy
How strategy includes and builds upon objective setting and forecasting
The four general types of strategies
The bias toward growth strategies

This chapter focuses on how top-level administrators identify and exploit opportunities. It is about *strategy,* a concept that encompasses the objectives and forecasts discussed in the previous chapter but adds a plan of action for the achievement of these objectives in a competitive environment. Strategy, therefore, is concerned with both means and ends.

An effective strategy is comprehensive, integrative, dynamic, synergistic, and properly timed. Let us look at what this means.

A strategy is comprehensive in that it covers all major aspects of the organization: the products or services offered, how they are marketed, the organization's financial viability, and the input-output processes, to name a few of the more important. A strategy is also integrative, which means all of its parts are compatible with each other and fit smoothly together.

A strategy needs to be dynamic because it must be flexible enough to meet the ever-changing environment in which organizations exist. For those who wonder what happens to organizations who fail to develop a dynamic strategy, we need only ask if you are familiar with the Central Leather Company? It is not exactly a household name these days. But Central Leather was the seventh largest company in the United States in 1909! Unfortunately for Central Leather, plastics came along and provided consumers with a good substitute for leather at a significantly lower price. And Central Leather was unsuccessful in producing an effective counterstrategy.

Wherever possible, strategies should be made to utilize positive synergy. Synergy is a combination of two or more resources that results in an output different from the sum of the inputs. For example, positive synergy would be 2 + 2 = 5; negative synergy would be 2 + 2 = 3. To increase the effectiveness of our strategies, we should look for positive synergies wherever possible. Economies of scale, or elimination of one or more departments through mergers or consolidations, represent positive synergistic effects. General Motors can operate Chevrolet, Pontiac, Oldsmobile, Buick, and Cadillac divisions less expensively together than if each were a separate corporation. In the same way, small school systems frequently join together to form a consolidated high school district, since no one of them can efficiently operate a secondary school alone.

The final quality that frequently differentiates an effective and an ineffective strategy is the matter of *when* it is initiated. The best idea and plan of action can fail if instituted at the incorrect time. Therefore, we must take into consideration the social, political, economic, and technological environment, as well as the anticipated action of our competitors, when we institute a particular strategy. Although the Edsel failed in 1958, it might have been an unquestioned success if introduced in 1952. Similarly, an organization's decision to engage in a massive expansion program, which will require extensive borrowing, is poorly timed if interest rates are at all-time highs and considerable reduction in the rate is anticipated in the near future.

What do strategies look like?

Because it is an integrative concept, strategy formation is concerned with defining the organization's purpose and developing forecasts. This forces administrators to consider the organization's mission and the scope of its activities. Will it operate locally, nationally, or internationally? Who will be its clients or customers? Should the organization carry a full line of services or products or put its efforts into specialization? Can administrators expect high inflation in the next several years and, if so, how will this affect the organization's revenues? These are the types of questions that should have come about from the objective setting and forecasting efforts discussed in chapter 6. The result should be a sharpening of the top administration's focus on what the organization is trying to do, how changes in the future will impact on the attainment of the organization's objectives, and what opportunities and threats lie ahead.

Next, strategy formation is concerned with analyzing the organization's capabilities. This is achieved through a resource audit. Determination of the organization's human, physical, and financial resources, when merged with the external forecast, will be a major input in determining which specific direction the organization will take.

Of course another important input is an assessment of what you expect others to do. This is an attempt to determine the actions of your competitors. All organizations, whether private or public, have competitors, either direct or indirect. If the competition is not for markets, then it is for the organization's resources. Although public agencies frequently have monopolies in terms of market, they rarely have such powers in commanding resources. A state public-welfare department has to compete with budget requests from tens and possibly hundreds of other departments within state government for its yearly budget allocation.

When an organization has defined itself, established forecasts, identified future opportunities and threats, analyzed its capabilities, and assessed the anticipated actions of its competitors, it is ready to establish its short-term, intermediate, and long-term subplans.

Areas in which these subplans might be established include pricing, marketing, research and development, new products, cost reductions, and growth. For example, if one of the objectives of an organization was growth at a certain rate each year, a subplan might suggest the best method for achieving that growth: increase current market share, sell new products or services, or acquire other organizations. These plans may cover periods of time as short as one year, or extend five, ten, or fifty years into the future.

Finally, strategy formation requires the determination of actions necessary to achieve the subplans. Traditionally, this includes the development by top administrators of programmed decisions—the rules, methods, procedures, and policies—that will guide lower-level decision makers toward the attainment of previously established objectives.

What do we know about organizations' practice of developing overall strategies? Unfortunately, not much. We have splinters of data, but as with our knowledge of general planning practices, it is almost exclusively based on the practice of billion-dollar-plus corporations.

We can begin by extending the time horizon information we learned about in overall planning to strategy formation. Given that administrators emphasize the short term, due to the difficulty of forecasting accurately beyond the short term, and because organizations reward short-term performance, a lack of formal strategy by organizations would not be surprising. Indeed, this assessment seems to be substantiated.

A survey of forty widely diversified *Fortune* 500 firms led one researcher to conclude that "the extent to which major corporations use formal strategic planning has been overstated vastly in the literature."[1] The cases of billion-dollar corporations like Borg-Warner and Westinghouse support this statement.

After the 1974–75 recession, Borg-Warner was confronted with a shrinking return on equity, swollen inventories, soaring production costs, and a massive amount of debt, problems that have been explicitly attributed to the lack of a strategy by the company.[2] Westinghouse, until the early 1970s, did no top-level strategic planning. "In place of an overall corporate design for growth and development, the company ran during most of the 1960s by the output of a computerized planning system that got most of its input from middle management sources."[3]

What about smaller organizations? Any statement can only be conjecture, but strategic planning is probably significantly less than that practiced in the largest firms. Much of it may be happenstance or may reside in the head of the top executive where it remains, untransmitted to lower-level administrators.

Rather than dwell on what strategy formation is about, let's take a close look at the various types of strategies.

[1] K. A. Ringbakk, "Organized Corporate Planning Systems: An Empirical Study of Planning Practice and Experiences in American Big Business," unpublished doctoral dissertation, University of Wisconsin, 1968.

[2] "Borg-Warner: Scrapping Old Lines for New Products and Services," *Business Week*, January 30, 1978, p. 92.

[3] "The Opposites: GE Grows While Westinghouse Shrinks," *Business Week*, January 31, 1977, p. 61.

Types of strategies

Strategies are generally classified either in general terms, such as retrenchment or growth, or by specific area, such as a market or financial strategy. In the following pages, we will describe the various types of strategies and provide an extensive array of examples that illustrate some highly successful efforts and some that were less successful.

General strategies

It has been proposed that organizations generally follow one of four strategies: stability, growth, retrenchment, or a combination approach.[4]

Stability   A stable strategy generally seeks to maintain the status quo. Administrators continue to serve the same clients by offering the same product or service. When an organization is performing at a satisfactory level, this strategy is quite attractive. It is most likely to be effective in a stable and unchanging environment.

It is not easy to identify organizations that are pursuing a stability strategy, if for no other reason than few top administrators are willing to admit to pursuing stability. North Americans resist acceptance of the status quo. It implies satisfaction or even smugness. Growth has had universal appeal, and retrenchment is often accepted as a necessary evil; but to actively seek to maintain the status quo is rarely seen in a positive light. For those who question this interpretation, they need only look at how the stock market treats stability. Corporations that consistently demonstrate strong but stable earnings typically sell at low price-earnings multiples. This describes, for example, firms in the publishing industry. Those companies that appear to offer high growth potential, even though their past record is one of minimal earnings, sell at the highest multiples. This typified the fast-food franchises in the mid-1960s and gambling equipment manufacturers in the late 1970s. Within this context, administrators do not relish having their organizational strategies labelled as stable.

It would probably be correct to describe International Business Machines (IBM) as following a stability strategy in the 1970s. With sales nearing $20 billion a year, high profitablity, and possession of most of the market for products such as computers and electric typewriters, its executives have correctly tried to keep a "a good thing going." In addition, an aggressive growth strategy might initiate fresh antitrust charges.

Most urban hospitals today can also be described as pursuing a stability strategy. Such hospitals overbuilt in the 1960s, resulting in empty beds. These organizations, therefore, currently find themselves trying to hold their own against skyrocketing costs and low bed-occupancy rates.

[4] William F. Glueck, *Business Policy: Strategy Formation and Executive Action* (New York: McGraw-Hill, 1972), p. 186.

Growth   As we have noted, the pursuit of growth has traditionally had magic appeal to North Americans. Bigger is better! The more the merrier! In our terms, growth means increasing the level of the organization's operations. Popular measures include more revenues, more profits, more employees, and a larger percentage of the market. Growth can be achieved through straight expansion, merger, or diversification. Examples abound of organizations who have followed growth strategies.

Successful cases include Seiko and Texas Instruments in the digital segment of the watch market. An infant industry as recently as 1974, with U.S. sales of about a million units, sales in 1978 approached 20 million units. And both Seiko and Texas Instruments successfully pursued growth strategies to take advantage of the surge in demand for this product.

Seiko concentrated its efforts in the upper end of the market—in the $65 to $350 price range.[5] Seiko had average annual increases of 16 percent between 1968 and 1978 based on exploiting its technological know-how and developing a strong marketing network. It successfully anticipated shifting consumer tastes at the upper end of the watch market, particularly the trend toward quartz digitals. The company spent heavily on technology and developed a reputation as an innovator. As U.S. electronics companies plunged into cheap, light-emitting diode watches, Seiko steadily broadened their line of quartz products and spent heavily on advertising, while Swiss and American competitors hesitated. Now, as quartz watches capture an even bigger share of the market, Seiko has an advantage that will be hard to overcome: sheer size and marketing power.

Texas Instruments has attacked the lower end of the digital watch market.[6] As a semiconductor producer, TI sought to use its technological know-how and mass production capabilities to overwhelm its competitors. In 1975, the lowest priced digitals were $50. Then, TI dropped its first bombshell—a $20 model that industry and retailers alike were not expecting for at least another year. This was a dramatic gamble to take over the mass market which had been dominated by the traditional watch companies such as Timex. Going after market share with a vengeance, TI slashed the retail price of its cheapest model by more than half in mid-1977, to $7.50, below the price of any mechanical timepiece for the first time. The result: Gruen, a well-known name in timepieces, filed for bankruptcy; another competitor—National Semiconductor Corp.—began to fail; a potential competitor—Gillette Co.—was frightened away; all resulting in an explosive gain in unit sales for TI.

An example of a growth strategy that went awry was the plan followed by Rohr Industries, an aerospace company.[7] Rohr executives decided in the

---

[5] "Seiko's Smash: The Quartz Watch Overwhelms the Industry," *Business Week,* June 5, 1978, pp. 86–97.

[6] "The Great Digital Watch Shake-Out," *Business Week,* May 2, 1977, pp. 78–80.

[7] "How Rohr's Move Into Transportation Backfired," *Business Week,* January 19, 1976, pp. 46–48.

late 1960s that their firm should diversify in order to protect itself against the instability of airplane manufacturing which is profitable in times of military build-up or war but suffers badly in peacetime. This diversification goal would, Rohr administrators concluded, spread the risk. The opportunity they saw was in mass transit vehicles, an area they forecasted as a booming growth market. They estimated that mass transit spending in the 1970s and 1980s would match the federal government's 20-year $72 billion highway spending program. This external forecast, when combined with the company's reputed technological capability in aircraft design, seemed a natural combination. Rohr would use its technical expertise in transportation systems to bring mass transit into the twenty-first century. The company's approach was aggressive: bid low in order to get a foothold in the market, and bid on almost every available major project in order to develop the all-important expertise. This aggressiveness would give them the upper hand on other firms that also wanted to get in on this growth market—companies like General Electric, Pullman, and Boeing.

So what went wrong with this strategy? To begin with, the mass transit act of 1974 authorized only $11.2 billion through 1980. Rohr had dramatically underestimated the clout of the highway lobby. In addition, the price of transit systems skyrocketed while, at the same time, municipalities were confronting severe financial problems. So Rohr was right about the potential demand for mass transit systems, only the potential purchasers did not have the required money. Finally, Rohr ran into its own problems in adapting technology and with cost overruns on fixed price contracts. Its two biggest projects—the Bay Area Rapid Transit (BART) system for San Francisco and the Washington Metropolitan Area Transportation Authority (WMATA) system for Washington, D.C.—proved disastrous. Three years after the first BART cars entered service, they were still operating poorly. BART has sued Rohr for $100 million, plus unspecified punitive damages; Rohr has countersued. The company has lost over $40 million on the WMATA project. Rohr's attempt to develop seven turbine trains for Amtrak added another $31 million loss. The overall result of Rohr's growth strategy has proven to be a financial disaster for the company.

Retrenchment   What may have been a dirty word in the go-go years of the 1960s—retrenchment—may be the most popular strategy of the 1980s. The optimism of the 1960s is gone; natural and human resources are no longer inexpensive, and North American productivity has stagnated. The most valuable skill in the 1980s may be the ability to manage decline.

A retrenchment strategy can mean cutting back the scope of current operations or objective attainment, becoming a captive of another organization, divestment, or liquidation. The evidence suggests that retrenchment has become increasingly necessary for state governments, urban school districts, and many small private colleges.

The passage in the summer of 1978 of Proposition 13 forced California to develop a retrenchment strategy. Cutbacks were made necessary throughout the state. The governor placed a freeze on hiring and identified a number of areas for cutbacks in services. Reports of other states following a similar retrenchment strategy have been increasing.

Urban school districts have suffered as more and more families move to the suburbs, resulting in fewer children attending urban schools, the loss of taxes as both people and businesses move to the suburbs, and a reduced willingness of taxpayers to fund schools. Many urban school superintendents have had to outline strategies for their districts which include the closing of some schools, termination of faculty, reduction in maintenance and other support services, elimination of capital improvements, and drastic reductions in athletic programs.

Inflation and the fact that there are now fewer college-age individuals have wreaked havoc during the past decade with small private colleges, especially those that lack sizeable endowments. As the cost of a year in a private college moves beyond $5000, many people who would have preferred attending a private college are bypassing college, delaying the decision, or opting for less expensive public institutions. Though many of these smaller schools have responded by introducing more attractive curriculums, offering increased financial aid, or by attempting to attract older students for evening and summer programs, many have had to drastically reduce the scale of their operation, and dozens have literally had to close their doors.

In the private sector, Westinghouse offers a good example of a firm that has had to cut back its ambitious growth objectives in an attempt to compensate for its past mistakes. The diversified company has sales of over $6 billion a year and is a major producer of utility power equipment, industrial electric products, and until recently, consumer appliances. In 1977, however, Westinghouse was shedding businesses, cutting back overseas operations, and working desperately to shore up its finances.[8]

Since the mid-1960s, Westinghouse had pursued rapid growth with minimal regard to risk. Unfortunately, there was no integrated strategy or solid control over its divisions. This led Westinghouse into a series of money-losing ventures in fields unfamiliar to its administrators. It set up its Urban Systems Development Corp. to put up low-cost, multi-family housing on government contracts, leading eventually to $61.5 million in losses during the two years prior to its being shut down. It lost another $64 million from its efforts in the mail order and record club businesses. "Instead of clear plans, Westinghouse fostered a laissez-faire attitude. Said Vice-Chairman Evans: 'We were able to say to our people—and mean it—that if they had a good business proposition, we could finance it.' But top management provided no guidance on what a good proposition was, nor any analysis of whether the company should enter the field in the first place."[9]

[8] "The Opposites," pp. 60–66.
[9] Ibid., p. 62.

Combination A combination strategy can be either the pursuit of two or more of the previous strategies simultaneously but in different parts of the organization, or the use of two or more of the strategies over time.

Borg Warner (BW) is pursuing the first type of combination strategy.[10] BW, which traditionally manufactured automotive components, is simultaneously adding or bolstering certain parts of the company and scrapping others. They have acquired Baker Industries, which provides armored trucks and courier services and produces fire-detection systems. The company is pouring money into new fields such as submersible pumps and energy-efficient heat pumps. However, at the same time, BW has scrapped hundreds of marginally profitable products and begun cut-backs in the transportation equipment segment of the company.

One of the more fascinating examples of the efforts to pursue a combination strategy simultaneously occurred in the tobacco industry in the mid-1960s. Scared by the Surgeon General's report on the negative effects of smoking on one's health, the major producers such as American Tobacco and Reynolds Tobacco began active diversification programs. Anticipating that tobacco would be a declining product line, they looked for other areas which would provide growth. American Tobacco added Jim Beam, Sunshine Biscuit, Andrew Jergens, and Master Lock, then changed its name to American Brands. Reynolds became R. J. Reynolds Industries and purchased Del Monte, Chun King, Hawaiian Punch, and began to develop and produce petroleum products.

The irony of the above combination strategy is that it ultimately became a compounded growth strategy. The reason: the anticipated decline in the demand for tobacco products never came about. For instance, in the mid-1970s, tobacco operations made up 46 percent of Reynolds' sales but accounted for 69 percent of earnings. Similarly, among many other such companies, tobacco products continued to account for a disproportionately large part of the organizations' profits.

To conclude our illustrations of combination strategies, we suggest that many large cities have recently taken on strategies which will change over time. If you look at some of the Sunbelt cities like Houston and Atlanta, you find that they have gone from growth to stability. Planners in these cities sought to take advantage of the attractiveness of the Sunbelt with its warm climate, low cost of living, and plentiful labor pool. But, they have also attempted to control the growth so that when it stabilizes, they will not have suffered the negative consequences. On the flip side, northeastern cities like Detroit and Cleveland have sought to arrest retrenchment. Faced with population decline, loss of tax revenues as taxpayers move out, loss of jobs as industry has fled, and loss of the middle class as job opportunities diminished, they have sought stability strategies which have included subplans for new housing, industrial development, and cultural centers.

[10] "Borg-Warner," pp. 92–94.

Where general strategies exist, the evidence indicates that between 1930 and 1974, growth (47 percent) was most popular, followed by stability (22 percent), retrenchment (17 percent), and combination (14 percent).[11] However, general strategies closely parallel the economic cycle. During depressions and recessions, retrenchment strategies become much more frequent (32 percent). Stability strategies are used most often during recovery (32 percent) and during depression (25 percent). During periods of prosperity, growth (49 percent) and combination (17 percent) strategies hit their high points.[12]

The 1960s saw extensive use of growth strategies, particularly through diversification, in order to reduce risks.[13] This, of course, was the period when conglomerates such as Gulf & Western, Litton Industries, and Signal Corporation were Wall Street favorites. During the 1970s, though, retrenchment strategies hit their modern-day peak,[14] especially for many of the diverse, multiproduct conglomerates. The 1980s may prove to be a heavy retrenchment period, particularly for publicly funded organizations such as school districts, social service agencies, city services, colleges, and state governments.

Specific strategies

Specific strategies identify more precise ways for the organization to match its capabilities with potential opportunities. The four most relevant specific strategic areas relate to the product or service that the organization offers, conversion processes, marketing, and finances.

Product or service What is it that the organization provides? How should it be designed? If it's a physical product, how should it be styled? If a service, what skills should our employees have, and how can we insure that these skills are kept current? These are questions that need to be considered.

The public accounting firm needs to know its service: financial auditing, tax, management advice, some combination of these, or other services. Similarly, hospitals and government agencies must assess the design and quality of the services they render. Manufacturing firms, of course, will be concerned with product development and design, obsolescence, styling, and quality control. For example, GM's 1973 decision to commit $6 billion to downsize its full line of cars by 1979 was a product strategy.

Process Process strategies are concerned with the quality and quantity of inputs and the way they will be combined to result in the final product or service. In nonmanufacturing organizations, this is closely intertwined with the service strategies. In manufacturing firms, however, decisions need to be

[11] William F. Glueck, *Business Policy: Strategy Formation and Executive Action* (New York: McGraw-Hill, 1976).
[12] Ibid.
[13] R. Rumelt, *Strategy, Structure, and Economic Performance* (Cambridge, Mass.: Harvard University Press, 1974).
[14] Glueck, 1976.

made regarding sources of materials, their quality and quantity, the equipment that the firm will utilize, plant layout, inventory levels, and so forth.

Market   Decisions relating to price, packaging, advertising, and distribution channels are typically part of the market strategy. Polaroid, for example, has historically pursued a "skimming the cream off the top of the market" pricing strategy. When a new camera is developed, it is first priced high and then dropped over time. The SX-70 began at over $200, but within a year Polaroid was producing a model in a plastic case for less than $125. Another illustration of a market strategy was Avon's decision to sell their cosmetics through salespeople who called at your home rather than using the traditional drug and department stores.

Financial   Since organizations require money to operate, they should have a financial strategy to identify where funds will come from—donations, government appropriations, revenues from customers, incurring of debt, sale of equity. Should a university require all of its nonscholarship students to pay tuition, fees, room and board up front, at the beginning of the term, or should it allow installment payments? Maybe it should accept Visa and Master Charge! How much should be set aside for capital purchases—for equipment, buildings, automobiles, and so on? These are issues to which a financial strategy should provide answers.

summary of major points

1. In addition to setting objectives and making forecasts, an organizational strategy specifically identifies future opportunities and threats; analyzes the organization's capabilities; assesses the actions of competitors; and establishes subplans and the actions necessary to achieve the subplans.

2. Effective strategies should be:
   a. Comprehensive
   b. Integrative
   c. Dynamic
   d. Synergistic
   e. Properly timed

3. Organizations follow one of four general strategies:
   a. Stability
   b. Growth
   c. Retrenchment
   d. Combination

4. Organizations should also have specific strategies for:
   a. Products or services that are offered
   b. Conversion processes
   c. Marketing
   d. Finances

STRATEGY FORMATION

167

FOR DISCUSSION

1. What is *strategy formation?*
2. How does strategy relate to planning?
3. "Strategy formation is generally the province of top administrators." Do you agree or disagree with this statement? Defend your position.
4. What does it mean when we say that "effective strategies should be comprehensive and integrated"?
5. How might strategic planning be used by the federal government?
6. Why is there a bias toward growth strategies in North America?
7. In what ways can a retrenchment strategy be pursued?
8. If you were in the business of producing and marketing baby food, how might your strategies have changed between 1960 and 1980?

case exercise

Union Carbide surprises Gulf Oil

In the summer of 1978, Gulf Oil Corporation's chemical division received news that would significantly influence its five-year goal of gaining and holding the no. 2 position in the market for low-density polyethylene film. A major competitor, Union Carbide Corp., announced that it had developed a new process to make low-density polyethylene at a cost that was 20 percent less than Gulf's conventional method.

In 1976, Gulf's chief executive officer, Jerry McAfee, had participated in establishing a five-year plan that would maintain Gulf's no. 2 position in the market for low-density polyethylene film, boost its high density film business from third to second place in that market, and build a polypropylene business from scratch to no. 2 or no. 3 in the market by 1980. The chemical division's goals seemed realistic given its executives' appraisal of industry growth potential, the competition, Gulf's market position, and any inherent risks, as well as the funds needed to reach its goals. Their forecasts projected growth in demand at 10 percent or more through 1981, and the likelihood of technological breakthroughs in the manufacture of polyethylene to be very low. Emphasis was thus placed on increasing production capacity by planning for the construction of a new plant in 1979 and minimizing research and development spending.

Market growth turned out to be 8 percent annually, rather than 10 percent, and the plans for the new plant were tabled, but it was Union Carbide's announcement that really put a wrench in the works. Executives at Gulf were assessing what to do. "Is what Union Carbide saying about their technology real? If so, does it apply to both high- and low-clarity film? Our main market segments are in film used for food wrap, while theirs has been film of the green garbage-bag type. If their new process is only for that segment, we might be able to shift our focus to different segments." Does the threat cover the entire market? Should they immediately intensify their own research to come up with a similar or better process? Union Carbide has indicated willingness to license its technology but only at a very high cost. Would this be a viable alternative? And in a year or two, when Gulf has to add capacity if they do not have a cost-cutting technology comparable to Union Carbide's, they will have to abandon the business.

Questions

1. How did Gulf's forecasts influence its strategy?
2. What are the down-side risks and up-side rewards with their current options?
3. What should Gulf's executives do?

FOR FURTHER READING

Andrews, K. R., *The Concept of Corporate Strategy.* Homewood, Ill.: Dow Jones-Irwin, 1971. A classic on strategic planning, this book presents concepts of strategy that have evolved at the Harvard Business School.

Chandler, A. D., Jr., *Strategy and Structure: Chapters in the History of Industrial Enterprise.* Cambridge: M.I.T. Press, 1962. An historical study of changing corporate strategy based on a survey of 100 large U.S. industrial companies.

Cohen. K. J., and R. M. Cyert, "Strategy: Formulation, Implementation and Monitoring," *Journal of Business* (July 1973), pp. 349–67. Attempts to structure the various problems inherent in the process of formulation, implementing, and monitoring corporate strategy in modern business firms.

Hofer, C. W., "Research on Strategic Planning: A Survey of Past Studies and Suggestions for Future Efforts," *Journal of Economics and Business* (Spring–Summer, 1976), pp. 261–86. One of the most comprehensive sources on the various aspects of strategy formation.

Rothchild, W. E., *Putting It All Together: A Guide to Strategic Thinking.* New York: American Management Association, 1976. The author, a specialist in strategic planning at General Electric, looks at various options and techniques.

Vancil, R. F., "Strategy Formulation in Complex Organizations," *Sloan Management Review,* Winter 1976, pp. 1–18. Provides a detailed description of how strategy can be determined so that it can keep pace with changing environments.

Chapter 8

Management By Objectives

AFTER
STUDYING
THIS CHAPTER,
YOU SHOULD
BE ABLE TO—

Define and explain the following key terms and concepts:	Management By Objectives MBO Process MBO Philosophy	Locke's theory of goal setting Action planning

Describe:

Steps in the MBO process
Differences between public and private organizations and how they
     might impact on an MBO effort
The value of hard goals
The value of specific goals
The impact of assigned and participative goals on performance
Three desirable characteristics that objectives should have
Pitfalls to MBO success

If an organization is committed to comprehensive planning, how can it convert its strategies into a series of more detailed operating plans, which can be further translated into specific objectives for organizational units and individual administrators? One answer is management by objectives or, as it is more popularly called, MBO. It is an approach which operationalizes the planning function through cascading objectives. In this chapter we will seek answers to the following questions: What is MBO? Does objective setting really lead to higher individual performance? How is MBO implemented? What problems or pitfalls should one be aware of before establishing an MBO program?

What is MBO?

Management by objectives was first advocated about a quarter of a century ago.[1] On an abstract level, it can be described as a philosophy of management or administration that seeks to convert organizational goals to personal goals to satisfactory performance outcomes. In more practical terms, it can be viewed as a process made up of four major elements: goal setting, action planning, self-control, and periodic reviews.[2] The organization establishes goals and actions plans to attain these goals at the highest level of the organization; then, by pushing the goal-setting activity down through all levels of the organization, it insures that lower administrative levels understand, accept, and control their own efforts toward the accomplishment of these higher level goals.

But MBO is not a unilateral edict: all employees, whether administrators or not, participate in the development of objectives and exercise some control in accomplishing them. The linking of goals from the top of the organization to the bottom is not only important for coordinating efforts to achieve the organization's objectives, but also for providing a mechanism to derive specific from general objectives. Objectives will be general for the organization as a whole, but as objectives cascade down through the levels of the organization they become more focused and specific as they reach individuals. So, while a community hospital may have a goal like reducing cost by 7 percent in the next calendar year while maintaining the same level of productivity, the admittance unit of this hospital might seek to reduce the standard entry processing time of a patient from 23 minutes to 19 minutes and to have 95 percent of all admission forms to the accounting department within three hours of check-in. Continuing this same example, Ms. Taylor,

---

[1] The concept is generally attributed to Peter F. Drucker, as proposed in *The Practice of Management* (New York: Harper & Row, 1954).

[2] Anthony P. Raia, *Managing By Objectives* (Glenview, Ill.: Scott, Foresman & Co., 1974), pp. 15–18.

an admissions clerk, will have her own set of objectives, which might include: achieve a zero level of complaints, submit all daily Medicaid forms to the accounting department by 5:15 P.M. each day, and successfully complete the local university's short course in hospital administration.

A process

The above presents MBO as a process or technique where "the superior and subordinate managers of an organization jointly identify its common goals, define each individual's major areas of responsibility in terms of the results expected of him and use these measures as guides for operating the unit and assessing the contribution of each of its members."[3] But it can also be presented as a philosophy of management. In this context, it is treated as a general way of managing rather than as a technique.

A philosophy

It is a philosophy which reflects a "proactive" rather than a "reactive" way of managing. The emphasis is on trying to predict and influence the future rather than on responding and reacting by the seat of the pants. It is also a "results-oriented" philosophy of management, one which emphasizes accomplishments and results.... It is a philosophy which encourages increased participation in the management of the affairs of the organization at all levels. Its "participative management" style is one which is consistent with the needs and demands of a modern society.[4]

It is correct, therefore, to view MBO as both a process and a philosophy. While it is most frequently discussed in the context of profit-making organizations, it is by no means limited only to business. It may be more difficult to state the objectives of public service organizations, for example, but this can be done. As one author noted, the objectives of a parks and recreation department—to "improve health," "provide recreation," or "develop good citizens"—must be restated in tangible and objective terms so that they can be measured and appraised.[5] We will have more to say about MBO's applicability to public sector organizations later in this chapter.

A summary

In attempting to answer the question "what is MBO?" a number of assumptions and characteristics have been presented. Management by objectives:

1. Promotes explicit objectives.
2. Provides a mechanism for the overall goals of the organization to be transmitted downard and operationalized.
3. Assumes units and individuals are evaluated on measurable results.
4. Assumes objectives are set jointly by consultation between subordinate and superior.
5. Ensures evaluation by providing for feedback and measurement of results.

[3] George S. Odiorne, *Management By Objectives* (New York: Pitman, 1965), pp. 55–56.
[4] Raia, p. 11.
[5] Herbert A. Simon, *Administrative Behavior* (New York: Macmillan, 1945), p. 176.

Let us now turn our attention to the research evidence on goal setting which builds the empirical support for the enthusiasm about MBO.

Can objective setting lead to higher performance?

At the level of the individual, there is some convincing evidence to support the value of setting goals. In this section, we will review this evidence and draw conclusions relative to the MBO philosophy.

Locke's theory of goal setting

In 1968, Edwin Locke proposed a theory of goal setting which has proven to be an important contribution to the administrative literature.[6] Synthesizing more than a dozen studies, Locke concluded that hard or difficult goals result in a higher level of performance than do easy goals and that specific hard goals result in a higher level of performance than do no goals or a generalized goal of "do your best." From this theory, other propositions have been presented regarding the importance of participation and feedback in goal setting. In the following pages, we will review the research pertaining to hard vs. easy goals, specific vs. generalized goals, assigned goals or participative goals vs. "do your best," and feedback vs. no feedback on goals.

Hard vs. easy goals

Locke proposed that, if factors like ability and acceptance of the goals are held constant, the more difficult the goals, the higher the level of performance. This was supported by a number of laboratory studies reported by Locke.[7] Although individuals with very hard goals achieved their goals far less often than those with very easy goals, the former consistently performed at a higher level than the latter. However, Locke noted, it is important that this hard goal-high performance relationship be moderated by goal acceptance. Many people "reject difficult tasks which are assigned to them and probably more people reject very hard tasks than reject moderately hard tasks. But the point is that once a hard task *is* accepted, the only logical thing to do is to try one's hardest until one decides to lower or abandon the goal."[8] Since proposed, others have sought to test the validity of this relationship.

In summary, seven studies have examined the relationship between goal difficulty and performance. With one exception, support was found in each study for Locke's proposition that hard goals lead to greater performance than do easy goals, as long as the goals are accepted. . . . It can be concluded that there is strong support for Locke's goal difficulty proposition.[9]

But can goals be too hard? The obvious answer is yes! When a goal is perceived as impossible instead of challenging, an individual's willingness to

[6] Edwin A. Locke, "Toward a Theory of Task Motivation and Incentives," *Organizational Behavior and Human Performance,* May 1968, pp. 157–89.
[7] Ibid.
[8] Ibid., p. 168.
[9] Gary P. Latham and Gary A. Yukl, "A Review of Research on the Application of Goal Setting in Organizations, *Academy of Management Journal,* December 1975, p. 835.

strive toward that goal will decline significantly. If a goal is perceived as too hard, one response is to reject the goal. If this is not possible (i.e., the boss *tells* you that your sales quota is 140 percent of last year's sales), it may result in the reporting of invalid data and other forms of dysfunctional behavior. This was found to be the case for plant managers in the Soviet Union, who were on production-based pay incentive plans, when assigned unreasonably high production goals. These high goals, when combined with a bonus system designed to reward the accomplishment of these goals, resulted in the production of unplanned products, the concealment of production capacity, the falsification of reports, and the deterioration of quality.[10]

From a contingency perspective, perception and individual differences should not be ignored. The evidence indicates that employees are likely to accept difficult goals if they perceive that (1) the goals are reasonable, (2) achievement of the goals will result in a personally desirable outcome, and (3) the employee has a high degree of self-assurance and a previous record of more successes than failures in goal attainment.[11]

It is irrelevant whether the goals are actually reasonable or whether they, in fact, will result in a personally positive outcome. What is relevant is that individuals perceive this to be true. If individuals actively participate in setting goals, it increases the probability that they will be seen as reasonable. In addition, a clear linking of results to rewards that are viewed as personally attractive should increase a goal's attractiveness.

Individual differences will influence whether difficult goals are seen as challenging rather than impossible. That is, certain individual differences lead people to view the same goals dissimilarly. Individuals who are assured and confident, as well as people whose track record includes more successes than failures, tend to be more optimistic. This translates into a greater willingness to accept difficult goals as a challenge that can be attained rather than as an insurmountable obstacle.

Specific vs. generalized goals

Locke proposed that *specific* hard goals produce a higher level of output than the generalized goal of "do your best."[12] He found that in six of his eight studies, individuals trying for specific hard goals performed at a significantly higher level than individuals trying to "do their best."

Subsequent research has borne out Locke's preliminary findings.[13] In ten out of eleven studies, evidence was found to support the effectiveness of specific goals. "Only one study failed to find any support for the goal specificity proposition of Locke's theory, and the measure of goal setting in this study was of dubious validity."[14]

[10] Joseph S. Berliner, "The Situation of Plant Managers," in *Soviet Society: A Book of Readings*, eds. A. Inkeles and K. Geiger (Boston: Houghton Mifflin, 1961), p. 369.
[11] Latham and Yukl, "A Review," p. 835.
[12] Locke, p. 169.
[13] Latham and Yukl, pp. 827–30.
[14] Ibid., p. 830.

PLANNING

Studies indicate that assigned (unilaterally determined) or participative (bilaterally determined) goals are consistently more potent than instructions to "do your best." For example, one experiment among skilled technicians compared participation, assigned, and nongoal groups. The results generally indicated that technicians with assigned and participation goals performed more effectively than the "do your best" group of skilled technicians.[15] Another study, using college students in simulated clerical tasks, found that individuals with assigned goals performed better than the groups without assigned goals.[16]

The above suggests that specific goals, whether assigned or participatively determined, result in higher performance than instructing people to merely "do your best." But what about different types of specific goals? Is there any difference in performance when individuals are assigned goals than when individuals participate in setting their own goals? Let's see.

Intuitively, it would seem reasonable to hypothesize that when individuals contribute to setting their own goals, rather than having them unilaterally assigned, performance would be significantly higher. Participation should increase an individual's commitment to the goals, since he or she would have been actively involved in their formation. The research evidence does not, however, clearly support this hypothesis.

A study conducted among educated logging workers found no superiority of participative over assigned goal setting, though workers who were classified as educationally disadvantaged did demonstrate higher performance under participative goal-setting conditions.[17] Another investigation explored the effects of participative versus assigned goal setting on goal difficulty.[18] It was found that under participative conditions, individuals established more difficult goals which, when combined with the earlier findings regarding hard goals, suggests that participation may have a positive impact on performance.

The study of skilled technicians, reported earlier, could not attribute any advantage to participation.[19] In fact, the results indicated a slight superiority of assigned goal setting over participative goal setting. The researcher qualified his findings, however, by suggesting that the results may have been

[15] John M. Ivancevich, "Different Goal Setting Treatments and Their Effects on Performance and Job Satisfaction," *Academy of Management Journal,* September 1977, pp. 406–19.

[16] Sam E. White, Terence R. Mitchell, and Cecil H. Bell, Jr., "Goal Setting, Evaluation Apprehension, and Social Cues as Determinants of Job Performance and Job Satisfaction in a Simulated Organization," *Journal of Applied Psychology,* December 1977, pp. 665–73.

[17] Gary P. Latham and Gary A. Yukl, "Assigned Versus Participative Goal Setting With Educated and Uneducated Wood Workers," *Journal of Applied Psychology,* June 1975, pp. 249–302.

[18] Gary P. Latham, Terence R. Mitchell and Dennis L. Dosett, "Importance of Participative Goal Setting and Anticipated Rewards on Goal Difficulty and Job Performance," *Journal of Applied Psychology,* April 1978, pp. 163–71.

[19] Ivancevich.

due to the fact that these skilled workers were educated (as were the logging workers, noted above) or that the typical procedure in the organization where the study was conducted was to assign goals. The results might reflect a resistance to a goal-setting procedure that was dramatically different from the one that the workers were used to.

These findings, along with other studies comparing participative and assigned goals, provide mixed results. While research generally confirms the superiority of specific and hard goals, the evidence is not consistent with regard to participation. "Although most of the studies found some evidence supporting the superiority of participative goal setting, a significant difference is found only under certain conditions or with certain types of employees.[20] The results suggest that this subject needs further research before we can draw any substantive conclusions.

Feedback on goals vs. no feedback

Locke proposed that performance feedback or knowledge of results would lead to higher performance because:

> (a) feedback may induce a person who previously did not have specific goals to set a goal to improve performance by a certain amount; (b) feedback may induce a person to raise his goal level after attaining a previous goal; (c) feedback that informs a person that his current level of effort is insufficient to attain his goal may result in greater effort, and (d) feedback may inform a person of ways in which to improve his methods of performing the task.[21]

The belief that feedback on one's performance will facilitate the goal setting-performance relationship seems intuitively logical. More importantly, however, is the fact that research evidence tends to confirm this belief.[22]

Summary and implications

Our discussion on goal setting has provided strong support for Locke's proposition that specific goals increase performance and that difficult goals, if accepted, result in higher performance than easy goals. These conclusions, as should be obvious, have some very real implications for MBO.

MBO argues for the value of specific, measurable goals, an argument that is supported by research findings. As to how challenging these goals should be, Locke's theory would propose making goals difficult rather than easy. Further, MBO proponents state that joint goal setting (participation) be used for establishing goals. Here, the evidence is mixed. While one is tempted to conclude that participation in setting goals will increase their chance of acceptance, this has not been validated. In fact, the evidence indi-

---

[20] Latham and Yukl, "A Review," p. 840.
[21] Ibid., p. 835.
[22] See, for example, Miriam Erez, "Feedback: A Necessary Condition for the Goal Setting—Performance Relationship," *Journal of Applied Psychology*, October 1977, pp. 624–27.

cates that assigned goals will be accepted and lead to higher performance provided they are realistic and not based on whim or caprice.[23] At this time, the claim that MBO should include participative goal setting because it will lead to greater acceptance and higher performance is not consistently supported. Finally, MBO includes a review and evaluation procedure based on the belief that feedback enhances the effectiveness of goal setting. The evidence generally confirms this belief.

Before we leave Locke's theory, we want to briefly present an example of how the theory was used at the Weyerhauser Company to improve the performance of logging trucks and produce a substantial cost savings for the company.[24]

The experiment sought to increase the net weight carried by these trucks in their hauls from the woods to the mill. Normally, the trucks would carry between 60 and 120 logs, the difference attributable to the varying size of the trees. It was the responsibility of the truck drivers to decide how many logs they would carry.

The researchers studied this operation and concluded that the trucks were frequently carrying far less than the maximum legal net weight. The truckers had traditionally been told to simply "do their best" in assessing weight loads. The researchers decided upon 94 percent of truck net weight as a "difficult" but attainable performance goal. This goal was assigned to the truck drivers along with clarification that this was an experimental program, they would not have to make any more truck runs, nor would there be any retaliation if performance were to suddenly increase and then decrease. In addition, truckers would be given feedback on their results. Since the truck weights had always been available to each individual driver as soon as the truck was weighed in, this feedback would not alter the findings. To minimize the effect of extraneous factors, the participants were given no monetary reward, fringe benefits, or special training. The only direct benefit was the verbal praise given for improving performance. The base period for comparing performance was the three months prior to the study when the drivers were operating under "do your best" conditions. The comparison would be to their nine-month performance with the 94 percent goal.

The results were quite impressive. There was a substantial improvement in performance that held throughout the nine-month period. The company's policy prevented any explicit discussion of the study's impact, however. "It can be said that without the increase in efficiency due to goal setting it would have cost the company a quarter of a million dollars for the

[23] See, for example, Gary P. Latham and Sydney B. Kinne III, "Improving Job Performance Through Training in Goal Setting," *Journal of Applied Psychology*, April 1974, pp. 187–91; and Gary P. Latham and J. James Baldes, "The 'Practical Significance' of Locke's Theory of Goal Setting," *Journal of Applied Psychology*, February 1975, pp. 122–24.
[24] Latham and Baldes, *op. cit.*

purchase of additional trucks in order to deliver the same quantity of logs to the mills. This figure does not include the cost for additional diesel fuel that would have been consumed or the expenses for recruiting and hiring additional truck drivers."[25]

This Weyerhauser example demonstrates Locke's theory that setting a specific hard goal, rather than using a generalized goal of "do your best," leads to a substantial increase in performance.

Implementing MBO

We can now get down to the issue of how to implement an MBO program. Earlier in the chapter we mentioned that MBO is made up of four essential elements: goal setting, action planning, self-control, and periodic reviews. Figure 8-1 expands on this to specify eight steps that an organization would follow in establishing an MBO program.

The MBO process

In goal setting, we establish objectives from the overall goals of the organization down to the level of the individual. This cascading approach insures that the various levels within the organization have a common direction. Whatever the organizational level, however, these objectives are formulated through consultation between superior and subordinate.

In action planning, we work on the means to the ends established in goal setting. This is, we develop realistic plans to attain our objectives. This step includes identifying the activities necessary to accomplish the objective, establishing the critical relationships between these activities, assigning responsibility for each activity, estimating the time requirement for each activity, and determining the resources required to complete each activity.

By self-control, we mean systematic monitoring and measuring of performance—ideally, by having the individual review his or her own performance. Inherent in allowing individuals to control their own performance is a positive image of human nature. The MBO philosophy is built on the assumptions that individuals can be responsible, can exercise self-direction, and do not require external controls and threats of punishment to motivate them to work toward the organization's objectives. MBO, therefore, is based upon a set of humanistic assumptions about the nature of man—of which participation and control of one's own performance are logical extensions.

Finally, with periodic progress reviews, corrective action is initiated when behavior deviates from the standards established in the goal-setting phase. Again, consistent with the MBO philosophy, these superior-subordinate reviews are conducted in a constructive rather than punitive manner. Reviews are not meant to degrade the individual but to aid in future performance. These reviews should take place two or three times a year.

When the above process is implemented successfully, a number of

[25] Ibid., p. 124.

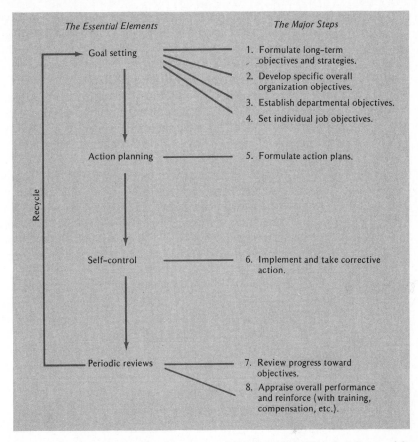

The Essential Elements | The Major Steps

Goal setting
1. Formulate long-term objectives and strategies.
2. Develop specific overall organization objectives.
3. Establish departmental objectives.
4. Set individual job objectives.

Action planning
5. Formulate action plans.

Self–control
6. Implement and take corrective action.

Periodic reviews
7. Review progress toward objectives.
8. Appraise overall performance and reinforce (with training, compensation, etc.).

Recycle

Adapted from *Managing by Objectives* by Anthony P. Raia. Copyright © 1974 by Scott, Foresman & Co. Reprinted by permission of the publisher.

FIGURE 8-1   The MBO process

benefits accrue to the organization, some of which we have already noted. MBO makes objectives explicit; identifies conflicting objectives; provides individuals with the opportunity to participate in those decisions which affect them; ensures an evaluation mechanism by providing for measurement of accomplishments, feedback, and periodic reviews; and reduces performance vagaries because evaluation is based on results.

Scope of objectives   What will objectives look like? They should be tangible, measurable, and verifiable! That means that, wherever possible, we should avoid qualitative objectives and substitute in their place quantifiable statements. For example, a quantitative objective might be "to initiate a direct check purchase-order system for all orders under $500 by December 31," or "to increase donations next year by 15 percent."

179

Too often, however, we are faced with broad qualitative-type objectives. An example might be a purchasing department's goal "to improve speed in processing purchasing orders." Obviously, such an objective is vague. It does not meet our criteria of being tangible, measurable, and verifiable. We must break down that qualitative statement into subparts that meet our requirements—for example, "mail or call in an order within 24 hours from receipt of the purchase order," or "to initiate by phone an order to vendors within a 30-mile radius of our office, and follow up with a purchase order." We have taken a vague qualitative objective and turned it into something that is quantifiable.

Clearly, objectives cannot be set for everything. Therefore, we must be selective, so that resources and efforts are concentrated in critical or key areas. Objectives are necessary in all areas on which the survival of the organization depends.[26] This point is demonstrated in objectives for the Convair Division of General Dynamics. Their 1968 statement of objectives outlined four critical areas: quality, management, economics, and new business:

QUALITY: Achieve 100 percent success in all Atlas and Centaur launch and flight operations. Improve quality by 20 percent as measured by Convair Craftsmanship Program. Win Air Force "Craftsmanship" award.

MANAGEMENT: Improve safety record by 10 percent to status of best in aerospace industry. Develop maximum effectiveness in "Convair Integrated Management Systems," by implementing on all new programs. Maintain progress on management upgrade by highlighting communication and management personnel selection and development.

ECONOMIC: Make or exceed budgeted profit on all programs. Save $1 million in "conservation" program.

NEW BUSINESS: Win two new Atlas and/or Centaur missions. Win major improvement program for F-106. Exceed production sales forecast by ten percent. Initiate development of a proprietary program. Win military aircraft program. Win key technology contracts leading to major space programs for 1970s.[27]

Not all the Convair objectives are in quantifiable terms, but most are measurable, verifiable, and tangible. With a few exceptions, they are specific enough to allow measurement, comparison, and determination of whether they have been achieved.

Findings suggest that the level of the individual within the organization is an important factor in determining what objectives will look like. Specifically, the ability to establish tangible, verifiable, and measurable performance goals for an individual should tend to be inversely related to that individual's level in the organization.

It is relatively easy to quantify the performance criteria for most oper-

[26] Peter F. Drucker, *Management: Tasks, Responsibilities and Practices* (New York: Harper & Row, 1974), pp. 99–100.
[27] *Convair Quarterly Report,* January 8, 1969, A-2-A-5. With permission.

atives. As we review the jobs of people higher up in the organization, we find that these job descriptions grow progressively more vague and that it becomes increasingly difficult to formulate tangible, verifiable, and measurable standards for them. The higher a person "rises in an organization and the more varied and subtle his work, the more difficult it is to pin down objectives that represent more than a fraction of his effort."[28] The result is that positions higher in the organization may require more subjective measures than lower positions. Although both objective and subjective measurement data have the potential to be manipulated, it is probably more likely that individuals would try to distort the subjective measures.[29] This also suggests that it is easier to successfully implement MBO at lower levels in the organization.

Is MBO widely adopted by organizations? A study of *Fortune* 500 companies showed that 120 had tried MBO, that of these, only 30 percent discussed their objectives as often as once a month, and only 10 of these firms believed they had highly successful applications.[30] A survey of approximately 200 hospitals found 41 percent using a formal MBO program.[31] Of obviously poorer reliability, but nevertheless interest, is the report of a noted management expert:

> Recently I polled the participants in a management course of mine as to the experience of their companies with MBO. These managers came from a broad range of manufacturing firms. Of the approximately 25 percent who came from companies who had tried MBO, about one-third said the experience had been bad; in most of these companies MBO had been either formally dropped or, more commonly, it had just faded away. In another third, MBO was judged a success, and in the final third the experience was mixed. This is hardly my idea of rigorous research, but I suspect more careful studies would come to roughly the same conclusions.[32]

Some problems in implementation Before one begins to regard MBO as a panacea for an administrator's problems, we should consider some pitfalls in implementing an MBO program. Some writers have numbered as many as twenty problems,[33] but we will discuss only the major ones.

[28] Harry Levinson, "Management By Whose Objectives?," *Harvard Business Review,* July–August 1970, p. 126.

[29] Edward E. Lawler III and John Grant Rhode, *Information and Control in Organizations* (Pacific-Palisades, Ca.: Goodyear Publishing Co., 1976), p. 97.

[30] Fred Schuster and Alva F. Kendall, "Management By Objectives, Where We Stand—A Survey of the Fortune 500," *Human Resource Management,* Spring 1974, pp. 8–11.

[31] Fred Luthans, "Management By Objectives in the Public Sector: The Transference Problem," paper presented at the 35th Annual Academy of Management Conference (New Orleans, Louisiana, 1975).

[32] George Strauss, "Management by Objectives: A Critical View," *Training and Development Journal,* April 1972, p. 15.

[33] Dale D. McConskey, "20 Ways to Kill Management by Objectives," *Management Review,* October 1972, pp. 4–13.

Requires top management commitment A lack of top management involvement and support will quickly undermine any MBO program. It may be an unwillingness to back up the efforts of lower-level administrators who attempt to apply MBO in their units. Or it may take the form of failing to do the sustained follow-up work necessary to make MBO effective. Either way, MBO is likely to be ineffective and may be a total failure.

Three approaches have been proposed by which administrators can implement MBO: (a) authoritarian—top administrators decide MBO will be used and *dictate* same; (b) persuasion—top administrator's *sell* MBO to lower-level administrators; and (c) education—the MBO philosophy is discussed until it is well *understood* and accepted.[34] While the education approach is the one usually advocated, contingency variables should not be overlooked. For instance, the authoritarian style can be effective if the top executive has absolute power and is willing to use it; if lower-level administrators are clearly dependent upon their superiors; and if the internal environment of the organization is one where subordinates accept, and expect to receive, unexplained orders from above. Where these conditions exist, the authoritarian approach has been successful.[35]

Reliance on the persuasion approach alone leads to disillusionment. Inspirational talks on the benefits of MBO quickly lose their luster. However, this approach may be useful in the early stages of implementation, if only to get people to submit to education.

Must be consistent with top management's philosophy If MBO is initiated in an environment where the administrative philosophy tends to emphasize external controls and threats, we can expect it to fail. MBO is a philosophy that supports the value of the individual on the job; therefore, administrators must accept a positive view of the nature of man if MBO is to work.

One author argues that MBO, while designed to loosen administrative controls, rarely achieves this in practice.[36] Despite a degree of participation at all levels, senior administrators typically establish the organization's basic objectives. Subordinates may have some freedom in setting secondary goals, voicing objections, and determining how to carry out the basic objectives, but essentially participation means the freedom to determine means, not ends.

There are constraints in the public sector The differences between public and private sector organizations have been downplayed up to this point. However, the area of objective setting, particularly in the MBO framework,

---

[34] George S. Odiorne, "The Politics of Implementing MBO," *Business Horizons,* June 1974, pp. 13–21.
[35] Ibid.
[36] George Strauss, p. 13.

is one place we should spend some time talking about these differences. Although MBO is applicable to all organizations, there are important differences between public and private organizations which can influence its effectiveness and, therefore, deserve some discussion.

Public sector administrators find that many of their decisions are preempted by laws, rules, and regulations. Programmed decisions far exceed nonprogrammed decisions, even in the middle and lower-upper regions of government. And nonprogrammed decisions frequently have greater constraints on them than their counterpart in the private sector. This environment, as might be obvious, limits the opportunities for individuals to participate in setting objectives.

There are other factors that are different in the public sector. Many forms of rewards are set by law. For example, promotions are frequently allocated on seniority or test scores, rather than performance on the job. Pay increases also heavily emphasize seniority. Additionally, since many top-level federal, state, and local government officials are elected and come up for reelection every two or four years, their time horizon for goal setting rarely extends beyond twenty-four or thirty-six months.

In business firms, performance is defined in terms of results, and these results revolve around the concept of maximizing return on investment. Therefore, it is possible to translate objectives into tangible, measurable and verifiable components. For instance, the search for growth, market leadership, or product innovations are all consistent with maximizing return on investment. In the public sector, there is no such equivalent. Objectives are more vague and require some creative thinking to come up with ways to make them substantive.

> "The development of the whole personality" as the objective of the school is, indeed, "intangible." But, "teaching a child to read by the time he has finished third grade" is by no means intangible; it can be measured easily and with considerable precision.
>
> "Abolishing racial discrimination" is equally unamenable to clear operational definition, let alone measurement. But to increase the number of black apprentices in the building trades is a quantifiable goal, the attainment of which can be measured.[37]

The above problems are not unique to the public sector. Business firms also suffer from a number of the ills which are often attributed solely to public organizations. But it is unrealistic to ignore the fact that decision constraints do tend to be greater in public organizations; as does discretion surrounding reward allocations, and the ability to define and measure objectives.

Reports of what happened when MBO was implemented in the massive U.S. Office of Management and Budget (OMB) are not especially en-

[37] Peter F. Drucker, "Managing the Public Service Institution," *Public Interest* (Fall 1973), p. 49.

couraging.[38] Introduced in 1973 throughout 21 major federal agencies, initial response was good. Within five months, OMB filed 237 objectives with the White House. The second year produced more than 225 additional objectives. Agencies were encouraged to submit objectives of any type as long as: (1) the issue was important to the President; (2) there was a means of determining whether it had been achieved; and (3) no additional financial or legislative resources would be required. The lack of more elaborate specifications for goals resulted in most agencies submitting precise, short-term, small, and noncommittal objectives.

The White House found that getting action on objectives was very different from getting objectives listed on paper. The sponsors of MBO at OMB began to lose interest within months of its launching, illustrated, for example, by top executives frequently canceling the periodic review meetings between OMB directors and agency heads to discuss progress toward their objectives. Closer analysis indicated why the program was destined to evaporate. Eighty percent of the objectives chosen were apolitical.

> The objectives were noncontroversial, because they referred to consensual aims such as the preparation of a report by a given date without any commitment as to content; the implementation of a new act of Congress that was their responsibility to fulfill; or actions that had low likelihood of causing protest by politically active groups. The absence of controversy made such objectives safe for bureaucrats to present to political superiors. But it also meant that busy Executive Office staff had no positive incentive to take an interest in them, and paid a high opportunity cost in time to monitor noncontroversial achievements of government, when there were many controversial issues to seek to influence.[39]

The study concluded that the effort agencies gave to making MBO a success was related to the extent to which the agencies saw MBO as primarily benefitting their department, rather than as a channel of information and control by OMB.

When input rather than output measures are used In cases where quantitative outputs cannot be easily measured, as with many service jobs, the tendency is to use inputs or effort as a measure of performance. Although this can happen in public or private organizations, criticism is most often directed at the public sector. The argument usually goes something like this: rewards are allocated on good intentions, on not alienating important constituencies, and for development of new programs rather than, for example, tangible evidence of the effectiveness of new programs. What happens, therefore, is that "results" in public organizations are translated into mean-

[38] Richard Rose, "Implementation and Evaporation: The Record of MBO," *Public Administration Review,* January–February 1977, pp. 64–71.
[39] Ibid., p. 68.
[40] Drucker, "Managing the Public Service Institution," p. 50.

ing a larger budget.[40] "Performance" becomes the ability to maintain or increase one's budget. "And the budget is, by definition, related not to the achievement of any goals, but to the *intention* of achieving those goals."[41] This budget-orientation focuses the attention of public administrators not on efficiency or cost control, but on attaining larger budgets, increasing the size of their staff, and insuring that the full budget allotment is spent. To achieve results with a smaller budget or smaller staff is not "performance." To fail to spend the current budget can only mean a smaller budget next year. So what happens? Administrators in the public sector define "performance" and "results" as what will maintain or increase their budget rather than in providing better services for lower costs.

Tendency to select easily measurable and visible goals   MBO can become ineffective when easily quantifiable objectives are chosen for expediency. If it is difficult to devise good quantitative goals, poor ones may be chosen, resulting in misdirected efforts. The desire for objective standards is admirable, but such standards "often force the subordinate to *look* good rather than *be* good and to emphasize the measurable rather than the unmeasurable."[42] Fascination with quantifiable goals can limit the attention paid to important aspects of an individual's performance merely because they cannot be easily expressed in numerical terms. That is, there is a tendency to select easily measurable and visible goals, which are not necessarily the most important.

The fact that most organizations do not use MBO and, of those that do, there are many failures, can be attributed to MBO being inconsistent with modern administrative-man decision making. Specifically, risk is not rewarded in most organizations so objectives tend to cover the short term, cover safe and noncontroversial issues, and tend to err on the conservative side—being too easy rather than too hard.

Cannot automatically resolve conflicts   Another pitfall is the problem of merging individual and organizational objectives. It is one thing to say that goals should be determined jointly, but that does not insure that differences can be resolved. People will only pursue organizational goals to the extent that they complement and further their own personal goals. If the individual perceives his goals to be in conflict with those of the organization, one choice is to resolve the conflict directly in his favor. He might, for example, distort or falsify his performance results, expand his unit when it is not in the best interests of the organization, or make business trips at organization expense which are personally gratifying but do not further the organization's objectives. Another choice is to indirectly choose in his own favor by trying to please his boss.

[41] Ibid.
[42] George Strauss, "Management by Objectives," p. 15.

. . . knowing that his boss is the one who hands out rewards, the typical subordinate may look anxiously for some indication of what the boss thinks are proper goals. Once these become clear, he will quickly adopt them with "enthusiasm." Indeed, some subordinates might prefer that their boss indicate his wishes frankly from the start, instead of putting them through guessing games.[43]

The previously cited OMB experience suggests consensus is achieved by formulating noncontroversial objectives. Consensus can also be achieved by keeping objectives abstract. As long as they remain intangible, everyone can be happy and feel that their interests are being served.[44] But as soon as goals are made clear, specific and verifiable, conflict arises. One author suggests that the MBO process inadequately deals with this conflict of organization and individual goals: "What are the manager's personal objectives? What does he need and want out of his work? How do his needs and wants change from year to year? What relevance do organizational objectives and his part in them have to such needs and wants?"[45]

Organizations do not necessarily reward performance Although we traditionally say that organizations reward performance, there is often a breakdown in the performance-reward linkage in organizations. Instead of rewarding good performance alone, means to that end are frequently rewarded—things like getting along with people, good work habits, physical appearance, personality, and harmonious relations in one's department. Each of these criteria *could* lead to better performance—but not necessarily. When organizations reward those people who get along well with others, for instance, they are basing reward distributions on a popularity-contest view of performance rather than on getting the job done.

Why do organizations reward people who "look like" an administrator rather than those who perform like administrators? Why do they assign more importance to their being at work on time and staying late than to their getting the job done? The evidence indicates that in many organizations, there is more concern with how actions look than with the effect of these actions. "Style" is valued over "substance." This occurs because performance evaluation is not a science. For MBO to function as the theory says, the evaluation of an individual's efforts should be relatively objective and bias-free. Most of us recognize that this doesn't occur.

[43] Ibid., p. 11.
[44] W.K. Warner and A.E. Havens, "Goal Displacement and the Intangibility of Organizational Goals," *Administrative Science Quarterly*, vol. 12, 1968, p. 543.
[45] Harry Levinson, p. 128.

. . . since every subordinate is a component of his superior's effort to achieve his own goals, he will inevitably be appraised on how well he works with his superior and helps the latter meet his needs. A heavy subjective element necessarily enters into every appraisal and goal-setting experience.[46]

Requires differentiating rewards   The final potential problem we will consider is that many organizations do not make great enough distinctions in the rewards that are offered, thus undermining the concept of MBO. In many cases, there is no significant difference in salaries between people who are obviously performing outstandingly at their jobs and those who perform marginally. When organizations homogenize rewards, performance will be reduced to the level of the weakest link in the chain.

The experience of the Purex Corporation reflects the importance of people perceiving that rewards are contingent on performance; that is, on how well they achieve their goals. Purex established MBO in the early 1960s with generally favorable results.[47] At the end of eighteen months, average productivity in its manufacturing plants had increased by over 6 percent. This was against decreasing productivity of 0.4 percent per month before the introduction of the program. A follow-up study a year later found productivity still high, but leveled off to an annual increase of only about 2.5 percent. After eighteen months, the program was still not fully implemented at lower levels, and several problems emerged. A number of people complained about an overreliance on production and quantitative goals and reported that it had become a statistics game which was based upon unrealistic objectives. Complaints were also offered about the program's failure to provide any tangible benefits for individual administrators: "What does it really mean to the individual when he successfully meets his goals? How does he personally benefit, other than by a feeling of accomplishment and inner satisfaction?"[48]

In conclusion, MBO is potentially a powerful philosophy of managing. However, many organizations are designed and managed so as to undermine the MBO philosophy. Whether a formal MBO program exists or not, there appears considerable evidence to support the argument that the use of objectives redirects individual effort toward particular standards of performance. Objectives clarify for employees the behavioral patterns that are desirable on the job and, in the majority of situations, improve employee performance.

[46] Harry Levinson, p. 127.

[47] Anthony P. Raia, "Goal Setting and Self-Control," *Journal of Management Studies,* February 1965, pp. 34–53.

[48] Anthony P. Raia, "A Second Look at Management Goals and Controls," *California Management Review,* Summer 1966, pp. 49–58.

1. MBO (management by objectives) is a philosophy of management or administration that seeks to convert organizational goals to personal goals to satisfactory performance outcomes. The MBO process is made up of four major elements:
    a. Goal setting
    b. Action planning
    c. Self-control
    d. Periodic reviews

2. Locke's theory of goal setting proposes that hard goals result in a higher level of performance than do easy goals, and specific hard goals result in a higher level of performance than do no goals or a generalized goal of "do your best."
    a. If other things like ability and acceptance of the goals are held constant, the more difficult the goals, the higher the level of performance.
    b. Specific goals are more effective than generalized goals.
    c. Most research confirms that participative goal setting is superior to assigned goals, though the evidence is not as impressive as with hard and specific goals.
    d. Knowledge of results facilitates the goal-setting–performance relationship.

3. MBO objectives should be tangible, measurable, and verifiable.

4. Potential problems in implementing MBO include:
    a. Lack of commitment by top management
    b. Inconsistent with top management's philosophy
    c. Constraints in the public sector
    d. The use of input rather than output measures
    e. Selection of easily measurable and visible goals
    f. Resolution of conflicts is not automatic
    g. Failure of organizations to reward performance
    h. Failure to provide differentiating rewards

FOR DISCUSSION

1. Relate MBO to the total planning process.
2. What qualities of MBO can provide for improved organizational performance?
3. Contrast the philosophy of MBO with the process of MBO.
4. What is Locke's theory of goal setting?
5. Relate Locke's theory with the MBO process. Are they fully compatible?
6. How will objectives change at various levels in the organization?

PLANNING

7. What factors in the public sector might work against an effective MBO program?

8. Contrast MBO with the description of modern administrative man and pinpoint potential problems.

Implementing large classes at Metro University

Metro University is an urban school in a large cosmopolitan city. From its early years, around the turn of the century, it built its reputation as a "first-generation" university; that is, it offered higher education to students who, for the most part, would be the first in their families to attend college. Being publicly supported, it provided courses at low cost. Additionally, class size was purposely kept small to facilitate high student-faculty interaction. By the late 1970s, however, Metro U. found that its mission had changed. More and more of its students were selecting Metro because of its location rather than its reputation for small classes and concern for students. Enrollments had exploded—from 6000 students in 1970 to over 25,000 in 1980. It became obvious to the university's president that the school had entered a new era in its history and would have to do something to contend with a limited budget for hiring new faculty and pressures from the legislature to continue to service *any* qualified student who applied.

In the spring of 1980, the president called his three vice presidents and six academic deans to his office. He clearly reviewed the enrollment statistics with them. He concluded that Metro U. was faced with no choice but to drop the rule that no class could have more than forty students. The president said he was prepared to immediately convert the basement of the Student Center into two lecture halls, each capable of seating 300 students. Further, the university's auditorium, with a capacity of 1000, could also be used for lectures.

The initial response of the vice-presidents and deans could have been predicted. Although they were empathetic to the problem, they were uniformly resistant to such a move. The president's reply was simply: "Given the legislature's open admission position, we have no other choice." The discussion then turned to which classes would be taught in this large lecture format.

The six deans each spent several minutes attempting to convince those in attendance that the courses in their areas did not lend themselves to the large lecture format. More realistically, the deans knew that each would probably have to offer some large classes. The actual problems, though no one had the courage to overtly address them, were: How could the faculty be sold on the idea of large classes, and what faculty member would want to give up classes of twenty or thirty, for ones of three hundred or maybe a thousand?

The president summarized his observations and then stated, "O.K., I've explained the problem. I've told you what we need to do. Now, how do we make it work?"

Questions

1. Is the president's approach compatible with MBO? Explain.
2. If MBO were to be used in this situation, how could it be specifically implemented?
3. If you were the president, would you have handled the meeting any differently? If so, how?

FOR FURTHER READING

Brady, R.H., "MBO Goes to Work in the Public Sector," *Harvard Business Review,* March–April 1973, pp. 65–74. Because of the absence of the profit motive, MBO in the public sector must be managed somewhat differently from the private sector. There are a number of obstacles, but the author argues that they can be overcome.

Hughes, C.L., *Goal Setting: Key to Individual and Organizational Effectiveness.* New York: American Management Association, 1965. In depth coverage of goal formation, goal achievement orientation, goal processes, and goal setting systems. Also addresses the integration of individual and organizational goals.

Levinson, H., "Management By Whose Objectives?," *Harvard Business Review,* July–August 1970, pp. 125–34. The author argues that because MBO is based on a reward-punishment psychology, when combined with performance appraisal, it is self-defeating.

Migliore, R.H., *MBO: Blue Collar to Top Executive.* Washington, D.C.: Bureau of National Affairs, 1977. A practical book describing MBO, how managers can apply it, and methods for evaluation.

Odiorne, G.S., "How to Succeed in MBO Goal Setting," *Personnel Journal,* August 1978, pp. 427–29ff. Based on research of 12 companies who said they did it right, this article provides 27 rules for improving MBO goal setting.

Odiorne, G.S., "MBO: A Backward Glance," *Business Horizons,* October 1978, pp. 14–24. Reviews MBO's history, the anti-MBO movement, and recent developments.

ORGANIZING

Chapter

Organization Structure

**AFTER
STUDYING
THIS CHAPTER,
YOU SHOULD
BE ABLE TO—**

Structure	Graicunas' theory
Complexity	Tall structures
Formalization	Flat structures
Centralization	Technology
Bureaucracy	Environmental uncertainty
Division of labor	Mechanistic organizations
Span of administration	Organic organizations
Departmentation	Differentiation
Unity of command	Integration

The three components of structure
The advantages and limitations of bureaucracy
The importance of division of labor
The advantages and limitations of a wide span of administration
The need for departmentation
The best time to enforce the unity of command
The impact of technology on structure
The impact of environment on structure
The difference between differentiation and integration
The difference between mechanistic and organic structures

Organization structure exists, but it can't be seen. It is not a chart hanging in the personnel office, it is not the physical walls, nor is it the layout of factories, stores, or offices, though they are all part of it. By organization structure, we mean the tasks people are assigned, who they report to, who they work with, and who they must interact with in order to get their job done.

When most of us think of an organization we usually take its structure for granted. If it is a small organization, it will probably have just a few departments. If it is large, it will have many departments, subdepartments, and maybe even a few divisions. And, of course, large organizations have a proliferation of individuals with titles like senior vice-president, director, and executive assistant. But an organization structure should be the result of considerable forethought. The fact that a chief of police reports to the city manager and not the mayor should be justified in terms of organizational effectiveness rather than convenience.

The design of an organization should not just evolve randomly; instead, it should reflect the organization's objectives and the strategies chosen. The right organization design will significantly facilitate the achievement of those objectives. The decisions made in the planning function impact on organizing by providing the guidelines for determining what type of organization will best facilitate the attainment of the organization's objectives. In this chapter, we will present you with the major components that make up structure and then review how we can develop an effective organization design.

Key components of organization structure

For our analysis, we will use a simplified description of structure. For our purpose, *structure is composed of three components: complexity, formalization, and centralization.* Complexity involves how much differentiation there is within the organization. This includes the degree of division of labor, departmentation, and the number of levels in the organization's hierarchy. The degree to which the organization relies on rules and procedures to direct the behavior of employees is formalization. Centralization considers where the locus of decision-making authority lies. These three variables, then, make up the term *structure*.

To illustrate these three components, let us look at a concept we have all heard many times but which is often unjustly maligned: bureaucracy.

By bureaucracy, we do not mean red tape, paper shuffling, and inefficiency. While this is a common meaning given to the term, this is *not* part of its definition. In fact, we cannot assume that a bureaucracy is necessarily inefficient. All we can say is that bureaucracy is a type of structure, one that

German sociologist Max Weber called an "ideal type" early in this century.[1] This ideal structure would contain each of the following:

Division of labor. Each person's job is broken down into simple, routine, and well-defined tasks.

Well-defined authority hierarchy. There is a multilevel formal structure, with a hierarchy of positions or offices. Each lower office is under the supervision and control of a higher one.

Formal guides to behavior. To insure uniformity and to regulate the behavior of job holders, there is a heavy dependence on formal policies, procedures, and rules.

Impersonal nature. Sanctions are applied to avoid involvement with personalities and personal preferences of its members.

Employment decisions based on merit. Selection and promotion decisions are based on education, experience, and other qualifications of the candidates.

In a bureaucracy, goals are clear and explicit. Positions are arranged in a pyramidal hierarchy, with authority increasing as one moves up in the organization. This authority lies in the positions, rather than in the people who occupy them. Selection of members is based on their qualifications, and requirements of the position determine who shall be employed and in what position. Now, let's relate this description of bureaucracy to the three components we used to define structure.

A bureaucracy generally has high complexity, high formalization, and high centralization. It makes use of division of labor to create specialized units and departments. It has many rules and procedures to guide employees. Decisions usually flow from the top, with the most important decisions being made by senior executives.

The above illustration may invite the question: "Given the way you have defined a bureaucracy, aren't almost all organizations, then, bureaucracies?" For most of the organizations you deal with, the answer is probably yes. Your state or provincial government; large supermarkets and department stores; the companies that make your home appliances, automobiles, and textbooks; and even the fast food franchise you are apt to frequent—McDonald's, Arthur Treacher's Fish and Chips, Taco Bell, or Kentucky Fried Chicken—are all bureaucracies!

Are there organizations that are not bureaucracies? Sure there are! Almost all small organizations do not meet our definition of a bureaucracy. Neither do many professional firms like public accountants and management consultants. But most organizations with twenty or more employees take on bureaucratic characteristics. Why? Because it is frequently the most efficient way to organize. In fact, early writers in administration generally believed that high complexity, formalization, and centralization were ideal for all organizations. Today, we do not accept this notion.

[1] Max Weber, *The Theory of Social and Economic Organizations,* ed. Talcott Parsons, trans. A.M. Henderson and Talcott Parsons (New York: Free Press, 1947).

Since the type of activities that people in organizations engage in is different, it appears only reasonable that structure be adjusted to fit the situation. We are no longer trying to determine what *the* ideal or perfect organization should be. Rather, our efforts are being directed at identifying those situational variables that most influence the structure of an organization and the resulting impact on the organization's effectiveness.

In this chapter, we will review the cornerstones in the classical structure and then introduce some modern insights into organization design. As you will see, we began in search of "the one best way to organize." The road, however, leads us to the conclusion that the "best way" depends on the situation.

The classical cornerstones

The cornerstones of organization can be traced back to the early writers in administrative thought. The subjects of division of labor, span of administration, departmentation, and the unity of command were discussed comprehensively by these classical writers more than half a century ago. Out of their analysis and discussion came normative statements.

Division of Labor

The concept of division of labor, or what some have referred to as specialization, was carefully scrutinized 200 years ago by Adam Smith, in his *Wealth of Nations.*[2] Smith noted that ten men, each doing particular tasks in the manufacturing of pins, could produce about 48,000 pins a day between them. He proposed, however, that if each were working separately and independently, the ten workmen combined would be lucky to make 200, or even ten, pins in one day. If each had to draw the wire, straighten it, cut it, pound the heads for the pin, sharpen the point, and solder the head and pin shaft, it would be quite a feat to produce ten pins a day!

Though the division of labor that Smith described was unique for its time, the process of having each worker perform a minute and specialized task would become the standard form of manufacturing during the Industrial Revolution. During the early twentieth century the concept would be expanded to include nonmanufacturing jobs as well.

Why does division of labor work? First, in highly sophisticated and complex operations, no one person can perform all the activities or tasks due to physical limitations.

Second, limitations of knowledge act as a constraint. Some tasks require highly developed skills; others can be performed by the untrained. If many of the tasks require a large amount of skill, it may be impossible to find people capable of performing all the activities involved. Further, if all workers are engaged in each step of, say, an organization's manufacturing

[2] Adam Smith, *An Inquiry into the Nature and Causes of the Wealth of Nations,* 4th ed., ed. Edward Cannan (London: Methuen, 1925). Originally published in 1776.

process, all must have the skills necessary to perform both the most demanding and the less demanding jobs. The result would be that, except when performing the most skilled or highly sophisticated tasks, employees would be working below their skills levels. Since skilled workers are paid more than unskilled, and their salaries should reflect their highest level of skill, it represents poor usage of resources to pay a person for his ability to do complex and difficult tasks while requiring him to do easy ones.

3) Another element in favor of division of labor is efficiency. One's skill at performing a task successfully increases through repetition. Efficiency is also exhibited in reducing time spent in changing tasks; the time spent in putting away one's tools and equipment from a prior step in the work process and getting ready for another are eliminated through specialization. Additionally, training for specialization is more efficient from the organization's perspective. It is easier and less costly to train workers to do a specific and repetitive task than to train them for difficult and complex activities. Finally, 4) division of labor increases efficiency and productivity by encouraging the creation of special inventions and machinery.

These justifications for division of labor all center around economics. Not one point in our argument emphasizes the human element; and unfortunately, that is just where the disadvantage of division of labor lies. People who perform highly specialized tasks find, over time, that their work becomes boring, monotonous, fatiguing, and anxiety-creating. The result is worker dissatisfaction or alienation, which in turn reflects itself in lower output and reductions in the quality of product or services rendered.

A person's work activities can be viewed along a continuum; at one extreme, a minutely small activity is performed over and over again

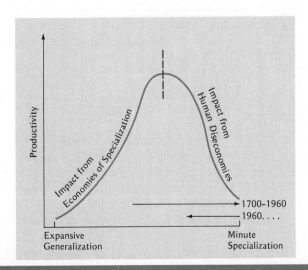

FIGURE 9-1   Specialization—expansion job continuum

throughout the workday, and at the other extreme, a whole process is carried through from beginning to end. Until recently, as noted in Figure 9-1, the modern era (1700–1960) could generally be described as a movement toward the specialization or right side of the continuum, which produced the economies mentioned previously.

However, there is a point along the continuum where the diseconomies from human dissatisfaction begin to offset the economic advantages of specialization. As a result of the realization that division of labor is not a source of unlimited productivity, we find that in a number of organizations, there has been a recent movement (since 1960) toward enlarging, rather than narrowing, the scope of job activities. For these organizations, productivity can be increased by generalizing jobs: giving employees more activities and greater responsibility. Figure 9-1 refers to organizations as a whole. Some organizations, however, may be able to continue to increase productivity through greater specialization.

It is generally acknowledged that jobs in North America are highly specialized.[3] Not only on assembly lines, but in offices and in the professions, we make extensive use of the division of labor concept. In spite of the movement in recent years toward improving the quality of work life through the expansion of jobs, it is still correct to describe the North American workforce as engaging in job activities that have been highly divided and specialized. We can conclude, therefore, that the benefits of the division of labor cornerstone in designing an organization have been accepted and put into use by practicing administrators.

Span of administration How many subordinates can an administrator efficiently and effectively direct? That question has received a considerable amount of attention by academics and practitioners during the last half century. It is an issue of great importance to the design and structuring of organizations.

> Simple arithmetic will show that the difference between an average managerial span of, say, four, and one of eight in a company of 4,000 nonmanagerial employees can make a difference of two entire levels of management and of nearly 800 managers![4]

The above is illustrated in Figure 9-2. You will note that each of the operative (lowest) levels contains 4096 employees. All the other levels represent administrative positions: 1365 administrators (levels 1–6) with a span of 4, 585 administrators (levels 1–4) with a span of 8. The span of four (narrow span) creates a tall organizational pyramid. The span of eight (a wider span) creates a flatter organization. If we could assume that the organization with

---

[3] See, for example, Studs Terkel, *Working* (New York: Pantheon, 1974).
[4] Harold Koontz, "Making Theory Operational: The Span of Management," *Journal of Management Studies,* October 1966, pp. 227–43.

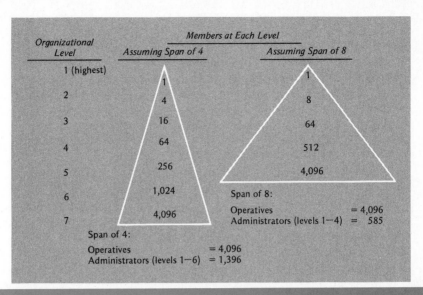

Organizational Level	Members at Each Level	
	Assuming Span of 4	Assuming Span of 8
1 (highest)	1	1
2	4	8
3	16	64
4	64	512
5	256	4,096
6	1,024	
7	4,096	

Span of 8:
Operatives   = 4,096
Administrators (levels 1—4)   =   585

Span of 4:
Operatives   = 4,096
Administrators (levels 1—6)   = 1,396

FIGURE 9-2   Contrasting spans of administration

a span of eight would operate as effectively as the one with four, think of the savings! If the average administrator makes $20,000 a year, a span of eight would save the organization 780 administrative positions (1365-585), or a total of $15,600,000 a year! Of course, the debate centers around whether wider spans are as effective as narrower spans.

Although there is no scientific manner in which an exact optimum span of administration can be determined, we do find general agreement among scholars that the span that is effective at the top level in an organization is not necessarily the one that will be effective for first-line supervisors.

For example, Ralph Davis prescribed that the *executive* span should *3-9* range somewhere between three and nine, whereas the *operative* should be *10-30* between ten and thirty.[5] Lyndall Urwick thought an ideal top-management span would be four, with others supervising between eight and twelve.[6]

So even though there is no agreement on an exact number of subordinates one person can successfully supervise, there is fairly strong agreement that the span should become smaller as one moves farther up the organization. This is explained in terms of the greater interlocking between those at higher levels in the organization than that at lower levels. That is, more of an executive's time is spent in leading activities of an unusual nature, and requiring nonprogrammed action.

[5] Ralph C. Davis, *The Fundamentals of Top Management* (New York: Harper & Row, 1957), p. 276.
[6] Lyndall Urwick, "Axioms of Organization," *Public Administration Magazine*, October 1955, pp. 348–49.

In the 1930's, a French management consultant, V.A. Graicunas, attempted to mathematically formulate the complexity of interlocking relationships.[7] Graicunas's theory can be expressed mathematically as $n(2^n/2 + n - 1)$, where n represents the number of subordinates reporting directly to an administrator. Verbally translated, the formula states that as the number of subordinates reporting to an administrator increases arithmetically, the number of potential interactions increases geometrically. For example, utilizing this formula, we would find that the number of potential interactions for three, four, five, and six subordinates would be 18, 44, 100, and 222, respectively. While the number of subordinates in our example increases 33 percent, 25 percent, and 20 percent as we move from three to six subordinates, the potential relationships increase by 150 percent, 138 percent, and 122 percent, respectively. As a result of this formulation, Graicunas suggested great care in the adding of additional subordinates.

However, he did fail to recognize that not all relationships are the same. The Graicunas mathematical model assumes that relationships are of the same importance and, further, that their frequency is constant. Therefore, the number of relationships that Graicunas calculates represents only *potential* interactions. We find a number of factors that directly affect this potential. The complexity of the work to be done affects the amount of time an administrator has to spend supervising. Additionally, the degree of similarity of tasks being performed, the degree of interdependence, the degree of standardization of work activities, the training and general capability of subordinates, and amount of initiative these subordinates demonstrate must all affect the determination of an optimum span of administration.

The evidence is clouded on whether the tall or flat organization is more preferable. Tall structures provide closer supervision and tighter "boss-oriented" controls, and coordination and communication become complicated because of the increased number of layers directives must go through. Flat structures have a shorter and more simple communication chain, less opportunity for supervision since each administrator has more people reporting to him, and reduced promotion opportunities as a result of fewer levels of administration.

An early study at Sears, Roebuck lent support for the flat organization or wide span case.[8] Two groups of Sears' stores, having between 150 and 175 employees, were the subject of the investigation. One group of stores was characterized by having only two levels of management: the store manager and approximately thirty department managers. The second group, in contrast, had three levels: a store manager, group managers, and merchandise managers. The conclusions drawn from this investigation were that, among

[7] V.A. Graicunas, "Relationship in Organization," in *Papers on the Science of Administration*, ed. L. Gulick and L. Urwick (New York: Institute of Public Administration, 1937), pp. 181–87.

[8] James C. Worthy, "Organization Structure and Employee Morale," *American Sociological Review*, vol. 15 (1950), pp. 169–79.

the stores studied, the two-level organizations with the wider spans out-performed the three-level stores on sales volume, profit, and morale criteria.

Later investigations suggest that there are other factors that moderate the relationship between the span and performance. A review of a number of studies found no support for the general thesis that flat organizations are preferable.[9] The evidence suggested that the larger the organization, the less effective flat organizations were. Increased size brings with it complexity and more demands on every administrator's time. Tall structures, with their narrow spans, reduce the administrator's day-to-day supervisory responsibilities and give more time for involvement with the administrator's own boss. In addition to the size of the organization, the type of job and the individual characteristics of the job holder will moderate the span-performance relationship. Certain jobs require more direction, while others require less. Certain individuals, because of their education, skills, and personality characteristics, prefer varying degrees of freedom or control. Traveling sales positions, for instance, are frequently sought because of the freedom they offer. It should not be surprising to find then that sales representatives in flat organizations demonstrate greater job satisfaction, less stress, and greater productivity than those in medium and tall organizations.[10]

Efforts to determine the optimal span of administration recognize that there are contingency factors. One of the most important of these efforts took place in the early 1960s at Lockheed.[11]

In 1961, the upper- and top-level spans at Lockheed were between five and ten. The span of administration at the middle level fluctuated at around three, and the span of supervisory personnel was between fifteen and eighteen. On a composite basis, top and middle administrative spans were averaging between three and four, with lower levels at approximately twelve. A thorough analysis of the spans resulted in a major reshuffle. Figure 9-3 presents Lockheed's attempt to develop a contingency model for span decisions. Six key variables were isolated (similarity of functions, geographic dispersion, complexity of function, direction and control, coordination, and planning; five degrees of difficulty cited; and weightings assigned to reflect relative importance. After scores for each position were obtained, the scores were adjusted downward to account for the amount of organizational assistance available to the administrator. The total corrected span scores were then compared against a standard representing effective units with wide spans within the organization (Figure 9-4).

By 1965, the span for top- and middle-level managers at Lockheed had been expanded to approximately four, with the first-line supervisory span

[9] Lyman W. Porter and E.E. Lawler III, "Properties of Organization Structure in Relation to Job Attitudes and Job Behavior," *Psychological Bulletin* (July 1965), pp. 23–51.

[10] John M. Ivancevich and James H. Donnelly, Jr., "Relation of Organization and Structure to Job Satisfaction, Anxiety-Stress, and Performance," *Administrative Science Quarterly,* June 1975, pp. 272–80.

[11] Harold Koontz, "Making Theory Operational," pp. 227–43.

FIGURE 9-3 A contingency model for span of administration

Span factor					
Similarity of functions	Identical	Essentially alike	Similar	Inherently different	Fundamentally distinct
	1	2	3	4	5
Geographic dispersion	All together	All in one building	Separate building, 1 plant location	Separate locations, 1 geographic area	Dispersed geographic areas
	1	2	3	4	5
Complexity of functions	Simple, repetitive	Routine	Some complexity	Complex, varied	Highly complex, varied
	2	4	6	8	10
Direction and control	Minimum supervision and training	Limited supervision	Moderate periodic supervision	Frequent continuing supervision	Constant close supervision
	3	6	9	12	15
Coordination	Minimum relation with others	Relationships limited to defined courses	Moderate relationships, easily controlled	Considerable close relationship	Extensive mutual non-recurring relationships
	2	4	6	8	10
Planning	Minimum scope and complexity	Limited scope and complexity	Moderate scope and complexity	Considerable effort required, guided only by broad policies	Extensive effort required; areas and policies not charted
	2	4	6	8	10

Source: Harold Koontz, "Making Theory Operational: The Span of Management," *Journal of Management Studies,* October 1966, p. 239. With permission.

FIGURE 9-4 Standardized span index

Total span factor weightings	Suggested standard span
40–42	4–5
37–39	4–6
34–36	4–7
31–33	5–8
28–30	6–9
25–27	7–10
22–24	8–11

Source: Harold Koontz, "Making Theory Operational: The Span of Management," *Journal of Management Studies,* October 1966, p. 240. With permission.

ORGANIZING

increased to seventeen. In the four-year period, the total number of company personnel declined 10 percent; however, reductions in administrators above the supervisory level equaled 15 percent, while supervisory personnel were reduced by one-third.[12]

The Lockheed program suggests that there are some clear disadvantages to narrow spans.[13] Specifically, it was found that at Lockheed, narrow spans were associated with a decrease in initiative and morale, higher costs, added levels that delayed decision making, decreased opportunities for self-development, and *too much direction.*

What is the relation between theory and practice in the application of the span of administration? A number of studies have been conducted to answer this question. Let us review some of their findings.

Ernest Dale studied 141 companies and found that at the top executive level, the average span among large companies was between eight and nine, and in small companies between six and seven.[14] Another study conducted by Dale surveyed 100 companies and also found that the top executive had between eight and nine persons reporting to him.[15] James Healey studied the span for top executives at 620 industrial plants in Ohio and found that more than 70 percent had between three and eight subordinates reporting directly to them.[16] Fewer than 15 percent of these managers had nine or more subordinates. Another study compared the spans of chief executives in fourteen small businesses with those of chief executives at twenty colleges and universities.[17] The researchers found that more than 60 percent in each group had a span of between four and six, with a range of from two to thirty-one. The researchers concluded that the size of span in the two types of organizations was quite similar.

In practice, the span of administration at the executive level tends to be larger than, say, Urwick's recommendation of four, yet it rarely exceeds nine. Observations would also allow us to conclude that the span of administration in the lower ranks of an organization are usually larger than the span of senior administrators. For the most part, top-level executives have smaller spans than first-level supervisory positions in the same organization. This, of course, would be consistent with the theory.

[12] Ibid.

[13] Ibid.

[14] Ernest Dale, *Planning and Developing the Company Organization* (New York: American Management Association, 1952).

[15] Ernest Dale, *Organization* (New York: American Management Association), pp. 94–96.

[16] James H. Healey, *Executive Coordination and Control* (Columbus: Ohio State University, 1956).

[17] Doris R. Entwisle and John Walton, "Observations on the Span of Control," *Administrative Science Quarterly,* March 1961, pp. 522–23.

Organizations have tasks that need to be performed. These tasks are combined into activities. Because there are economies in specializing activities, we end up with a number of people with specific talents. These people need to be coordinated, and because we know that no one person has an unlimited ability to efficiently and effectively direct others, there is a need to form specialized groups of people who can perform their related activities under the direction of an administrator. These specialized groups are called departments, and they can be created on the basis of simple numbers, function, product or service, client, geography, or process. Most complex organizations will use all the methods. For instance, the basic segmentation may be by function (i.e., finance, manufacturing, sales, personnel). Sales, in turn, may be segmented by geography, manufacturing by product, individual production plants by process, and so forth. The way tasks and activities are combined into departments should reflect on what grouping will best contribute to the attainment of the organization's objectives and the goals of individual units.

Simple numbers One of the easiest ways to group activities is through allocating people on the basis of simple numbers. For example, if we have three supervisors and forty-five operative employees, we could divide the forty-five employees into three groups of fifteen and provide a supervisor for each. Although not sophisticated, the method is fast and easy and provides superficial equity. In small organizations, or at the lower levels of complex organizations, it may be justified.

Function One of the most popular ways to group activities is by functions performed. A hospital might have departments devoted to research, patient care, accounting, and so forth. A manufacturing firm would have units for production, marketing, finance, personnel, and research and development. In a professional football organization, one might find units entitled Player Personnel, Ticket Sales, and Travel and Accommodations. Functional departmentation is most appropriate where there is a need for highly specialized expertise to be consolidated.

Product or service At General Motors, product departmentation is used when activities are allocated to various divisions: Chevrolet, Pontiac, Oldsmobile, Buick, and Cadillac. Each of these divisions operates with considerably autonomy, supported by its own manufacturing, sales, and research and development groups. Wherever there are diverse and rapidly changing product or service lines, this form of departmentation is advantageous.

Client The particular type of customer the organization seeks to reach can be the primary way in which it is departmentalized. For example, we may have sales units that handle only retailers, wholesalers, jobbers, or distributors. Similarly, a large law office may be segmented on the basis of corporate and individual clients: or a college along the lines of credit and noncredit courses. This method is appropriate where the differentiated needs of a clientele require consolidation for more rapid or comprehensive service.

Geography   Still another way to departmentalize can be on the basis of geography or territory. A sales organization may have western, midwestern, and eastern sales divisions. A large school district may have six high schools, to provide for each of the major geographic territories within the district. This method of departmentation takes advantage of localized knowledge for more rapid decision making with comprehensive information.

Process   When a customer or product must go through a series of units because of specialized equipment or manpower needs, the process form of departmentation may be best suited. Since each process requires different skills, this method offers a basis for the homogeneous categorizing of activities.

The issuance of motor vehicle licenses in one state office provides an example. The process is made up of three steps, each representing a separate department: (1) validation, by Motor Vehicles; (2) processing, by Licensing; and (3) payment collection, by Treasury.

If we take a look at departmentation practices in complex organizations, one conclusion becomes inevitable: most complex organizations use all the bases discussed in this chapter. To illustrate, we have dissected the organization chart of a large metals manufacturer, which we will call the XYZ Metals Company.[18] Methods of departmentation in this firm appear generalizable to many organizations. Figure 9-5 shows some pieces from the dissected chart.

The vice-presidents' positions are allocated on the basis of function: research and development, finance, manufacturing, personnel, sales, and purchasing.

Within the sales function, there are four divisions—west, east, north, and south; and within each of these geographical departments, there are sales personnel who specifically handle only automotive, retail, distributor, jobber, or architectural accounts. In other words, sales is a functional department, but within it there are sub-units classified on the basis of client and geography.

The next level under the vice-president of manufacturing consists of divisions: can, extrusion, sheet, and fabrication. These divisions and their management have been departmentalized on the basis of product. Within each plant, we again find a functional segmentation. Within one plant superintendent's responsibility, we find five processing units, by which departments have been created: casting; presses; tubing; finishing; and inspect, pack, and ship. Therefore, in Figure 9-5 we find each of our departmentation methods represented. We might add that the controller's sections,

[18] The information in this example is from an actual metals manufacturer who has asked not to be identified.

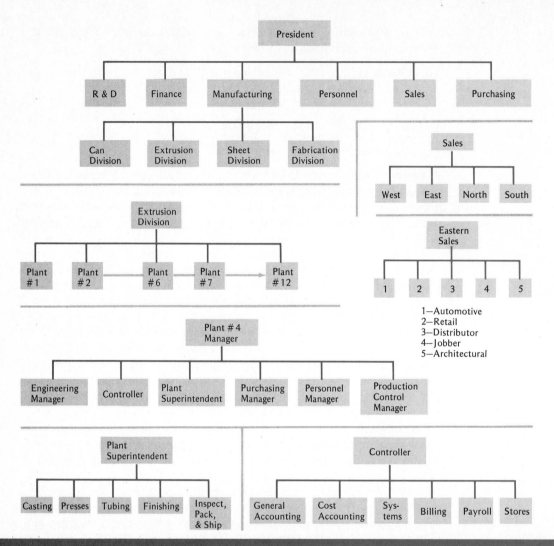

FIGURE 9-5   XYZ Metals Company: selected segments from organization chart

within Plant No. 4, were not selected as much on the basis of process or function as upon simple numbers. It was the controller's desire to keep each supervisor responsible for between three and seven personnel. Therefore, when any unit increased in size beyond what he perceived as a reasonable range, he would act to create another section.

What we find, then, in organizations, is that there is little difference between what is normatively prescribed and what is actually operationalized. There are six ways in which an organization may departmentalize, and

ORGANIZING

observation indicates that complex organizations utilize many or all of them.

The Bible states that "no servant can be the slave of two masters; for either he will hate the first and love the second, or he will be devoted to the first and think nothing of the second."[19] The classical writers in administration accepted this statement and argued that "no person can serve two masters." As a result, the unity of command is a major cornerstone in the classical determination of organizational structure. In those rare instances when this rule had to be broken, it was always explicitly stated that there should be a clear separation of activities and a supervisor responsible for each.[20] Without the unity of command, classical writers argued, individuals might have more than one superior, with the possible result of ambiguity as to whom they are directly responsible and even the potential that they might receive conflicting orders.

The unity of command concept was logical when organizations were comparatively simple in nature. The few large organizations that existed could achieve their goals in a structured form. More recently, as will be discussed in the next section, we have come to recognize that complex organizations need not be bureaucratic, with a clear division of labor, a defined hierarchy of formal relations, clear rules and policies, and impersonality. However, in those cases where a relatively rigid structure is necessary because of the organization's technology and environment, the dictum that each person have only one direct superior is still sound advice.

Current administrative practice suggests that there are numerous instances where the unity of command concept is violated. Anyone who has some work experience can attest to one or more instances when they were confronted with conflicting requests by their "supposed" superior and some other administrator, who may be either several levels above one's immediate boss or at the same level. Administrator X wants a certain report by tomorrow afternoon; Administrator Y wants another report by the same time; and there is only enough time to complete one report. An unusual instance? Not really! In some cases, it merely represents a powerful administrator attempting to give directives to an individual where no authority relation exists. In other cases, it can be the result of the top administration's attempt to facilitate coordination by creating overlapping authority relationships. For example, in chapter 12, we will discuss innovations in the design of organizational structures which purposely create multiple superiors and, hence, violate the unity of command.

[19] Matthew 6:24.

[20] For example, Frederick Taylor discussed the concept of *functional foremanship,* which gave the worker a foreman for each of the tasks he performed (e.g. tools, setups, punch press, etc.). However, the concept never gained wide acceptance.

The modern view

The classical cornerstones we have described, with their strong bureaucratic tone, are effective in certain circumstances. For instance, the evidence suggests that "when tasks people perform are well understood, predictable, routine, and repetitive, the bureaucratic structure is most efficient."[21] But these circumstances do not represent *all* organizations. Since the type of activities people in organizations engage in is different, it is only reasonable that structure be adjusted to fit the situation.

It is one thing to say we should adjust the structure to the situation, but what constitutes "the situation"? Research indicates that the critical situational factor is the degree of *uncertainty*. Administrators seek to reduce uncertainty, and structure can be used as such a buffer. The reason, therefore, that organizations are structured differently is because they encompass different degrees and types of uncertainty.

To illustrate how uncertainty effects structure, consider the case of a major New York management consulting firm which employs several hundred consultants. Employees in this organization are assigned to consulting jobs as they are contracted. Consultants in this firm have varied talents—some are financial experts, some are computer professionals, and still others design production systems. When a job is assigned to a project leader, he reviews the consulting firm's inventory of consultants and selects his team based on available consultants who he believes will be able to assist in the completion of the project. In this firm, consultants are paid whether they are assigned to projects or not. However, if a consultant is consistently passed over by project leaders when they are creating their teams, the partners conclude that the employee is not able to carry his or her weight and should be terminated. Internally, this consulting firm allows the "survival of the fittest" doctrine to determine who stays and who goes, or who works on project X or project Y. The good consultants are highly sought and fought over by project leaders. Those who have been on projects and made marginal contributions find their services in considerably less demand. Importantly, in this firm, there are no *permanent* assignments of consultants to projects or even functional specialty departments like finance, production, planning or systems.

Now, how does this consulting organization differ from Bethlehem Steel Corporation or the U.S. Department of Health, Education and Welfare, with their multitude of permanent departments, high degree of specialization, and formal rules and procedures to guide job assignments and promotions? Their structures are undoubtedly quite dissimilar, but notice that they face dramatically different degrees of uncertainty. The consulting firm is confronted with rapid and constant change and high uncertainty and

[21] Charles Perrow, *Complex Organizations: A Critical Essay* (Glenview, Ill.: Scott Foresman, 1972), p. 166.

therefore requires a more flexible structure than HEW or Bethlehem Steel, which face relatively little uncertainty.

At this point, you may be thinking: O.K., uncertainty is the critical determinant of structure. But this is such a vague concept. Is it possible to be more specific? In more operational terms, what does uncertainty mean?

Uncertainty can be dissected into two subsets. The first refers to elements inside the organization, what we will call *technology*. The other involves elements outside the organization or the *environment*. Let us briefly clarify these two terms and then review the research which has led us to acknowledge their importance.

Technology has been used in a number of ways by organization researchers. It is not our purpose to review the myriad of meanings but rather to isolate the critical content in the term. We define technology as what the organization uses to convert inputs to outputs. To attain its objectives, the organization uses equipment, materials, knowledgeable and/or experienced individuals, and puts them together into certain types and patterns of activities. Whether the organization produces goods or services, the change which inputs undergo to become outputs involves activities which may be very routine and standardized; or they may be very diverse with lots of problems that require constant attention.

To illustrate, if a small machine shop has a number of clients for whom they machine different parts, they probably have many changes to deal with; they have to change the material inputs, machining dies, the speed at which the machines operate, and realign the workforce to balance out scheduling problems. In contrast, the product line stays relatively unchanged in an oil refinery. The relationship of the workforce to their jobs is relatively known and predictable. Other than the concern for equipment breakdown, an oil refinery operates a relatively routine production process with little interruption. Routine technologies like oil refineries are confronted with less uncertainty than are organizations which utilize diverse technologies, and we will see how the degree of routinization influences structure through its control and coordination demands.

In addition, the environment within which an organization operates also influences structure. This includes all the individuals, institutions, and cultures that affect the organization, such as the number and diversity of customers, suppliers, regulatory agencies, competitors, and so forth. Because administrators actively seek ways to control their environment, we will find that structure offers an excellent vehicle to buffer, reduce, or even eliminate environmental uncertainty. So, we find that organizations that confront relatively stable environments are structured differently from firm's facing dynamic environments.

Importance of technology   Very few theorists today would disagree that an organization's structure adapts to its technology, yet this conclusion was reached relatively recently.

209

In the next several pages, we will trace the development of research linking technology and structure, from its beginnings in the early 1950s.

Tavistock group   One of the earliest studies on the relationship between technology and structure was conducted by researchers from the Tavistock Institute in London.[22] The investigation focused on the effects of a change from mining coal using the manual method to the machine-assisted long-wall method. With the manual method, members worked closely in teams of two or three. A team would remove the coal from the seam, load and remove the coal from the mine, and perform other necessary functions such as building roof supports and maintaining their tools. Because members of the team shared jobs, performed a variety of tasks, and were rewarded on the group's performance, satisfaction and cohesiveness were high. The social structure and task requirements could be said to be congruent.

When the long-wall method was introduced, teamwork was replaced by highly specialized individual work assignments. Each specialty had a different pay rate. Although this increased specialization expanded the need for some mechanism to improve communication, coordination, and supportive relationships among workers, this was not provided. The result was a high rate of absenteeism, low morale, and significant reductions in productivity. To reduce the negative effects resulting from the introduction of the long-wall method, the Tavistock researchers introduced a modified long-wall method which allowed an entire work shift to perform all the activities.

The modification proved highly successful. Unnecessary absenteeism dropped from over four percent to less than one-half of one percent; absences due to sickness and accidents dropped to half. Productivity increased more than 20 percent over the unmodified highly specialized structure. With the conventional long-wall method, workers ran behind schedule 69 percent of the time, whereas with the modified long-wall method this was reduced to only 5 percent. Based on these results, the researchers concluded that if the social structure does not change to fit the technology and needs of the workers, performance and satisfaction is adversely affected.

Woodward   While the Tavistock researchers emphasized the specialization component of technology, Joan Woodward stressed the length of production runs in her efforts to relate the technology of manufacturing firms' operations and their organization structure.[23]

Woodward studied nearly 100 small manufacturing firms in the south of England to determine the extent to which bureaucratic concepts like span of administration and unity of command were related to firm success. She was unable to derive any consistent pattern from her data until she segmented her firms into three categories based on the size of their production

[22] E.L. Trist and K.W. Bamforth, "Some Social and Psychological Consequences of the Longwall Method of Coal-Getting," *Human Relations* (February 1951), pp. 3–38.

[23] Joan Woodward, *Industrial Organization: Theory and Practice* (London: Oxford University Press, 1965).

run. These three categories, representing three distinct technologies, had increasing levels of complexity and sophistication. The first category comprised unit or small-batch producers, manufacturing custommade products like tailor-made suits and turbines for hydroelectric dams. Large-batch or mass-producing manufacturers, making items such as refrigerators and automobiles, made up her second category. The third and most complex group was of continuous-process producers, such as oil and chemical refiners.

Woodward found that there were distinct relationships between these classifications according to technology and the subsequent structure of the firms. For example, the more complex technologies had taller hierarchies and significantly different spans of administration. Small-batch producers had the widest spans and the flattest structures, averaging three levels of hierarchy. Mass and process producers averaged four and six levels of hierarchy, respectively. First-line supervisors in small-batch producers were directly responsible for between 21 and 30 subordinates, mass-production supervisors between 31 and 50, and process supervisors between 11 and 20. Mass-production producers, for example, tended to have the widest spans because duties and responsibilities on the assembly line were the most clear-cut and required the least amount of special attention.

Woodward concluded that specific structures were associated with each of the three categories and that successful firms met the requirements of their technology by making structural adjustments. Within each category, the firms that most nearly conformed to the median figure for each structural component were the most successful. Her investigation suggested that there was no one best way to organize manufacturing firms and that technology was an important determinant of the structure most likely to be related to success.

Perrow   One of the major limitations of Woodward's perspective on technology was that it was manufacturing-based. Since manufacturing firms represent less than half of all organizations, technology should be operationalized in a more general way if the concept is to have meaning across all organizations. To gain such a perspective on technology, Charles Perrow looked at knowledge technology rather than production technology.[24]

Perrow proposed that technology could be viewed in terms of (1) whether problems are analyzable or not and (2) whether the problems are familiar (incurring few exceptions) or unfamiliar (with many exceptions). This latter dimension is analogous to programmed and nonprogrammed decisions, discussed in chapter 4. Based on these two dimensions, he suggested a matrix (see Figure 9-6) with four cells or technologies: routine, craft, engineering, and nonroutine.

If problems can be systematically studied, using logical and rational analysis, cells A or B would be appropriate. Problems that can be handled

[24] Charles Perrow, *Organizational Analysis: A Sociological Perspective* (Belmont, Calif.: Wadsworth, 1970).

ORGANIZATION
STRUCTURE

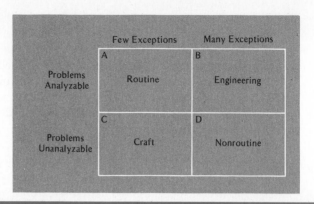

FIGURE 9–6   Perrow's Technology Classification

only by intuition, guesswork, or unanalyzed experience require the technology of cells C or D. Similarly, if new, unusual or unfamiliar problems appear regularly, they would fall in either cells B or D. If problems are familiar, then cells A or C are appropriate.

Using this four-cell scheme, Perrow would argue that organizations in cell A would tend to be structured bureaucratically. Cell B would be characterized by decentralized authority so problems could be solved by individuals who best understand them. Craft technology, in cell C, requires problem solvers with experience and craftsmanlike knowledge. Finally, the most complex cell is D, with nonroutine technology, which requires a structure that is least burdened by the rules and formality of a bureaucracy. For example, cell D organizations would be decentralized, have high interaction among all key members, and have goals which emphasize risk, growth, and innovation.

The two-by-two matrix of technologies, and the predictions of what structure is most compatible with these technologies, was not empirically tested by Perrow. However, one study of fourteen medium-sized manufacturing firms which looked only at cells A and D (routine and nonroutine technologies) found support for Perrow's predictions concerning the relationship between technology, task structure, and goals.[25]

When we attempt to operationalize Perrow's theory, we find that we come back to the same conclusion that Woodward and the Tavistock group arrived at—organization structure should match its technology. If an organization's technology changes, so should its structure. However, this suggestion continues to overlook the differences that exist within organizations. In other words, the researchers have failed to address the fact that *within* an organization, different activities have different technologies. For example, a

[25] Karl Magnussen, *Technology and Organizational Differentiation: A Field Study of Manufacturing Corporations,* unpublished doctoral dissertation, University of Wisconsin, Madison, 1970.

manufacturing firm may have a routine production operation, but that same company's research and development group is almost certain to have a nonroutine technology. The sales and finance functions of this same manufacturing firm probably rely on a technology lying somewhere between the routine and nonroutine, leaning toward the former. When we discuss the influence of environment on structure, we will find that researchers have begun to alter their theories to recognize these differences within organizations.

Aston group   A group of researchers from the University of Aston in Britain have produced a number of empirical studies which have generated a lot of attention by academics.[26] The Aston researchers defined technology as having three parts: operations, materials, and knowledge. Their studies, however, have been concerned only with the first—operations. Using a sophisticated composite measure of operations technology, the researchers were unable to find a relationship between their measure and the structural components of centralization, formalization, and complexity. What they did find, however, was the impact that size had upon structure. The total number of employees in the organization was positively related to complexity and formalization and negatively related to centralization. Larger organizations demonstrated more specialization, more standardization, and more formalization than smaller organizations, but *less* centralization. In other words, the Aston group argues that size is a more significant determinant of an organization's structure than its technology.

They propose that earlier studies which supported a causal relationship between technology and structure did so because technology and size were confused. "The effects which were attributed primarily to technology, were as likely to be due to the simultaneous growth in the size of the organization observed."[27]

Additional research reported during the 1970s has also found size to be important. A study of employment security agencies found complexity to increase with size, though at a decreasing rate.[28] An investigation of nearly 200 government departments also found that size determined complexity.[29] Still other studies have found large size to be related to decentralized decision making.[30] It can be argued that as size increases, the complexity of coor-

[26] See, for example, D.F. Hickson, D.S. Pugh, and D.C. Pheysey, "Operations Technology and Organizational Structure: An Empirical Reappraisal," *Administrative Science Quarterly,* September 1969, pp. 378–97; and D.S. Pugh, D.J. Hickson, S. Hinings, and C. Turner, "The Context of Organization Structure," *Administrative Science Quarterly,* March 1969, pp. 91–114.

[27] Hickson, et al., p. 389.

[28] P. Blau and R. Schoenherr, *The Structure of Organizations* (New York: Basic Books, 1971).

[29] M. Meyer, "Size and the Structure of Organizations: *A Causal Analysis," American Sociological Review* (August 1972), pp. 434–40.

[30] Blau and Schoenherr, *op. cit.* and P.M. Khandwalla, "Mass Output Orientation of Operations Technology and Organization Structure," *Administrative Science Quarterly,* March 1974, pp. 74–97.

dination prohibits centralized decision making, especially if the organization has geographically separated units.

The above should not be construed as a denouncement of the technology imperative. A re-examination of the Aston data, for example, has generated some alternative explanations for its findings.[31] Since the Aston researchers only looked at part of their definition of technology, it is possible that the other two components offer the clues to the technology-structure relationship. Another explanation that has considerable appeal is that technology determines structure, which in turn determines size.

Conclusion Clearly, there is no simple explanation of the technology-structure relationship. We know that there *is* a relationship and that to ignore technology as a major determinant of structure is naive. Size is also a factor, but whether it is causal or caused requires further research. In the final analysis, no definitive answer can be obtained until there is agreement among researchers as to what constitutes technology and how it can be validly measured.

Importance of environment Since organizations seek to control their environments in order to reduce uncertainty and their dependence on others, the external conditions that an organization faces should be an important determinant of structure. In this section, we will show that the evidence supports this contention.

Burns and Stalker Burns and Stalker studied twenty English and Scottish industrial firms and found that the type of structure that existed in rapidly changing and dynamic environments was significantly different from that in organizations with stable environments.[32] The researchers labeled the two structures as organic and mechanistic, respectively.

Mechanistic organizations have the characteristics we have come to identify with bureaucracy: high specialization, formalization, and centralization. They are characterized by routine activities, programmed behaviors, and relatively slow responses to the unfamiliar. Organic organizations have relatively flexible and adaptive structures, with emphasis on lateral rather than vertical communications, influence based on expertise and knowledge rather than authority of position, loosely defined responsibilities, and emphasis on exchange of information rather than giving directions.

Burns and Stalker believed that the most effective structure is one which adjusts to the requirements of the environment, which means using a mechanistic design in a stable, certain environment, and an organic form in a turbulent environment. However, they recognized that the mechanistic and organic forms were only the extremes of a continuum. No organization

---

[31] Howard Aldrich, "Technology and Organization Structure: A Re-examination of the Findings of the Aston Group," *Administrative Science Quarterly* (March 1972), pp. 26–43.

[32] Tom Burns and G.M. Stalker, *The Management of Innovation* (London: Tavistock Publications, 1961).

selects one or the other but rather moves toward one or the other. Additionally, they were aware that the preferences of organizational members had to be considered. If they preferred relatively routine tasks with a minimum of ambiguity, the mechanistic structure would better suit their needs. In contrast, for those employees who seek autonomy, variety, flexibility and openness, the organic form is more desirable.

Emery and Trist One of the clearest characteristics of environment was offered by Emery and Trist.[33] They distinguished four kinds of environment that an organization might confront: (*1*) *placid, randomized;* (*2*) *placid, clustered;* (*3*) *disturbed, reactive; and* (*4*) *turbulent field.* Each is increasingly more complex than the previous one.

1. The placid, randomized environment is relatively unchanging. Demands are randomly distributed, and changes take place slowly over time. A state workman's compensation agency is an example of an organization facing a placid, randomized environment.

2. The placid, clustered environment also changes slowly, but threats to the organization are clustered rather than random. Survival requires a strategy of anticipation rather than one of reaction. The organization requires a concentration of resources and specific competencies, hence these structures tend toward centralization. The Bell System illustrates an organization facing this environment.

3. The disturbed-reactive environment has many competitors seeking similar ends. There are plans, actions, and counteractions. Competition requires flexibility to survive, and this structure tends toward decentralization. Cigarette manufacturers like Philip Morris face this type of environment.

4. The turbulent-field environment is the most dynamic and has the highest uncertainty. The organization may be required to consistently develop new products or services to survive. Also, it may have to continually reevaluate its relationship to government agencies, customers, and suppliers. This characterized the pocket calculator and digital watch industries in the late 1970s.

Though Emery and Trist offered no specific suggestions as to the type of structure best suited to each environment, their classifications are not difficult to reconcile with Burns and Stalker's terminology. Emery and Trist's first two environments will be organized more mechanistically, while the dynamic environments will require structure that offers the advantages of the organic form. Regardless of the terms used, the theme underlying Emery and Trist's environmental classification is also compatible with the research findings on technology; that is, the greater the uncertainty, the less effective bureaucratic qualities are and the more important it is to create flexible structural forms. Stability is best handled by structures which have well-coordinated and highly structured forms. Uncertainty means instability and the potential for major and rapid changes. Only a flexible structure can respond promptly to such changes.

[33] F.E. Emery and E.L. Trist, "The Causal Texture of Organizational Environments," *Human Relations,* February 1965, pp. 21–32.

Lawrence and Lorsch   The last research we will review was conducted by two Harvard researchers, Lawrence and Lorsch.[34] They studied ten firms in three industries—plastics, food, and containers. The industries were chosen because they operated in what the researchers believed to be diverse environments. The plastics industry was highly competitive. The life cycle of any product is historically short, and firms are characterized by considerable new product and process development.The container industry, on the other hand, was quite different. There had been no significant new products in two decades. Sales growth had kept pace with population growth, but nothing more. Lawrence and Lorsch described the container firms as operating in relative certainty, with no real threats to consider. The food industry was midway between the two. There was heavy innovation, but new product generation and sales growth were less than plastics and more than containers.

Lawrence and Lorsch sought to match up the internal environments of these firms with their respective external environments. They hypothesized that the more successful firms within each industry would have better matches than the less successful firms. But what constitutes an organization's internal environment? Lawrence and Lorsch looked at two separate dimensions: *differentiation* and *integration.*

The term "differentiation" as used by Lawrence and Lorsch is more encompassing than our definition at the beginning of this chapter since it includes the dividing up of the organization into parts (which we previously called departmentation). But in addition to task segmentation, Lawrence and Lorsch argued that administrators in various departments can be expected to hold different attitudes and behave differently in terms of their goal perspective, time frame, and interpersonal orientation. Different interests and differing points of view mean that members in each department often find it difficult to see things the same way or agree on integrated plans of action. Therefore, the degree of differentiation becomes a measure of complexity and indicates greater complications and more rapid changes. The other dimension that Lawrence and Lorsch were interested in was integration, which refers to the quality of collaboration between interdependent units or departments.

Lawrence and Lorsch postulated that the more turbulent, complex, and differentiated the external environment facing an organization, the greater would be the degree of differentiation between its subparts. If the external environment is very diverse and the internal environment is highly differentiated, they further reasoned that there would be a need for an elaborate internal integration mechanism to avoid having units going in different directions. The need for increased integration to accommodate increases

[34] Paul Lawrence and Jay W. Lorsch, *Organization and Environment: Managing Differentiation and Integration* (Boston: Harvard Business School, Division of Research, 1967).

in differentiation related to the different goals of departmental managers. In all three industries, the researchers found manufacturing people to be most concerned with cost efficiency and production matters. Research and engineering people emphasized scientific matters. Marketing people's orientation was toward the marketplace.

In reference to their three industries, they hypothesized that the plastics firms would be the most differentiated, followed by food and container firms, in that order. And this is precisely what they found. When Lawrence and Lorsch divided the firms within each industry into high, moderate, and low performers, they found that the high performing firms had a structure which best fit their environmental demands. In diverse environments, subunits were more differentiated than in homogeneous environments. In the turbulent plastics industry, this meant both high differentiation and high integration. The production units had relatively routine activities, in contrast to sales and research and engineering. Where the greatest standardization existed, in the container industry, there was the least differentiation and the least integration. Departments within the container firms generally had similar structures. The food firms, as postulated, were in the middle ground.

What does all this mean? Simply that there are two opposing forces that operate in an organization: creating differentiation between departments to deal with specific problems and tasks facing the organization, and getting people to integrate and work as a cohesive team toward the organization's goals. The more successful organizations have more nearly solved the dilemma of providing both differentiation and integration by matching their internal subunits to the demands of the subenvironment.

Conclusion   Our discussion of technology and environment leads us to conclude that there is no one structure that is right for every organization. What is "right" depends on what is necessary to achieve a correct fit. More mechanistic organizations are effective in a stable environment where specific goals, narrow job definitions, routine technology, and employees who seek certainty exists. Activities of state and federal governments, as well as the armed services and the Bell System, probably closely represent these assumptions. On the other hand, where goals are more vague, where the environment is dynamic, and where innovation is necessary, organic forms of organizations are probably more appropriate. Examples of organizations that tend to approximate these latter assumptions would probably include consulting firms, advertising agencies, and organizations like the 1984 Olympic Committee in Los Angeles.

In theory, rationality of design is inferred after the fact in order to make sense out of things that have already happened. For instance, the *rational process* of designing the structure to reduce technological and environmental uncertainty may be a highly unusual occurrence in practice. Organization designs are frequently unplanned and represent only responses among conflicting interests for control over the organization.[35] Because of conflicting demands, imperfect information, and contests for power, rational designs are by definition virtually impossible. Recollecting our discussion of decision making in chapter 5, the idea of preplanned design requires foreknowledge and agreement upon objectives, constraints, and alternatives. We know this is not the case. Therefore, a more realistic view of organization design should recognize that in many cases, it is emergent rather than purposely planned. An organization's design, like its strategy, is more often reactive rather than anticipatory.

It should also be noted that the design of the overall organization and its major subunits—the topic of this chapter—is not what organizing means to many middle-level administrators and to most lower-level administrators. All administrators may have organizing responsibilities, but the function takes on a different orientation at various levels in the organization. Senior administrators are more likely to be concerned with designing the overall organization and major subunits. Questions like how many departments should be created, on what basis these departments should be formed, the span of administration, and the degree of centralization desired are issues that will get the attention of the organization's senior executives. For lower-level administrators, the organization's design is basically a given. This means they organize and schedule work flow, activities of departments, and tasks of individual employees. They are involved with questions concerning who is to do what, who is to report to whom, and what work is to be done in what order.

[35] Karl E. Weick, "Educational Organizations As Loosely Coupled Systems," *Administrative Science Quarterly,* March 1976, pp. 1–19; and Jeffrey Pfeffer and Gerald Salancik, "Organization Design: The Case for a Coalition Model of Organization," *Organizational Dynamics,* Autumn 1977, pp. 15–29.

summary of major points

1. "Organization structure" is composed of three components:
   a. Complexity
   b. Formalization
   c. Centralization
2. There are four classical concepts that have historically been considered the foundations upon which structure is built:
   a. Division of labor
   b. Span of administration
   c. Departmentation
   d. Unity of command

ORGANIZING

3. Division of labor increases productivity by exploiting the economic advantages of specialization:
   a. It recognizes that there are physical limitations to all tasks.
   b. It takes advantage of differing skill levels.
   c. It increases skill levels by repetition.
   d. It reduces time expended in changing tasks.
   e. It encourages the creation of special inventions and machinery.

4. The span of administration defines the number of subordinates an administrator can effectively direct.

5. Departments are similar groupings of work tasks and activities. There are six bases of departmentation:
   a. Simple numbers
   b. Function
   c. Product or service
   d. Client
   e. Geography
   f. Process

6. The unity of command concept states that subordinates should have no more than one superior to whom they are directly responsible.

7. The modern view of organization design states that the reason organizations are structured differently is because they incur different degrees and types of uncertainty.

8. Uncertainty can be dissected into two subsets:
   a. Technology—What the organization uses to convert inputs to outputs.
   b. Environment—All the individuals, institutions, and cultures which have an impact on the organization.

9. An organization's structure adapts to its technology.
   a. The Tavistock group's research concluded that if the social structure is not changed to fit the technology and needs of the worker, performance and satisfaction will be adversely affected.
   b. Joan Woodward found that there was a distinct relationship between specific technology classification and structure among successful firms.
   c. Charles Perrow expanded Woodward's view of technology beyond manufacturing firms. He proposed a knowledge-based technology definition.
   d. The Aston group provocatively argued that size is a more significant determinant of an organization's structure than its technology.

10. An organization's structure also adapts to its environment.
    a. Burns and Stalker identified mechanistic and organic organizations and argued that structure should be different in dynamic and turbulent environments than in stable environments.
    b. Emery and Trist distinguished four kinds of environments: (1) placid, randomized; (2) placid, clustered; (3) disturbed, reactive; and (4) turbulent field.
    c. Lawrence and Lorsch argued that there are two opposing forces that operate in an organization: provision of differentiation between departments to deal with specific problems and tasks facing the organization, and getting people to integrate and work as a cohesive team toward the organization's goals. The more successful organi-

zations have more nearly solved the dilemma of providing both differentiation and integration by matching their internal subunits to the demands of its subenvironment.

FOR DISCUSSION

1. What is meant by the term *organization structure?*
2. Define a bureaucracy. Identify its key components.
3. How many subordinates can an adminstrator effectively oversee?
4. What are the ways in which an organization can be departmentalized?
5. Would the objectives of (1) having as few organizational levels as possible to foster coordination, and (2) having a narrow span of administration to facilitate control be in conflict? Explain.
6. Define and give examples of what is meant by the terms *technology* and *environment.*
7. What role does uncertainty play in the design of an organization?
8. Contrast mechanistic organizations with organic organizations.

case exercise

Nudas: America's Fastest Growing Sport Shoe

In 1965, the American public thought of sport shoes as a pair of six-dollar Keds. Has that image ever changed in fifteen years!

The sport shoe market expanded in the late 1960s and early 1970s, and in the mid-1970s literally exploded. With running having become the largest participant sport in the country—an estimated 25 million people are reported to be regular joggers—the market for running and sport shoes has grown exponentially. So, too, has the competition, with German and Japanese shoes, selling in the $25 to $35 range, becoming the strongest forces in the market.

The Nudas Shoe Co. operated out of Japan and in 1979 sold more than five million pairs of its shoes in the U.S. with its advertising campaign slogan: "You'll never know you have them on." These sales were achieved through utilization of an American jobber-distributor, who warehoused Nudas shoes and provided a sales staff to call on shoe retailers. For providing this service, Nudas gave the jobber-distributor a 35 percent discount on wholesale. So, for example, a pair of Nudas' Speedos, which retail for $30 and wholesaled for $21, were sold to the jobber-distributor for $13.65.

Nudas ultimately decided that they could distribute their shoes more effectively and efficiently if they did it themselves. In 1981, they chose as a goal to sell seven million pairs of their shoes at an average wholesale unit price of $23. They promoted a local sales executive, Henry Okuda, to head the U.S.

marketing operations. As Henry assessed his new task, he recognized the immediate need to develop a U.S. sales organization. On the assumption that a good salesperson would generate between $600,000 and $800,000 of sales, he computed the need to hire about 200 salespeople.

Questions

1. How many sales managers will Henry need to supervise his sales staff?
2. How might he differentiate sales territories?
3. Compute a rough comparison of the cost of Nudas providing their own sales organization versus using a jobber-distributor.

FOR FURTHER READING

Champion, D.J., *The Sociology of Organization.* New York: McGraw-Hill, 1975, chapters 1–9. Sophisticated look at organizational models, typologies, variables, and the formal organization structure.

Ford, J.D., and J.W. Slocum, Jr., "Size, Technology, Environment and the Structure of Organizations," *Academy of Management Review,* October 1977, pp. 561–75. Extensive review of the literature pertaining to the structural influence of size, technology, and environment.

Hall, R.H., *Organizations: Structure and Process,* 2nd ed. Englewood Cliffs, N.J.: Prentice-Hall, Inc., 1977, chapters 5–7. Reviews the literature on complexity, formalization, and centralization.

Scott, W.G., "Organization Theory: An Overview and An Appraisal," *Journal of the Academy of Management,* April 1961, pp. 7–26. Presents the development of three theories of organization: classical, neoclassical, and modern. Argues for a systems focus.

Scott, W.G., "Organization Theory: A Reassessment," *Academy of Management Journal,* June 1974, pp. 242–54. The 1961 article was based on a paradigm of growth, abundance, and consensus. What happened in the 1960s forces us to question this paradigm and propose the possibility of a radical replacement.

Thompson, J.D., *Organizations in Action.* New York: McGraw-Hill, 1967. Possibly the most important publication on organization which came out in the 1960s. Argues that the fundamental problem facing complex organizations is uncertainty.

Chapter

10

Authority

AFTER
STUDYING
THIS CHAPTER,
YOU SHOULD
BE ABLE TO—

Define and explain the following key terms and concepts:

Authority	Responsibility
Traditional view	Accountability
Acceptance theory	Centralization
Zone of indifference	Decentralization
Line authority	Legitimate power
Staff authority	Coercive power
Functional authority	Reward power
Chain of command	Expert power
Delegation	Referent power

Describe:

Sources of authority
The differences between line, staff, and functional authority
The value of maintaining the chain of command
Why delegation is often difficult to do
The difference between operating and ultimate responsibility
Whether authority has been losing its influence in North America
The difference between authority and power
The five bases of power

Halfway through the term in your "Statistics I" course, the instructor begins the class with the following instructions: "Take out a piece of paper. We're going to have a pop quiz." Question: Would you comply with your instructor's request? The answer is probably yes. The reason you did what your instructor asked was that you perceived her as having the "authority" to give a pop quiz. But what if your instructor had asked each student to give her $1000 in "small, unmarked bills" if they wanted to pass the course? Would you comply with this request? Probably not. Why? Because it is unlikely that you perceive this latter request to be within her "authority" as your instructor.

The above illustration is meant to demonstrate the value of authority in an organization. It is probably the most important method for obtaining compliance. In this chapter we will define authority; consider its source and the role it plays in determining the chain of command; describe three different types of authority; analyze the relationship of authority to responsibility, delegation, decentralization, and power; and conclude with an assessment of whether there is, as some experts claim, an increasing resistance to authority in organizations today.

Authority is a right

The classic analysis of authority is generally attributed to Max Weber.[1] He described authority as the willing and unconditioned compliance of people, resting upon their belief that it is legitimate for the superior to impose his will on them and illegitimate for them to refuse to obey. Henry Fayol, in his classic *General and Industrial Administration,* defined authority as "the right to give orders and the power to exact obedience."[2]

In our discussion, we will view authority as the right to act, or command others to act, toward the attainment of organizational goals. The most important term in our definition is the word *right*. It is this term that specifies legitimacy in our organizational context.

Authority, therefore, is related to one's position within the organization. Each administrative position has specific inherent rights that incumbents acquire from the position's rank or title. It has nothing to do directly with the person. Authority lies in the position. The expression "The King is dead; long live the King" illustrates the concept of authority. Since the rights are inherent in the job, as soon as one accepts a position, one assumes the

---

[1] Max Weber, *The Theory of Social and Economic Organizations*, ed. Talcott Parsons, trans. A.M. Henderson and Talcott Parsons (New York: Free Press, 1947).
[2] Henri Fayol, *General and Industrial Administration* (London: Sir Isaac Pitman, 1949).

authority that goes with it. Of course, when that position is vacated, the rights are lost.

Source of authority

What is the source of authority? Why is it that individuals in organizations, for the most part, tend to comply with the requests of their superior who is "in authority"? The traditional view was that a superior's right to exact compliance from subordinates developed at the top and moved down through the organization. The top, in this case, did not necessarily mean the chief executive officer or his governing board. The ultimate source of administrative authority is the society that allows the creation of social institutions. Officers of the U.S. Army obtain their authority from the U.S. Constitution, which provides for national defense. The president of the Coca-Cola Company acquires his rights from the state of Delaware, where Coca-Cola is incorporated, which allows business firms to incorporate; and ultimately from the U.S. Constitution, which creates the concept of private property. Similarly, the superintendent of New York City schools and the administrators at Boston's Mount St. Mary's Hospital acquire their authority from the society which permits and sanctions the formation of school systems and which allows the formation of churches and, further, permits them to support institutions such as hospitals.

A contrasting position on authority was presented by Chester Barnard, who argued that authority comes from below rather than from above.[3] We call this position an acceptance theory of authority. Barnard proposed that authority is based on the willingness of subordinates to accept it; that is, a subordinate perceives the consequences of following directives to outweigh the consequences of rejecting them. Therefore, there can be no such thing as persons of authority, but only persons to whom authority is addressed. Should a subordinate disobey a superior's communication, his disobedience is a denial of that communication's authority for him. Where authority appears to exist but is not accepted by subordinates, in reality there exists no authority.

Barnard elaborated by describing four requirements that are necessary before authority can be accepted. First, subordinates must be able to understand the communication. Second, at the time of his decision, the subordinate must believe that what is asked of him is not inconsistent with the purposes of the organization. Third, at the time of his decision, the subordinate must believe that what is being asked of him is compatible with his personal interests as a whole; consequently, immoral or unethical requests, if they are viewed as such by the subordinate, may be disobeyed. Finally, Barnard suggested that the subordinate must be able mentally and physically to

[3] Chester Barnard, *The Functions of the Executive* (Cambridge, Mass.: Harvard University Press, 1936).

comply with the request. A demand that is only "a little impossible" is still impossible and therefore beyond the capability and compliance of the subordinate.

During the war in Southeast Asia in the 1960s, the story was told of "Charlie" Company, a U.S. Army unit that had a remarkably low fatality rate. After it had been together for a number of months, a new commanding officer was placed in charge of the unit. The members of "Charlie" Company believed that the major reason for their low fatality rate was the prior commanding officer's insistence that all traveling be done off designated roads, which was an unusual practice, since the standard method for travel was along marked roads. The new commanding officer, believing that the more traditional approach of moving his men along designated paths was to be preferred, ordered his company to move out along the marked trails. To his surprise, the company, in total, disobeyed his orders and refused to move unless they could travel away from the marked paths. Even after considerable discussion, the officer was unable to get compliance from his men. The problem was not resolved until higher-ranking officers were brought in to help reconcile the conflict.

The main point to note in this incident is that although the commanding officer had the authority to command these subordinates, the subordinates had the right to disobey those orders. So, to generalize from this example, superiors have no authority if their subordinates do not accept that authority. In other words, subordinates have the ultimate right to negate what we have traditionally thought of as the legitimate authority of positions in organizations.

Barnard further presented a concept he called the "zone of indifference" which, in addition to his four requirements noted previously, explains the unquestioning acceptance of authority. Within this zone, subordinates do not care what is specifically asked of them. Outside the zone are requests which for one reason or another the subordinate finds unacceptable. Whether an administrator's zone is interpreted as wide or narrow depends upon the degree to which the subordinate perceives that the inducements outweigh the costs or sacrifices involved. A police officer may be indifferent as to whether he is assigned traffic patrol or vice detail, but he may absolutely refuse to accept a walking patrol assignment in the city's high crime zone without a partner.

The ideal state for an administrator is to have his subordinates maintain a broad view of their zone of indifference to his directives. When this state exists, along with Barnard's four requirements, the administrator finds that his requests are complied with. Generally, we find that people who are upward mobile, particularly middle- and upper-level administrators, tend to interpret their zone more widely. At the other extreme, the plumber who refuses his foreman's order to work around some wires, since the plumber views this to be the work of an electrician, has defined his zone, in relation to his foreman, in narrow terms.

AUTHORITY

225

Types of authority

Early administrative writers made a distinction between two forms of authority relationships: line authority and staff authority. They defined the former as having direct responsibility for accomplishing the objectives of the organization, and the latter as supporting the line in attaining these objectives. The difficulty of separating direct and supportive activities in modern complex organizations makes this differentiation somewhat obsolete today.[4] However, since these terms are used frequently by practitioners, we should clarify the distinction.

The concept of line authority is not confusing. Basically, it is the superior-subordinate authority relationship, in which we accept a superior's direct authority over a subordinate. The only constraint to defining line authority is that it must contribute to the *direct* achievement of organizational objectives.

Staff authority, however, is more complex. It supports line authority by advising, servicing, or evaluating others. The reason that efforts have been made to distinguish between line and staff authority is the recognition that staff authority is limited. In an advisory role, staff personnel give advice. They have no rights, in the sense that their suggestions need not be obeyed. In a service role, such as an assistant position, they act as an extension of an administrator; however, they possess no direct authority. In an evaluation role, staff personnel may perform functions such as inspection or auditing activities. Some positions, such as accounting in a manufacturing operation, can perform all three of these staff functions; that is, they may give advice, perform a service, and be responsible for checking on the performance of others. For example, a director of general accounting may have no direct say in what capital equipment can be purchased by a production department, but he can utilize the veto power inherent in his evaluation role to influence capital expenditures. Further, he may give advice to a line administrator concerning whether a certain purchase is an expense or a capital item, or he may have his office maintain cost figures on specific projects as a service to line personnel.

The separation between line and staff is often confused by relating the terms to departmental activities, rather than on the basis of relationships. Thus, the accounting function is considered staff at General Motors, but it is viewed as line at the public accounting firm of Price, Waterhouse. Similarly, personnel activities at the Montreal General Hospital are staff, whereas at a placement-service organization, such as Snelling & Snelling, personnel is line. The factor that determines whether a function is line, then, is the objectives of the organization. At a small liberal-arts college, teaching may be the only line activity; at a large university, line functions may include teaching, research, and community service.

[4] Gerald G. Fisch, "Line-Staff Is Obsolete," *Harvard Business Review*, September–October 1961, pp. 67–79.

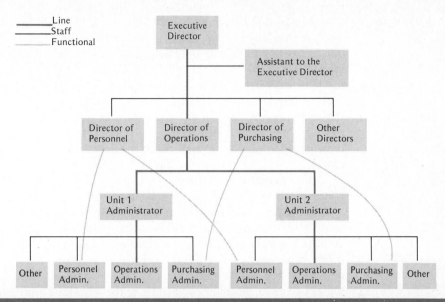

FIGURE 10-1   Organization chart depicting line, staff, and functional authority relations

Is the distinction between line and staff important? A favorable argument can be made for supporting the distinction. For example, there is a difference between the *assistant hospital administrator* and the *assistant to the hospital administrator;* the former is line, the latter is staff. The former has direct authority, whereas the latter must work through the authority of his supervisor. As one person remarked after being promoted from staff assistant to his boss's line position, "I never realized there was such a difference between making a decision and making a suggestion."

The counterargument states that the distinction is not that important because while staff personnel may not have legitimate authority, they have influence as a result of their expertise and their contacts with the organization's senior decision makers. It has been found that staff personnel are different from line, in that they are generally younger, better educated, and more articulate, have greater technical competence in specific areas, possess high-level organizational contacts, and are less loyal to the organization than are line personnel.[5] As a result, they utilize their superior articulation, technical competence, status, and ability to apply sanctions in ways that make them extremely powerful. It is differences such as these, in outlook and position, that inevitably create conflicts between line and staff personnel. As long as an organization differentiates between line and staff authority, certain forms of conflict are inevitable.

[5] Melville Dalton, "Conflicts between Staff and Line Managerial Officers," *American Sociological Review*, June 1950, pp. 342–51.

AUTHORITY

227

In addition to line and staff, there is a third form of authority, which we have overlooked up to this point: functional authority. It is the authority one has over individuals or units outside one's own direct areas of command. Figure 10-1 is an example from a manufacturing organization where the personnel department is responsible for the employment termination process. When the personnel department, acting on another department's recommendation, calls in an employee and informs him that his employment has been terminated, it is using functional authority. Similarly, when the controller stipulates to operating managers the type of accounting system to be used, he acts on the basis of his functional authority.

In organizations that are extensively dispersed geographically—for instance, firms with manufacturing plants, distribution centers, or sales offices spread across the country or overseas—you often see considerable use of functional authority. In a manufacturing plant, there may be a plant purchasing manager and several purchasing agents. The plant manager is the direct supervisor of this purchasing manager. But overall corporate purchasing policy, which guides the day-to-day activities of the plant purchasing department, probably comes from the corporate purchasing office. In other words, it is not unusual for departments within geographically dispersed organizational units to get directions from the unit manager as well as head-office administration. Again, using our purchasing example, head office may use its functional authority to tell plant purchasing personnel that all purchases for items in excess of $100 require three price bids, but the plant manager retains the authority to hire, fire, reward, and punish all the employees in his plant, including the plant purchasing manager.

Obviously, functional authority can create problems. It causes overlapping relationships and increases the possibility of dysfunctional conflict between units. However, in large organizations, such authority can increase efficiency, because of specialization of skills and also improved coordination when those responsible for a particular activity have commensurate authority to ensure its attainment.

Authority and the chain of command

Figure 10-2 shows the organization chart of a metropolitan hospital. Like all organization charts, it shows authority relationships. More specifically, it identifies the chains of command. These are the superior-subordinate connections, and they begin at the top of the organization and fan out in an increasing number at the lower levels of the organization.

For example, one chain in Figure 10-2 would be as follows: Board of Directors → Executive Director → Assistant Executive Director → Director of Finance → Purchasing → Receiving. Another chain is: Board of Directors → Executive Director → Assistant Executive Director → Director of Professional Services → Director of Community Services → Outpatients.

The combination of these individual chains forms the organization's overall chain of command. Every position fits into the organization's overall chain of command at some point. This cohesive linking insures that every individual in the organization reports, either directly or indirectly, to the chief executive and the governing board.

The chain of command sets up an authority hierarchy. Theoretically, all formal communications within the organization take place along this chain or line of authority. When the chain is broken, it undermines some administrator's authority. If the Director of Children's Services in Figure 10-2 bypasses the Director of Professional Services and takes her problems to the Assistant Executive Director, it challenges the authority of the Director of Professional Services and threatens morale and performance in the organization. Of course, there are times when emergencies require that the chain be short-circuited. But in order for those in authority to be kept informed of activities under their jurisdiction and to avoid individuals receiving orders from two or more "bosses," individuals should go through the official channels.

Delegation and decentralization

Delegation

One of the most difficult activities for young administrators to accept and perform adequately is the process of delegation. Yet it is this process that is the key to the organization, since it gives subordinate administrators the means with which to operate and so makes organization possible. It is the means for granting authority downward to subordinate administrators, thereby giving them both certain rights and providing certain prescribed limits for them to operate within. More specifically, it includes the assigning of duties to subordinates, the granting of authority to allow these duties to be fulfilled, and the acceptance by the subordinates of both the responsibility and the accountability for the satisfactory performance of these duties.

Why is delegation one of the most difficult activities for an administrator to practice? First, there is the notion that "if you want something done right, do it yourself!" This idea carries security, but we must get over it, since no successful administrator can function for very long following the guidance of that expression. Of course, if you lack trust in others, it is very easy to rationalize doing things yourself rather than delegating them. Successful delegation requires confidence in a subordinate's abilities and in his conscientiousness in completing tasks.

Then, since administrators recognize that they are ultimately responsible for the activities of their subordinates, many are just unwilling to let go—to allow others to make mistakes. Additionally, some administrators are fearful of having subordinates gain power through learning particular tasks and becoming expert in them. And also, some administrators just enjoy doing detail work that can be done better by a subordinate. Finally, some

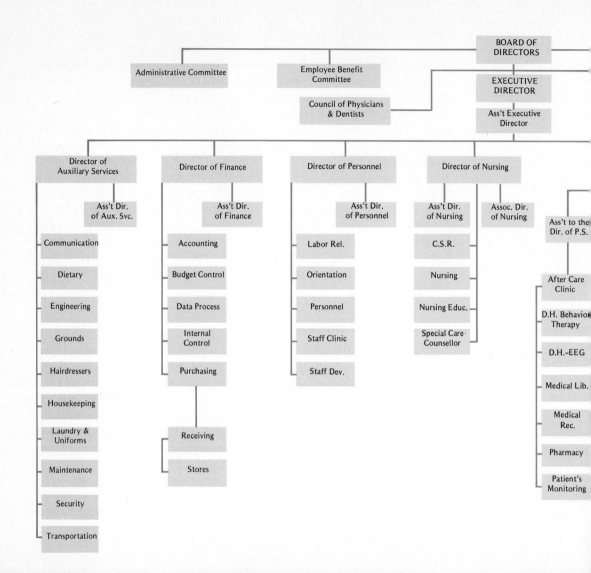

FIGURE 10-2   Hospital organization chart

administrators naively believe that delegating is abdicating, and is therefore something that good administrators avoid. Clearly, this is incorrect. In fact, not to delegate is not to administer.

Although the enumeration above is not comprehensive, it does include the major reasons why administrators fail to share their authority with their subordinates. However, effective administrators do not delegate everything they do. On the contrary, they initiate controls to ensure that those activities

ORGANIZING

230

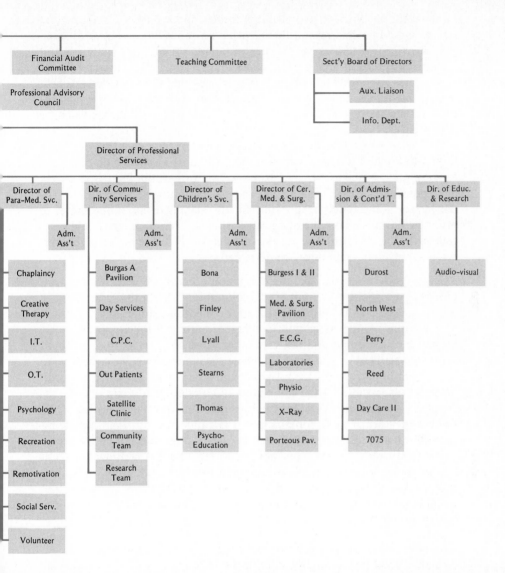

that are delegated are completed and performed satisfactorily. The truly great administrators recognize the importance of delegation. To paraphrase Alfred Sloan, an early president of General Motors, "My greatest talent was getting good people to work for me."

Equating authority and responsibility When we delegate authority, we must allocate commensurate responsibility. That is, when one is given "rights," one also assumes a corresponding "obligation" to perform. To al-

AUTHORITY

locate authority without responsibility creates opportunities for abuse, and no one should be held responsible for what he or she has no authority over.

Classical writers recognized the importance of equating authority and responsibility. Additionally, they stated that responsibility cannot be delegated. They supported this contention by noting that the delegator was held responsible for the actions of his delegates. One may ask, How is it possible to have authority and responsibility equal, if responsibility cannot be delegated?

The answer is that we recognize two forms of responsibility: operating responsibility and ultimate responsibility. Administrators pass on operating responsibility, which in turn may be passed on further. But there is an aspect of responsibility—its ultimate component—that must be retained. An administrator is ultimately responsible for the actions of his subordinates to whom he has passed on operating responsibility. Therefore, he should delegate operating responsibility equal to the delegated authority; however, ultimate responsibility can never be delegated.

Accountability   To complete the delegation process, we need not only authority and responsibility, but also accountability. Authority is the right to act, responsibility the obligation to perform delegated duties and tasks, and accountability is the obligation to a higher authority for satisfactory performance of the duties and tasks. In other words, responsibility is the obligation to carry out what is assigned, while accountability is the obligation to one's superior to carry out the assignment in a satisfactory manner. Subordinates are responsible for the completion of tasks assigned them and are accountable to their superiors for the satisfactory performance of that work. Former president Nixon, for example, was guilty of confusing ultimate responsibility and accountability when he stated about the Watergate break-in, "I accept responsibility, but not the blame." Such a comment suggests that responsibility can somehow exist apart from accountability. In Nixon's case, he was ultimately responsible and accountable to the American public, not only for his own actions but for the actions of those to whom he had delegated authority.

A review of administrative practices reveals that organizations do not do a very good job of holding administrators responsible for the decisions they make. Why? In mechanistic organizations, the hierarchy allows the "buck" to be passed. If a decision proves poor, the "system" usually provides opportunities to place the blame on another level of the organization. In organic organizations, you frequently have group or committee decisions, so it is difficult to identify *who* is accountable. The result, therefore, is that responsibility is clouded by the effort of individuals to protect themselves against the risk of being held accountable for faulty decisions.

**Decentral-
ization**

The concepts of centralization and decentralization are closely tied to delegation. The extent to which delegation is used defines the extent of centralization or decentralization within an organization. As with many of the terms we find in administration, *centralization* and *decentralization* are frequently misunderstood. Let us begin by clarifying what we mean by these terms.

The most widely held interpretation of decentralization is either (1) the dispersion of authority, or (2) the geographical dispersion of the organization. The latter interpretation is incorrect, for the concepts of centralization/decentralization are meant only to reflect the degree of authority that is delegated to lower levels in the organization. The error is caused by the fact that organizations that are geographically dispersed are usually decentralized in nature. Therefore, although an organization with offices or units across the country or throughout the world is decentralized, its decentralization consists of the degree to which authority has been delegated to different levels within it. Alone, the term says nothing about geographical dispersion.

Interestingly, certain organizational activities are more likely to be centralized than are others. For example, financial and legal functions are rarely decentralized. The reason is simple: Certain functions, because of economies or for evaluating purposes, are more readily handled at the centralized level than when they are dispersed down in the organization. On the other hand, sales and personnel functions are frequently decentralized, since they are uniquely tailored to the needs of the customer and employee respectively, and lower-level organizational members are frequently better able to make effective decisions.

It is difficult to generalize as to which direction the centralization/decentralization trend is taking. To generalize about all organizations, the 1950s and 1960s were periods highlighted by intensive decentralization efforts. Much of these were made possible by the widespread use of computers, which allowed for effective evaluation of performance at lower levels. But as a result of a number of factors, including larger computers that require high usage to be economically justifiable, a shortage of qualified administrators, and increased government regulations, the 1970s saw a strong movement back toward centralization.

However, this generalization cannot be applied to individual organizations, most of which fluctuate between centralizing and decentralizing activities, and in which, rather than following a predetermined course, authority has moved upward and downward to react to the changing needs of the organization. No organization should be fully centralized or fully decentralized. These are relative rather than absolute terms, representing extreme positions between which organizations fluctuate.

Whether decision making in an organization should favor centralization or decentralization depends on a large number of contingency factors. For example, the larger the organization, the more decisions that will have to be made. Since the top administrators in an organization have only so much time and can obtain only so much information, as organizations get larger they become increasingly dependent upon lower-level administrators to make decisions. Hence, they should be more decentralized.

The significance of decisions influences the degree of centralization-decentralization. The more significant a decision, as expressed in terms of cost and impact on the future of the organization, the greater the probability that it should be made by top executives. Important decisions are made at higher levels of the organization, while those with minimal impact are delegated downward. A department head may have sole authority to make expenditures up to $500, and a division head's sole authority may allow her to make purchases to $5000, while a vice-president's discretion may extend up to $100,000.

The complexity of tasks should influence where decisions are made. The greater the complexity of the tasks to be done, the more difficult it is for top administrators to keep current and possess sufficient technical information to make effective decisions. As tasks become more complex, they require greater expertise, and decisions about these tasks should be delegated down to whatever level includes this degree of technical expertise.

When the values of the organization's top administrators support and indicate trust in subordinates, authority is more likely to be decentralized. However, if the senior executives do not have confidence in the abilities of lower-level administrators, they will hold on to their authority and create a centralized organization.

In addition to the values held by senior administrators, the realistic qualities of the subordinates will affect the degree of delegation. Decentralization requires individuals with the skills, abilities, and motivation to make good decisions. If this is lacking, top executives will be reluctant to relinquish authority. Individual differences are also relevant in regard to subordinates' willingness to accept decisions imposed from above. If it is crucial that employees carry out a decision, and these employees desire to actively participate in those decisions that affect them, then administrators will be well advised to seriously consider decentralizing decision making.

In addition, it is usually desirable to centralize those functions within the organization that continually interact with the environment. For example, financial, government relations, and labor relations activities are most often centralized to allow the organization to maintain continuity and isolate its greatest expertise in reaching investment sources, reacting to changing government regulations, and negotiating national labor contracts.

Before we leave decentralization, a comment should be made regarding the importance of control systems when decentralization is employed. Decentralization includes giving subordinates authority, selecting the decisions that are to be made at lower levels, giving and stating policy to guide decision making, and selecting and training people to fill those subordinate roles. If adequate controls are not instituted, the administrator has not delegated, but abdicated. This situation is exemplified by the problems that General Electric, Westinghouse Corporation, and several other heavy industrial-equipment manufacturers had in the late 1950s. Because controls were not effectively instituted, and because of broad decentralization, division administrators were able to establish fixed prices and collude on bid prices with other manufacturers. This activity divided up the market nicely and resulted in handsome profits for the firms; however, the top executives were indicted and found guilty of the collusion crimes committed by their underlings. Since ultimate responsibility and final accountability cannot be delegated, decentralization requires adequate control systems.

Finally, let us take a look at decentralization in practice. Studies of American[6] and British[7] organizations confirm that size is a critical determinant of decentralization. The larger the organization, the more likely it is to be decentralized. Moreover, organic organizations tend to be more decentralized than mechanistic organizations in order to maintain adaptability.[8] These findings, which almost seem paradoxical since organizations tend to become more mechanistic as they grow, emphasize the importance of flexibility. Centralized decision making can be effective when an organization is small, or when it is large if this increased size is accompanied by a stable technology and environment.

Is respect for authority on the decline?

It has become increasingly popular to argue that there has been an important change in society's attitude toward authority. From a narrow perspective, it is being said that today's youth are no longer willing to accept authority. Others, however, believe that authority has become obsolete to both young and old:

> We have been, for better or for worse, an authoritarian society. And now, suddenly, it isn't working anymore. Authority is built on subordination. People must be willing to accept subordinate roles, limiting definitions of themselves. And Americans everywhere are becoming insubordinate, unmanageable.[9]

The above quotation coincides with this increasingly popular notion that authority is on the decline, if not altogether obsolete. Unlike our fathers and mothers, the argument is made, we are increasingly unwilling to accept that we must obey orders merely because the boss is "boss." As a group, we are supposed to be more questioning, challenging, and democratically

[6] Ernest Dale, *Organization* (New York: American Management Association, 1967), p. 110.

[7] John Child, "Predicting and Understanding Organization Structure," *Administrative Science Quarterly*, June 1973, pp. 168–85.

[8] Tom Burns and G.M. Stalker, *The Management of Innovation* (London: Tavistock Publications, 1961).

[9] Richard Cornuelle, *De-Managing America* (New York: Random House, 1975), p. 14.

oriented. However, the evidence suggests that this view of authority may be considerably exaggerated.

Milgram's obedience study

Stanley Milgram, a psychologist at Yale University, wondered how far individuals would go in following commands. If you were placed in the role of a teacher in a learning experiment and told by an experimenter to administer a shock to a learner each time that learner made a mistake, would you follow the commands of the experimenter? Would your willingness to comply decrease as the intensity of the shock was increased? To answer these questions, Milgram set up the following study.[10]

Subjects were originally male volunteers who were paid $4.50 for taking part in the experiment, but Milgram eventually expanded his subjects to include a wide range of ages, occupations, and educational levels. Each subject was led to believe that the experiment was to investigate the effect of punishment on memory. Their job was to act as a teacher and administer punishment whenever the learner made a mistake on the learning test.

Punishment was administered by an electric shock. The subject sat in front of a shock generator with 30 levels of shock—beginning at zero and progressing in 15-volt units to a high of 450 volts. The demarcations of these positions ranged from "Slight Shock" at 15 volts to "Danger: Severe Shock" at 450. To increase the realism of the experiment, the subject received a sample shock of 45 volts and saw the learner—a pleasant, mild-mannered man, about 50 years old—strapped into an "electric chair" in an adjacent room. Of course, the learner was an actor and the electric shocks were phoney, but the subject did not know this.

Taking his seat in front of the shock generator, the subject was directed to begin at the lowest shock level and to increase the shock intensity to the next level each time the learner made a mistake or failed to respond.

When the test began, the level of shock intensity rose rapidly because the learner made many errors. The subject got verbal feedback from the learner: at 75 volts the learner began to grunt and moan; at 150 volts he demanded to be released from the experiment; at 180 volts he cried out that he could no longer stand the pain; and at 300 volts he insisted that he be let out, yelled about his heart condition, screamed, and then failed to respond to further questions.

Most subjects protested and, fearful they might kill the learner if the increased shocks were to bring on a heart attack, insisted they could not go on with their job. Hesitations or protests by the subject were met by the experimenter's statement, "You have no choice, you must go on! Your job is to punish the learner's mistakes."

If you were the subject in this experiment, to what degree would you have obeyed authority? When forty psychiatrists were asked this question, they predicted that most subjects would not go beyond 150 volts and that

[10] Stanley Milgram, *Obedience to Authority* (New York: Harper & Row, 1974).

less than 4 percent of the subjects would continue beyond 300 volts. But what were the actual results?

As you might expect, the majority of the subjects dissented. But dissension does not mean disobedience! Sixty-two percent of the subjects increased the shock level to the maximum of 450 volts! The average level of shock administered by the remaining 38 percent was nearly 370 volts!

What does this mean? Apparently, there is a willingness to conform with directives, in spite of the social undesirability of this behavior, if given official sanction. This study may explain how it was possible for Hitler to recruit individuals to willingly carry out orders that destroyed millions of Jews in the gas chambers of the concentration camps. To consider the implications in a more recent context, one study of Americans' response to the trial of Lt. William L. Calley for his actions in Vietnam found that 67 percent of the respondents thought that most people would have acted as did Calley. About half said they too would have followed orders and shot men, women, and children.[11]

Zimbardo's
mock prison

Stanford psychologist Philip G. Zimbardo and his associates created a mock prison in the basement of the Stanford psychology building; hired two dozen emotionally stable, physically healthy, law-abiding students who scored "normal-average" on extensive personality tests at $15 a day; randomly assigned them the role of either "guard" or "prisoner" and established some basic rules. They then stood back to see what would happen.[12]

At the start of the study, there were no measurable differences between those men assigned to be guards and those chosen to be prisoners. Additionally, the guards received no special training in how to be prison guards. They were told only to "maintain law and order" in the prison, not to take any nonsense from the prisoners, and that physical violence was forbidden. To further simulate the realities of prison life, the prisoners were allowed visits from relatives and friends, but while the mock guards worked eight-hour shifts, the mock prisoners were kept in their cells around the clock, allowed out only for meals, exercise, toilet privileges, head count lineups, and work details. As you might expect, it took the mock guards little time to adjust to their new authority. Nor was there resistance by the "prisoners," who accepted the authority positions of the guards.

The primary forms of interaction on the part of the guards were commands, insults, degrading references, verbal and physical aggression, and threats. Every guard, at some time, engaged in abusive, authoritarian behavior. After an initial rebellion was crushed by the guards, the prisoners reacted passively as the guards daily escalated their aggression.

Given the fact that the participants in this study were chosen specifi-

[11] Herbert C. Kelman and Lee H. Lawrence, "American Response to the Trial of Lt. William L. Calley," *Psychology Today*, June 1972, pp. 41–45, 78–81.

[12] P.G. Zimbardo, C. Haney, W.C. Banks, and D. Jaffe, "The Mind Is a Formidable Jailer: A Pirandellian Prison," *New York Times*, April 8, 1973, pp. 38–60.

cally because they had normal, healthy, stable personalities, we can conclude that any of us can be expected to use and accept authority in roles that are stereotyped as highly authoritarian (such as prison guards, teachers, corporate executives, or police).

Jones' third wave

Another illustration of our willingness to accept and obey authority lies in the startling results of one American high school teacher's effort to show his students how it was possible for so many Germans to be aware of what the Nazis were doing to the Jews in the late 1930s and early 1940s, yet claim they didn't know what was going on.[13]

Ron Jones was teaching his high school history class about Nazi Germany and decided to introduce his students one Monday to a key Nazi concept: discipline. He began by introducing new rules in the classroom, such as requiring students to stand behind their desks when asking or answering a question, to start each statement by saying "Mr. Jones," and to give short, crisp answers to all questions.

The students' responses amazed Jones. By the end of the first day, everyone had begun to offer questions and answers, even students who had previously been hesitant. The questions being asked were better than usual, and answers to questions were accurate. The students even seemed more cooperative.

On Tuesday, the classroom environment was becoming significantly different. Upon entering his room, for example, Jones found everyone sitting at attention. While a few students were smiling, most were staring rigidly ahead. How far could Jones carry this? He went to the blackboard and wrote two slogans in big letters: "STRENGTH THROUGH DISCIPLINE" and "STRENGTH THROUGH COMMUNITY." Then Jones had the class chant the slogans over and over. At the end of the period, he introduced a salute to be used by class members—the right hand raised to the shoulder, fingers curled. He called it the Third Wave salute.

By now, the Third Wave "Movement" was spreading. Jones and his students exchanged the salute outside the classroom. On Wednesday, the original thirty members of Jones' class were joined by thirteen curious students who cut their regular classes to learn more about the Third Wave. Jones issued membership cards to the forty-three students and appointed three students to report any members who failed to comply with class rules. This apparently was unnecessary for, on Wednesday alone, twenty students "squealed" to Jones on students not saluting or failing to uphold membership rules.

When Jones entered his history class on Thursday, which now had grown to eighty students, he announced "the real reason for the Third Wave." It was no classroom experiment but a nationwide program "to find

---

[13] "The Third Wave: Nazism in a High School," reported in Ron Jones' *No Substitute for Madness* (San Francisco: Zephyros, 1976).

students willing to fight for political change." In fact, he informed the class that, at noon the next day, a presidential candidate would appear on national television to announce the Third Wave. For Third Wave members, there would be a special rally in the school's auditorium to watch the announcement.

As noon on Friday approached, the auditorium had more than 200 students. Jones closed the doors and posted guards to keep others out. He then addressed the audience, asking them to "demonstrate the extent of our training." He saluted, and 200 arms rose in response. He shouted, "Strength Through Discipline," again and again, and each time the response got louder and louder.

At 12:05, Jones turned off the auditorium lights and walked to the TV set and turned it on. Minutes passed without any "presidential candidate." After about five minutes, one student yelled out, "There isn't any leader, is there?" Jones switched off the set and began a brief lecture on how all 200 participants had been duped. "There is no such thing as a national youth movement called the Third Wave. You've been used, manipulated, shoved by your own desires to where you are now. You're no better or worse than the German Nazis we've been studying. You thought you were the elite—better than those outside this room. You bargained your freedom for the comfort of discipline. . . . Oh, you think you were just going along for the fun, that you could extricate yourself at any moment. But where were you heading? How far would you have gone?"

Jones reminded his audience that, as with those who pleaded ignorance at the German war crimes trials, "Everyone must accept the blame. No one can claim that they didn't in some way take part." The students were ordinary, decent people who, like Nazi followers, got caught up. But, again like the Nazi followers, they could always claim that they didn't know what was happening.

Jones then told the now silent students that the real test would take place in the next few minutes or perhaps years. "If our enactment of the fascist mentality is complete, not one of you will ever admit to being at this Third Wave rally. . . . You won't admit to being manipulated to accepting this madness as a way of life. . . . It's a secret I shall share with you."

Exceptions don't make the rule

The above studies should dramatize that in spite of all the democratic dialogue we hear, we are unusually willing to accept authority and authoritarian environments and to comply with authority figures. Most of us would probably enjoy having and using the authority that goes with a powerful position.

At this point, you may be tempted to ask: What about people like John Dean, Daniel Ellsberg, and the Vietnam war resisters? What about the people we read about who quit their jobs rather than comply with directives that they find personally objectionable? The answer seems to be that these are exceptions to the rule. Regardless of how much we might be repulsed by

AUTHORITY

239

the conclusion that most of us readily accept authority without question, the overall evidence seems to support this position.

It is easy to attack our society's reliance on authority. It is currently fashionable to argue for free, democratic, and participative organizations. Yet we should not forget the value of authority in maintaining order. We are still a society that relies on authority. It is the cement that holds organizations together. Most importantly, regardless of the attention given in recent years to the growing democracy in organizations, the vast majority of people are still willing to comply with the directives of those in authoritative positions.

Though there is much talk, especially among academics, about the demise of authority, the evidence does not support this contention. Administrators like authority and there is little indication that they are giving it up. Practicing administrators worked hard and played the "game" to acquire their authority. They do not relish those who yell, "Time out. We're changing the rules of the game. We are now all equal. Democracy lives!" Administrators covet the rights inherent in their positions and continue to rely heavily on these rights when decisions need to be made.

Authority and power

Authority and power are two terms that are frequently confused. While they do have a common denominator, the difference between the two is significant. Although this point was made in chapter 5, it is important enough to be reiterated and expanded upon.

We previously defined authority as a right, having legitimacy based on one's position in an organization. When we speak of power, we mean an individual's capacity to influence decisions. As such, authority is actually part of the larger concept of power; that is, the ability to influence based on an individual's legitimate position is one of the sources of power. However, it is not the *only* source of power. So, in summary, we can say that authority is composed of rights that are inherent in a formal position in the organization—these rights go with the position rather than the person. Power, on the other hand, is the ability to influence the decision-making process which may or may not be based on a formal authority position in the organization.

The topic of power and dependency has very recently achieved a great deal of attention by both behavioral scientists and practicing administrators. We have now come to realize that one need not be an administrator to have important influence in an organization; nor should we surmise that one's influence increases directly the higher one rises in the organization. In the next several pages, therefore, we will review four other bases of power and then demonstrate, by way of a brief example, how power worked in one organization.

More than twenty years ago, French and Raven identified five types of power.[14] They explained the sources or bases from which power emanates and called these bases legitimate, coercive, reward, expert, and referent. Since we have already devoted considerable attention to the first, let us look closely at the other four.

Coercive power   The coercive base is defined by French and Raven as depending on fear. One reacts to this power out of fear of the negative ramifications that might result if one fails to comply. It rests on the application, or the threat of application, of physical sanctions such as infliction of pain, deformity, or death; the generation of frustration through restriction of movement; or the controlling through force of basic physiological or safety needs.

In the 1930s, when John Dillinger went into a bank, held a gun to the teller's head, and asked for the money, he was incredibly successful at getting compliance with his request. His power base? Coercive. A loaded gun gives its holder power because others are fearful that they will lose something which they hold dear—their life.

> Of all the bases of power available to man, the power to hurt others is possibly most often used, most often condemned, and most difficult to control . . . the state relies on its military and legal resources to intimidate nations, or even its own citizens. Businesses rely upon the control of economic resources. Schools and universities rely upon their right to deny students formal education, while the church threatens individuals with loss of grace. At the personal level, individuals exercise coercive power through a reliance upon physical strength, verbal facility, or the ability to grant or withhold emotional support from others. These bases provide the individual with the means to physically harm, bully, humiliate, or deny love to others.[15]

We can say that Smith has coercive power over Jones if Smith can dismiss, suspend, or demote Jones, assuming Jones values his or her job. Similarly, if Smith can assign Jones work activities that Jones finds unpleasant or treat Jones in a manner that Jones finds embarrassing, Smith possesses coercive power over Jones.

The above examples of coercive power make it evident that coercive and legitimate power bases are not independent. In fact, most formal positions include certain coercive powers; however, individuals in an organization can acquire coercive powers without ever attaining a formal administrative position.

Reward power   The opposite of coercive power is the power to reward. People comply with the wishes of another because it will result in positive benefits; therefore, one who can distribute rewards that others view as valu-

[14] John R.P. French, Jr., and Bertram Raven, "The Bases of Social Power," in *Group Dynamics: Research and Theory*, ed. Dorwin Cartwright and A.F. Zander (New York: Harper & Row, 1960), pp. 607–23.
[15] David Kipnis, *The Powerholders* (Chicago: University of Chicago Press, 1976), pp. 77–78.

able will have power over them. These rewards can be anything that another may value. In an organizational context, we think of money, favorable performance appraisals, interesting work assignments, friendly colleagues, and preferred work shifts or sales territories.

Coercive and reward power are actually counterparts of each other. If you can remove something of positive value from Jones or inflict something of negative value upon him, you have coercive power over him. If you can give Jones something of positive value or remove something of negative value, you have reward power over Jones. Consistent with this interrelationship, we should also recognize that reward power tends to exist along with legitimacy, although it is not restricted to such authority positions.

Expert power   Expert power is that influence one wields as a result of one's expertise, special skill, or knowledge. If Dr. J. (Julius Irving), the incredible basketball star of the Philadelphia 76ers, makes suggestions to a young rookie on how to improve his jump or dunk shots, we would expect that the rookie would listen and probably attempt to comply with Dr. J's suggestions. Why? His record indicates high expertise in such shots. In contrast, if your author made the same suggestions to the rookie, they would most likely be ignored.

Valid knowledge is one of the most powerful sources of influence. For example, the accountant with twenty years' experience in the organization, who is the only one that understands the general accounting system, has power. Just such a case existed in a manufacturing firm a few years ago. It caused considerable discomfort for the controller, since he was solely dependent on this long-standing employee (let us call him A.J.) in areas pertaining to general accounting. The area supervisor was a young college graduate with little experience in how the system worked. In addition, no other employee except A.J. had performed all the general accounting functions. By reason of his expertise, A.J. had made himself almost irreplaceable *and powerful.*

Powerful positions based solely on expert power are held by people in almost every group or organization. Physicians, in white coats and with stethoscopes around their neck, have expert power. We listen to our doctors because the five years they spent in medical school gives them credibility. Walter Cronkite's nightly comments on the state of the world probably carry greater impact than the comments of your Aunt Alice. In spite of the fact that you have known Aunt Alice all your life, love her dearly, and that you are unknown to Walter Cronkite, he has greater credibility on world affairs than your aunt. However, if you are looking for the family recipe for chocolate chip cookies, Aunt Alice's credibility will certainly outweigh Mr. Cronkite's.

In recent years, as a result of the explosion in technical knowledge that is required in order to do most jobs, expert power has become an increasingly potent power force. As jobs become more specialized, we become increasingly dependent on "experts" to achieve the organization's goals. As members increase their knowledge of information that is critical to the operation of the group, the more is their expertise power enhanced. If our computer system is critical to our unit's work, and if I know how to repair it and no one else within 200 miles does, then the unit is dependent on me. I wield expert power. If such a situation existed, you might expect the administrator to have others trained in the workings of the computer or hire someone with this knowledge in order to reduce my power. As others become capable of duplicating your activities, your expertise power diminishes.

Referent power The last category of influence that French and Raven identified was referent power. Its base is identification with a person who has the resources or personal traits one believes are desirable. If Smith admires and identifies with Jones, power can be exercised by Jones because Smith wishes to please Jones.

Referent power develops out of admiration of another and a desire to be like that person. If you admire someone to the point of modeling your behavior and attitudes after him, he possesses referent power over you. This power base can be operative without the power holder even recognizing it. B can potentially influence A even without attempting to do so, or without B's awareness. Referent power explains, incidentally, why celebrities are paid millions of dollars to endorse products in commercials. Marketing research shows that people like Margaux Hemingway, Joe Namath, Farrah Fawcett-Majors, and Robert Blake have power in influencing your buying behavior for products like perfumes, popcorn makers, hair conditioners, and oil additives. With a little practice, you or I could probably deliver as smooth a sales pitch as these individuals, but the buying public does not identify with you and me. On the other hand, if you have younger brothers or sisters who look up to you and want to be like you, you may have extraordinary abilities to influence them. In other words, you hold referent power in your relationship.

Complexity of power

It can be seen from the previous discussion that we view power as potentially existing between individuals and positions at any level, from lowest-level operatives to chief executives. It is certainly not the sole property of administrators. Power is a two-way street, possessed by both administrators and their subordinates. Administrators have legitimate power and the accompanying power over money, security, opportunity for advancement, and satisfying work assignments. Subordinates can demonstrate their power through slowdowns, absenteeism, knowledge, production of poor-quality output, or waste of organizational resources. Additionally, subordinates can unite to increase their influence on organizational decisions.

Similarly, there are *external* power forces that may utilize any of the five influence bases. Suppliers, clients, unions, neighbors, and federal, state, and local governments represent examples of individuals, groups, organiza-

AUTHORITY

243

tions, and institutions that can influence an organization from the outside. Depending on the organization's reliance upon these external forces, they can affect the internal decision-making structure moderately or quite dramatically.

Real world administrators recognize the need to develop a broader power base than that which they receive through their formal position. Power is necessary in order to influence decisions in ways that are politically beneficial, and practitioners become astutely aware of this reality often before they ever attain administrative responsibilities. Observational evidence upholds almost without exception that organizational members actively seek influence beyond that which is acquired by position.

Those who become enthralled with authority to the exclusion of the broader issue of power fail to recognize that in organizations, administrators are not the only individuals who make decisions, nor is it valid to assume that higher-level administrators automatically have greater influence than lower-level administrators. Power, when held by nonadministrative personnel, can be used to influence outcomes. Therefore, to look at decision making as something engaged in only by people holding formal authority is naive. Similarly, it is naive to believe that lower-level administrators do not actively seek and occasionally achieve power equal to or greater than the formal influence of their superiors.

Milo: a case study in power

A study in the 1950s by Melville Dalton was one of the classic investigations of how power works in one organization, the Milo Fractionating Center, a fictional name given to a midwestern industrial firm with 8,000 employees.[16] The study represents Dalton's perceptions as an employee of the firm. It is comprehensive beyond our needs; but we will present his findings regarding the effect of power on altering the idealized state of where decisions were supposed to be made.

Figures 10-3 and 10-4 represent a simplified formal organization chart of Milo, and the structure as it was actually functioning as perceived by Dalton. A close study of the power structure finds instances of assistant managers who have influence equivalent to that of their superiors, and equivalently positioned managers on the formal chart being viewed somewhat differently in terms of their influence. Let us look particularly at the differences as they affected the manager (Stevens), assistant plant manager (Hardy), superintendent of industrial relations (Rees), and superintendent of Division C (Springer).

Dalton considered Hardy and Stevens as equivalent. For example, although Stevens opened staff meetings, Hardy quickly took charge and

[16] Melville Dalton, *Men Who Manage* (New York: John Wiley, 1959).

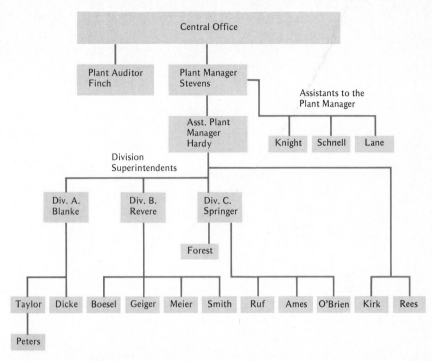

Central Office

Plant Auditor
Finch

Plant Manager
Stevens

Assistants to the
Plant Manager

Asst. Plant
Manager
Hardy

Knight   Schnell   Lane

Division
Superintendents

Div. A.
Blanke

Div. B.
Revere

Div. C.
Springer

Forest

Taylor Dicke Boesel Geiger Meier Smith Ruf Ames O'Brien Kirk Rees

Peters

Source: Melville Dalton, *Men Who Manage* (New York: John Wiley, 1959), p. 21.

FIGURE 10-3   Simplified formal organization chart of Milo

dominated. Hardy's approval was viewed as indispensable for important promotions; when breakdowns or emergency stops occurred, it was Hardy that supervisors feared. Further, many staff men viewed Hardy as the man to convince in order to get projects accepted.

Rees occupied a position that had previously been uninfluential. The prior incumbent had been promoted to an unimportant position as "assistant" to Stevens. Rees, however, had considerable power, which was apparently derived from his close association with corporate headquarters. These power alignments outside the plant differentiated him. He was in a different relationship to Stevens and Hardy. Dalton concluded that Hardy exceeded his legitimate power in every field of plant activity except those that Rees had broadly described as being within his industrial-relations sphere.

Although Springer was formally equal to the other two superintendents, he carried influence considerably greater than that of his peers. In fact, the other two superintendents consistently conferred with Springer before asking Hardy for favors. This power was apparently derived from

AUTHORITY

245

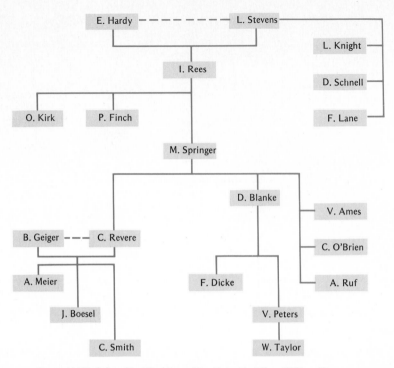

Source: Melville Dalton, *Men Who Manage* (New York: John Wiley, 1959), p. 22.

FIGURE 10-4   Power structure of Milo

Hardy, whom Springer had worked with for four years at corporate head-quarters and with whom he shared a close relationship.

This study dramatizes the difference between formal patterns of legitimate power and the realities and complexity of power patterns. Most important, the Milo study should not be viewed as an unusual or exceptional case. It is a picture of only one organization, but generally speaking, complex power derivations exist in all but the smallest of organizations.

summary of major points

1. Authority is the *right* to act, or command others to act, toward the attainment of organizational goals.
2. The traditional view of authority's source is society. A contrasting position

ORGANIZING

bases authority on the subordinate's willingness to accept and comply with a request.

3. The zone of indifference represents the legitimate authority within any position. There is no questioning of a superior's authority within this zone.

4. Three types of authority are frequently identified:
   a. Line, which contributes directly to the organizational objectives.
   b. Staff, which advises, services, or evaluates.
   c. Functional, which is authority over individuals or units outside one's own direct areas of command.

5. The chain of command consists of the authority connections between superior and subordinate, from the top to the bottom of the organization.

6. Delegation is the granting of authority downward to subordinate administrators, giving them both certain rights and providing certain prescribed limits for them to operate within.

7. Responsibility is the obligation to perform delegated duties and tasks.

8. Accountability is the obligation to a higher authority for satisfactory performance of the duties and tasks.

9. Decentralization refers to the degree to which authority has been delegated downward.

10. The evidence indicates that authority is generally as powerful an influence base as it was half a century ago.

11. Authority is a subset of power. Power refers to the ability to influence decisions, and authority is the legitimate dimension of that capability.

12. In addition to legitimate authority, there are four other power bases:
    a. Coercive
    b. Reward
    c. Expert
    d. Referent

FOR DISCUSSION

1. What is *authority*? How does it compare to power?

2. Contrast two divergent views on the source of authority.

3. Contrast *delegation* and *decentralization*.

4. What differentiates line, staff, and functional authority?

5. How are authority and organization structure interlocked?

6. "You need authority to make decisions." Build an argument to support this statement. Then build an argument against this statement.

7. What factors influence the degree to which an organization should be decentralized?

8. Identify and define the five bases of power. State whether each is derived primarily from the organization or from the individual.

Who's in charge here?

Diane Fitzgerald has just submitted her two-week notice to Dr. Davis, the administrative director of the Toronto General Hospital. She explains her decision to resign.

"I can't take it any longer here, Dr. Davis," Diane began. "I've been a nursing supervisor in the maternity wing for four months, but I can't get the job done. How can I do a job when I've got two or three bosses, each with different demands and priorities? Listen, I'm only human. Let me give you an example, but believe me, this is no atypical case. Things like this are happening *every* day.

I came into my office at 7:45 yesterday morning. I find a message on my desk from Dana Jackson (the hospital's head nurse). She tells me that she needs the bed-utilization report by 10:00 A.M. that day, so that she could make her presentation to the Board in the afternoon. I knew the report would take at least an hour and a half to prepare. Thirty minutes later, Joyce (the nursing floor supervisor and Diane's immediate supervisor) comes in and asks me why two of my nurses aren't on duty. I told her that Dr. Reynolds (head of surgery) had taken them off my floor and was using them to handle an overload in the Emergency Surgical wing. I told her I had objected, but Reynolds said there were no other options. So what does Joyce say? She tells me to get those nurses back in the maternity section immediately. What's more, she would be back in an hour to insure that I got things straightened out! I ask you, Dr. Davis, is this any way to run a hospital?"

Questions

1. What is the formal chain of command?
2. Who has acted outside his or her authority?
3. What can Dr. Davis do to improve conditions?
4. What types of informal power might Ms. Fitzgerald have developed to deal with competing demands?

FOR FURTHER READING

Albanese, R., "The Management of Authority," *SAM Advanced Management Journal*, January 1974, pp. 57–64. There are pressures decreasing the role of authority in organizations, as well as subtle pressures to increase it. Net result: it is changing but will not be eliminated.

Machiavelli, N., *The Prince*, ed. T.G. Gergin. New York: Appleton-Century-Crofts, 1964. The classic treatise on power and politics. Analyzes what practices had brought success in the past and deduces from them what principles ought to be followed for success in the present.

Mowday, R.T., "The Exercise of Upward Influence in Organizations," *Administrative Science Quarterly*, March 1978, pp. 137–56. Presents five methods of influence. Found that manipulation of information gives the greatest flexibility.

ORGANIZING

Pfeffer, J., "Power and Resource Allocation in Organizations," in *New Directions in Organizational Behavior*, ed. B.M. Staw and G.R. Salancik, pp. 235–65. Chicago: St. Clair Press, 1977. Looks at power, with particular attention paid to the role of social influence, the processes by which this influence is exercised, the bases of this influence, and the consequences of this perspective on organizations.

Sikula, A.F., "Administrative Authority," *Business and Society*, Spring 1975, pp. 22–30. Illustrates the similarities and differences among authority, power, responsibility and accountability. Discusses the sources of authority.

Zald, M.N., ed., *Power in Organizations*. Nashville, Tenn.: Vanderbilt University Press, 1970. A collection of papers and commentaries that serve to examine the role power and politics play upon control, decision making, and effecting and inhibiting change.

Chapter 11

Staffing the Organization

**AFTER
STUDYING
THIS CHAPTER,
YOU SHOULD
BE ABLE TO—**

**Define and
explain the
following
key terms
and
concepts:**

Job analysis
Job description
Bonafide occupational
qualifications

Type I errors
Type II errors
Assessment centers

Describe:

How information can be obtained as to what jobs are being done in an
organization

The value of a job description

The sources for identifying potential candidates

The validity of application forms, tests, interviews, and personal references as selection devices

An organization needs people. It requires both administrative and nonadministrative personnel to complete a variety of tasks and activities. Getting competent people is critical to the success of every organization, whether profit or nonprofit, public or private. Therefore, part of the organizing function is filling positions—putting the right person into the right job.

In this chapter we want to overview how administrators go about securing personnel (both other administrators and nonadministrators) to fit into the organization. Basically, this overview can best be achieved by breaking down the staffing activity into three major parts: job analysis, recruitment and selection.

Job analysis: assessing our needs

In chapters 9 and 10 we explained why it is necessary to divide work up and create authority relationships to facilitate coordination. When this is done, we are faced with jobs that have to be staffed. Staffing activity begins for most administrators with their finding out what jobs are being done and what skills are being utilized in these jobs. We call this "finding out" procedure *job analysis*. It is used to determine the kind of people needed to fill the job and culminates with a job description that identifies specific details about the job and the qualifications necessary to successfully complete it.

How do administrators get this information? Usually by studying people currently doing the job. Popular techniques include the following:

Observation Method—The employee is either watched directly or filmed on the job.

Individual Interview Method—Selected job incumbents are extensively interviewed, and the results of a number of these interviews are combined into a single job analysis.

Group Interview Method—Same as individual except that a number of job incumbents are interviewed simultaneously.

Structured Questionnaire Method—Employees check or rate the items they perform in their job from a long list of possible task items.

Technical Conference Method—Specific characteristics of a job are obtained from "experts," who usually are supervisors with extensive knowledge of the job.

Diary Method—Job incumbents record their daily activities in a diary or notebook.

A study, performed by California State College in Long Beach to determine the extent of job analysis being used across the United States, found that among the approximately nine hundred responding organizations, ranging in size from less than five hundred employees to over one hundred thousand, three-quarters indicated that they used job analysis.[1] For the respondents that did not use job analysis, the reasons most often cited were: (1) "It could serve no useful purpose," (2) "An acceptable system has not been found," (3) "It is too expensive," and (4) "It takes too much time." Of relevance was the researchers' finding that an organization's size was a good predictor of usage. Those with fewer than five hundred employees were less likely to have job analysis than larger organizations.

Information gathered by using one or more of the above methods allows the administrator to draw up a job description. Generally speaking, job descriptions are written statements of the tasks, duties, and behaviors required in a given job and the qualifications the job incumbents must possess. A common format for a job description might look as follows:

1. Job title.
2. Duties to be performed.
3. Distinguishing characteristics of the job.
4. Authority and responsibilities.
5. Specific qualifications necessary, such as required knowledge, skills, abilities, training, and experience.
6. Criteria by which job incumbents will be evaluated.

The job description acts as an important standard to guide administrators in determining whether candidates are qualified to fill job vacancies, and provides a point of comparison to determine whether individuals' actual job activities correspond to the duties outlined in the job description. For illustrative purposes, Figure 11-1 shows a description for the position of city engineer in Plattsburgh, New York.

Recruitment: finding potential candidates

Once we know our personnel needs, we can begin to do something about them. More specifically, we want to develop a comprehensive set of potential candidates to fill the positions identified in the job analysis.

But where can an administrator look to recruit potential candidates? There are a number of sources, but recruitment efforts are likely to be more successful if the source chosen reflects the type of position to be filled. For example, an ad in the Sunday *New York Times* Business Employment Section is more likely to be read by an executive seeking an administrative position in the $50,000 to $75,000-a-year bracket than by a watch repairman seeking to find employment. Similarly, a recruiter visiting a two-year vocational school in search of a recent college graduate with a background in the liberal arts and a master's degree in social work, to head a community social action agency, is obviously looking "for the right person in the wrong

[1] Jean J. Jones, Jr., and Thomas A. DeCotiis, "Job Analysis: National Survey Findings," *Personnel Journal*, October 1969, pp. 805–09.

FIGURE 11-1   A job description

Title: City Engineer; Plattsburgh, New York

General Statement of Duties: Has responsible charge of the professional engineering work of the city; does related work as required.

Distinguishing Features of the Class: This is an important professional engineering position involving responsibility for the planning and supervising of engineering activities. The work is performed under general supervision, with considerable leeway for the exercise of independent judgment in planning the details of projects and assuming responsibility for technical results. An incumbent in this position serves as a consultant to all city officials and departments on the engineering aspects of city projects.

Examples of Work: (Illustrative only)
Directs and coordinates the design of engineering projects, including
    plans, estimates, specifications and working drawings;
Checks and approves plans and specifications for street paving and
    grading, sewer and water line extensions, park development, recreational facilities and related public construction and repair projects;
Acts as consultant to other municipal departments on engineering
    problems;
Prepares specifications for projects to be put out for bids and reviews
    all bids submitted;
Reviews all construction work performed by private contractors;
Reviews ordinances and resolutions which relate to some aspect of
    civil engineering.

Required Knowledges, Skills and Abilities: Thorough knowledge of the principles and practices of civil engineering; thorough knowledge of procedures involved in the initiation, planning and development of engineering projects; ability to coordinate complex phases of an engineering program; ability to lay out the working details of engineering projects; initiative and resourcefulness; good professional judgment; good physical condition.

Acceptable Experience and Training: Four years of professional engineering experience, of which one year shall have been in a responsible capacity in the design and construction of streets, sidewalks or related projects, and graduation with a degree in civil engineering from an engineering school registered by the University of the State of New York; or any equivalent combination of experience and training.

Special Requirements for Acceptance of Applications: Eligibility for a license to practice as a professional engineer in New York State.*

* Possession of license will be required at time of appointment.

place." What we find, therefore, is that certain methods of recruitment are more effective for filling certain types of jobs.

Additionally, the scope of recruitment and the amount of effort devoted to it will be affected by the size of the organization and the level of the vacancy. We can hypothesize that the larger the organization, the easier it should be to recruit job applicants; and the higher the job is in the hierarchy, the greater should be the geographic scope for recruiting candidates to fill it. The ability to recruit qualified applicants appears to be strongly influenced by the size of the organization. There are at least three possible explanations for this. First, the larger the organization, the larger the pool of internal candidates. The City of Detroit Police Department will have more internal candidates to choose from when recruiting for detective positions than will the Police Department in Racine, Wisconsin. So, internal search is facilitated by size. Second, larger organizations have greater visibility. Though this can, at times, be a negative factor (if the organization has been the subject of unfavorable media attention, for example), visibility tends to be an asset. Support for this statement can be seen by visiting most college placement offices. Organizations like IBM, General Motors, Ford, and Shell Oil have large numbers of students who want to interview with them; while small or less well-known firms have significantly fewer students interested in interviewing. The third reason that large size makes recruiting easier is that potential candidates perceive larger organizations as offering greater opportunities for promotion. Especially where an organization emphasizes internal promotions, the larger its size and the more levels in its hierarchy, the more positions to which an individual can aspire.

Middle and top-level administrators in large organizations will have greater responsibilities (in terms of number of subordinates and costs) than their counterparts in smaller organizations, therefore, the search for candidates to fill such slots can justify wider and more thorough recruiting efforts. Similarly, top-level executives will have greater responsibilities than middle-level executives, so again a broader recruiting campaign can be justified based on the potential impact of their decisions on the future of the organization. Let us now take a look at the major sources administrators can look to in the search for job candidates.

Internal search

Most large organizations will attempt to develop their own employees for those jobs beyond the lowest level entry positions. When organizations give priority to internal candidates, we say they promote from within. There are a number of advantages to promotion from within: (1) it is good public relations, (2) it builds morale among employees, (3) it encourages good people who are ambitious, (4) it can act as a training device for developing middle- and top-level administrators, (5) it improves the probability of a correct selection decision, since information on the individual's performance is readily available, (6) it is less costly than going outside to recruit, and (7) internal selectees already know the organization.

ORGANIZING

254

Internal sources, of course, also have their disadvantages. Obviously, it would be self-defeating for the organization to utilize inferior internal sources simply because they are there, if excellent candidates are available on the outside. In addition, reliance on internal candidates can restrict diversity, new ideas, and people with fresh approaches to old problems.

In small organizations, an internal search can be done informally by merely reviewing a list of employees, their background and abilities, and their past performance appraisals. In large organizations, formal personnel files will usually be available to provide information. In fact, administrators in large organizations can use their computer information system to generate an output of those individuals within the organization who possess the characteristics desired. In those instances where administrators want to promote from within, but no satisfactory candidate is currently available, the internal search may identify individuals who, with some special training, may be able to assume promotion to higher and more complex tasks. In such cases, on-the-job training or the taking of some development courses may be just the thing to prepare internal candidates for future vacancies.

Advertisements

Advertisements are one of the most popular methods to communicate to the public that an organization has a vacancy. These advertisements might be placed on a sign outside a manufacturing firm's plant (i.e., "Now Hiring—Machinists"); or in community newspapers, regional periodicals, or nationally distributed professional journals.

The higher the position or the more specialized the skills sought, the more widely communicated the advertisement is likely to be. The search for a top executive might include advertisements in a national periodical, for example. On the other hand, the advertisement of blue-collar jobs is usually confined to the local daily newspaper or regional trade journals.

Advertisements are obviously an excellent way to reach the public concerning entry-level vacancies. However, even for organizations that rely almost completely on the internal search approach for filling vacancies, advertisements may have value. Ads can be used to "test" the market or to insure that internal candidates are reasonably competitive with external candidates. Advertisements have also gained in importance as evidence that the organization is making efforts to comply with government regulations stipulating that an organization's search for candidates does not discriminate against individuals because of race, color, religion, sex, or national origin. Broad exposure of information on vacancies increases an organization's opportunity to locate qualified females and minorities who may otherwise not be aware of the vacancy.

Employee referrals

One of the best sources of individuals who will perform effectively on the job is a recommendation from a current employee. At Michigan Bell, for example, it was found that 40 percent of employee-referred applicants were acceptable to the organization compared with only 11 percent from all other sources.[2]

It is not surprising that employee referrals are an excellent source of recruits. An employee will rarely recommend someone unless he believes that the individual can perform adequately. Such a recommendation reflects on the recommender, and when someone's reputation is at stake, we can expect the recommendation to be based on relatively strong beliefs. If there is any truth to the saying that "birds of a feather flock together," we might conclude that if the recommender is a good performer, there is a high probability that the applicant also would be effective on the job. And if the recommender is satisfied with his job and the organization as a whole, this can act as a stimulant to encourage his friends and acquaintances to consider employment opportunities in the organization.

Of course, one of the negative aspects of employee referrals is that recommenders may confuse friendship with job competence. Individuals often like to have their friends join them at their place of employment for social and even economic reasons (they can share transportation to work, for example), but this desire may cloud the recommender's perception of how effective the referral might be in successfully performing the job.

Employment agencies   Administrators may use employment agencies as sources for their staffing needs. For organizations that are small and have no formal personnel function, these agencies are often better equipped to identify quickly, and at lower cost, viable job candidates. Of course, employment agencies can be and are used by large organizations, too, because certain types of agencies possess the expertise and contacts that even the large organizations, with their huge personnel departments, do not have. We will describe three common forms of employment agencies: public, private, and executive search.

Public agencies   In North America, all U.S. states and Canadian provinces have a public employment service which provides services free or at nominal cost to employers and applicants. For example, in the U.S., a federal-state partnership was established in 1933 to help job seekers find suitable employment and to help employers find suitable workers. In the mid-1970s, these twenty-four hundred local employment service offices were processing more than 15 million applicants and close to 8 million job openings a year.[3]

Public agencies are a good source for securing individuals who are unskilled or possess minimum training and a poor source for individuals with high skills or extensive training. Why? It is not due to intent, but rather to the way in which the image of public agencies has evolved. Public agencies are perceived by prospective applicants as having few high-skilled and

---

[2] "Recruiting and Selecting Employees," *Studies in Personnel Policy,* no. 144 (New York: National Industrial Conference Board, 1954), p. 19.

[3] "The U.S. Employment Service," *Employment and Training Report of the President* (Washington, D.C.: Government Printing Office, 1976), pp. 121–22.

high-paying jobs, and employers tend to see such agencies as having few high-skilled applicants. Therefore, public agencies tend to attract and place predominantly low-skilled, blue-collar workers. The agencies' image as perceived by both applicants and employers tends to bring about a self-fulfilling prophecy: Few high-skilled individuals place their names with public agencies, and few employers look to these agencies for high-skilled applicants.

Private agencies How does a private agency which charges for its services compete with public agencies who give their services away? Clearly, they must do something different from that which the public agencies do, or at least give that impression.

The major difference between the public and private employment agencies is their image. That is, private agencies are believed to offer positions and applicants of a higher caliber. Additionally, private agencies provide a more complete line of services. They advertise the position, they screen applicants against the criteria specified by the employer, and they usually provide a guarantee of six months or a year as protection to the employer should the applicant not perform satisfactorily.

Executive search consultants The third agency source consists of executive search, management consulting, or what has been rather derogatorily called "head-hunting" firms. Rather than being a category completely separate from private employment agencies, they are more accurately described as a special case. Executive search agencies specialize in the placement of middle-level and top-level administrators.

The features that distinguish executive search agencies from most private employment agencies are the level at which they recruit; their fee, which is quite substantial; their nationwide contacts; and the thoroughness of their investigation. They will canvass their contacts and do some preliminary screening. They will seek out a highly effective executive who has the skills to do the job, can effectively adjust to the searching organization, and most importantly, is willing to consider new challenges and opportunities.

One of the major advantages of the executive search firm is that it can act as a buffer for screening candidates, yet keep the prospective employer anonymous. Only during the final stages of the search, when it is evident that both parties are interested, need the senior executives in the prospective organization move into the negotiations.

Temporary help services Organizations like Manpower, Incorporated and Kelly Girl Service can be a source of employees where individuals are needed on a short-term and temporary basis. Temporary rentals are particularly valuable in meeting short-term fluctuations in personnel needs. While traditionally developed in the office administration area, the temporary help service has recently expanded its coverage to include a broad range of skills. It is now possible, for example, to "rent" an engineer or a librarian as well as a secretary.

257

Schools, colleges and universities

Educational institutions at all levels offer opportunities for recruiting recent graduates. Most educational institutions operate placement services where prospective employers can review credentials and interview graduates. Whether the education sought involves a high school diploma, specific vocational training, or a college background with a bachelor's, master's, or doctoral degree, educational institutions are an excellent source of potential employees for entry-level positions in organizations.

But educational institutions are not only sources for young, inexperienced entrants to the workforce. It is not uncommon to find individuals with considerable work experience using an educational institution's placement service. This includes those who have work experience but recently returned to school to upgrade their skills, as well as former graduates interested in changing jobs and utilizing their school's placement center. So administrators seeking applicants can find not only new diploma recipients at the school, college, or university placement bureau, but also former graduates interested in pursuing other opportunities.

Professional organizations

Many professional organizations, including labor unions, operate placement services for the benefit of their members and employers. The professional organizations include such varied occupations as public administrator, industrial engineer, psychologist, and seafarer.

Many of these organizations publish rosters of job vacancies and distribute these lists to members. Administrators can usually have their vacancies listed for no charge. It is also common practice to provide placement facilities at regional and national meetings where those looking for employment and those looking for employees can find each other.

Unsolicited applicants

"Walk-ins," whether they reach an employer by letter, telephone, or in person, can be a major source of prospective applicants. Although the qualifications of unsolicited applicants will depend on economic conditions, the organization's image, and the perceived types of jobs that might be available, this source does provide an excellent supply of applicants. Even if there are no particular openings when the applicant makes contact, the application can be kept on file for later needs. If the individual is already employed, this source can still be referred to many months later and can provide applicants who are (1) interested in considering other employment opportunities and (2) regard the organization as a possible employer.

Other

In the search for particular types of applicants, nontraditional sources should be considered. For instance, Employ the Handicapped associations can be a source of highly motivated workers, a Forty-Plus Club can be an excellent place to find mature and experienced workers; and organizations like the National Organization for Women often provide placement services. Minorities can be located by contacting urban league offices, schools in the inner cities, and by using minority-oriented media.

ORGANIZING

We should not be surprised to find that recruiting is not a fully rational and distinct process. Many small employers keep no records of recruitment and use a variety of methods, whereas many large employers combine community relations and recruitment in a single endeavor.

The most frequently referenced and comprehensive study that sought to appraise the methods employers use in recruiting considered the hiring patterns of San Francisco Bay Area employers.[4] Results of this study suggested that no single method of recruitment was predominant in the area and that recruitment practices were adapted to job vacancies, employment rates, and other circumstances faced by the employer. In a follow-up to this study, researchers concluded that recruiting by employers was generally an informal process, influenced by structural elements in the labor market.[5]

Staffing practices in the U.S. federal government are coordinated under the jurisdiction of the U.S. Civil Service Commission, which makes generalizations somewhat more valid. Federal agencies' main sources are internal to the agency doing the searching or other units of the federal administration. In practice, only about 11 percent of the senior slots in the federal service are filled from the outside.[6]

For organizations in general, the following comment on recruiting is probably quite accurate: "Once a decision to hire has been made . . . many sophisticated systems adopt a Seat-of-the-Pants approach, and personnel managers depend on their 'feel' of the labor market in their choice of recruitment methods."[7]

Selection: making successful choices

The most critical stage in staffing is selection. All selection activities, whether they be the completion of an application form or the administering of interviews or tests, exist for the purpose of making effective selection decisions. That is, administrative decision makers seek to predict which job applicants will be successful if hired.

Purpose of selection activities

The selection decision dilemma is depicted in Figure 11-2. Notice that an administrator can only make two choices—to accept or reject a candidate. If we assume that candidates will either succeed or fail on the job, we end up with four possible outcomes. Two of these outcomes would be correct; two would be errors.

[4] F.T. Malm, "Recruiting Patterns and the Function of Labor Markets," *Industrial and Labor Relations Review,* July 1954, pp. 507–25.

[5] L. Ulman, M. Gordon, and H. Wilensky, "A Study of Employer Policies in a Large Metropolitan Labor Market Area," published under Federal Control No. 81-05-67-24 by the Institute of Industrial Relations, University of California, 1967.

[6] David T. Stanley, *The Higher Civil Service* (Washington: D.C.: Brookings Institution, 1964), p. 95.

[7] Robert W. Ericson, "Recruitment: Some Unanswered Questions," *Personnel Journal,* February 1974, p. 136.

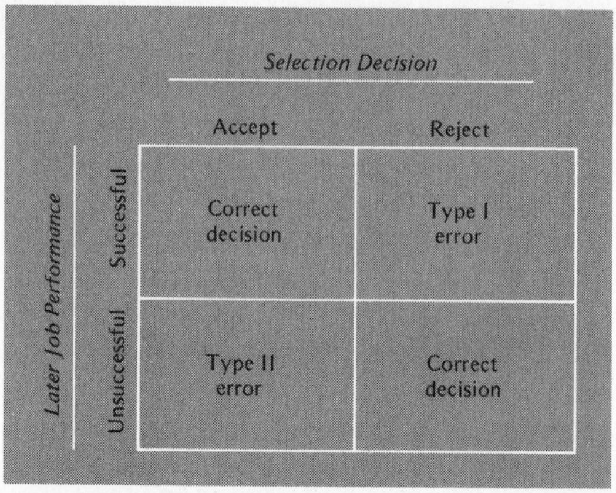

FIGURE 11-2   Selection decision outcomes

Correct decisions are those where the applicant we predicted to be successful later proved to be successful on the job, or where the applicant was predicted to be unsuccessful and would perform accordingly if hired. In the former case, we have successfully accepted; in the latter case, we have successfully rejected. Thus, the purpose of selection activites is to make accurate predictions; that is, to develop outcomes shown as "correct decisions" in Figure 11-2.

Problems occur when we make errors—by rejecting candidates who would later perform successfully on the job (Type I error) or accepting those who subsequently perform poorly (Type II error). These problems are, unfortunately, far from insignificant. Type I errors historically meant only that the costs in performing selection activities would be increased. Today, selection devices that result in Type I errors open the organization to charges of discrimination, especially if certain categories of applicants (i.e., women, minorities) are disproportionately rejected. Type II errors, on the other hand, have very obvious costs to the organization: training the employee, or firing the employee and incurring subsequent costs of further recruiting and selection screening. The major thrust of any selection activity, therefore, is to reduce the probability of making Type I and Type II errors, while increasing the probability of making correct decisions.

Selection devices

Administrators can use a number of selection devices to reduce Type I and II errors. The most popular of these devices are an analysis of the prospect's completed application form, employment tests, interviews, background investigation, and in some cases even a physical examination. In the next several pages, we will briefly review each of these devices, plus a recent phenomenon called the assessment center, giving particular attention to how effective each of these devices is in successfully predicting job performance.

260

The application form   The application form may require only that the prospect give his or her name, address, and telephone number. At the other extreme, an organization may use a comprehensive personal history profile, detailing the activities, skills, and accomplishments of the applicant.

Legislation during the past fifteen years has significantly affected what can and cannot be asked on an application form. For example, unless it can be shown to be a bona fide occupational qualification, in the United States it is illegal to ask information about sex, religion, race, marital status, or national origin. But legislation has not ruled out asking individuals hard biographical data; that is, items that can be verified (for example, your rank in your high school graduating class). Nor should administrators discount the value of using weighted applications, where information that has proven, over time, to be predictive of future success on the job is given a greater numerical weight in the application's assessment. For instance, some organizations have compared current and previous employees based on length of employment and biographical items such as local address, age, previous salary, and age of children, and have been able to develop a relatively high degree of reliability in predicting turnover for various types of jobs.

Employment tests   The same legislation that placed restrictions on what questions could be asked on applications has impacted even more heavily on employment testing. Today, the law stipulates that it is the responsibility of the employer to demonstrate that any test given—intelligence, aptitude, ability, interest—is job related. This is important because many tests in the past unintentionally discriminated. We know, for example, that minority candidates, as a group, score below the general population average on a number of selection tests. But this does not necessarily mean that their performance on the job would be below average. The reason is that almost all these tests were standardized against answers from white middle-class candidates.

How good are tests at predicting future job performance? Reviews of the research suggest that, for middle and senior-level executives, the evidence is mixed, with the majority of the findings indicating that tests are not effective predictors. Some studies report that personality and interest measures can indicate future administrative effectiveness,[8] but most fail to be accurate predictors.[9] Similarly, some find that intelligence, as measured by

---

[8] Edwin E. Ghiselli, *The Validity of Occupational Aptitude Tests* (New York: John Wiley, 1966); and G. Grimsley and H.F. Jarrett, "The Relation of Managerial Achievement to Test Measures Obtained in the Employment Situation: Methodology and Results," *Personnel Psychology,* Spring 1973, pp. 31–48, and Summer 1975, pp. 215–31.

[9] See, for example, Robert M. Guion and R.F. Gottier, "Validity of Personality Measures in Personnel Selection," *Personnel Psychology,* Spring 1965, pp. 135–64; Abraham K. Korman, "The Prediction of Managerial Performance: A Review," *Personnel Psychology,* Summer 1968, pp. 295–322; and A.N. Nash, "Vocational Interests of Effective Managers: A Review of the Literature," *Personnel Psychology,* Spring 1965, pp. 21–37.

verbal ability tests, is a useful predictor,[10] while others are unable to support such conclusions.[11] On a more positive note, the relationship of intelligence to successful job performance is more clear at the first-line supervisory level. Here the evidence indicates that intelligence is a fair predictor.[12] At the operative level, tests of intellectual ability, spatial and mechanical ability, perceptual accuracy, and motor ability all appear to have a moderate level of predictive capability for many semi-skilled and unskilled jobs in industrial organizations.[13]

What kind of conclusions can we draw from the above? It is probably accurate to state that the value of tests to predict job proficiency decreases as we move up the hierarchy. Tests are good predictors for jobs that are made up of clearly defined and routine activities. Typing and filing skills, as well as running a drill press, a lathe, and monitoring a radar display unit in an air control tower are examples of tasks that lend themselves to selection based heavily on the results of test scores. At the other extreme, it is difficult to develop valid job-related tests that can accurately predict success at performing such tasks as decision making and creating advertising slogans.

Employment interviews   It is indeed the rare candidate who is hired without an interview. The opportunity to talk directly with a candidate has a very special appeal; much of it probably originating in an administrator's belief that he or she has a talent for judging people and that the interview offers a satisfactory vehicle for getting information that the administrator can use in appraising whether this individual will be a successful job performer.

In spite of its popularity, the value of the interview in making better selection decisions has been the subject of considerable debate, with most of the evidence stacking up against the interview as an effective predictive tool. It has been described as a "costly, inefficient and usually invalid procedure."[14] In brief, the criticism surrounding the interview centers on prejudgments and inconsistent interpretations made by the interviewer.

The evidence generally concludes that interviewers develop a stereotype of a good job applicant and that this stereotype clouds objective judgments. Interviewers tend to believe that it is desirable for employees to be trustworthy, dependable, conscientious, responsible, stable, and so forth, leading one set of researchers to conclude that "being a Boy Scout will get an applicant to first base in nearly any occupation."[15]

[10] Grimsley and Jarrett, op. cit.
[11] Korman, op. cit. and A.I. Kraut, "Intellectual Ability and Promotional Success Among High Level Managers," *Personnel Psychology*, Summer 1969, pp. 281–90.
[12] Grimsley and Jarrett, op. cit.; and Korman, op. cit.
[13] Edwin E. Ghiselli, "The Validity of Aptitude Tests in Personnel Selection," *Personnel Psychology*, Winter 1973, p. 475.
[14] Marvin D. Dunnette and Bernard M. Bass, "Behavioral Scientists and Personnel Management," *Industrial Relations*, May 1963, p. 117.
[15] Milton D. Hakel and Allan J. Schuh, "Job Applicant Attributes Judged Important Across Seven Diverse Occupations," *Personnel Psychology*, Spring 1971, pp. 45–52.

Another unsettling fact about interviews is that interviewers generally draw early impressions which become very quickly entrenched, and negative information exposed early in the interview tends to be more heavily weighted than if that same information were conveyed later.[16] Studies indicate that most interviewers' decisions change very little after the first four or five minutes of the interview. As a result, information elicited early in the assessment process carries greater weight than does information elicited later, and a "good applicant" is probably characterized more by the absence of unfavorable characteristics than by the presence of favorable characteristics.

Finally, because interviews usually have so little consistent structure, an individual may "look" good in one instance and not in another. Even where studies have sought to have interviewers treat interviewees consistently, there are still inconsistencies in the interviewers' interpretation of the data they obtain.[17]

Does the above mean the interview is worthless? NO! We suggest that the more nonroutine the job, especially among top administrative positions, the more weight that should be placed on the interview as a selection device. The interview, as a relatively subjective predictor of specific job skills, has demonstrated that it is a reasonably effective method for discerning an individual's interpersonal skills and level of motivation.[18] In jobs where these characteristics are important in determining success, the interview can be a valuable selection input. In nonroutine activities, especially top-level administrative positions, failure (as measured by involuntary terminations) is more frequently caused by a poor fit between the individual and the organization than by lack of competence on the part of the individual. So interviewing can be useful when it emphasizes the ability of the candidate to fit into the organization rather than specific technical skills.

Background investigations The background investigation may be merely asking the applicant to supply "three letters of reference," or it may include direct contact with former employers to confirm the employee's work record and to learn of their appraisal of her performance, contacting other job-related references and personal references, and/or verifying the educational accomplishments shown on the application.

Several studies have suggested that administrators should take the time to verify the information given on an application. One found nearly a quarter of the returned reference checks indicated significant deviations from information supplied by the applicant on dates of employment, job

[16] See, for example, Edward C. Webster, *Decision Making in the Employment Interview* (Montreal: Industrial Relations Center, McGill University, 1964); and Lawrence H. Peters and James R. Terborg, "The Effects of Temporal Placement of Unfavorable Information and of Attitude Similarity on Personnel Selection Decisions," *Organizational Behavior and Human Performance,* April 1975, pp. 279–93.
[17] Eugene C. Mayfield in Neal Schmitt's "Social and Situational Determinants of Interview Decisions: Implications for the Employment Interview," *Personnel Psychology,* Spring 1976, p. 81.
[18] Ibid., p. 97.

title, past salary, or reasons for leaving a prior position.[19] Another study found that when application form information was checked with the applicant's previous employer, more than half had a discrepancy concerning either the duration of previous employment or previous salary earned.[20] The average overestimation by former employees of time spent on their previous job was sixteen months and, incredibly, 15 percent of the employers stated that the applicant had *never* worked for them!

While verifying data on the application form may provide information that aids in making the selection decision, the same cannot generally be said for personal references or performance evaluations supplied by previous employers. Who among us does not have at least three friends who will attest to our "fantastic attitude, abilities and motivation"? Since we can assume that almost everyone has a few friends, the value of personal references must be heavily discounted. Positive appraisals, or lack of, by previous employers should also be viewed skeptically. Many employers are reluctant to speak candidly about a former employee's job performance. Personal likes and dislikes will heavily influence the type of recommendation given. It is not unheard of for a mediocre employee to be given a high recommendation to encourage another employer to hire him away, or for an excellent employee to be given a low appraisal to discourage those interested in his services from pursuing him further. Finally, it is necessary to question the basic validity of performance evaluation. Since it is far from a science, what does a good or bad evaluation really mean? Moreover, can we assume that the employee will perform the same way on her new job as she did on her old one?

Physical examination   For jobs that require certain physical characteristics, the physical examination may provide relevant selection information. However, few jobs can meet this requirement today. Minimum height and weight requirements, for example, are not prima facie evidence that one has the strength to be a police officer or a life guard. When physical strength is a requirement for a job, specific strength tests should be administered. This will minimize the possibility that the requirements will become a form of sex discrimination. It is probably fair to conclude that the physical examination offers little in the way of relevant information in the selection decision other than to insure that the candidate meets the minimum standards for the organization's group life and medical insurance programs.

Assessment centers   The last selection device we will discuss is the assessment center, a procedure for appraising an individual's ability to perform executive activities. It is an effective way of identifying and evaluating administrative ability. Most importantly, it has consistently demonstrated re-

[19] Robert Hershey, "The Application Form," *Personnel,* January–February 1971, pp. 36–39.
[20] Irwin L. Goldstein, "The Application Blank: How Honest Are the Responses?" *Journal of Applied Psychology,* October 1971, pp. 491–92.

sults that predict later job performance,[21] in organizations as diverse as AT&T, Standard Oil, Sears, Roebuck, and the Social Security Administration. Its strength appears to lie with the fact that assessment center judgments are not based on some substitute for performance, but rather the applicant's exhibited behavior which parallels the behavior required on the job.

Assessment centers provide an opportunity for line executives and supervisors to view candidates who have been considered for a particular job. In the presence of the assessors, the candidates go through an evaluating procedure consisting of from six to eight "games" in order to simulate real problems that the successful candidate may confront in an administrative position. Based on a list of descriptive dimensions that the actual job incumbent will have to meet, activities might include an interview, an in-basket exercise, case discussion, simulation exercises, and decision games.

As we have noted, the results from the use of assessment centers has been quite impressive. They do an excellent job of predicting those who will move ahead in an organization. However, a recent review of research on assessment centers concluded that though results are impressive and consistent, they are based on relatively few studies and, most importantly, many of these studies may be biased by using promotion as a predictive criterion.[22] Given that promotions are rarely based solely on performance, assessment evaluators will come up with effective results if they know what factors administrators actually use to make promotion decisions.

A review of selection devices in the hiring of administrators in Canadian business firms is probably generalizable to North America. This study revealed that interviews were used the most frequently (73.5%), followed by references (72.1%), application forms (64.7%), and tests (27.9%).[23] Other studies confirm interviews to be the primary selection device, with its frequency in some cases exceeding 98% of the surveyed organizations.[24] What is disturbing, particularly given the interview's low predictive capability, is the apparent weight that administrators give this device in the overall selection decision. Though the evidence is skimpy, impressions from the interview

---

[21] See, for example, B.M. Cohen, J.L. Moses, and W.C. Byham, *The Validity of Assessment Centers: A Literature Review,* Monograph II (Pittsburgh: Development Dimensions Press, 1974); Allen I. Kraut, "A Hard Look at Management Assessment Centers and Their Future," *Personnel Journal,* May 1972, pp. 317–26; and John R. Hinrichs, "An Eight-Year Follow-Up of a Management Assessment Center," *Journal of Applied Psychology,* October 1978, pp. 596–601.

[22] Richard J. Klimoski and William J. Strickland, "Assessment Centers—Valid or Merely Prescient," *Personnel Psychology,* Autumn 1977, pp. 353–61.

[23] Harish C. Jain, "Managerial Recruitment and Selection in the Canadian Manufacturing Industry," *Public Personnel Management,* May–June 1974, pp. 207–15.

[24] William R. Spriegel and Virgil A. James, "Trends in Recruitment and Selection Practices," *Personnel,* November–December 1958, pp. 42–48; and D.E. Robertson, "Personnel Testing Practices in Wisconsin Industry," (unpublished master's thesis, University of Wisconsin, 1965).

appear to be weighed more heavily than test scores, application blank information, or previous employer references.[25]

The usage of tests tends to be generally a function of the size of the organization. A recent review of testing practices at 2500 companies found that 36.5 percent of the firms did no testing, but that ranged from 61 percent for those with fewer than one hundred employees to less than 40 percent for employers with five thousand or more employees.[26] Of greater importance were the respondents' comments regarding changes in testing practice: 75 percent had reduced their usage, and nearly 14 percent expected to soon discontinue testing.[27] A survey of local city and county government practices in Arizona revealed that 66 percent of the large jurisdictions used written tests for selection, while only 14 percent of the small jurisdictions did.[28]

Finally, evidence suggests that, in the selection of administrative personnel, the assessment center is growing in popularity. Approximately two thousand organizations are now involved in some form of assessment project,[29] and given the assessment center's consistently high ratings, its usage should grow rapidly during the 1980s.

[25] H. Charles Pyron, "The Use and Misuse of Previous Employer Reference in Hiring," *Management of Personnel Quarterly,* Summer 1970, pp. 15–22.

[26] "Employee Testing and Selection Procedures: Where Are They Headed?" in *Personnel Management Policies and Practices* (Englewood Cliffs, N.J.: Prentice-Hall, Inc., 1975).

[27] Ibid.

[28] V.M. Lochr et al., "Personnel Selection Methods Used in Arizona Local Government," *Public Personnel Management,* September–October 1973, pp. 327–31.

[29] W.C. Byham, "The Assessment Center as an Aid in Management Development," *Training and Development Journal,* December 1971, pp. 10–22.

summary of major points

1. Part of the organizing function is ensuring that the right person is put into the right job.
2. Job analysis ascertains what jobs are being done and the skills utilized in these jobs.
3. Data to do a job analysis can be obtained through the:
    a. Observation method
    b. Individual interview method
    c. Group interview method
    d. Structured questionnaire method
    e. Technical conference method
    f. Diary method
4. Job descriptions are a written statement of the tasks, duties, and behaviors required in a given job and the qualifications the job incumbents must possess.

5. The recruitment method should reflect the type of position to be filled. Popular methods include:
   a. Internal search
   b. Advertisements
   c. Employee referrals
   d. Employment agencies
   e. Temporary help services
   f. Schools, colleges, and universities
   g. Professional organizations
   h. Unsolicited applicants
6. The most critical stage in staffing is selection; that is, predicting which job applicants will be successful if hired.
7. The most popular selection devices include:
   a. Application forms
   b. Employment tests
   c. Interviews
   d. Background investigations
   e. Physical examinations
8. The most effective device for selecting administrators is the assessment center.

FOR DISCUSSION

1. Write a job description for your instructor. Where would your college recruit to fill such a job? What selection devices might improve the quality of the selection decision?

2. Write a job description for a clerk at a nearby grocery store. Where would this store recruit to fill such a job? What selection devices might improve the quality of the selection decision?

3. "The perfect advertisement will be so worded that only one applicant will respond and he or she will be the ideal candidate." Do you agree or disagree with this statement? Support your position.

4. Why would an organization pay a private employment agency to recruit candidates for a position when a public employment agency provides its service for free?

5. What are Type I and Type II errors in applicant selection? Discuss the effects of each of these errors on a unit's performance.

6. Describe the strengths and weaknesses of each of the following as an effective selection device:
   a. Tests
   b. Interviews
   c. References

7. Demonstrate how our discussion of the realities of decision making in chapter 5 relates to the topic of interviewing.

8. How can the assessment center be used to improve selection?

Wanted: superintendent of schools

The Tucson Public School District includes 32 elementary, 8 junior high, and 7 high school sites, with a combined enrolment of 40,000 students. To staff the system, TPS employs 1,300 teachers, 125 administrators, and over 400 supportive personnel. The superintendent of the district, Dr. Lee, has held his position for over 20 years but has announced his intention to retire next year.

The school board recognizes the importance of obtaining an effective educator to head up TPS. In their most recent meeting they agreed that they should begin recruiting for a replacement for Dr. Lee as soon as possible. They also agreed on some general qualities they would expect in the successful candidate: an understanding of the role of elementary and secondary public education in the community; an effective and dynamic speaker; the ability to develop and administer budgets; a sensitivity to the needs of minorities; a progressive philosophy toward creative learning; and a track record that will command the respect of teachers, parents, students, and influencial members of the community.

Questions

1. What recruiting sources should the board consider?
2. What criteria would predict successful performance in the job of school superintendent?

FOR FURTHER READING

Adler, S., "Using Assessment Centers in Small Organizations," *Personnel Journal,* September 1978, pp. 484–87. Reviews the assessment center concept, giving special consideration to its use in small organizations.

Fine, S., "What's Wrong with the Hiring System?" *Organizational Dynamics,* Autumn 1975, pp. 55–67. The author argues that hiring procedures are ineffective and discriminatory. A better procedure—differential placement—involves self-selected employment based on matching capabilities with job requirements.

Novit, M.N., *Essentials of Modern Personnel Management.* Englewood Cliffs, N.J.: Prentice-Hall, Inc., 1979, chap. 2. Reviews the major laws and regulations that govern the staffing function.

Rice, B., "Measuring Executive Muscle," *Psychology Today,* December 1978, pp. 95–110. Interesting description of how the assessment center is used at American Airlines.

Robbins, S.P., *Personnel: The Management of Human Resources.* Englewood Cliffs: N.J.: Prentice-Hall, Inc., 1978, chap. 4 and 5. A more comprehensive review of recruitment and selection.

Wanous, J.P., "Tell It Like It Is at Realistic Job Previews," *Personnel,* July–August 1975, pp. 50–60. Realistic job previews increase the probability of job survival but do not reduce the flow of capable applicants.

ORGANIZING

Chapter 12

Organizing for Maximum Performance

AFTER STUDYING THIS CHAPTER, YOU SHOULD BE ABLE TO—

Quality of work life
Job rotation
Work modules
Task force
Ombudsperson
Job enrichment

Shorter workweek
Flex-time
Matrix structure
Committee structure
Enriched environment

The potential problems created by bureaucracies

The difference between minor and major structural modifications

The similarities and differences between job rotation and work modules

How project, committee, and matrix structures facilitate coordination

The role of an ombudsperson

The advantages and disadvantages of job enrichment

The advantages and disadvantages of the shorter workweek and flex-time

The differences between enriched environments and enriched jobs

What do we know about work design that can guide administrators in altering structural elements so as to maximize employee performance? It will be the purpose of this chapter to offer some answers to this crucial question.

During the past decade there has been an extensive effort to experiment with structural techniques that might improve the quality of work life. These techniques have, for the most part, sought to encourage employee involvement in his or her work, increase freedom and autonomy, reduce boredom, and lessen conflict with the goals of the organization. This effort has evolved out of a concern that the bureaucratic model, as described in chapter 9, limits human and organizational potential. It has been argued, for example, that improvements in the quality of work life might lead to more positive feelings toward one's self, toward one's job, and toward the organization; might further lead to improved physical and psychological health, and to greater growth and development of the individual as a person and as a productive member of the organization; and finally, can lead to decreased absenteeism and turnover, fewer accidents, and higher quality and quantity of output of goods and services.[1]

The above is a rather optimistic perspective, but it nevertheless summarizes what some scholars and practitioners believe: that redesigning jobs is a powerful approach to improving worker performance. Though much of this enthusiasm is almost evangelical in nature, with a questionable research foundation, some studies have demonstrated startling results. What we will attempt to do, therefore, is review a broad selection of structural techniques or modifications, giving particular attention to the presence or absence of data that will allow us to conclude how successful each might be in improving a worker's performance and an organization's effectiveness.

However, as you review the content of this chapter, it is a good idea to keep in mind that the relevance of these techniques tends to increase with the size of the organization. We propose that the larger an organization becomes, the more its administrators should consider structural modifications to offset potential declines in employee satisfaction.

We previously discussed the fact that bureaucracy is not, in and of itself, bad. However, the majority of individuals in bureaucracies find the rules and impersonality disagreeable, hence the value of structural modifications. In contrast, the benefits provided by most of the structural modifications discussed in the chapter are rarely needed by the small organization; it already is flexible and adaptive, and employees rarely experience the alienation to their work that can accompany extensive division of labor.

---

[1] J. Lloyd Suttle, "Improving Life at Work—Problems and Prospects," in *Improving Life at Work,* ed. J. Richard Hackman and J. Lloyd Suttle (Santa Monica, Ca.: Goodyear Publishing, 1977), p. 9.

Different degrees of structural modification

We have chosen to present the techniques for structural modification within a framework of two categories. The first we have called "Minor Structural Modifications" and the other "Major Structural Modifications." Before we review each category, let us note the purpose behind this division.

The labels "minor" and "major" are somewhat arbitrary names. What they attempt to demonstrate is that some structural modifications are relatively simple and straightforward and can be implemented with minimal disturbance to the organization. In contrast, other modifications are complex and are difficult to implement without creating substantial disturbance throughout the organization.

We, therefore, propose the following: Minor structural modifications, in contrast to the major techniques, tend to be less complex, require less commitment from the top administration in order to be effective, and can be implemented in an isolated administrative unit without significant ramifications to the organization as a whole (although they can certainly be implemented on an organizationally-wide scale). The minor techniques fall within the discretion of many lower- and middle-level administrators; whereas the comprehensiveness, complexity, or visibility of the major techniques, if they are to be effective, require top executive support.

Minor structural modifications

We have identified four modifications as being relatively easy to implement within a given department or division with minimal negative effects on other organizational units. These are: job rotation, work modules, projects and task forces, and the creation of an ombudsperson position.

Job rotation

Job rotation allows workers to diversify their activities and offset the occurrence of boredom. There are two types of rotation: vertical and horizontal. Vertical rotation is really nothing more than promoting a worker into a new position. However, since bureaucracies exist in pyramid-shaped organizations and therefore have a continually reduced opportunity for promotion, we will emphasize the horizontal dimension of job rotation, or what may be better understood as lateral transfer.

Horizontal job transfers can be instituted on a planned basis—that is, by means of a training program whereby the employee spends two or three months in an activity and is then moved on. This approach, for example, is common among large Wall Street law firms where new associates work for many different partners before choosing an area of specialization. Horizontal transfers can also be made on a situational basis—moving the person to another activity when the first is no longer challenging or when the needs of work scheduling require it. In other words, people may be put in a continual transfer mode. As employed by many large organizations in their programs to develop administrative talent, rotation may include moving people between line and staff positions, often allowing an employee to understudy a more experienced organizational member.

The advantages of job rotation are clear. It broadens employees and gives them a range of experiences. Boredom and monotony, which develop after a person has acquired the skills to perform his or her task effectively, are reduced when transfers are made frequently. Finally, since a broad experience permits a greater understanding of other activities within the organization, people are prepared more rapidly to assume greater responsibility, especially at the upper echelons. In other words, as one moves up the organization, it becomes increasingly necessary to understand the intricacies and interrelationships of activities; and these skills can be more quickly acquired by moving about within the organization.

On the other hand, job rotation is not without its drawbacks. Training costs are increased and productivity is reduced by moving a worker into a new position just when his or her efficiency at the prior job was creating organizational economies. An extensive rotation program can result in having a vast number of employees situated in positions where their experience is very limited. And even though there may be significant long-term benefits from the program, the organization must be equipped to deal with the day-to-day problems that result when inexperienced personnel perform new tasks, and when rotated administrators make decisions based on little experience in the activity at hand. Job rotation can also demotivate intelligent and aggressive trainees who seek specific responsibility in their chosen specialty. Finally, there is some evidence that rotation that is imposed involuntarily on employees increases absenteeism and accidents.[2]

Formal job rotation appears to be used more as an executive development technique than as a device to reduce job boredom, yet even in this usage it is far from widespread. A survey of over 250 line administrators from both industry and government, inquiring into organizational practices in employee development, found that less than 2 percent of their organizations were using job rotation.[3] It would appear, even though there is little empirical evidence to support this contention, that informal rotation practices are much more prevalent.

Work modules If we can conceive of extremely rapid job rotation, to the point where one would assume new activities every few hours, we can comprehend the technique of work modules. It has been suggested as a solution to meet the

[2] Martin J. Gannon, Brian A. Poole, and Robert E. Prangley, "Involuntary Job Rotation and Work Behavior," *Personnel Journal*, June 1972, pp. 446–48.

[3] Benjamin B. Tregoe, "What is OD?," *Training and Development Journal*, March 1974, p. 18.

problem of fractionated, boring, and programmed work, at an acceptable price, with undiminished quality and quantity of product.[4]

Prof. Robert Kahn, of the University of Michigan, has defined a work module as a time task unit, equal to approximately two hours of work at a given task. A normal forty-hour-a-week job would then be defined in terms of four modules a day, five days a week, for between 48 and 50 weeks a year.

Through the use of modules, it would be possible to increase diversity for workers. Undesirable work could be spread about, for example, by having everyone take a module or two each day. The result would be that people would change activities through changing work modules. Or, as we noted previously, it can be viewed as a very rapid job rotation system.

The benefits of work modules lie in increasing diversity for the employees, by dividing up and sharing the undesirable work activities, expanding work independence to the bottom of the hierarchy, and constructing the job to meet the needs of the individual, rather than forcing people to fit a particularly defined job.

However, work modules do present some problems. Considerable time and money are involved in planning and executing the changeover. Dysfunctional conflicts can develop over the question of equity and the allocation of modules. Bookkeeping, and payroll-computation costs increase. Finally, as we noted with a rotation program, there is a loss of expertise, and with it, an increased possibility of errors.

It is safe to say that use of work modules, in practice, is rare. Your author is familiar with several business firms that have taken a certain group of jobs and organized them so that workers trade activities each day after lunch, but these are isolated practices representing fewer than 100 employees in corporations that employ tens of thousands.

Projects or task forces

In organizations faced with a dynamic and changing environment, it may be desirable to structure some activities with considerable flexibility. Such structures could be highly adaptive and temporary, existing only for the life of an activity. This describes project structures or task forces.

These are temporary organizational units, developed for the purpose of achieving a given objective. Once that objective is attained, the unit disbands. The achievement of the objective is the only time limit involved. The project administrator may select his staff from across the present organization lines—taking a few accountants from accounting, a purchasing agent from the purchasing department, engineers from engineering, and so forth—or he may hire outside to fill slots in his project. This interdisciplinary unit, then, can attack a problem without the coordination difficulties

[4] Robert L. Kahn, "The Work Module," *Psychology Today,* February 1973, pp. 35–39.

that would arise if individuals with varying expertise worked on the problem while still entrenched in their separate departments.

The use of projects became highly developed in the 1960s by the aerospace industry, which used them as a structural way to deal with the uncertainty inherent in bidding on government contracts: the awarding of contracts occurs irregularly, and they have a given objective with a limited life span. However, the concept is not unique to the aerospace industry. Consumer-product firms, such as Procter & Gamble, use the structure to design and develop new products. In the creation of a new toothpaste, for example, people with expertise from finance, manufacturing, marketing, product design, research, and other relevant units may be brought together to create the product, design its package, determine its market, compute its manufacturing cost, and determine its profit. Once the problems have been fully worked out of the product and it is ready to be produced in quantity, the task group disbands and the toothpaste is integrated into the functional operation of the organization.

Although project structures are now used primarily by aerospace firms, consulting organizations, the federal government, and to some extent by business and industry, with the growth of knowledge-centered organizations, we might postulate a growing usage of project structures in the future.

The ombudsperson

Still another structural technique to improve an organization's performance is the creation of an ombudsperson position.[5] An ombudsperson's role is to provide a means by which employees can get an objective review of their complaints and appeals by a third party. Further, the role is independent, attempting to favor neither the organization or employee.

This position may be formally created and filled by a fulltime incumbent. For small organizations this may not be practical, but the concept can still be used. The ombudsperson may, for example, simply be an individual elected or appointed to handle grievances in addition to his or her normal duties. Or in large organizations, a department or division may choose to have an ombudsperson as an outlet for internal disputes.

An ombudsperson can contribute to a more effective organization by creating a fact-finding mechanism and an outlet for employee grievances when the traditional channels fail. Issues that typically are aired with an ombudsperson include complaints over salary, performance evaluation, promotion decisions, and layoffs. But the ombudsperson is not meant to circumvent the traditional authority lines within the organization. Employees first take the complaint to their immediate superior. If the employee is not satisfied with the outcome, he or she then takes the complaint to the om-

---

[5] Isidore Silver, "The Corporate Ombudsman," *Harvard Business Review,* May–June 1967, pp. 77–87.

budsperson. If the grievance appears valid or deserves further investigation to determine its validity, the ombudsperson attempts to get the facts and work out a satisfactory solution. Importantly, the ombudsperson will discuss the grievance with the employee's immediate administrative superior only if the employee agrees. In most cases, if the employee, the administrator, and the ombudsperson cannot work out a settlement that the ombudsperson thinks is fair, the ombudsperson can go to the administrator's administrator and, if necessary, to a senior executive (usually vice-president or higher). But the ombudsperson has no authority to overrule an administrator's decision. Since the ombudsperson position itself usually reports to such a senior executive, in order to maintain its required independence, the ombudsperson usually has the ear and support of the organization's top administration in resolving grievances.

The ombudsperson idea appears to have gained little momentum. In the early 1970s, the idea appeared to be spreading through U.S. industry, but it never really caught on. By the mid-1970s, Xerox Corp. and General Electric were cited by *Business Week* as having one or more ombudspeople, although Boeing Vertol had phased theirs out.[6] The ombudsperson's greatest acceptance has been in government. Many large cities, states and provinces, and the federal government use the ombudsperson both to adjudicate problems between citizens and government and to work with employee complaints.

Major structural modifications

The structural modifications that follow tend to require major efforts and commitments by the top administration of an organization. If nothing else, implementation of these suggestions is usually highly visible, thus making it difficult for individual lower-level administrators to implement them unobtrusively. The modifications we will discuss will be job enrichment, the shorter workweek, flex-time, matrix structures, committee structures, and programs which bring administrative job privileges to *all* employees.

Job enrichment

The technique that has received the widest attention in the search to improve the quality of work life is job enrichment.

A job is enriched by allowing the worker to assume some of the tasks executed by his or her supervisor. Enrichment requires that workers do increased planning and controlling of their work, usually with less supervision and more self-evaluation. From the standpoint of increasing the internal rewards from a job, it has been proposed that job enrichment offers great po-

[6] "Where Ombudsmen Work Out," *Business Week,* May 3, 1976, pp. 114–16.

tential.[7] However, job enrichment is successful only when it increases responsibility, increases the employee's freedom and independence, organizes tasks so as to allow workers to do a complete activity, and provides feedback to allow individuals to correct their own performance.

A successful job enrichment program should ideally increase employee satisfaction. But since organizations do not exist to create employee satisfaction as an end, there must also be direct benefits to the organization. There is evidence that job enrichment produces lower absenteeism and reduced turnover costs; but on the critical issue of productivity, the evidence is inconclusive. In some situations, job enrichment has increased productivity; in others, productivity has been decreased. However, when it decreases, there does appear to be consistently conscientious use of resources and a higher quality of product or service. In other words, in terms of efficiency, for the same input a higher quality of output is obtained.

In order to get a better idea of what enriched jobs are like, we will briefly review job enrichment efforts at the Buick division of General Motors, Volvo in Sweden, and a pet food plant of General Foods in Topeka, Kansas.

The Buick experiment[8] The Buick Product Engineering group decided in the early 1970s to analyze the job of Assembler for enriching. An Assembler is a skilled hourly mechanic, responsible for performing experimental changes in fleet cars as ordered by the Design Engineers and for keeping the fleet cars in top operating condition. The Product Engineering group included forty-five Assemblers.

The Assembler's content of daily tasks was restructured and redefined, but the job description itself was not changed. Job modifications included such things as allowing the Assembler to:

Correct any deficiencies discovered and to record the action on a work sheet (this job modification was selected as the most practical for initial introduction).
Choose his own work assignment.
Contact the Design Engineer directly.
Inspect his own work.
Establish his own completion dates and job hour content.

Presentations concerning the proposed job restructuring were made to departmental management, the Design Engineers, and the union. An informal approach was used to introduce the program to the Assemblers. Each foreman handled implementation according to his assessment of the best

[7] See, for example, F. Herzberg, B. Mausner, and B. Snyderman, *The Motivation to Work* (New York: John Wiley, 1959); Louis E. Davis, *Design of Jobs* (London: Penguin, 1972); and R.N. Ford, *Motivation Through the Work Itself* (New York: American Management Association, 1969).
[8] F.J. Schotters, "Job Enrichment at Buick Products Engineering," *GM Personnel Development Bulletin*, no. 22, June 4, 1973.

way to approach his employees. He determined the feelings in his own group and in most cases introduced additional job modifications on a man-to-man basis. Acceptance of the project was also fostered by the Assemblers themselves—who often "sold" the program to each other through informal discussions.

One of the ways that each supervisor tracked project progress was by recording the reactions from his Assemblers. In some cases implementation of the job modifications was too fast and negative feedback occurred— "How come I have to write these tickets? Did they take all the pencils away from the engineers?"

During the early stages of the program, some Design Engineers also expressed objections to the redefined duties. However, as communication between Assemblers and Design Engineers improved and as additional phases of job restructuring were introduced, most difficulties were worked out through face-to-face discussion.

This interpersonal approach prevented the program from becoming a "management directive" and resulted in management credibility and in employee acceptance of the project.

Since implementation of the job enrichment program, the following changes have been observed by Product Engineering supervision:

> Productivity has increased nearly 13 percent (as measured by increased work tickets per Assembler per month).
>
> Petty grievances (where no discipline is assessed) have been virtually eliminated.
>
> Fleet cars are kept in better mechanical condition because Assemblers have shown initiative in discovering and repairing such discrepancies as rattles, steering gear whine, defective exhaust systems, and engine starting problems.
>
> Departmental morale has improved considerably, along with increased pride and interest in the work.
>
> Communication and personal relationships between and among Assemblers, foremen and Design Engineers have increased and improved. (Assemblers now call or visit engineers to personally discuss projects.)

The Volvo experiment[9] The Kalmar plant of Volvo was designed to avoid the traditional assembly-line design for automobile manufacturing. The plant was designed to facilitate the building of cars in groups or teams. The reason for Volvo's decision to experiment with building cars in teams was far from altruistic. Productivity per se was not a major issue; rather the problem was high employee withdrawal rates. The company was experiencing levels of absence and turnover that had become increasingly expensive, and Volvo felt that it had to do something to make automobile assembly jobs more interesting. In contrast to North America, where auto-

[9] Adapted from Richard E. Walton, "From Hawthorne to Topeka and Kalmar," in *Man and Work in Society,* ed. E.L. Cass and F.G. Zimmer (New York: Van Nostrand Reinhold, 1975), pp. 120–21.

mobile manufacturers are also concerned with high levels of withdrawal behavior, Volvo had a more critical problem because the Swedish system pays rank-and-file workers regardless of whether or not they show up for work.

Each assembly team at Volvo is composed of fifteen to twenty-nine individuals and given the responsibility for a complete function or component of the car. The shop floor space given each team permits an average of six car bodies to be worked on simultaneously. The production goal in the Kalmar plant is one new car every three minutes; therefore a team can keep each car within its work area for approximately eighteen minutes.

The teams at Kalmar are given considerable freedom. Employees on each team decide how the work of their team is to be distributed. Team members are also encouraged to learn each other's jobs. Responsibility for material supplies in their work area, output, and quality control all lie with the individual teams.

The Volvo experiment goes far beyond merely the creation of work teams, though this is the core of their enrichment program. Employees are also treated more humanely than in most North American automobile assembly plants. For instance, Volvo employees enjoy a work environment that is light, airy, and low in noise level, with wall-to-wall carpeted "coffee corners" and changing rooms with washroom and cupboards for clothes.

The objective at Kalmar is to create an environment where employees will have high job identification, greater understanding of the various tasks encompassed in building a car and flexibility in being able to perform these tasks, improved communication between workers and with their foremen and engineers, and increased job satisfaction and motivation. While these are ambitious objectives, Kalmar management claims lower labor turnover, more employee participation, improved quality, and fewer final adjustments.

As an aside, we should note that North American automobile workers might not respond as favorably to comprehensive enrichment as did Swedish workers at Volvo. An experiment in which six American automobile workers spent four weeks in a modern Swedish auto plant assembling complete engines in assembly teams was viewed unfavorably by five of the six participants.[10] Some felt, after a point, that teamwork could become tedious. Complaints were also expressed that enriched jobs demanded greater concentration and a faster pace. One of the experimenters, a ten-year veteran at Ford, said, "If I've got to bust my ass to be meaningful, forget it—I'd rather be monotonous."

The General Foods Topeka plant[11] In 1971, General Foods began an experiment in their new Topeka, Kansas, plant which produces Gaines pet food. As at Kalmar, the General Foods plant utilizes work teams. These teams have from seven to fourteen members and hold collective responsibil-

---

[10] "Doubting Sweden's Way," *Time*, March 10, 1975, p. 44.
[11] Walton, "From Hawthorne to Topeka and Kalmar," pp. 118–19.

ity for large segments of the production process. The team's responsibilities include the traditional functional departmentation in a plant—maintenance, quality control, industrial engineering, and personnel. For instance, teams do their own screening of applicants to locate replacements that are qualified and who will fit into the teams. Workers make job assignments, schedule coffee breaks, and even decide team members' pay raises.

A unique feature at the Topeka plant is the absence of job classification grades. All operators have a single classification and earn pay increases based on their ability to master an increasing number of jobs. No limits are placed on how many team members can qualify for the higher pay brackets, therefore encouraging employees to teach each other their jobs.

When the experiment began, team leaders were appointed to facilitate team development and decision making. However, after several years, the teams became so effective at managing themselves that the team leader positions were being eliminated.

The work environment also received considerable attention. Differential status symbols were minimized. The physical design of the plant was created to facilitate rather than discourage the congregating of workers during working hours.

What impact did this work environment have on the employees' and the plant's performance? In 1973, employees were generally praising the variety, dignity, and influence that they enjoyed; and they liked the team spirit, open communication, and opportunities to expand their mastery of job skills. While the experiment was not without criticizers, they generally believed that the work system as a whole was better than any other they knew about. From the management side, the plant operated with 35 percent fewer employees than similar plants organized along traditional lines. Additionally, the experiment resulted in higher output, minimum waste, avoidance of shutdowns, lower absenteeism, and lower turnover. However, the plant has recently been a source of problems to General Foods.[12] While General Foods' administrators still describe the plant's operation as "very successful," some former employees say that, after the initial euphoria, the system has steadily eroded. Much of the blame seems to be a conflict between the team concept and the corporation's bureaucracy. Whether there are serious problems or not, it is interesting that General Foods, which once encouraged publicity about the Topeka plant, has now become publicity shy about it.

Individual differences impact on job enrichment effectiveness There has been considerable research attempting to identify why job enrichment is accepted in some situations and not in others. The research indicates that there are individual differences that moderate the job enrichment-performance and job enrichment-satisfaction relationship.

It appears that employees who have strong growth needs and who are

[12] "Stonewalling Plant Democracy," *Business Week,* March 28, 1977, pp. 78–81.

also satisfied with contextual factors—pay, seniority, co-workers and supervision—respond more positively to enriched jobs than do employees who have less need for growth and/or are dissatisfied with contextual factors in their job.[13] Efforts to enrich jobs have been found to be associated with increased job performance for employees who have a strong need for achievement, but not for those who demonstrate low achievement need.[14] Apparently, enriched jobs stimulate the achievement motive for those with a high need, leading to greater effort and performance. There is also evidence suggesting that job enrichment is preferred by upwardly mobile employees with moderate to high incomes.[15] This would be consistent with the high achievement findings, since high achievement tends to lead to higher incomes.

With very little trouble, it would be possible to fill a good-sized ballroom with the quantity of articles and books on job enrichment that have emerged in the last decade. In fact, in many circles, "quality of worklife" and "job enrichment" are seen as synonymous terms. It is often touted as a panacea for worker alienation and dissatisfaction.

Given this attention by academics, it may surprise you to find that there is apparently a tremendous discrepancy between job enrichment's theoretical potential and its practical application in organizations. In spite of the frequent reference to the fact that name organizations like Texas Instruments, IBM, AT&T, Procter & Gamble, Corning Glass, Maytag, Motorola, Monsanto, Weyerhauser, Exxon, and Polaroid have reported some degree of success with job enrichment, a recent study covering some of the largest American corporations found that only 4 percent actually had ongoing formal job enrichment programs, with another 25 percent practicing job enrichment on an informal basis.[16]

One researcher, after extensively reviewing the job enrichment literature, went so far as to state that there are few, if any, genuine cases where job enrichment has been applied successfully to a large, heterogeneous work force.[17] He proposes that most applications either were common sense job redesign or occurred among a select group who responded to the Hawthorne effect (success was a result of the special attention received rather than the program's content).

[13] Greg R. Oldham, J. Richard Hackman, and Jones L. Pearce, "Conditions Under Which Employees Respond Positively to Enriched Work," *Journal of Applied Psychology,* August 1976, pp. 395–403.

[14] Richard M. Steers and Daniel G. Spencer, "The Role of Achievement Motivation in Job Design," *Journal of Applied Psychology,* August 1977, pp. 472–79.

[15] Bill Tudor, "A Specification of Relationships Between Job Complexity and Powerlessness," *American Sociological Review,* October 1972, pp. 596–604.

[16] William E. Reif, David N. Ferrazzi, and Robert J. Evans, Jr., "Job Enrichment: Who Uses It and Why?" *Business Horizons,* February 1974, pp. 73–78.

[17] Mitchell Fein, "Job Enrichment: A Re-evaluation," *Sloan Management Review,* Fall 1973, pp. 69–88.

The 1970s saw an increasing interest by administrators in developing shorter workweeks for employees. Experiments have generally covered workweeks of three 12-hour days, four 9-hour days, and four 10-hour days, with the latter receiving the greatest attention.[18] For our discussion, we will limit our scope to the four 10-hour-days program.

Proponents of the four-day, forty-hour-workweek have argued that, in addition to having a favorable effect on employee absenteeism, job satisfaction, and productivity, a four-day workweek provides employees with more leisure time, decreases commuting time, decreases requests for time off for personal matters, makes it easier for the organization to recruit employees, and decreases time spent on tasks such as setting up equipment. Others, however, have noted some potential disadvantages. Among these are a decrease in worker's productivity near the end of the longer workday, a decrease in service to customers and clients, unwillingness to work longer days when needed to meet deadlines, and underutilization of equipment.[19] While the evidence does generally support that the shorter workweek increases employee enthusiasm and morale and reduces turnover and absenteeism, the evidence is mixed on the issue of productivity.

A paper-box company has reported being able to operate machines at a 20 percent faster pace, which has increased productivity, and also having saved $25,000 a year from reduced spoilage. Another company reported a 10 percent increase in productivity after implementing the four-day workweek.[20]

An investigation of 470 clerical and supervisory employees in an accounting function found that 62 percent of the workers saw their jobs as more tiring, and administrators complained about the difficulty of coordinating work loads. However, there was a resultant reduction in overtime of 10 percent, and 78 percent of the employees did not want to revert back to the traditional five-day workweek once the program had been operating for six months. Although analysis of productivity figures indicated that they were unaffected either positively or negatively, supervisors were generally unenthusiastic about the program. Fifty-three percent of them saw it as detrimental to their work area; only 18 percent saw it as beneficial.[21]

It appears that there is a long-term and short-term impact of the

---

[18] For interesting 12-hour experiments, see C. Kenneth Crump, "The Twelve-Hour Shift in Nursing Services," working paper no. 112, University of Western Ontario, School of Business Administration, Research and Publications Division; and David Robison, "Dupont's 12-Hour Shift Experiment Turns Up Surprising Benefits," *Personnel Journal,* May 1978, pp. 234–269.

[19] Dan Olson and Arthur P. Brief, "The Impact of Alternative Workweeks," *Personnel,* January–February 1978, p. 73.

[20] Don Hellriegel, "The Four-Day Work Week: A Review and Assessment," *MSU Business Topics,* Spring 1972, pp. 39–48.

[21] James G. Goodale and A.K. Aagaard, "Factors Relative to Varying Reactions to the 4-Day Workweek," *Journal of Applied Psychology,* February 1975, pp. 33–38.

shorter workweek.[22] When first implemented, the shorter workweek achieves many of the results claimed by its advocates: improved morale, reduced dissatisfaction, and reduced absenteeism and turnover figures. However, after approximately one year, many of these advantages disappear. Employees then begin to complain about increased fatigue and the difficulty of coordinating their jobs with their personal lives—the latter a particular problem for working mothers. Administrators also find drawbacks. More scheduling of work is involved, overtime rates must frequently be paid for the hours worked over eight during the workday, and general difficulties arise in coordinating work. Additionally, administrators still tell employees when to arrive and when to leave, so the shorter workweek does little to increase the worker's freedom, specifically in selecting the work hours that suit him best.

As a result, despite the high expectations held for the shorter workweek, the lack of overwhelming enthusiasm for those programs that have been instituted suggests that the four-day workweek is no panacea for dealing with the problems inherent in bureaucratic structures. It has been suggested, however, that the desire for increased worker freedom can be achieved through flexible work hours.

The shorter workweek has been experimented with on a reasonably wide basis, but there appears to be no significant movement away from standard eight-hour, five-day workweeks, which have dominated since the late 1930s. In the mid-1970s, it was estimated that 4,000 companies in the U.S. had four-day workweeks operating,[23] though this may err on the high side since other estimates place the number between 700 and 1,000.[24] As an example of usage, a *Personnel* inquiry of human resources executives in 52 organizations found that only four of these organizations had implemented and were continuing four-day workweek programs, and all four limited involvement to certain employees in selected departments or divisions.[25]

Lest anyone think that these studies have overlooked organizations that have made major changes in the workweek, they need only to review the U.S. Bureau of Labor Statistics' figures. In 1974, 82 percent of employees worked five days a week, 16 percent from five and one-half to seven days, and only 2 percent from three to four and one-half days.[26]

The use of the four-day workweek appears to be centered heavily in local public administration. While these organizations account for only 2 percent of all fulltime workers, they represented 18 percent of those on

[22] John M. Ivancevich and Herbert L. Lyon, "The Shortened Workweek: A Field Experiment," *Journal of Applied Psychology,* February 1977, pp. 34–37.

[23] Alan Edmonds, "Waking Up Happy—The New Way to Beat the Alarmclock Blues," *Quest,* December 1974, p. 23.

[24] C.A. Chard and D.L. Caruth, "A Look at the Four-Day Workweek," *Business Studies,* vol. 12, 1973, pp. 40–48.

[25] William H. Wagel, "Alternative Work Schedules: Current Trends," *Personnel,* January–February 1978, pp. 4–5.

[26] Janice Neipert Hedges, "How Many Days Make a Workweek?" *Monthly Labor Review,* April 1975, pp. 29–36.

shorter workweeks.[27] It may be, however, that the recent popularity of flex-time, which leaves the number of work days per week unchanged, may have slowed the shorter workweek movement.

Flex-time

Flex-time is a system whereby employees contract to work a number of hours a week, but are free to vary the hours of work within certain limits. Each day consists of a common core, usually six hours, with a flexibility band surrounding the core. For example, the core may be 10:00 A.M. to 4:00 P.M., with the office actually opening at 7:30 A.M. and closing at 6:00 P.M. All employees are required to be at their jobs during the common-core period, but they are allowed to accumulate their other two hours from before and/or after the core time. Additionally, some flex-time programs allow extra hours to be accumulated and turned into a free day off each month.

Under flex-time, the employee assumes responsibility for completing his or her job, and that increases the person's feeling of self-worth. It is consistent with the view that people are paid for producing work, not for being at their job stations for a set period of hours.

Flex-time has been implemented in a number of diverse organizations, and the response has been generally favorable. An evaluation of Mutual of New York's flex-time program rated it very successful. There was an increase in employee productivity, fewer errors, improved employee morale, and a significant reduction in lateness and absenteeism.[28] A flex-time program initiated in several administrative departments at a large General Motors of Canada plant received similarly favorable notices.[29] Workers liked the program, and the company found that lateness and absences were reduced, offices were staffed for a longer period each day, and overtime costs were reduced. The State of New York's Commerce Department has also given its flex-time experiment high ratings.[30] Based on use by over 150 employees, the program has been described as "an astounding success," with improvements in departmental productivity and worker morale. Said one executive, "The idea is to treat state employees like civilized adult people instead of like kindergarteners. It's very simple: If you treat people with maturity, they respond with maturity. But if you treat them like children, then the game becomes how to cheat the system."[31]

Unfortunately, a comprehensive evaluation of flex-time programs in those organizations where it has been implemented has not been undertaken. Therefore, the early optimism must necessarily be guarded. The concept frequently contributes to decreased tardiness, reduced absenteeism, less job fatigue, increased organizational loyalty, and improved recruitment.

[27] Ibid.
[28] Cynthia J. Fields, "Variable Work Hours—The MONY Experience," *Personnel Journal,* September 1974, pp. 675–78.
[29] "Flexitime at GM of Canada," *Personnel,* January–February 1978, pp. 41–43.
[30] Molly Ivins, "Bill in Albany Asks Flexible Work Time," *New York Times,* March 13, 1977, p. 45.
[31] Ibid.

Where flex-time has been implemented, 80 percent or more of the employees report that they want it continued.[32] However, flex-time should not be viewed as void of drawbacks. It produces problems for administrators in directing subordinates outside the core time period, causes confusion where there is shift work, increases difficulties when someone with a particular skill or knowledge is not available, and makes planning and controlling work more cumbersome and costly for administrators.[33]

There appears to be a rapid growth in the implementation of flex-time since its introduction in the U.S. by Control Data Corporation in 1972. It is gaining popularity in the civil service and in service industries where operations are relatively independent. The Social Security Administration in Baltimore has over 2,000 employees on flex-time. It is widely used by banks and insurance companies.[34] But, exclusive of the government where over 70,000 employees are on flex-time,[35] usage seems to be limited to smaller organizations. It is estimated, for example, that only about one hundred companies employing thirty thousand or more have implemented flex-time.[36]

Matrix organization

An increasingly popular approach to improving organizational performance is the use of the matrix organization. In simplistic terms, the matrix organization is a combination of departmentation by function and by product. Another way of describing the matrix organization is to say that it is a project structure superimposed on a basic functional hierarchy. However, because the matrix structure is permanent, in contrast to the project or task force, we view it as a major structural modification.

Figure 12-1 shows a matrix organization chart for a College of Administrative Studies. The academic departments of accounting, economics, and so forth represent functional units. Specific programs offered by the college are overlaid on the functions. As a result, the director of the undergraduate program may have Professor Jones teaching an introductory course in this program, yet Professor Jones is also a member of the accounting department which has its own chairman.

What becomes quickly obvious is that the matrix organization breaks the unity of command, for it creates dual lines of authority. Employees in a matrix structure have a dual assignment: to their functional department and to their task group. While this duality can create problems, its advantage is creating a flexible and adaptive structure which can achieve a series of ob-

[32] Robert T. Golembiewski and Carl W. Proehl, Jr., "A Survey of the Empirical Literature on Flexible Workhours: Character and Consequences of a Major Innovation," *Academy of Management Review,* October 1978, pp. 837–53.

[33] J. Carrol Swart, "What Time Shall I Go to Work Today?" *Business Horizons,* October 1974, pp. 19–26.

[34] Robert J. Kühne and Courtney O. Blair, "Flexitime," *Business Horizons,* April 1978, p. 41.

[35] "Start When You Please," *Time,* January 10, 1977, p. 52.

[36] Janice Neipert Hedges, "New Patterns for Working Times, *Monthly Labor Review,* February 1973, p. 4.

Programs / Academic Departments	Undergraduate	Master's	Ph.D.	Research	Executive Programs	Community–Service Programs
Accounting						
Administrative and Environmental Studies						
Economics						
Finance						
Marketing						
Organizational Behavior						
Political Science						
Quantitative Methods						

FIGURE 12-1   Matrix organization for a college of administrative sciences

jectives that uses the knowledge and skills of participating specialists without relying on a one-way flow of work or a rigid functional allocation of authority. It "pushes decision making down to more people, puts a premium on teamwork and, its users hope, restores a measure of small-company flexibility to the large and complex organizations using it.."[37]

Program administrators in a matrix structure have authority over project personnel relative to the program's objectives. However, decisions such as promotions, salary recommendations, and the annual review of each employee are still a part of the functional or departmental administrator's responsibility.

Obviously, with the traditional line-staff distinctions and the unity of command disregarded, the matrix organization requires a great deal of informal interaction if program administrators are to achieve their program's objectives. Since their authority is highly restricted, they must rely on other bases of power to achieve their objectives.

Although the matrix deviates from bureaucratic hierarchical structures, its advantages are impressive if flexibility is important: a focus on one person for all matters concerning the program, manpower flexibility, generally faster response to program needs and client desires, and motivation for organizational members by providing greater freedom and more opportunities to take responsibility for the attainment of specific objectives.

[37] "How to Stop the Buck Short of the Top," *Business Week,* January 16, 1978, pp. 82–83.

ORGANIZING
FOR MAXIMUM
PERFORMANCE

Committee structures

An interesting deviation from the pyramid-shaped structure is a committee form of organization. In those instances when it is desired that a broad range of experience and backgrounds be brought to bear on a decision, when those who will be affected by a decision are allowed to be represented, when it is believed desirable to spread the work load, or during periods of administrative transition when no single individual is ready to lead the organization, committees may prove highly effective.

Committees may be of a permanent or a temporary nature. When permanent committees are established at the top level of the organization, we frequently refer to the positions as forming a plural executive. Du Pont, for example, has utilized top-level committee decision making for a number of decades. Westinghouse and General Electric, similarly, use a three-man administrative group at the top. Each man still retains certain lines of authority, but they work as a group on planning and attacking long-range company problems of a nonoperating nature. We see increasing evidence of this form of structure in complex organizations. A number of universities now have an "office of the president," rather than merely the position of president. So, too, we are finding an "office of the governor," rather than merely a singular position.

Although there are advantages to this form of structure, it also has distinct disadvantages. It can tend to delay the decision-making process, as Aetna Life and Casualty found out.[38] After using the executive-group concept for four years, the largest publicly owned insurer in the U.S. gave up on the structure, apparently because it impeded decision action. But there are other problems as we noted in chapters 4 and 5. When a number of executives are involved in the decision-making process, the cost of making those decisions is increased. Also, there is a risk that the decision will be compromised. Rather than having the best decision come forward, consensus may become the rule of the day, thereby substituting "safe" decisions in place of those that might be in the best interests of the organization. And finally, the problem of accountability arises.

Administrative privileges for all

The last structural modification we will discuss is a recent effort taken by some organizations to increase productivity by treating all employees to the privileges and prerogatives traditionally associated only with administrative positions.

The objective is to give equal treatment to all employees. Weekly salaries replace hourly wages; blue-collar workers participate in the organization's pension program and receive paid sick leave; time clocks are removed; and gone also are supervisors reading a long list of disciplinary rules to new workers. The organization, in other words, replaces the traditional formal system of rules and penalties that had applied to nonadministrative personnel with the same trust shown administrators.

---

[38] "Aetna: Where Group Management Didn't Work," *Business Week*, February 16, 1976, p. 77.

The Eaton Corp. has adopted this program in over a dozen of its new plants.[39] One executive noted that the company is attempting to enrich the environment rather than the job. Enriching jobs "would have required major changes in technology in our new plants that were not practical, and we weren't sure that a lot of people wanted job enrichment."[40]

This view that many people may not want enriched jobs, but rather the other benefits and amenities that have traditionally been the province of administrators, has some support.[41] Blue-collar workers are not necessarily after more responsibility and continuity in their jobs. A large number want the prerogatives long enjoyed only by administrators—things like arriving and leaving at will and taking extended lunches if they so choose.

Does the spreading of administrative privileges improve performance? The Eaton results have been promising. Product output in the new plants using this approach ranges up to 35 percent higher than at older plants; however, part of these gains are attributable to more advanced equipment. But there have been other encouraging statistics: absenteeism rates at the new plants range between 0.5 percent to 3 percent compared with 6 percent to 12 percent in the old plants; and voluntary quits were reduced from as high as 60 percent a year in the old plants to 4 percent in the new ones.

Techniques such as the matrix organization, committee structures, and allocating administrative privileges to every employee all suffer from low usage. The matrix is popular in large universities, in consulting firms, and is reportedly in use by several large companies, including General Electric, Equitable Life Insurance, TRW Systems, Citicorp, Dow Corning, and Shell Oil.[42] But academic interest in the matrix far overwhelms its current application. The same can also be said for creating "office of the executive" structures or enriched environments.

Based on the almost universal rejection by organizations of structural modification suggestions, one is inclined to ask: Why have administrators not adopted these innovations? Three frequent replies are: (1) "Too costly," (2) "Evidence of their effectiveness in actually improving productivity is questionable," or (3) "Our administrators don't feel comfortable breaking away from the traditional authority." The most valid reason, however, may be: "Employees don't want them."

Surveys conducted by the University of Michigan Survey Research Center, the National Opinion Research Center, and the University of California Survey Research Center covering the years 1958 through 1977 demonstrate two facts: (1) the vast majority of workers are satisfied with their

[39] "Where White-Collar Status Boosts Productivity," *Business Week*, May 23, 1977, pp. 80–85.
[40] Ibid. p. 80.
[41] R. Schrank, "Work in America: What Do Workers Really Want?" *Industrial Relations,* vol. 13 (1974), pp. 124–129.
[42] "How to Stop the Buck Short of the Top," p. 82.

jobs; and (2) workers, as a group, were more satisfied in 1977 than in 1958.[43] During the nineteen-year period, the percentage of workers who reported that they were satisfied with their jobs never fell below 80 percent; in 1977, 88.4 percent of the respondents said they were "very" or "somewhat" satisfied with their jobs. It is results such as these that suggest that work, for the vast majority of people, is not the unpleasant task that many in the media would have us believe.

[43] U.S. Department of Labor, *Job Satisfaction: Is There a Trend?*, Manpower Research Monograph, no. 30, Manpower Administration, 1974, p. 4; and "Many Found Less Content in Jobs," *New York Times*, December 17, 1978, p. 1.

summary of major points

1. The issue of "quality of work life" has recently received considerable attention as a reaction to the negative repercussions from bureaucracy.

2. It has become increasingly popular for behavioral scientists to redesign jobs in order to improve worker performance.

3. Job redesign techniques can be placed into one of two categories: minor and major.

4. Minor modifications tend to be relatively simple and straightforward, implemented with minimal disturbance to the organization. Included in this category are:
   a. Job rotation—moving individuals from job to job, either on a planned or situational basis.
   b. Work modules—breaking work tasks into two-hour modules, allowing the equal dispersal of pleasant and unpleasant activities.
   c. Projects or task forces—temporary interdisciplinary organizations developed for the purpose of achieving a given objective that disband when this objective is attained.
   d. The ombudsperson—an independent position created to allow employees a channel for getting an objective review of complaints.

5. Major modifications tend to be complex and difficult to implement without creating substantial organization-wide disturbance. Included in this category are:
   a. Job enrichment—workers do increased planning and evaluating of their own work.
   b. Shorter workweek—employees work fewer days and longer hours; usually four days, ten hours a day.
   c. Flex-time—employees work a number of hours a week, but are free to vary the hours of work within certain limits.
   d. Matrix organization—a permanent combination of departmentation by function and by product, with dual lines of authority.
   e. Committee structures—group decision-making bodies, which include the plural executive.
   f. Administrative privileges for all—all employees are treated equally, given the benefits and amenities usually restricted to administrators.

1. What is the argument behind those who strongly support the "quality of work life" movement?

2. What structural modifications are most likely to be successful if implemented by a first-line supervisor? Why?

3. "An employee should have a job that gives him or her autonomy and diversity." Build an argument in favor of this statement. Then build an argument against this statement.

4. What is job enrichment? When is it likely to be effective?

5. "People don't want enriched jobs; they want an enriched environment." Do you agree or disagree? Support your position.

6. What are the similarities and differences between project and matrix structures?

7. Do you think jobs will be designed in a significantly different way in the year 2000 than they are now? Support your position.

8. How do you explain all the media attention given to worker discontent when nearly 9 out of 10 workers indicate that they are generally satisfied with their jobs?

case exercise

Life in the computer department

The computer systems department at the North City Bank runs twenty-four hours a day, five days a week. The department's six computer operators have traditionally worked three alternating shifts on a rotation basis. The longevity of each shift is two weeks. All shifts commence on Mondays and terminate on Fridays. Shift one is between 12:00 A.M. and 8:00 A.M.; shift two from 8:00 A.M. to 4:00 P.M.; and the third shift is between 4:00 P.M. and midnight.

In the four years since the bank opened, the computer operators consistently had a quit-rate of at least three times any other position in the bank. Last year, for instance, fifteen different people had filled the six computer operator jobs.

Joan Hernandez, the new computer department's supervisor, decided that she had to do something to reduce this chronic turnover rate. She began talking to the operators and heard the same complaint from each. The comments of Carl Cooper, one of the operators, pretty well summed up the feelings of the group.

"This swing shift business is crazy. The only good shift is from 8:00 A.M. to 4:00 P.M. On the second shift, at least you can live a normal life. But not for long. It takes about three days to adjust after a shift change. You get into the groove for about 10 days, then it's chaos again. And that third shift really is useless! The part of the day you're free, the rest of the world is working. Then when everyone's on the way home, you start your working day. By the time you get home, at one in the morning, everybody's sleeping. Not much of a social life during those two weeks, needless to say.

"Shift number one is not much better. When people are home sleeping at midnight, you start your day. You battle through the quiet, monotonous morning hours, waiting for the sun to tell you it's almost time to go home.

"The thing is not so much the swinging of the shifts, but the fact that you're stuck here for five days a week at these odd hours. The weekend is hardly enough time to get into a normal day cycle. But even if you could, Monday and the odd hours are there before you know it. I'm tired of it, and I've only been here six weeks. The money is okay, and the people here are real nice. But I can't march to the beat of a different drum much longer."

Questions

1. What is the cause of the high turnover among computer operators?
2. What alternatives are there to deal with this problem?
3. What do you think is the best solution and why?

FOR FURTHER READING

Hackman, J.R., "The Design of Work in the 1980s," *Organizational Dynamics,* Summer 1978, pp. 3–17. The author looks at two routes to work design in the 1980s—designing jobs to people or people to jobs. He is pessimistic, envisioning that the latter is more likely.

Kaplan, H.R., and C. Tausky, "Humanism in Organizations: A Critical Appraisal," *Public Administration Review,* March–April 1977, pp. 171–78. Authors argue that the data indicates that organizational humanists may be overstating the utility and benefits derived from increased worker participation in organizational decision making.

O'Toole, J., "Lordstown: Three Years Later," *Business and Society,* Spring 1975, pp. 64–71. The 1972 strike at the Lordstown plant of General Motors is often cited as evidence that workers find the assembly line dehumanizing. The author reviews the Lordstown case and the myths that have grown out of it.

Porter, A.L., and F.A. Rossini, "Flexiweek," *Business Horizons,* April 1978, pp. 45–51. The authors propose an alternative that has some features of both the shorter workweek and flex-time, and then explore its potential.

Schrank, R., "How to Relieve Worker Boredom," *Psychology Today,* July 1978, pp. 79–80. Jobs should be designed to allow employees to "schmooze"—to talk, fool around, and do other things unrelated to their assigned work.

Whitsett, D.A., "Where Are Your Unenriched Jobs?," *Harvard Business Review,* January–February 1975, pp. 74–80. Job enrichment cannot be applied everywhere. The author lists and describes clues for identifying opportunities where it will succeed.

PART

V

LEADING

Chapter

Motivation

**AFTER
STUDYING
THIS CHAPTER,
YOU SHOULD
BE ABLE TO—**

Motivation
Needs
Hierarchy of needs theory
Physiological needs
Safety needs
Love needs
Esteem needs
Self-actualization needs
Lower-order needs
Higher-order needs
Theory X

Theory Y
Achievement need (*nAch*)
Affiliation need (*nAff*)
Power need (*nPow*)
Motivation-hygiene theory
Intrinsic job factors
Extrinsic job factors
Expectancy theory
Equity theory
Activity trap

The motivation process
The priority of different needs
Two distinct views of man
The difference between motivation and hygiene factors
The expectancy model of motivation
The importance of equity
The role of money as a motivator

Why do people act as they do? Given comparable abilities, why are some people outstanding performers and others lazy or irresponsible? What activates and conditions a person's inner drives, desires, and wishes? How can we get employees to exert greater effort? The answers to these questions lie in the subject of motivation.

What is motivation?

We might define motivation in terms of some outward behavior. People who are "motivated" exert a greater effort to perform than those who are "not motivated." However, such a definition is relative and tells us little. A more descriptive but less substantive definition would say motivation is the willingness to do something, and is conditioned by this action's ability to satisfy some need for the individual. A need, in our terminology, means some internal state that makes certain outcomes appear attractive. This motivation process can be seen in Figure 13-1.

FIGURE 13-1   Basic motivational process

An unsatisfied need creates tension which stimulates drives within the individual. These drives generate a search behavior to find particular goals that, if attained, will satisfy the need and lead to the reduction of tension.

Motivated employees are in a state of tension. In order to relieve this tension, they engage in activity. The greater the tension, the more activity will be needed to bring about relief. Therefore, when we see people working hard at some activity, we can conclude that they are driven by a desire to achieve some goal that they perceive as having value to them.

Some early motivation theories

The previous description of the motivation process does little to specifically explain employee behavior. Let us, therefore, look at four theories which were formulated in the 1950s, received considerable attention, and are still frequently offered as explanations of, or approaches to, motivation. These theories were proposed by Abraham Maslow, Douglas McGregor, David McClelland and Frederick Herzberg.

FIGURE 13-2   Maslow's hierarchy of needs

Maslow's hierarchy of needs

The most well-known theory has been proposed by Abraham Maslow.[1] He hypothesized that within every human being there exists a hierarchy of five needs. These needs are:

1. Physiological: includes hunger, thirst, shelter, sex, and other bodily needs
2. Safety: includes security and protection from physical and emotional harm
3. Love: includes affection, belongingness, acceptance, and friendship
4. Esteem: includes internal esteem factors such as self-respect, autonomy, and achievement; and external esteem factors such as status, recognition, and attention
5. Self-actualization: the drive to become what one is capable of becoming—includes growth, achieving one's potential, and self-fulfillment

As each of these needs becomes substantially satisfied, the next need becomes dominant. In terms of Figure 13-2, the individual moves up the hierarchy. From the standpoint of motivation, the theory would say that although no need is ever fully gratified, a substantially satisfied need no longer motivates.

Maslow separated the five needs into higher and lower levels. Physiological and safety needs were described as lower-order, and love, esteem, and self-actualization as higher-order needs. The differentiation between the two orders was made on the premise that higher-order needs are satisfied internally to the person, whereas lower-order needs are predominantly satisfied externally (by such things as money wages, union contracts, tenure). In fact, the natural conclusion to be drawn from Maslow's classification is that in times of economic plenty, which has generally described the North American society since the mid-1940s, almost all permanently employed workers have had their lower-order needs substantially met.

Maslow's need theory has received wide recognition, particularly among practicing administrators. This can be attributed to the theory's in-

[1] Abraham Maslow, *Motivation and Personality* (New York: Harper & Row, 1954).

tuitive logic and ease of understanding. Unfortunately, however, research does not generally validate the theory. Maslow provided no empirical substantiation, and several studies that sought to validate the theory found no support.[2]

Old theories, especially ones that are intuitively logical, apparently die hard. One researcher reviewed the evidence and concluded that "although of great societal popularity, need hierarchy as a theory continues to receive little empirical support."[3] Further, the researcher stated that the "available research should certainly generate a reluctance to accept unconditionally the implication of Maslow's hierarchy."[4] Another review came to the same conclusion.[5] Little support was found for the prediction that need structures are organized along the dimensions proposed by Maslow; the prediction of a negative relationship between the level of need gratification and the activation of that need; or the prediction of a positive relationship between the level of need gratification and the activation level of the next higher need.

McGregor's theory X and theory Y

Douglas McGregor proposed two distinct views of man: one basically negative, labeled Theory X, and the other basically positive, labeled Theory Y.[6] After viewing the way administrator's dealt with employees, McGregor concluded that an administrator's view of the nature of man is based on a certain grouping of assumptions, and that he tends to mold his behavior toward subordinates according to these assumptions.

Under Theory X, the four assumptions held by the administrator are:

1. Employees inherently dislike work and, whenever possible, will attempt to avoid it.
2. Since employees dislike work, they must be coerced, controlled, or threatened with punishment to achieve desired goals.
3. Employees will shirk responsibilities and seek formal direction whenever possible.
4. Most workers place security above all other factors associated with work, and will display little ambition.

In contrast to these negative views toward the nature of man, McGregor listed four other assumptions that he called Theory Y:

[2] See, for example, Edward E. Lawler III and J. Lloyd Suttle, "A Causal Correlational Test of the Need Hierarchy Concept," *Organizational Behavior and Human Performance,* April 1972, pp. 265–87; and Douglas T. Hall and Khalil E. Nongaim, "An Examination of Maslow's Need Hierarchy in an Organizational Setting," *Organizational Behavior and Human Performance,* February 1968, pp. 12–35.
[3] Abraham K. Korman, Jeffrey H. Greenhaus, and Irwin J. Badin, "Personnel Attitudes and Motivation," in *Annual Review of Psychology,* ed. Mark R. Rosenzweig and Lyman W. Porter (Palo Alto, Calif.: Annual Reviews, 1977), p. 178.
[4] Ibid. p. 179
[5] M.A. Wahba and L.G. Bridwell, "Maslow Reconsidered: A Review of Research on the Need Hierarchy Theory," *Organizational Behavior and Human Performance,* vol. 15 (1976), pp. 212–40.
[6] Douglas McGregor, *The Human Side of Enterprise* (New York: McGraw-Hill, 1960).

1. Employees can view work as being as natural as rest or play.
2. Man will exercise self-direction and self-control if he is committed to the objectives.
3. The average person can learn to accept, even seek, responsibility.
4. Creativity—that is, the ability to make good decisions—is widely dispersed throughout the population, and not necessarily the sole province of those in administrative functions.

What are the motivational implications if you accept McGregor's analysis? The answer is best expressed in the framework presented by Maslow. Theory X assumes that lower order needs dominate individuals. Theory Y assumes that higher order needs dominate individuals. McGregor, himself, held to the belief that Theory Y assumptions were more valid than Theory X. Therefore, he proposed ideas like participation in decision making, responsible and challenging jobs, and good group relations as approaches that would maximize an employee's job motivation.

Unfortunately, there is no evidence to confirm that either set of assumptions is valid, or that acceptance of Theory Y assumptions and altering one's actions accordingly will lead to more motivated workers. As will become evident later in this chapter, either Theory X or Theory Y assumptions may be appropriate in a particular situation.

McClelland's achievement, affiliation, and power motives

David McClelland has proposed that there are three major relevant motives or needs in work place situations:

1. The need for achievement—the drive to excel, to achieve in relation to a set of standards, to strive to succeed
2. The need for affiliation—the desire for friendly and close interpersonal relationships
3. The need for power—the need to make others behave in a way that they would not have done otherwise

Some people have a compelling drive to succeed for the sake of success alone. McClelland calls this the drive for achievement, which he has abbreviated as *nAch*.[7] From his research into the achievement need, McClelland found that high achievers differentiate themselves from others by their desire to do things better. They seek situations where they can attain personal responsibility for finding solutions to problems, where they can receive rapid feedback on their performance, and where they can set moderately challenging goals. High achievers dislike succeeding by chance. They like to keep score, they are competitive, and they look for challenges. Importantly, they avoid what they perceive to be very easy or very difficult tasks.

The characteristics of *nAch* closely align with qualities necessary for successful entrepreneurship. As a result, we should not be surprised to find high achievers attracted to business, and particularly to fields such as com-

[7] David C. McClelland, *The Achieving Society* (New York: Van Nostrand Reinhold, 1961).

missioned sales, where there are challenging risks, rapid feedback, and opportunities to influence outcomes through personal efforts.

The need for affiliation (*nAff*) and the need for power (*nPow*) tend to be closely related to administrative success, according to McClelland.[8] His research gives strong evidence that the best administrators are high in their need for power and low in their need for affiliation.

Attempts to validate McClelland's research and conclusions have met with reasonable success. However, practitioners have given greatest attention to the achievement need. Given that *nAch* drives people to act on the basis of an internally induced stimulus rather than relying on externally imposed motivators, there are several implications for administrators. First, since the *nAch* attributes can be taught and have been positively related to higher work performance, administrators can consider having employees undergo *nAch* training to stimulate this need. Second, the understanding of the concepts behind *nAch* and the characteristics which individuals high in *nAch* seek in their jobs, can assist in explaining and predicting employee behavior.

Herzberg's motivation-hygiene theory	In the belief that a person's relation to his work is a basic one and that his attitude to his work can very well determine his success or failure, Frederick Herzberg investigated the question, "What do people want from their jobs?"[9]

Herzberg asked people to describe, in detail, situations when they felt exceptionally good or bad about their jobs. These responses were tabulated and categorized. The responses of a group of accountants to his open-end questionnaire are diagrammed in Figure 13-3.

From the categorized responses, Herzberg concluded that the replies people give when they feel good about their jobs are significantly different from the replies given when they feel bad. As seen in Figure 13-3, certain characteristics tended to be consistently related to job satisfaction, and others to job dissatisfaction. Intrinsic factors, such as achievement, recognition, the work itself, responsibility, and advancement seemed to be related to job satisfaction. When those questioned felt good about their work, they tended to attribute these characteristics to themselves. On the other hand, when they were dissatisfied, they tended to cite extrinsic factors, such as company policy and administration, supervision, interpersonal relations, working conditions, and salary.

The data suggest, says Herzberg, that the opposite of satisfaction is not dissatisfaction, as was traditionally believed. In other words, removing dissatisfying characteristics from a job does not necessarily make the job satisfying, nor vice versa. As illustrated in Figure 13-4, Herzberg interpreted his

---

[8] "McClelland: An Advocate of Power," *International Management,* July 1975, pp. 27–29.

[9] Frederick Herzberg, *Work and the Nature of Man* (New York: World Publishers, 1966).

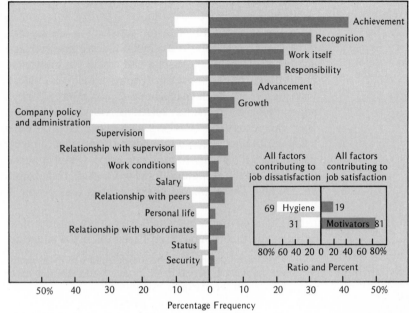

Factors characterizing 1,844 events on the job that led to *extreme dissatisfaction*

Factors characterizing 1,753 events on the job that led to *extreme satisfaction*

Achievement
Recognition
Work itself
Responsibility
Advancement
Growth

Company policy and administration
Supervision
Relationship with supervisor
Work conditions
Salary
Relationship with peers
Personal life
Relationship with subordinates
Status
Security

All factors contributing to job dissatisfaction | All factors contributing to job satisfaction

69 Hygiene 19
31 Motivators 81

80% 60 40 20 0 20 40 60 80%
Ratio and Percent

50% 40 30 20 10 0 10 20 30 40 50%
Percentage Frequency

Source: Frederick Herzberg. "One More Time; How Do You Motivate Employees?" *Harvard Business Review*, January–February 1968, p. 57. With permission. Copyright © 1967 by the President and Fellows of Harvard College; all rights reserved.

FIGURE 13-3 Comparison of satisfiers and dissatisfiers

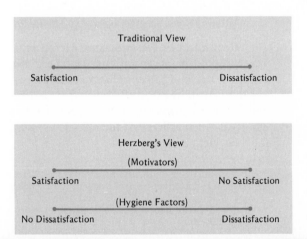

Traditional View

Satisfaction ——————————— Dissatisfaction

Herzberg's View
(Motivators)
Satisfaction ——————————— No Satisfaction

(Hygiene Factors)
No Dissatisfaction ——————————— Dissatisfaction

FIGURE 13-4 Contrasting views of satisfaction-dissatisfaction

findings to propose the existence of a dual continuum: the opposite of satisfaction being no satisfaction, the opposite of dissatisfaction being no dissatisfaction.

The factors leading to job satisfaction are separate and distinct from those that lead to job dissatisfaction, according to Herzberg. Therefore, by acting to eliminate factors that can create job dissatisfaction, one can bring about peace, but not necessarily motivation—can placate, rather than motivate. As a result, such characteristics as company policy and administration, supervision, interpersonal relations, working conditions, and salary have been categorized by Herzberg as hygiene factors. When they are satisfactorily maintained, people will not be dissatisfied; however, neither will they be satisfied. If we want to motivate employees, Herzberg suggests emphasizing achievement, recognition, the work itself, responsibility, growth, and advancement. These are the characteristics that people find intrinsically rewarding.

The motivation-hygiene theory is not without its detractors. The criticisms of the theory have been based upon five suggested weaknesses:

1. The procedure that Herzberg used is limited by its methodology. When things are going well, people tend to take credit themselves. Contrarily, they blame failures on the extrinsic environment.

2. The reliability of Herzberg's methodology is questioned. Since raters have to make interpretations, it is possible that they may contaminate the findings by interpreting one response in one manner while treating another response differently.

3. No overall measure of satisfaction was utilized. In other words, a person may dislike part of his job, yet still think the job is acceptable.

4. The theory is inconsistent with previous research. The motivation-hygiene theory ignores situational variables.

5. Herzberg assumes that there is a relationship between satisfaction and productivity. But the research methodology he used looks only at satisfaction, not at productivity. To make such research relevant, one must assume a high correlation between satisfaction and productivity.[10]

Regardless of the criticisms, Herzberg's theory has been widely read and accepted in organizations. Herzberg has suggested that his findings imply the value of job enrichment and increased autonomy to people utilizing self-control mechanisms over their work. Additionally, he has recommended the expansion of the personnel function beyond its traditional emphasis—that is, hygiene factors—so as to create jobs that offer motivation for their incumbents.

[10] Robert J. House and Lawrence A. Wigdor, "Herzberg's Dual-Factor Theory of Job Satisfaction and Motivation: A Review of the Evidence and a Criticism," *Personnel Psychology,* Winter 1967, pp. 369–89; and Donald P. Schwab and Larry L. Cummings, "Theories of Performance and Satisfaction: A Review," *Industrial Relations,* October 1970, pp. 408–30.

If organizations were widely practicing the theories espoused by Maslow and Herzberg, we would expect to see job enrichment, participative decision techniques, and other autonomy-oriented approaches being broadly implemented. Generally speaking, this is not the case. Administrators still tend to rely heavily on money as a motivator. Similarly, organizational rewards tend to emphasize wages, hours, and working conditions—all hygiene factors.

Motivation today: an expectancy approach

Although the early motivation theories offer insight into motivation, none offers a valid model for explaining an individual's drives. What is needed is an integrative model that considers such important elements as needs, the job design, the ability of the employee, and contingency aspects relevant to particular people in particular situations. Such a model has been formulated, and though it has not been immune to attack,[11] it is currently the clearest and most accurate explanation we have of individual motivation. We will call this model *expectancy theory.*[12]

What is expectancy theory?

Expectancy theory argues that the strength of a tendency to act in a certain way depends on the strength of an expectation that the act will be followed by a given outcome and on the attractiveness of that outcome to the individual. It includes, therefore, three variables:[13]

1. Attractiveness: the importance that the individual places on the potential outcome or reward that can be achieved on the job. This considers the unsatisfied needs of the individual.
2. Performance-reward linkage: the degree to which the individual believes that performing at a particular level will lead to the attainment of each job outcome.
3. Effort-performance linkage: the perceived probability by the individual that exerting a given amount of effort will lead to performance.

While this may sound pretty complex, it really is not that difficult to visualize. Whether one has the desire to produce at any given time depends on one's particular goals and one's perception of the relative worth of performance as a path to the attainment of these goals.

---

[11] See, for example, Herbert G. Heneman III and Donald P. Schwab, "Evaluation of Research on Expectancy Theory Prediction of Employee Performance," *Psychological Bulletin,* July 1972, pp. 1–9; and Leon Reinharth and Mahmoud A. Wahba, "Expectancy Theory as a Predictor of Work Motivation, Effort Expenditure, and Job Performance," *Academy of Management Journal,* September 1975, pp. 502–37.

[12] Victor H. Vroom, *Work and Motivation* (New York: John Wiley, 1964).

[13] Vroom refers to these three variables as valance, instrumentality, and expectancy, respectively.

| Individual Effort | → | Individual Performance | → | Organizational Rewards | → | Individual Goals |

FIGURE 13-5   Simplified expectancy model

Figure 13-5 is a considerable simplification of expectancy theory, but expresses its major contentions. The strength of a person's motivation to perform (effort) depends on how strongly she believes that she can achieve what she attempts. If she achieves this goal (performance), will she be adequately rewarded and, if she is rewarded by the organization, will the reward satisfy her individual goals? Let us consider the four steps inherent in the theory and then attempt to apply it.

First, what outcomes does the job offer the employee? Outcomes may be positive: pay, security, companionship, trust, fringe benefits, a chance to use talent or skills, congenial relationships. On the other hand, employees may view the outcomes as negative: fatigue, boredom, frustration, anxiety, harsh supervision, threat of dismissal. Importantly, reality is not important here; the critical issue is what the individual employee perceives the outcome to be, regardless of whether or not her perceptions are accurate.

Second, how attractive do employees consider these outcomes? Are they valued positively, negatively, or neutrally? This obviously is an internal issue to the individual and considers her personal values, personality, and needs. The individual who finds a particular outcome attractive—that is, positively valued—would prefer attaining it to not attaining it. Still others may be neutral.

Third, what kind of behavior must the employee produce in order to achieve these outcomes? The outcomes are not likely to have any effect on the individual employee's performance unless the employee knows, clearly and unambiguously, what she must do in order to achieve them. For example, what is "doing well" in terms of performance appraisal? What are the criteria the employee's performance will be judged on?

Fourth and last, how does the employee view her chances of doing what is asked of her? After the employee has considered her own competencies and her ability to control those variables that will determine her success, what probability does she place on successful attainment?[14]

Let us use the classroom organization as an illustration of how one can use expectancy theory to explain motivation.

An application of expectancy theory   Most students prefer an instructor who tells them what is expected of them in the course. They want to know what the assignments and examinations will be like, when they are due or to be taken, and how much weight each carries in the final term grade. They also like to think that the amount of ef-

[14] This four-step discussion was adapted from K.F. Taylor, "A 'Valance-Expectancy' Approach to Work Motivation," *Personnel Practice Bulletin*, June 1974, pp. 142–48.

fort they exert in attending classes, taking notes, and studying will be reasonably related to the grade they will make in the course. If we assume that the above describes you, consider that five weeks into a class you are really enjoying (we'll call it Admin. 110), an exam is given back. You have studied hard for this exam. You have consistently made "A's" and "B's" on exams in other courses where you have expended similar effort. And the reason you work so hard is to make top grades, which you believe are important for getting a good job upon graduation. Also, you are not sure but you may want to go on to graduate school. Again, you think grades are important for getting into a good graduate school.

Well, the results of that five-week exam are in. The class median was 72. Ten percent of the class scored an 85 or higher and got an "A." Your grade was 46; the minimum passing mark was 50. You're mad. You're frustrated. Even more, you're perplexed. How could you possibly have done so poorly on the exam when you usually score among the top grades in other classes by preparing as you had for this exam? Several interesting things are immediately evident in your behavior. Suddenly, you no longer are driven to attend Admin. 110 classes regularly. You find you do not study for the course either. When you do attend classes, you daydream a lot—the result is an empty notebook instead of several pages of notes. One would probably be correct in describing you as "lacking in motivation" in Admin. 110. Why did your motivational level change? You know and I know, but let's explain it in expectancy terms.

If we use Figure 13-5 to understand this situation, we might say the following: studying and preparation in Admin. 110 (effort) is conditioned by its resulting in answering the questions on the exam correctly (performance), which will produce a high grade (reward), which you believe will lead to the security, prestige, and other benefits that accrue from obtaining a good job (individual goal).

The attractiveness of the outcome—which in this case is a good grade—is high. But what about the performance-reward linkage? Do you feel that the grade you received truly reflects your knowledge of the material? In other words, did the test fairly measure what you know? If the answer is yes, then this linkage is strong. If the answer is no, then at least part of the reason for your reduced motivational level is your belief that the test was not a fair measure of your performance. If the test was of an essay type, maybe you believe the instructor's grading method was poor. Was too much weight placed on a question that you thought was trivial? Maybe the instructor does not like you and was biased in grading your paper. These are examples of perceptions that influence the performance-reward linkage and your level of motivation.

Another possible demotivating force may be the effort-performance relationship. If, after you took the exam, you believed that you could not have passed it regardless of the amount of preparation you had done, then your desire to study will drop. Possibly the instructor wrote the exam under the assumption that you had had a considerably broader background in the course's subject matter. Maybe the course had several prerequisites that you did not know about, or possibly you had the prerequisites but took them several years ago. The end result is the same: You place a low value on your effort leading to answering the exam questions correctly; and hence there is a reduction in your motivational level and you lessen your effort.

The key to expectancy theory, therefore, is the understanding of an individual's goals, and the linkage between effort and performance, between performance and reward and, finally, between the rewards and individual goal attainment. As a contingency model, expectancy theory recognizes that there is no universal principle for explaining everyone's motivations. Additionally, just because we understand what needs a person seeks to satisfy does not ensure that the individual himself perceives high performance as necessarily leading to the satisfaction of these needs. If you desire to take Admin. 110 in order to meet new people and make social contacts, but the instructor organizes the class on the assumption that you want to make a good grade in the course, the instructor may be personally disappointed should you perform poorly on the exams. Unfortunately, most instructors assume that their ability to allocate grades is a potent force in motivating students. But it will only be so if students place a high importance on grades, if students know what they must do to achieve the grade desired, and if the students believe there is a high probability of their performing well should they exert a high level of effort.

| *Summarizing expectancy theory* | Let us summarize some of the issues expectancy theory has brought forward. First, it emphasizes payoffs or rewards. As a result, we have to believe that the rewards the organization is offering align with what the employee wants. It is a theory based on self-interest wherein each individual seeks to maximize his expected satisfaction: "Expectancy theory is a form of calculative, psychological *hedonism* in which the ultimate motive of every human act is asserted to be the maximization of pleasure and/or the minimization of pain."[15] Second, we have to be concerned with the attractiveness of rewards, which requires an understanding and knowledge of what value the individual puts on organizational payoffs. We shall want to reward the individual with those things he or she values positively. Third, expectancy theory emphasizes expected behaviors. Does the person know what is expected of him and how he will be appraised? Finally, the theory is concerned with expectations. It is irrelevant what is realistic or rational. An individual's own expectations of performance, reward, and goal satisfaction outcomes will determine his level of effort, not the objective outcomes themselves. |

[15] Edwin A. Locke, "Personnel Attitudes and Motivation," in *Annual Review of Psychology,* ed. Mark R. Rosenzweig and Lyman W. Porter (Palo Alto, Calif.: Annual Reviews, 1975). p. 459.

Does expectancy theory work?

The space we have devoted to expectancy theory suggests that it is important, yet as we have seen before, few theories are irrefutable, without critics, or void of contradictory findings. Expectancy theory is no exception.[16] Attempts to validate the theory have been complicated by methodological, criterion, and measurement problems. As a result, many published studies that purport to support or negate the theory must be viewed with caution. Importantly, most studies have failed to replicate the methodology as it was originally proposed. For example, the theory proposes to explain different levels of effort within the same person under different circumstances, but almost all replication studies have looked at different people. By correcting for this flaw, support for the validity of expectancy theory has been greatly improved.[17] Some critics suggest that the theory has only limited use, arguing that it tends to be more valid for predicting in situations where effort-performance and performance-reward linkages are clearly perceived by the individual.[18] Since few individuals perceive a high correlation between performance and rewards in their jobs, the theory tends to be idealistic. If organizations actually rewarded individuals for performance, rather than criteria such as seniority, effort, skill level, or job difficulty, then the theory's validity might be considerably greater. However, rather than invalidating expectancy theory, this criticism can be used in support of the theory and for explaining why a large segment of the work force exerts a minimal level of effort in carrying out their job responsibilities.

Observations suggest that administrators are not providing accurate open feedback to individuals about their performance. Administrators find that identifying group task objectives and linking them to task responsibilities of individual members is a time-consuming operation. Mutual goal setting (the sharing of the goal-setting task with the subordinate) is avoided by some administrators because they believe this is an infringement of administrative prerogatives. In some cases, task objectives are identified, performance is evaluated, and the results are conveyed to the employee; yet the employee remains unsure of the administration's view of his or her accomplishments in terms of preestablished objectives. In summary, it appears that many administrators have failed to recognize the importance of establishing objectives and performance feedback as would be suggested by MBO and expectancy theory.[19]

[16] See footnote 11.
[17] Paul M. Muchinsky, "A Comparison of Within- and Across-Subjects Analyses of the Expectancy-Valance Model for Predicting Effort," *Academy of Management Journal,* March 1977, pp. 154–58.
[18] Robert J. House, H.J. Shapiro, and M.A. Wahba, "Expectancy Theory as a Predictor of Work Behavior and Attitudes: A Re-evaluation of Empirical Evidence," *Decision Sciences,* January 1974, pp. 481–506.
[19] Joel K. Leidecker and James J. Hall, "Motivation: Good Theory—Poor Application," *Training and Development Journal,* June 1974, pp. 3–7.

Furthermore, the literature suggests that administrators should ensure that high productivity and good work performance lead to the achievement of personal goals. Again a review of actual organizational practices reveals many exceptions. Organizations seldom allocate rewards in such a way as to optimize motivation, per the expectancy model. While individual performances tend to be widely divergent—that is, a few outstanding, a few very poor, and the majority surrounding the average—rewards tend to be allocated more uniformly. The result is the overrewarding of incompetence and the underrewarding of superior performance. Organizations, generally speaking, do not necessarily reward "Protestant ethic" behavior. Hard work does not necessarily pay off; and, therefore, many workers place low probability on its leading to organizational rewards and, eventually, the attainment of personal goals.

Internal politics is a vital determinant of who and what will be rewarded. For example, group acceptance may be a personal goal, and high productivity may hinder rather than support achievement of this goal. As a result, workers will reduce output and gain approval. The failing of our motivational theories tends to lie in their overemphasis on the rationality of administrators in allocating rewards, while understating the influence of politics in their distribution.

The above perceptions were upheld in a recent study of 270 lower-level administrators undertaken at a large utility company.[20] These administrators were asked to indicate what types of behavior and activities are rewarded at their company. While the researcher hypothesized that responses would all be performance-oriented, given the social desirability of such replies, the results were quite different. Approximately 40 percent of the respondents perceived political factors—"knowing the 'right' people" and "relations with one's immediate supervisor"—to be the major influences on how rewards were distributed. These results, which if incorrect probably err on the side of understating the weight that organizational politics plays in reward distribution, support our position that politics has considerable influence in determining who and what will be rewarded.

Another reality in organizations is what one writer has called "the activity trap."[21] Administrators tend to focus their attentions and rewards on effort, appearances, or activities rather than performance, to such an extent that employees emphasize style over substance. Signs of the activity trap are promotions and salary increases based on seniority or a performance evaluation system that rewards people on the basis of demonstrating desirable personality traits rather than accomplishments. When we reward people for having a nice smile, not complaining, not asking embarrassing questions,

[20] William J. Crampon, "The Development of Managerial Job Behavior-Reward Expectations" (unpublished doctoral dissertation, University of California, Irvine, 1976).

[21] George S. Odiorne, *Management and the Activity Trap* (New York: Harper & Row, 1974).

covering for their boss, or for being easy to get along with, we begin substituting style for substance

Is there any evidence to support the activity trap thesis? A study done in the 1960s concluded that, among a group of organizations surveyed, there was evidence to support the thesis. The study found that pay was being allocated at least as much for effort as for accomplishment.[22]

We find other evidence that suggests that the performance-reward relationship is not always strong. For instance, we cite a survey of nearly nine thousand workers, consisting of administrators and both salaried and hourly employees, which looked for factors that would predict pay.[23] For administrative positions, education proved to be the best predictor of compensation. The job level held and the age of the incumbent were also relatively good predictors of actual pay. "It appears that the better educated, higher level, older managers, who have been with the company somewhat longer, are better paid."[24] Among salaried employees, age was the most closely related variable to pay, closely followed by education and job level. Length of time on the job was the major predictor for hourly workers. Those hourly workers who had been with the company the longest were the highest paid. The researchers concluded:

> One inference that seems reasonable from all these data is that the amount of an employee's pay is likely to be determined by many factors, a large portion of which seem to be from those such as age, education, tenure, and job level. It is possible, however, that such factors have little or no relation to actual effectiveness or job performance.
>
> This finding casts considerable doubt that employee performance is related to pay.[25]

A survey of 493 large manufacturing and service companies provides further evidence to suggest that rewards are not based on performance criteria.[26] As Figure 13-6 shows, pay increases in these companies tended to be more influenced by external factors such as the national cost-of-living index and community pay policies than by individual worker productivity.

This same survey also revealed that less than one-third of the firms discuss with their employees how the company's pay system works.[27] Twenty-three percent tell employees what an average raise was, and merely 27 percent inform the employee how much of his pay increase was due to a

---

[22] Lyman W. Porter and Edward E. Lawler III, *Managerial Attitudes and Performance* (Homewood: Ill.: Richard D. Irwin, 1968), p. 158.

[23] W.W. Ronan and G.J. Organt, "Determinants of Pay and Pay Satisfaction," *Personnel Psychology,* Winter 1973, pp. 503–20.

[24] Ibid., p. 511.

[25] Ibid., p. 513.

[26] David A. Weeks, *Compensating Employees: Lessons of the 1970's,* Report No. 707 (N.Y.: The Conference Board, 1976), pp. 12–14.

[27] Ibid., pp. 19–20.

Factors determining pay increases

Employee Category:	Worker productivity	Company's financial results	Company's financial prospects	Internal equity among groups	Increases of industry leaders	Area surveys	Ability to hire	National bargaining settlements	Union demands	Cost-of-living index
* Officers and executives	4	1	2	6	5	3	7	9	10	8
* Exempt salaried	7	2	3	5	6	1	8	10	9	4
* Nonexempt salaried	5	3	4	6	8	1	7	10	9	2
* Nonunion hourly	3	5	4	6	7	1	10	8	9	2
* Union hourly	9	7	5	8	4	6	10	2	1	3

[1] Importance rating determined by frequency of mentions in first, second, or third place in a ranking from 1 to 10.
[2] Sample composed of manufacturing (44%), banking and insurance (38%), utility (15%), and retail (3%) firms.

Source: Adapted from David A. Weeks, *Compensating Employees: Lessons of the 1970's*, Report No. 707 (N.Y.: The Conference Board, 1976), pp. 12–14.

cost-of-living adjustment and how much was really due to good performance. As might be expected, fewer still—about 14 percent of these companies—make public to all employees the organization's full salary ranges and the pay structure.

Some special issues in motivation

There are a number of topics within the subject of motivation that have attracted special attention by researchers and practitioners. For example, does money motivate? Are the techniques that motivate workers in business different from those that motivate public employees? We have identified five of these special issues and will discuss them in the following pages.

Is equity important?

Does it surprise you to hear about a person who makes $200,000 a year, yet is unhappy with his salary? In fact, this was a frequent occurrence in the late 1970s among superstar professional athletes. In the early 1960s, the Mickey Mantles and the Wilt Chamberlains made $100,000 to $150,000 a year. Of course, this was a lot of money, but it set the outer limits on what upcoming superstars could hope to earn. But suddenly, in the mid-1970s, professional athletes making as much as $300,000 or more per year were talking in terms of being demotivated by their "low" salaries. In baseball, for example, as

fast as players signed long-term contracts, others were trying to "renego-
tiate" their current contracts. A million-dollar, five-year contract, was a
prize package in 1976. By 1978, after Reggie Jackson had signed for $3 mil-
lion and Rich Gossage got $2.7 million, baseball players were suddenly un-
happy with what was previously considered a very substantial income.[28] This
rapid escalation in baseball salaries leads us to ask: What should a baseball
superstar get? What is a proper salary based on? His teammates? Other players on baseball teams? Other professional athletes? His age? The number of
years he has been with the team?

This discussion of athlete's salaries has a direct parallel to employees
in all organizations. It dramatizes the fact that an individual's motivation is
not only affected by the absolute rewards given by the organization, but by
their relative worth to others. In other words, in addition to our level of effort being influenced by the absolute rewards we receive from our performance, we also make relative comparisons between our input-output ratio and
those of others. We perceive what we get from a job situation (outputs) in
relation to what we put into it (inputs), and then compare our input-output
ratio with the input-output ratio of relevant others. If we perceive our ratio
to be equal to the relevant others with whom we compare ourselves, a state
of equity is said to exist. If they are unequal, inequity exists; that is, we tend
to view ourselves as underrewarded or overrewarded. It has been proposed
that an equity process takes place in which people who view any inequity as
aversive will attempt to correct it.[29]

The referent that an employee selects adds to the complexity of equity
theory. Evidence suggests that the reference chosen is an important variable
in equity theory.[30] The three referent categories have been classified as
"other," "system," and "self." The "other" category includes other individuals with similar jobs in the same organization, and also includes friends,
neighbors, or professional associates. Based on information that employees
receive through word of mouth, newspapers, and magazines, on such issues
as executive salaries or a recent union contract, employees can compare
their pay to that of others.

The "system" category considers organizational pay policies and procedures, and the administration of this system. It considers organization-
wide pay policies, both implied and explicit. Precedents by the organization
in terms of allocation of pay would be a major determinant in this category.

The "self" category refers to input-output ratios that are unique to the

[28] Joseph Durso, "Big Problem Is Arising in Baseball: How Much Should a Superstar
Get?" *New York Times,* March 5, 1978, p. 51.
[29] J.S. Adams, "Inequity in Social Exchanges," in *Advances in Experimental Social
Psychology,* ed. Leonard Berkowitz (New York: Academic Press, 1965), pp. 267–300.
[30] Paul S. Goodman, "An Examination of Referents Used in the Evaluation of Pay,"
Organizational Behavior and Human Performance, October 1974, pp. 170–95.

individual and differ from the individual's current input-output ratio. This category is influenced by such criteria as past jobs or commitments that must be met in terms of family role.

The choice of a particular set of referents is related to the information available about referents as well as to their perceived relevance. Based on equity theory, we might suggest that when employees envision an inequity, they may take one or more of five choices:

1. Distort either their own or others inputs or outputs
2. Behave in some way so as to induce others to change their inputs or outputs
3. Behave in some way so as to change their own inputs or outputs
4. Choose a different comparison referent
5. Leave the field (quit their job)

Equity theory recognizes that individuals are concerned not only with the absolute amount of rewards they receive for their efforts; but also with the relationship of this amount to what others receive. They make judgments as to the relationship between their input and outputs and the inputs and outputs of others. Based on one's inputs, such as effort, experience, education, and competence, one compares outputs such as salary levels, raises, recognition, and other factors. When people perceive an imbalance in their input-output ratio relative to others, tension is created. This tension provides the basis for motivation, as people strive for what they perceive as equity and fairness. In the search to relieve this tension, employees may decrease their input while holding their output constant, or increase their outputs while holding inputs constant—possibly resulting in fighting the system, engaging in increasing absenteeism, or performing other undesirable behaviors.

Equity theory's implications for administrators should be clear. In addition to absolute rewards, relative rewards are also critical to employee motivation. Employee awareness of inequity can result in lower productivity, more absenteeism, or an increase in resignations.

Does money motivate?

When someone asks if money motivates, it is tempting to answer that it does only if one doesn't have any. Surprisingly, this statement has some semblance of truth.

Whether money motivates depends considerably on how much you have. Since money is rarely an end, but rather a means to purchasing ends, it can rather substantially gratify both physiological and safety needs. A $1,000 stimulus to a worker earning $5,000 a year may be interpreted as the means for a considerable improvement in his standard of living. But that same $1,000 given to someone making $40,000 a year would probably have little effect on his life style.

However, we must caution against broad generalizations. To some people, money is not important, whether they have a lot or a little. Others, no matter how much money they have, are continually driven by the desire to acquire more of it, possibly to satisfy their desire for status or their goal of being rich (esteem and self-actualization needs, respectively). Research indicates that for some, money can be instrumental in satisfying esteem and recognition needs as well as basic physiological needs.[31]

If money is to act as a motivator, it is necessary to assume a relationship between performance and rewards. Those who seek money will be motivated to higher performance only if they can clearly link higher performance to the reward of more money. Consistent with expectancy theory, money motivates high performance only to the extent that money is seen as being able to satisfy an individual's personal goals and is perceived as being dependent upon performance criteria.

Economic conditions necessarily affect the importance of money as a motivator. Money was a motivator for much of the population in 1932, during the Great Depression, but it may be considerably less effective in 1982! When a box boy in a supermarket is making $180 a week and has his own apartment, an automobile, a decent wardrobe, and some spending money, can we expect to motivate him with money, the means for predominantly satisfying lower-order needs?

Does everyone want to self-actualize? Prof. Chris Argyris of Harvard has introduced a maturation theory, proposing that all healthy people seek situations that offer autonomy, wide interests, treatment as equals, and the opportunity to exhibit their ability to deal with complexity.[32] Healthy people, says Argyris, seek employment situations that allow them the opportunity for self-actualization. Unfortunately, according to Argyris's interpretation, most organizations treat employees like children, making then dependent, subordinate, and narrowly constrained.

George Strauss has countered that not everyone seeks to satisfy self-actualization needs on the job, and that people also seek security in knowing what is expected of them. He attacked those who imply:

> ... that people should want freedom and self-actualization, that it is somehow morally wrong for people to be lazy, unproductive, and uncreative. It seems to me that the hypothesis overemphasizes individuals' desire for freedom and underemphasizes their desire for security .... mature behavior does not mean freedom from all restrictions: it means successful adjustment to them.[33]

Strauss continues his attack on Argyris:

---

[31] Edward E. Lawler III, *Pay and Organizational Effectiveness: A Psychological View* (New York: McGraw-Hill, 1971).

[32] Chris Argyris, *Integrating the Individual and the Organization* (New York: John Wiley, 1964).

[33] George Strauss, in *Individualism and Big Business,* ed. Leonard Sayles (New York: McGraw-Hill, 1963), pp. 67–80.

MOTIVATION

311

Argyris, for example, might reply that such individuals are immature personalities who have adjusted to organization restrictions by becoming apathetic and dependent; were the organization environment healthy, these individuals would react differently. But in many cases the restrictions which conditioned these people occurred in childhood or are present in the culture. Such individuals may be too far gone ... indeed, many people may have internalized and made part of their self-concept a low level of aspiration regarding their on-the-job responsibilities and their ability to handle them. ...

There is an additional value judgment in the basic hypothesis that the *job* should be a primary form of need satisfaction for everyone (as it is for professors). But the central focus of many people's lives is not the job (which is merely a way of getting a living), but the home or the community. Many people find a full measure of challenge, creativity, and autonomy in raising a family, pursuing a hobby, or taking part in community affairs.[34]

Strauss concludes that there is an overemphasis on the job as a source of need satisfaction and also an underemphasis on the role of money as a means of motivation:

Money is a means of satisfying higher needs too—ego, safety [*sic*], and for some, even self-actualization, e.g., the individual who (perhaps misguidedly) seeks to live his life off the job engaging in "creative" consumption.

True, employees expect much better physical, psychological, and social conditions on the job today than they did fifty years ago. But they also expect more money. There is little evidence that money has ceased to be a prime motivator.[35]

The debate between Argyris and Strauss is not easily resolved. Many employers do treat their people as immature, thus retarding their natural growth. The potential of great numbers of employees is suboptimized in organizations. However, as Strauss suggests, we cannot accept that all people equally desire autonomy and self-actualization. With various degrees of emphasis, they also want security and the knowledge of what is expected of them. In addition, although self-actualization may be important to all, there is no reason to conclude that that need must be satisfied on the job. Since work consumes only 35 percent of our waking hours, we have a good deal of opportunity to be autonomous and self-actualizing in our off-the-job activities.

Are public employees different?

It is frequently claimed that the productivity of public employees seriously lags behind that of employees in business.[36] One reason cited is that public employee motivation is low. But is this true? Are public employees less motivated than their counterparts in the private sector?

[34] Ibid.
[35] Ibid.
[36] See, for example, R.S. Rosenbloom, "The *Real* Productivity Crisis Is in Government," *Harvard Business Review,* September–October 1973, pp. 156–64.

The evidence indicates that there are differences, but probably not as marked as one generally assumes. Two dimensions are of particular relevance: job security and reward systems.

A study comparing employees in a city government organization with employees in five diverse business firms dispelled the stereotype of public employees as security-oriented.[37] The findings showed that security is perceived as less important for public employees than for those in the private sector. Also, in contrast to the standard stereotype, it was found that public employees had greater concern for self-actualization than did the employees in the business sample. While the researchers acknowledged that the low need for security by public employees may be due to the fact that they already possessed it, the researchers concluded that public employees viewed self-actualization as a more potent motivating factor than did their counterparts in business. They also showed that public employees were significantly more satisfied with direct economic benefits than private employees. This may be the result of efforts in recent years to equalize the public and private sector wage rates or could result from the fact that public employees hold lower expectation levels.

While public employees may not suffer from an exaggerated concern with security, the evidence generally supports that rewards in public sector jobs are not allocated in a way that would maximize their motivation potential.[38] Government efforts to measure performance are of a more recent vintage and have met with fewer successes than have similar efforts in business, particularly among business firms in the industrial sector. With performance being more ambiguous, rewards such as promotions and salary adjustments in government tend to be allocated on seniority rather than merit.

The above findings do not allow for any simple conclusions. There are some differences between public- and private-sector employees, but not necessarily in the direction that most people tend to think. While we certainly need more research on this topic, the general view that employees in the public sector are more security-oriented or lack the achievement drive of employees in business is not supported. What does seem apparent is that, though neither the public or private sector do a very good job of making rewards contingent on performance, the public sector is probably most deficient.

Do fewer people today want to be administrators? Our final motivation issue addresses the question of whether there is declining motivation among people to accept administrative positions. Surprisingly, in spite of the social desirability linked with achievement, advancement, the assumption of greater authority and responsibility, and

[37] John W. Newstrom, William E. Reif, and Robert M. Monczka, "Motivating the Public Employee: Fact vs Fiction," *Public Personnel Management,* January–February 1976, pp. 67–72.

[38] Walter L. Balk, "Why Don't Public Administrators Take Productivity More Seriously?" *Public Personnel Management,* July–August, 1974, pp. 318–24.

the earning of more money, the long-term picture demonstrates that there has been a continual decline in the willingness to manage in large organizations.

Evidence indicates that certain motives are consistently associated with administrative success in large organizations.[39] Three motives appear with regularity: (1) a positive attitude toward holding positions of authority; (2) the desire to engage in competitive endeavor, especially with peers; and (3) the desire to exercise power over others. While not as consistently relating to success, three other motives have shown promising results on occasion: (4) the desire to behave in accordance with the requirements of an assertive role; (5) the desire to assume a differentiated role relative to others in the work situation; and (6) the desire to accept routine administrative responsibilities.

Using the above motives, one researcher has found a notable decline in the motivation to manage among business students in college and young administrators.[40] Comparisons of students over several decades finds a significant drop in the desire to assume administrative responsibilities in large hierarchical organizations, to the extent that the researcher has forecasted "a coming shortage of managerial talent."[41] It is important to note, however, that the generalizability of this research is limited to large organizations. There is, for example, little evidence to suggest that any of the six previously mentioned motives are important for administrative success in professional organizations with a simple or minimal hierarchy. Since organic structures place different demands on administrators than do mechanistic structures, it should not be surprising that the motives that lead to success in one may not be significant in the other.

[39] John B. Miner, *Motivation to Manage: A Ten Year Update on the "Studies in Management Education" Research* (Atlanta: Ga.: Organizational Measurement System Press, 1977).

[40] John B. Miner, *The Human Constraint—The Coming Shortage of Managerial Talent* (Washington, D.C.: Bureau of National Affairs, Inc., 1974).

[41] Ibid.

summary of major points

1. *Motivation* is the willingness to do something, conditioned by this action's ability to satisfy some need.

2. Maslow, in his hierarchy of needs theory, said there are five needs. When each becomes substantially satisfied, it no longer motivates. These needs, in ascending order, are:
   a. Physiological
   b. Safety
   c. Love

    d. Esteem

    e. Self-actualization

3. McGregor proposed two distinct views of man: one basically negative, labeled Theory X; and the other basically positive, labeled Theory Y. McGregor believed that if administrators accepted Theory Y assumptions and adopted ideas like participative decision making, the creation of responsible and challenging jobs, and formation of good group relations, employee motivation would be maximized.

4. McClelland proposed that there are three major relevant needs in work place situations: achievement, affiliation, and power. A high need to achieve has been positively related to higher work performance.

5. Herzberg has proposed a two-factor motivation-hygiene theory. He argues that intrinsic job factors motivate, whereas extrinsic factors only maintain and placate employees.

6. The most accurate model for explaining motivation is expectancy theory. The theory states that an individual's desire to produce at any given time depends on his particular goals and his perception of the relative worth of performance as a path to the attainment of these goals.

7. Equity theory proposes that employees compare what they get from a job situation with what they must put into it and, where inequity exists, attempt to correct it.

8. The evidence suggests that money has motivational properties but has different value to different people.

9. Not all people desire autonomy and self-actualization in their jobs. Self-actualization can be achieved off the job as well as in the work place.

10. Public employees are often criticized as security-oriented, though this may be a myth. However, rewards in the public sector do not appear to be allocated in a way that would stimulate employee motivation.

11. The evidence indicates a notable decline by business students and young administrators in their motivation to manage in large hierarchical organizations.

FOR DISCUSSION

1. Define *motivation*. Describe the motivation process.

2. Contrast the hierarchy of needs theory with the motivation-hygiene theory.

3. "Theories X and Y are descriptions of administrative styles." Do you agree or disagree with this statement? Support your position.

4. What role would money play in the motivation-hygiene theory? In expectancy theory? For the individual with a high *nAch*?

5. What role would self-actualization play in the motivation-hygiene theory? In expectancy theory? For the individual with a high *nAch*?

6. "Government employees lack motivation and are preoccupied with security." Do you agree or disagree with this statement? Support your position.

7. What is equity theory? How does it relate to the expectancy model?
8. Contrast expectancy theory with research on *nAch*.

Alice doesn't work here anymore

If there was anyone who didn't sincerely like Alice Kelly, it sure was difficult to identify them. At 52 years of age, she looked and acted like the grandmother we never had. She was sweet, always polite, always helpful. She remembered the birthdays of everyone in the payroll office. She could tell you the name of everyone's husband or wife and children. She was the grand old lady of the payroll office—with twenty-eight years on the job. Since she began work with the City of Charleston, she had performed the same job, week after week, year after year.

While no one spoke about the fact that Alice's work output had dropped over the years, it was obvious to most everyone. Back in the early 1960s, Alice could process forty timecards an hour. Today, fifteen an hour was more likely.

The department's supervisor, Mike McGown, was trying to figure out how to motivate Alice. He concluded that Alice wasn't slowing down because of age. She was physically and mentally as strong as when she joined the department. Her family life had changed over the years—her youngest child had moved out in the early 1970s and her husband had died of a heart attack in 1974—but nothing to explain why her productivity continued to decline, almost on a uniform monthly basis. Mike figured that at her current rate of decline, in another eighteen months she would be putting in her forty hours a week, collecting pay for forty hours, but not really producing anything.

Alice was not financially independent. Her husband had left her a home free and clear and maybe $50,000 in life insurance. But it seemed to Mike that she still depended on her $14,000 a year salary to get by. Her kids were all on their own, doing quite well in fact, according to Alice.

Anything Mike contemplated would have to be consistent with city personnel policies. For example, while there was no union in the office staff, it was an unwritten rule that once a city employee had put in twenty years of service, termination would require not only the approval of the mayor but also the Board of Aldermen.

Questions

1. What additional information might you seek, if you were Mike, in order to help you to determine Alice's loss of motivation?
2. What are Mike's options?
3. What do you think is the best solution and why?

LEADING

FOR FURTHER READING

Chung, K.H., *Motivational Theories and Practices.* Columbus, Ohio: Grid, Inc., 1977. Reviews major theories of motivation, integrates them into a theoretical framework, and translates theory into specific motivational programs applicable to organizations.

Connolly, T., "Some Conceptual and Methodological Issues in Expectancy Models of Work Performance Motivation," *Academy of Management Review*, October 1976, pp. 37–47. Reviews expectancy theory and attempts to identify weaknesses and inconsistencies in empirical studies which have sought to validate the theory.

Deci, E.L., "Paying People Doesn't Always Work the Way You Expect It To," *Human Resource Management*, Summer 1973, pp. 28–32. Argues that when extrinsic rewards are used as payoffs for superior performance, the internal rewards from that performance are reduced.

Hunt, J.G., and J.W. Hill, "The New Look in Motivational Theory for Organizational Research," *Human Organization*, Summer 1969, pp. 100–109. Argues that the expectancy model is superior to either the Maslow or Herzberg models on both theoretical and empirical grounds.

Lawler, E.E., III, *Motivation in Work Organizations.* Monterey, Calif.: Brooks/Cole, 1973. Reviews the recent literature in work motivation and satisfaction.

Steers, R.M., and L.W. Porter, eds, *Motivation and Work Behavior,* 2nd ed. New York: McGraw-Hill, 1979. Some of the major articles in the study of work motivation are reprinted.

Chapter

14

Leadership and Supervision

AFTER STUDYING THIS CHAPTER, YOU SHOULD BE ABLE TO—

Define and explain the following key terms and concepts:	Leadership	LPC
	Trait theories	Leader-member relations
	Behavioral theories	Task structure
	Initiating structure	Position power
	Consideration	House path-goal model
	"High-high" leader	Job scope
	Employee-oriented	Supervision
	Production-oriented	Cosmopolitan
	Managerial grid	Local
	Fiedler contingency model	

Describe:
The difference between administrators and leaders
The limitations of trait theories
The limitations of behavioral theories
The difference between initiating structure and consideration
Why no leadership style is ideal in all situations
The strengths and limitations in current contingency theories
Why the supervisor's job deserves special attention
The differing views held of the supervisor's role

In November 1976, *Time* magazine allocated more than ten pages to an article, "Leadership: The Biggest Issue."[1] Their title underscores the importance that we in North America place on the subject. Rarely does a week go by that we don't read or hear about a leadership void. "Carter can't lead!" "Who will lead the AFL-CIO after Meany is gone?" "Where have all the leaders gone?"

If leadership is such an important issue, the critical question is: What makes a great leader? The tempting answer to give is: Great followers! While there is some truth to this response, the issue is far more complex.

The leadership literature is voluminous, and much of it is confusing and contradictory. In order to make our way through this "forest," we shall consider three basic approaches to explaining what makes an effective leader. The first sought to find universal personality traits that leaders had to some greater degree than nonleaders. The second approach tried to explain leadership in terms of the behavior that a person engaged in. Both of these approaches have been described as "false starts," based on their erroneous and oversimplified conception of leadership.[2] Most recently, we have looked to contingency models to explain the inadequacies of previous leadership theories in reconciling and bringing together the diversity of research findings. In this chapter, we shall present the contributions and limitations of each of the three approaches. However, let us first clarify the distinction between leaders and administrators. Writers frequently confuse the two, although they are not necessarily the same.

Administrators vs. leaders

Administrators are appointed. They have a legitimate power base and can reward and punish. Their ability to influence is founded upon the formal authority inherent in their positions. In contrast, leaders may either be appointed or emerge from within a group. Leaders can influence others to perform beyond the actions dictated by formal authority.

Should all leaders be administrators? Conversely, should all administrators be leaders? One of the few common threads in the literature is that effective leaders are important inputs to a successful organization. Therefore, all administrators should *ideally* be leaders. However, not all leaders necessarily have capabilities in other administrative functions, and hence, not all should hold administrative positions. The fact that a person can influence others does not tell us whether he can also plan, organize, or control.

[1] "Leadership: The Biggest Issue," *Time,* November 8, 1976, pp. 20–31.
[2] Victor H. Vroom, "The Search for a Theory of Leadership," in *Contemporary Management: Issues and Viewpoints,* ed. Joseph W. McGuire (Englewood Cliffs, N.J.: Prentice-Hall, Inc., 1974), p. 396.

Given that, if only ideally, all administrators should be leaders, we will pursue the subject from an administrative perspective. Thus, *leaders* in this chapter will mean those who have both the ability to influence others *and* administrative authority.

Trait theories

If one were to describe a leader based on the general connotations presented in today's media, one might list qualities such as intelligence, charisma, decisiveness, enthusiasm, strength, bravery, integrity, self-confidence, and so on—possibly eliciting the conclusion that effective leaders must be one part Boy Scout and two parts Jesus Christ. The search for characteristics such as those listed that would differentiate leaders from nonleaders occupied the early psychologists who studied leadership.

Is it possible to isolate one or more personality traits in individuals we generally acknowledge as leaders—Franklin D. Roosevelt, Adolph Hitler, Susan B. Anthony, Joe "Bananas" Bonnano, Martin Luther King, Jr., Joan of Arc, Mahatma Gandhi—that nonleaders do not possess? We may agree that these individuals meet our definition of a leader, but they represent individuals with utterly different characteristics. If the concept of traits were to be proved valid, there had to be found specific characteristics that all leaders possess.

Research efforts at isolating these traits resulted in a tremendous number of dead-ends. A summary of these studies resulted in inconsistent conclusions.[3] The best that can be said is that intelligence, extroversion, self-assurance, and empathy tend to be related to achieving and maintaining a leadership position; that is, leaders tend to possess these characteristics to a relatively greater degree than others within the group in which they lead. Except for data surrounding the variable of intelligence, however, the findings allowed for very little generalization.

By the late 1940s and early 1950s, many researchers were beginning to recognize that traits had not provided any substantive base upon which accurate predictions of leadership could be made. Further efforts appeared headed toward more dead-ends. Trait theories had inherent limitations: They ignored the needs of followers; they generally failed to clarify the relative importance of various traits; they ignored situational factors; and, probably most importantly, although they could specify traits that almost all leaders possess, these traits were frequently held also by a substantial number of nonleaders.

Perhaps it was a bit optimistic to believe that there could be consistent and unique personality traits that would apply across the board to all effective leaders no matter whether they were in charge of the Hells Angels, the

[3] C.A. Gibb, "Leadership," in *The Handbook of Social Psychology*, 2nd ed., ed. Gardner Lindzey and Eliot Aronson (Reading, Mass.: Addison-Wesley, 1969), pp. 216–28.

New York Yankees, Gulf Oil Corporation, the Massachusetts General Hospital, the Church of the Latter Day Saints, or Playboy Enterprises.

Behavioral theories

The inability to strike "gold" in the trait mines led researchers to look at the behaviors that specific leaders exhibited. They wondered if there was something unique in the way that effective leaders behave. For example, do they tend to be more democratic than autocratic?

Not only, it was hoped, would the behavioral approach provide more definitive answers about the nature of leadership but, if successful, it would have practical implications quite different from those of the trait approach. If trait research had been successful, it would have provided a basis for *selecting* the "right" person to assume formal positions in organizations requiring leadership. In contrast, if behavioral studies were to turn up critical behavioral determinants of leadership, we could *train* people to be leaders. The difference between trait and behavioral theories, in terms of application, lies in their underlying assumptions. If trait theories were valid, then leaders are born: You either have it or you do not. On the other hand, if there were specific behaviors that identified leaders, then we could teach leadership—we could design programs that implanted these behavioral patterns in individuals who desired to be effective leaders. This was surely a more exciting avenue for it would mean that the supply of leaders could be expanded. If training worked, we could have an infinite supply of effective leaders.

There were a number of studies that looked at behavioral styles. We shall briefly review the two most popular studies: the Ohio State group and the University of Michigan group. Then we shall see how the concepts that these studies developed could be used to create a grid for looking at and appraising leadership styles.

Ohio State University studies

The most comprehensive and replicated of the behavioral theories resulted from research that began at Ohio State University in the late 1940s.[4] These studies sought to identify independent dimensions of leader behavior. Beginning with over a thousand dimensions, they eventually narrowed the list into two categories that substantially accounted for most of the leadership behavior described by subordinates. They called these two dimensions initiating structure and consideration.

[4] Ralph M. Stogdill and Alvin E. Coons, eds., *Leader Behavior: Its Description and Measurement*, Research Monograph No. 88 (Columbus, Ohio State University, Bureau of Business Research, 1951). For an updated literature review of the Ohio State research, see Steven Kerr, Chester A. Schriesheim, Charles J. Murphy, and Ralph M. Stogdill, "Toward a Contingency Theory of Leadership Based Upon the Consideration and Initiating Structure Literature," *Organizational Behavior and Human Performance*, August 1974, pp. 62–82.

Initiating structure refers to the extent to which a leader is likely to define and structure his or her role and those of subordinates in the search for goal attainment. It includes behavior that attempts to organize work, work relationships, and goals. The leader characterized as high in initiating structure could be described in terms such as: assigns group members to particular tasks; expects workers to maintain definite standards of performance; and emphasizes the meeting of deadlines.

Consideration is described as the extent to which a person is likely to have job relationships that are characterized by mutual trust, respect for subordinates' ideas, and regard for their feelings. A leader high in consideration could be described as one who helps subordinates with personal problems, is friendly and approachable, and treats all subordinates as equals.

Extensive research, based on these definitions, found that leaders high in initiating structure *and* consideration (a "high-high" leader) tended to achieve high subordinate performance and satisfaction more frequently than those who rated low on either consideration, initiating structure, or both. However, the "high-high" style did not always result in positive consequences. For example, leader behavior characterized as high on initiating structure led to greater rates of grievances, absenteeism, turnover, and lower levels of job satisfaction for workers performing routine tasks. Other studies found that high consideration was negatively related to performance ratings of the leader by his superior. In conclusion, the Ohio State studies suggested that the "high-high" style generally resulted in positive outcomes, but enough exceptions were found to indicate that situational factors needed to be integrated into the theory.

University of Michigan studies	Leadership studies undertaken at the University of Michigan's Survey Research Center, at about the same time as those done at Ohio State, had similar research objectives: to locate behavioral characteristics of leaders that appeared to be related to measures of performance effectiveness.

The Michigan group also came up with two dimensions of leadership behavior which they labeled employee-oriented and production-oriented.[5] Leaders who were *employee-oriented* were described as emphasizing interpersonal relations; they took a personal interest in the needs of their subordinates and accepted individual differences among members. The *production-oriented* leaders, in contrast, tended to emphasize the technical or task aspects of the job—their main concern was in accomplishing their group's tasks and the group members were a means to that end.

The conclusions arrived at by the Michigan researchers strongly favored the leaders who were employee-oriented in their behavior. Employee-oriented leaders were associated with higher group productivity and higher

[5] R. Kahn and D. Katz, "Leadership Practices in Relation to Productivity and Morale," in *Group Dynamics: Research and Theory,* 2nd ed., ed. D. Cartwright and A. Zander (Elmsford, N.Y.: Row, Paterson), 1969.

job satisfaction. Production-oriented leaders tended to be associated with low group productivity and lower worker satisfaction.

The managerial grid

A graphic portrayal of a two-dimensional view of leadership style has been developed by Blake and Mouton.[6] They propose a managerial grid based on the styles of "concern for people" and "concern for production," which essentially represent the Ohio State dimensions of consideration and structure or the Michigan dimensions of employee-oriented and production-oriented.

The grid, depicted in Figure 14-1, has nine possible positions along each axis, creating eighty-one different positions in which the leader's style may fall. The grid does not show results produced, but rather the dominating factors in a leader's thinking in regard to getting results.

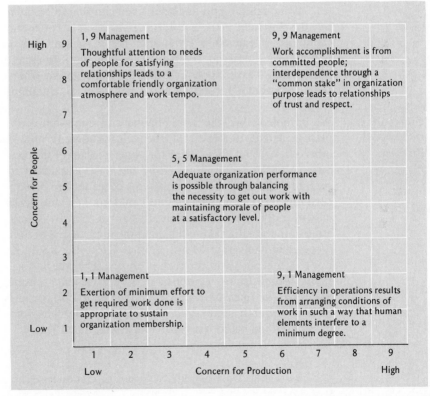

Source: Robert R. Blake, Jane S. Mouton, Louis B. Barnes, and Larry E. Greiner, "Breakthrough in Organization Development," *Harvard Business Review,* 42, November-December 1964, 136. With permission.

FIGURE 14-1   The managerial grid

[6] Robert R. Blake and Jane S. Mouton, *The Managerial Grid* (Houston: Gulf Publishing Co., 1964).

Based on the findings from the research Blake and Mouton conducted, they concluded that administrators perform best under a 9,9 style, as contrasted, for example, with the 9,1 (task-oriented) or the 1,9 (country-club type) leader. The five key positions on the grid and brief descriptions are offered by Blake and Mouton:

1,1: *Impoverished*—a minimum effort to accomplish the work is exerted by the leader.

9,1: *Task*—the leader concentrates on task efficiency but shows little concern for the development and morale of subordinates.

1,9: *Country-Club*—the leader focuses on being supportive and considerate of subordinates, to the exclusion of concern for task efficiency.

5,5: *Middle-of-the-Road*—adequate task efficiency and satisfactory morale are the goals of this style.

9,9: *Team*—the leader facilitates task efficiency and high morale by coordinating and integrating work-related activities.[7]

Although the grid has been given considerable play in the administrative-development area, it unfortunately offers a better framework for conceptualizing leadership style than for presenting any tangible new information in clarifying the leadership quandary. In spite of the grid's simplicity and intuitive appeal, there is little substantive evidence to support the conclusion that a 9,9 style is most effective in all situations.[8]

Summary of behavioral theories

We have described the most popular and important of the attempts to explain leadership in terms of the behavior exhibited by the leader. There were other efforts,[9] but they faced the same problem that confronted the Ohio State and Michigan findings: They had very little success in identifying consistent relationships between patterns of leadership behavior and successful performance. General statements could not be made because results would vary over different ranges of circumstances. What was missing was consideration of the situational factors that influence success or failure. For example, it seems unlikely that Martin Luther King, Jr., would have been a great leader of his people at the turn of the century, yet he was in the 1950s and 1960s. Would Jimmy Carter have risen to become president of the United States had he been born in 1905 rather than 1925, or in New York rather than Georgia? It seems quite unlikely, yet the behavioral approaches we have described could not clarify these situational factors.

[7] Ibid.

[8] L.L. Larson, J.G. Hunt, & R.N. Osborn, "The Great Hi-Hi Leader Behavior Myth: A Lesson from Occam's Razor," *Academy of Management Journal,* December 1976, pp. 628–41; and Paul C. Nystrom, "Managers and the Hi-Hi Leader Myth," *Academy of Management Journal,* June 1978, pp. 325–31.

[9] See, for example, the three styles—autocratic, participative, and laissez-faire—proposed by Kurt Lewin and Ronald Lippitt, "An Experimental Approach to the Study of Autocracy and Democracy: A Preliminary Note," *Sociometry,* 1, 1938, pp. 292–380; or the more recent 3-D Theory proposed by William J. Reddin, *Managerial Effectiveness* (New York: McGraw-Hill, 1970).

LEADING

324

Contingency theories

It became increasingly clear to those who were studying the leadership phenomenon that the predicting of leadership success was more complex than isolating a few traits or preferable behaviors. The failure to obtain consistent results led to a new focus on situational influences. The relationship between leadership style and effectiveness suggested that under condition *a*, style *x* was preferable, while style *y* would be more suitable for condition *b*, and style *z* for condition *c*. But what were the conditions *a*, *b*, *c*, and so forth? It was one thing to say that leadership effectiveness was dependent on the situation, and another to be able to isolate those situational conditions.

There has been no shortage of studies attempting to isolate critical situational factors that affect leadership effectiveness. One author, in reviewing the literature, found that the task being performed (i.e., complexity, type, technology, size of the project) was a significant moderating variable, but additionally uncovered studies that isolated situational factors such as style of the leader's immediate supervisor, group norms, span of administration, external threat and stress, time demands, and organizational climate.[10]

Several approaches to isolating key situational variables have proven more successful than others and, as a result, have gained wider recognition. We shall consider three of these: the autocratic-democratic continuum; and the Fiedler and path-goal models.

Autocratic-democratic continuum model

If autocratic and democratic styles were viewed only as two extreme positions, this model would be correctly labeled as a behavioral theory. However, they are merely two of many positions along a continuum. At one extreme the leader makes the decision, tells his subordinates, and expects them to carry out that decision. At the other extreme, the leader fully shares his decision-making power with his subordinates, allowing each member of the group to carry an equal voice. Between these two extremes fall a number of leadership styles, with the style selected dependent upon forces in the leader himself, his operating group, and the situation. Although this represents a contingency theory, we shall find, upon investigating other contingency approaches, that it is quite primitive.

As depicted in Figure 14-2, there is a relationship between the degree of authority used and the amount of freedom available to subordinates in reaching decisions. This continuum is seen as a zero-sum game; as one gains, the other loses, and vice versa.[11] However, much of the research using this model has been concentrated on the extreme positions.

After reviewing eleven separate studies, Filley, House, and Kerr found

---

[10] Jeffrey C. Barrow, "The Variables of Leadership: A Review and Conceptual Framework," *Academy of Management Review,* April 1977, pp. 231–51.

[11] Robert Tannenbaum and Warren H. Schmidt, "How to Choose a Leadership Pattern," *Harvard Business Review,* March-April 1958, pp. 95–101.

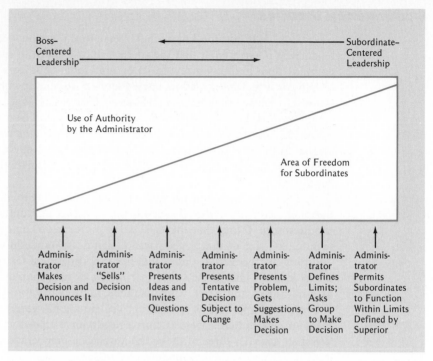

Boss-Centered Leadership ← → Subordinate-Centered Leadership

Use of Authority by the Administrator

Area of Freedom for Subordinates

| Administrator Makes Decision and Announces It | Administrator "Sells" Decision | Administrator Presents Ideas and Invites Questions | Administrator Presents Tentative Decision Subject to Change | Administrator Presents Problem, Gets Suggestions, Makes Decision | Administrator Defines Limits; Asks Group to Make Decision | Administrator Permits Subordinates to Function Within Limits Defined by Superior |

Source: Robert Tannenbaum and Warren H. Schmidt, "How to Choose a Leadership Pattern," *Harvard Business Review*, March-April 1958, 96. With permission.

FIGURE 14-2   Leadership-behavior continuum

seven to demonstrate that participative leadership has positive effects upon productivity while there were no significant effects in the other four. Though only three of the eleven investigations reported on participative leadership's effect on subordinate satisfaction, all showed positive results.[12]

Hamner and Organ reached a similar conclusion when they reviewed the research:

> Generally speaking, we find that participative leadership is associated with greater satisfaction on the part of subordinates than is nonparticipative leadership; or, at worst, that participation does not lower satisfaction. We cannot summarize so easily the findings with respect to productivity. Some studies find participative groups to be more productive; some find nonparticipative groups to be more effective; and quite a few studies show no appreciable differences in productivity between autocratically versus democratically managed work groups.[13]

[12] Alan C. Filley, Robert J. House, and Steven Kerr, *Managerial Process and Organizational Behavior,* 2nd ed. (Glenview, Ill.: Scott, Foresman, 1976), p. 223.

[13] W. Clay Hamner and Dennis W. Organ, *Organizational Behavior: An Applied Psychological Approach* (Dallas: Business Publications, 1978), pp. 396–97.

The above suggests a clear link between participation or the democratic style of leadership and satisfaction, but the relationship of this style to productivity is less apparent. The research can be interpreted as saying that people like democracy, but that it will not necessarily result in higher productivity.

A contingency approach would recognize that neither the democratic or autocratic extreme is effective in all situations. The following models more comprehensively appraise these situational characteristics.

Fiedler model   The first comprehensive contingency model for leadership was developed by Fred Fiedler.[14] His model proposes that effective group performance depends upon the proper match between the leader's style of interacting with his or her subordinates and the degree to which the situation gives control and influence to the leader. Fiedler developed an instrument, which he called the least-preferred co-worker (LPC) questionnaire, that purports to measure whether a person is task- or relationship-oriented. Further, he isolated three situational criteria—leader-member relations, task structure, and position power—that he believes can be manipulated so as to create the proper match with the behavioral orientation of the leader. In a sense, the Fiedler model is an outgrowth of trait theory, since the LPC questionnaire is a simple psychological test. However, Fiedler goes significantly beyond trait and behavior approaches by attempting to isolate situations, relating his personality measure to his situational classification, and then predicting leadership effectiveness as a function of the two.

The above description of the Fiedler model can appear somewhat abstract. Let us now look at the model in more pragmatic detail.

Fiedler's LPC questionnaire contains sixteen bipolar adjectives (such as pleasant-unpleasant, efficient-inefficient). The questionnaire asks the respondent to: "Think of all the co-workers you have ever had. Now describe, using the bipolar-adjective scale, one person you are least able to work with." Fiedler proposes that, based on the answer, he can determine the leadership orientation of the respondent. If the least-preferred worker is viewed in relatively favorable terms, Fiedler suggests, the respondent can be said to be primarily interested in good personal relations with his co-worker; he is what may be generalized as relationship-oriented. Contrarily, if the least-preferred co-worker is seen in relatively unfavorable terms, the respondent is primarily interested in performing well, or is task-oriented.

As we noted, the three contingency dimensions that Fiedler considers are leader-member relations, task structure, and position power. They are defined as follows:

1. Leader-member relations: how well liked, respected, and trusted the leader is
2. Task structure: the degree to which the job assignments are procedurized (i.e., structured or unstructured)

[14] Fred E. Fiedler, *A Theory of Leadership Effectiveness* (New York: McGraw-Hill, 1967).

3. Position power: the degree of influence a leader has over power variables such as hiring, firing, discipline, promotion, and salary increases

Fiedler states that the more positive the leader-member relations, the more highly structured the job activity, and the greater the position power, the greater the leader's influence. For example, a very favorable situation—that is, where the three variables are positive—might involve a payroll supervisor who is well respected and whose subordinates have confidence in her, in a job that provides considerable freedom for her to reward and punish her subordinates, where the activities to be done (i.e., wage computation, check writing, report filing) are specific and clear. On the other hand, an unfavorable situation might be the disliked chairman of a voluntary United Fund-raising team.

Fiedler's study of over 1,200 groups resulted in the graph shown in Figure 14-3. Basically, Fiedler says the shape of the curve in Figure 14-3 implies that task-oriented leaders tend to perform better in situations that are very favorable to them, and also in situations that are very unfavorable (the right and left sides of the curve, which fall below the dotted line). Relationship-oriented leaders, however, tend to perform better in moderately favorable situations—situations that give them neither great nor little control and influence.

One should not surmise that Fiedler has closed all the gaps and put to rest all the questions underlying leadership effectiveness. On the contrary—

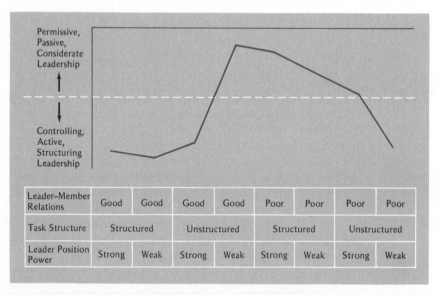

Leader–Member Relations	Good	Good	Good	Good	Poor	Poor	Poor	Poor
Task Structure	Structured		Unstructured		Structured		Unstructured	
Leader Position Power	Strong	Weak	Strong	Weak	Strong	Weak	Strong	Weak

Source: Fred E. Fiedler, ''The Effects of Leadership Training and Experience: A Contingency Model Interpretation,'' *Administrative Science Quarterly*, December 1972, p. 455. With Permission.

FIGURE 14-3 Findings from Fiedler model

the Fiedler model has been challenged on empirical, methodological, and theoretical grounds.[15] Its empirical validity is said to contain serious flaws: Sample sizes have been criticized as too small, creating statistical errors; and it has been claimed that, rather than having presented a theory, Fiedler has developed only a simple generalization, since the model's ability to predict is weak. However, in spite of the criticisms, the Fiedler model continues to be a dominant input in the development of a contingency explanation of leadership effectiveness. Its greatest contribution may be in the direction it has taken leadership research, rather than in any specific answers that it provides.

Path-goal model

Robert House, of the University of Toronto, has proposed a contingency model for leadership that integrates the expectancy model of motivation with the Ohio State leadership research.[16] The model considers the effort-performance and performance-goal satisfaction linkages, and the leadership dimensions of initiating structure and consideration. The model describes the leader as responsible for:

> . . . increasing the number and kinds of personal payoffs to the subordinates for work-goal attainment and making paths to these payoffs easier to travel by clarifying the paths, reducing roadblocks and pitfalls, and increasing the opportunities for personal satisfaction en route.[17]

Since the theory is described in terms of path clarification, need satisfaction, and goal attainment, it is referred to as the path-goal model of leadership. That is, initiating structure acts to "clarify the path" and consideration makes the path "easier to travel."

You will remember that the Ohio State group concluded that effective leaders would score high on both initiating structure and consideration. Yet, there were exceptions. What House has done, therefore, is to reconcile the apparent contradictions in the findings of the Ohio State group. The "high-high" leader is not always the most effective, so House asks: In what situations is initiating structure desirable? In what situations is consideration desirable?

House has concluded from his research that leaders who demonstrate a high degree of direction or initiating structure are more effective when their subordinates are working on unstructured or ambiguous tasks. Where

---

[15] George Graen, et al., "Contingency Model of Leadership Effectiveness: Antecedent and Evidential Results," *Psychological Bulletin,* 74 (1970), 285–96; Ahmed S. Ashour, "The Contingency Model of Leadership Effectiveness: An Evaluation," *Organization Behavior and Human Performance,* 9 (1973), 330–68; and Abraham K. Korman, "On the Development of Contingency Theories of Leadership: Some Methodological Considerations and a Possible Alternative," *Journal of Applied Psychology,* 58, no. 3 (1973), 384–87.

[16] Robert J. House, "A Path-Goal Theory of Leader Effectiveness," *Administrative Science Quarterly,* September 1971, pp. 321–28.

[17] Robert J. House and Terence R. Mitchell, "Path-Goal Theory of Leadership," *Journal of Contemporary Business,* Autumn 1974, p. 86.

the tasks to be done are not clear, subordinates appreciate the leader's clarifying the path to goal achievement. High consideration, on the other hand, results in high employee satisfaction when subordinates are performing structured, routine tasks. In clearly defined and structured tasks, efforts by the leader to explain tasks that are already clear will be seen by the employees as redundant or even insulting.

In summary, the path-goal model proposes that the scope of the job and the characteristics of the subordinates moderate the relationship between a leader's behavior and subordinate performance and satisfaction. More specifically, if there is ambiguity in the mind of the subordinate about his or her job, the leader should clarify the path to work-goal attainment; and if the path is already clear, a leader demonstrating high initiating structure will reduce subordinate satisfaction.

While the path-goal model is a relatively recent addition to the leadership literature, attempts to validate it have met with generally positive results, with some predictions of the model more successful than others. Revisions in the model to include more complex interactions of its variables appear necessary to improve its overall predictive capabilities. However, given the criticisms of Fiedler's model and the support for an expectancy theory of motivation, it appears that the direction the path-goal model is taking holds promise.

One way to look at leadership in practice is to review how organizations choose leaders. Given that an administrator *should be* a leader, do organizations attempt to match individual administrators with favorable situations? The answer is no! Rather than using a situational approach, there is a heavy reliance on selection of individuals with the right "traits" or background and the development of leadership skills through training. In other words, organizations tend to treat leadership as a skill possessed by an individual rather than as a function of the situation. As a result, organizations rely on personality and ability tests to identify individuals with leadership qualities, on training programs for developing leadership skills, on past experience as predictive of future performance, and on political factors as the basis for selecting formal leaders.

Tests are a frequently utilized input upon which leader selection is based. Personality, intelligence, interest, and aptitude tests can provide important information for the selection of structured jobs. However, administrative positions are rarely structured enough for tests to offer substantive predictive input.[18] The diversity of administrative functions and skills makes the design of reliable and valid tests extremely difficult.

Leadership training is a popular way for organizations to prepare individuals for leadership positions. Hundreds of millions of dollars are poured

[18] John P. Campbell, M.D. Dunnette, E.E. Lawler, and K.E. Weick, *Managerial Behavior, Performance and Effectiveness* (New York: McGraw-Hill, 1970).

into leadership training each year by organizations, yet "research has failed to show that leadership training makes organizations more effective."[19] An administrator may come away from a seminar more aware of his or her behavior, more knowledgeable about alternative styles, and even determined to behave and operate differently. However, there is no evidence whatsoever that administrators can, or have ever been able to, successfully change their fundamental behavior.[20]

Further, the empirical evidence does not support the idea that by the acquisition of experience, leadership effectiveness is improved. Studies of Belgian and Canadian military officers, research and development teams, shop foremen, post-office administrators, and school principals indicate that "experienced managers tend to be no more effective than the managers with little experience."[21] The thesis that experience is the best teacher does not appear to work for leadership. Alexander the Great at 18 led the select Macedonian cavalry to victory; William Pitt became prime minister of England at 24; Charles Percy became president of Bell & Howell at 29; Robert Hutchins was president of the University of Chicago at the age of 30.[22] And not one of these men was a highly experienced leader before he became successful.

Organizations often use a person's experience at one level to predict his success at another. The fact that promotions to formal leadership positions are usually used by the organization as rewards can be a problem when one moves to a situation requiring a different leadership pattern.

Laurence Peter's *Peter Principle*[23] offers insight into the fallacy of promoting people to positions of formal leadership. In actual practice, formal leaders are often appointed from the pool of operatives. However, do good teachers make good principals? Do accountants make effective controllers, scholars effective university presidents, doctors successful hospital administrators, or carpenters better carpentry foremen? The evidence suggests that prior operative experience is not an accurate predictor of leadership performance.

Finally, any realistic view of leader selection must consider political factors. Even though they seldom have anything to do with administrative competence, whom one knows, who owes whom favors, who has influence over the final decision, and how others perceive each candidate in terms of their own self-interest are some of the key factors that do influence the selection of formal leaders in organizations. Unfortunately, they are rarely ref-

[19] Fred E. Fiedler, "The Trouble with Leadership Training Is That It Doesn't Train Leaders," *Psychology Today,* February 1973, p. 23.

[20] Theodore Leavitt, "The Managerial Merry-Go-Round," *Harvard Business Review,* July–August 1974, p. 125.

[21] Fred E. Fiedler, "Leadership Experience and Leadership Performance: Another Hypothesis Shot to Hell," *Organizational Behavior and Human Performance,* January 1970, pp. 1–14.

[22] Ibid.

[23] "In a hierarchy, every employee tends to rise to his level of incompetence."

erenced in the literature. Test scores, experience, education, and other objective criteria can be, and frequently are, used to support decisions made on qualitative factors, which are highly susceptible to political influences.

Our conclusion, while somewhat disappointing, is realistic. Little of what most organizations do toward putting the right person into an administrative position is effective in obtaining that end. Specifically, few organizations are taking a sophisticated look at the situation and attempting to make decisions as to who should lead what unit based on matching individuals with situations.

Supervision: a special case of leadership

Supervision is often lumped conveniently together with all other levels in the administrative hierarchy, yet this camouflages the fact that supervisors are uniquely different from all other administrators. This difference is important enough to justify separate discussion. In the following pages we will highlight those factors that make the supervisory position a special case of leadership and we will show how the supervisor's role suffers from ambiguous interpretation.

Supervisors are first-level administrators

The term *supervision* is traditionally used to refer to the activity of immediately directing the activities of subordinates. In such a context, it can occur at all levels of the organization. However, in this section, we will use a narrower perspective: We will view supervision as first-level administration and supervisors as first-level administrators. That is, counting from the bottom of the traditional pyramid-shaped organization, they represent the first or lowest level in the administrative hierarchy.

As first-level administrators, supervisors must, by definition, occupy the only level of administration charged with the responsibility of directing the work of nonadministrative personnel. It is true, of course, that all administrators may direct activities of staff assistants or of their own secretaries, positions that may be nonadministrative; but the direct responsibilities of nonsupervisory administrators are for the work of other administrators. Therefore, supervisors are directly responsible for the daily, face-to-face, immediate operative activities of a group of personnel.

The uniqueness of being a supervisor

We have already noted one of the unique characteristics of supervision—that supervisors do not direct the activities of other administrators. Additionally, there are specific distinctive characteristics that create problems peculiar to first-level administrators. Supervision calls for:

1. Heavy reliance on technical expertise
2. Communication in two languages

332

3. Coping with role conflict
4. Coping with constrained authority
5. Being *the* representative of the administration to operatives

Heavy reliance on technical expertise   Supervisors are required to know the job they supervise. Unlike other administrators, who are heavily oriented toward planning and controlling, supervisors spend a large portion of their time directing and overseeing the activities of their subordinates. And because it is the supervisors who are confronted with the exceptions—the problems in their area—they must have expert knowledge of the jobs that their subordinates perform.

Communication in two languages   Communication is a problem at all levels in the organization; however, it is particularly a problem for supervisors. Middle- and top-level administrators converse with administrators both above and below them. In contrast, supervisors are required to communicate in two distinct languages—that of administrators, and that of the workers. Differing educational backgrounds, value systems, and points of reference are several of the major disparities between the two groups. For example, administrators tend to take on "organizational man" attributes, with high loyalty to the organization, whereas operatives generally see their organizational alliance as merely a way to make a living.

Another way of looking at the problem is through the descriptions of "cosmopolitan" and "local" job orientations suggested by Merton.[24] The cosmopolitan is characterized by a job orientation centered on occupational recognition. His occupation, professional colleagues, and associations are what he looks to for recognition and affiliation. The organization, then, is merely the vehicle that allows cosmopolitans to pursue their professional objectives. They judge their success in terms of growth in their professional community, rather than in the organization per se. For the most part, scientists, researchers, university scholars, physicians, engineers, many skilled tradesmen and union members, and staff personnel can be classified as cosmopolitans. In contrast, Merton describes locals as having job orientations centered on recognition within their employing organization.

These differing orientations require varied approaches to motivation. A particular concern to supervisors is that their superiors tend to have a local orientation—that is, that they owe their loyalty to the organization—whereas, in contrast, the people they directly supervise may owe their loyalty to some group different from the organization. Depending on the group orientation, the individuals themselves, and the degree of loyalty that the organization has enlisted from its workers, operatives may be either cosmopolitan or local in orientation. Asked, for example, about his or her work, a

[24] Robert K. Merton, *Social Theory and Social Structure,* rev. ed. (New York: Free Press, 1957), pp. 393–95.

cosmopolitan might respond, "I am a teamster," or "I am a nurse," whereas a local would respond, "I work for Consolidated Trucking," or "I am employed by the Miami General Hospital."

Supervisors tend to have a local orientation, since their rewards are closely attuned to the organization. Therefore, while top- or middle-level administrators, who themselves are local in orientation, lead subordinates who are also local in orientation, quite frequently first-line supervisors must direct and oversee the activities of people whose loyalties lie outside the organization. This obviously reduces the power bases upon which the individual supervisor can rely.

Coping with role conflict Supervisors are neither fish nor fowl. They are not operatives, and, although they are officially classified as administrators, they are often not accepted by other administrators. A supervisor may be assumed to be like any other administrator, but his activities, status, and security are quite different, for he heads a nonadministrative family—operatives. The additional fact that supervisors are frequently appointed from the operative ranks suggests that if their performance is not found satisfactory, they may be returned to their prior status. As a result, a supervisor's security and status are often less than those of other administrators. Finally, operatives who are promoted to supervisors may have difficulty in resolving how they are to relate to the people who were previously their co-workers, buddies, drinking pals, and so forth. This crisis often results in role conflict.

Coping with constrained authority A hundred years ago, supervisors or foremen had complete authority. That is not so today. For supervisors to survive in the 1980s, they must have a less autocratic style than their predecessors had, must adapt to the constraints imposed by union contracts, and must accept the intricate appeals systems that most organizations provide for the benefit of operatives. In contrast, middle- and upper-level administrators, because of their local orientation, traditionally interpret their superiors' zone of authority in broader terms.

Supervisors are required to interact in an authority relationship with two groups: operatives who are their subordinates, and administrators who are their superiors. It may even be argued that the task orientation of the administrative group ("Get the job done") and the relations orientation of the operative group ("Treat us as human beings and show concern for our feelings") are incompatible demands on supervisors, placing them in a role-conflict situation and in an environment with high responsibility and questionable authority.

The administrator's representative The final problem unique to supervisors is that, to the operatives, they are The Organization. Rules, policies, procedures, and other dictates from above are implemented at the supervisory level, so when operatives think of the administration, their main point of reference is their supervisors. This obviously places high responsibilities upon supervisors to accurately reflect the attitudes and philosophy of the administration, a task made even more difficult for them because they rarely participate in major policy decisions that affect the people they directly supervise.

Differing perspectives on the supervisor's role

The role that supervisors play in an organization is far from consistently interpreted. The position has been described as everything from the "critical link" in an organization to "a necessary evil." Keith Davis has synthesized five such descriptions of the supervisor's role in an organization.[25] They are visually depicted in Figure 14-4.

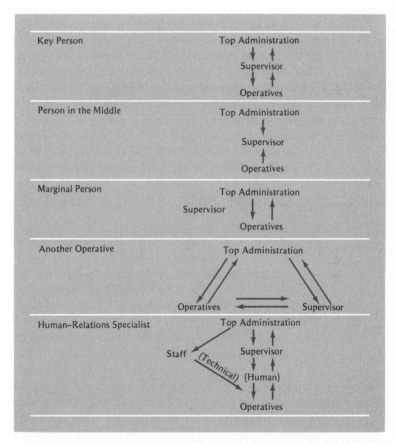

Source: Adapted from Keith Davis, *Human Behavior at Work: Human Relations and Organizational Behavior*, 4th ed. (New York: McGraw-Hill, 1972), p. 121. With permission.

FIGURE 14-4   Different viewpoints of the supervisor's role

[25] Keith Davis, *Human Behavior at Work: Human Relations and Organizational Behavior*, 4th ed. (New York: McGraw-Hill, 1972), pp. 120–23.

Key person in the administrative hierarchy   Supervisors may be viewed as the critical figures in getting the work done, primarily because of their ability to significantly facilitate or hinder the flow of information from operatives to the major decision-making group, or vice versa. They are the hub in the communication wheel, with every critical organizational activity related to generating the final product or service revolving around them.

Person in the middle   Consistent with our "neither fish nor fowl" description, a supervisor is often referred to as "the person in the middle." As noted earlier in this section, he is forced to interact with, and reconcile, the opposing social forces of administrators and operatives. These opposing positions can be attributed to differing frames of reference, value systems, and needs.

Administrators should be task-oriented—concerned with getting the work out and perceiving operatives as merely one of the resources needed to attain the objective. This puts task-oriented pressure on the supervisor. In contrast, operatives are human beings and seek to be treated as such, so they want supervisors who give them freedom, trust, and respect. They are concerned with congenial working conditions and a supervisor who is responsive to their problems and needs. Such expectations can be translated into the desire for a supervisor who is relationship-oriented rather than task-directed.

Obviously, these are difficult—perhaps even impossible—role perceptions to reconcile. Therefore, supervisors become buffers, or people in the middle.

Marginal person   Similar to that of the "person in the middle," but more derogatory, is the view that the supervisor is the powerless nebbish in the organizational hierarchy, left out of, or on the margin of, the principal decisions and influences that affect his unit.

Often unaccepted by administrators, ignored by the staff, and clearly not one of the workers, the supervisor is viewed as one who walks alone. Administrators have a number of other administrative levels in which to find associates, and operatives have their unions and informal groups, but supervisors have no one to interact with except each other.

The marginal status of supervisors is reinforced by their being held responsible for their units' performance, but with authority that is often extremely confining. They are often bypassed on union matters, which are negotiated above them, and constrained by grievance procedures, which subject their decisions to review. These contstraints, plus the abundance of rules and procedures, frequently make them literally powerless in dealing with their constituents.

Another operative   Through the late 1940s, the prevalent view of the supervisor was as an operative, but with a different title. However, the legal interpretation since then has been that supervisors are members of the administrative team. Unfortunately, the way they are treated is frequently at odds with their legal status.

In support of the view that the supervisor is not an administrator, but only another form of operative, are the facts that supervisors lack authority, that they are required to implement decisions that are made elsewhere, and that their role is merely one of following instructions. Further, since many administrators refuse to accept them as full-fledged executives, they lack the status of other administrators. Given the backgrounds of supervisors, which usually include experience at the operative level, it is not surprising that many middle-and upper-level administrators find it difficult to communicate effectively with them. The differences in their social backgrounds, education, values, and reference points frequently make interaction and understanding difficult.

Human relations specialist　A final view of the supervisor's role is that of a human-relations specialist—the equivalent of a staff specialist concerned with caring for the human or people side of the operations. A building never gets dejected, and a computer doesn't get jealous of other computers, but human beings do suffer from these kinds of maladies; hence the need for a people specialist. In their directing and overseeing activities, supervisors utilize their specialty in human relations. It can be said that supervisors get the work done by getting along with others and by their ability to gain cooperation and compliance from their operatives.

Synthesis　It is difficult to accept any of the descriptions above as characteristic of all supervisors, but arguments can be made that there is some truth in each of them. The presentation of these five roles has not been for the purpose of resolving a universal description of the supervisor, but rather to show the differing perceptions with which a supervisor is confronted. And, of course, one should conclude from it that the supervisor truly holds a unique position in the administrative hierarchy, one that is unlike any other administrative position.

> The key man concept prevails in management literature and speeches. Management apparently believes it. Research, however, confirms that the step from belief to practice is quite difficult, and that in practice the supervisor is less a key man.[26]

Supervisors are in the middle and they are marginal. They are not powerful enough to influence the key decisions they are required to carry out. Additionally, their authority and freedom to act are heavily constrained by policies, rules, and procedures that are also imposed from above. The fact

[26] Davis, *Human Behavior at Work,* p. 120.

that they must link two groups, differing significantly in value systems, places supervisors in a kind of purgatory—hopeful of attaining full membership in the administrative ranks, but recognizing the distinct possibility of being returned to the status of operative.

A descriptive view of the supervisor's functions must emphasize the job's demand for technical expertise. Often brushed aside in the literature is the fact that supervisors are the ones who are confronted with the problems among the operatives, and although these may be people problems, requiring human-relations skills, they are more often problems requiring some knowledge of the operations being performed. Supervisors need not be any more or less human-relations specialists than any other administrators in an organization. All administrators require human-relations skills, since they all lead the activities of subordinates.

However, in contrast to middle- and upper-level administrators, supervisors spend a large percentage of their time in the leading function—in the directing and overseeing of their subordinates' activities. As we noted in the earlier part of this book, the ability to move successfully from one position to another increases, all other things being equal, as one moves higher in the organization, owing to the fact that the functions of planning and controlling consume a larger percentage of one's time. Similarly, the leading function becomes *less* time-consuming as one moves higher in the organization. As a result, the need to develop specific technical expertise in the area administered becomes less important as one becomes more concerned with establishing policy than with carrying it out.

Finally, as we noted previously, the view that a supervisor is merely another operative by a different name is no longer an acceptable role description. The courts have determined that supervisors are members of the administrative hierarchy. They may not carry the status and security that middle- and upper-level administrators possess, but nevertheless, they cannot be described as merely "other workers."

summary of major points

1. Administrators and leaders need not be the same.
2. Trait theories dealing with the characteristics leaders are most apt to have, have not proved successful in predicting leadership.
3. Three behavioral theories are discussed:
   a. Ohio State University Studies
   b. University of Michigan Studies
   c. The managerial grid

LEADING

4. Three contingency theories are discussed:
   a. Autocratic-democratic continuum model
   b. Fiedler model
   c. House path-goal model
5. The autocratic-democratic continuum presents leadership styles as existing along a continuum, with autocratic and democratic styles as end points on the continuum. The style selected is dependent upon forces in the leader, the operating group, and the situation.
6. The Fiedler model attempts to match up an individual with a situation that is compatible with his or her basic orientation. Three situational variables are identified: leader-member relations, task structure, and the leader's position power.
7. The House path-goal model identifies two situational variables: job scope and individual characteristics of the subordinate.
8. Supervision is a special case of leadership. Supervisors are the only administrators who direct the activities of nonadministrators.
9. There are unique characteristics in the supervisor's position:
   a. Heavy reliance on technical expertise
   b. Communication in two languages
   c. Personal identity crisis
   d. Constrained authority
   e. Being the representative of the administration to operatives
10. The supervisor's role has a number of interpretations:
    a. Key person in the administrative hierarchy
    b. The person in the middle
    c. Marginal person
    d. Another operative
    e. A human-relations specialist

FOR DISCUSSION

1. "All administrators should be leaders, but not all leaders should be administrators." Do you agree or disagree with this statement? Support your position.

2. Trace the development of leadership research.

3. Discuss the strengths and weaknesses in the trait approach to leadership.

4. "Behavioral theories of leadership are static." Do you agree or disagree with this statement? Support your position.

5. What is the managerial grid? Contrast its approach to leadership with the Ohio State and Michigan groups.

6. What are the contingencies in Fiedler's contingency model? Develop an example where you operationalize the Fiedler model.

7. What are the contingencies in the path-goal model? What are the conclusions obtained from this model?

8. Why is a supervisor a unique type of administrator?

Getting off to a good start

Sue Raynolds is 22 years old and will be receiving her B.S. degree in Human Resources Administration from the University of Nebraska at the end of this semester. She has spent the past two summers working for Mutual of Omaha, filling in on a number of different jobs while people were on vacation. She has received and accepted an offer to join Mutual on a permanent basis upon graduation, as a supervisor in the policy-renewal department.

Mutual of Omaha is a large insurance company. In the headquarters office, where Sue will work, they employ 5,000 employees alone. The company believes strongly in the personal development of its employees. This translates into a philosophy, emanating from the top executive office, of trust and respect for all Mutual employees.

The job Sue will be assuming requires her to direct the activities of 22 clerks. Their jobs require little training and are highly routine. A clerk's responsibility is to insure that renewal notices are sent on current policies, tabulating any changes in premium from a standardized table, and advising the sales division if a policy is to be canceled as a result of nonresponse to renewal notices. Sue's group is composed of all females, ranging from 19 to 62 years of age, with a median of 23. For the most part, they are high school graduates with little prior working experience. The salary range for policy renewal clerks is $675 to $760 per month.

Sue is determined to get her career off on the right foot. As a result, she has been doing a lot of thinking about the qualities of an effective leader.

Questions

1. What are the critical factors that will influence the leadership style Sue uses?
2. Describe the style you think would be most effective for Sue.

FOR FURTHER READING

Driscoll, J.W., D.J. Carroll, Jr., and Timothy A. Sprecher, "The First-Level Supervisor: Still 'the Man in the Middle,'" *Sloan Management Review,* Winter 1978, pp. 25–37. From a survey in six plants of two large companies, the researchers assess what supervisors believe motivates their subordinates, the degree of control supervisors feel they have over these sources of motivation, and how accurately these beliefs are known by each supervisor's boss.

McCall, M.W., Jr., and M.M. Lombardo, eds. *Leadership: Where Else Can We Go?* Durham, N.C.: Duke University Press, 1978. Nine stimulating articles which basically assert that we need to redirect leadership research. The pursuit of rigor and precision has led to an overemphasis on techniques at the expense of knowing what is going on in a direct, human way.

Miner, J.B., "The Uncertain Future of the Leadership Concept: An Overview,"

Organization and Administrative Sciences, Summer–Fall 1975, pp. 197–208. The leadership concept has outlived its usefulness and should be abandoned in favor of a theory of control.

Schriesheim, C.A., J.M. Tolliver, and O.C. Behling, "Leadership Theory: Some Implications for Managers," *MSU Business Topics,* Summer 1978, pp. 34–40. Effective solutions to supervisory problems are not easily found in the leadership literature; practitioners are wise to move with caution.

Vroom, V.H. and P.W. Yetton, *Leadership and Decision-Making.* Pittsburgh: University of Pittsburgh Press, 1973. Presents a normative leadership-participation model with eight contingency variables and five alternative leadership styles.

Zaleznik, A., "Managers and Leaders: Are They Different?" *Harvard Business Review,* May–June 1977, pp. 67–78. A bureaucratic society which breeds managers may stifle young leaders who need mentors and emotional interchange to develop.

15

Managing Change, Communication, and Conflict

**AFTER
STUDYING
THIS CHAPTER
YOU SHOULD
BE ABLE TO—**

Define and explain the following key terms and concepts:	The 3-C's of leading	Decoding
	Change interventions	Communication channel
	Sensitivity training	Feedback loop
	Nondirective counseling	Selective perception
	Survey feedback	Conflict
	Team building	Conflict management
	Intergroup development	Functional conflict
	Behavior modification	Dysfunctional conflict
	Continuous reinforcement	Problem solving
	Intermittent reinforcement	Superordinate goals
	Transactional analysis	Avoidance
	Stroking	Smoothing
	Transcendental meditation	Compromise
	Communication message	Authoritative command
	Encoding	

Describe: The 3-C's and how they impact on each other
Why people resist change
The strengths and weaknesses of the various change interventions
The process of communication
How physical, individual, and semantic barriers affect communication
The difference between functional and dysfunctional conflict
The methods for resolving and stimulating conflict
The relationship between change interventions and conflict resolution
        techniques

The successful leader is responsible for stimulating *change*, promoting effective *communications,* and managing *conflict*. We will call these three responsibilities the three-C's of leading. In this chapter we will demonstrate the interrelationships between these concepts and offer some techniques that administrators can use to bring about change, facilitate more effective communications, and reduce the probability that conflict within the organization will reach destructive levels.

How the 3-C's interrelate

One of the most compelling objectives that an organization has is survival. Since nothing can be accomplished if the organization is unable to survive, administrators must seek survival as a minimal organizational objective. But survival can only result when the organization is able to adapt to changes in its environment. Obvious examples of these dynamic environmental factors include new technologies, changing demands of clients and customers, and new or modified government regulations. So, we can say that change brings about adaptation, and only through adapting can an organization survive.

Stimulating change in organizations, therefore, is a major responsibility of administrators. Unfortunately, as Figure 15-1 illustrates, the management of change is complex, being closely tied in with the concepts of communication and conflict. We particularly want to emphasize that communication precedes change and the interrelationship between communication and conflict.

Communication leads to change

For change to occur, ideas and information must be transmitted to others. If we want employees to do something different than they have been doing in the past, this must be conveyed. Similarly, if we decide to reorganize a given division to improve its performance, nothing can happen until this decision is communicated. Communication, therefore, is the only way an administrator can convey goals, plans, decisions, or directives to others.

Change, of course, is not restricted to altering organizational processes.

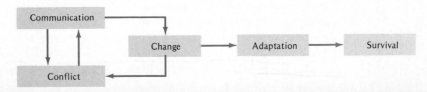

FIGURE 15-1   How the 3-C's interrelate.

It also includes efforts to modify the behavior of individuals—to reduce fears or stereotypes; to increase confidence in themselves; or to make them more open, cooperative, and trusting. In other words, behavioral characteristics may directly hinder an employee's job performance, and the effective administrator should desire to change these characteristics. As we will see later in this chapter, communication can be a means of bringing about this behavioral change.

Communication and conflict

When we communicate, we plant the seeds for conflict. The message that is communicated may be misinterpreted, which can create conflict, or the message might be clearly understood but be perceived as a threat. So, we should recognize that communication, even when it is couched in the positive framework of "increased and improved understanding," can result in conflict.

The reverse relationship also exists; that is, conflict can bring about communication. As we will see later in the chapter, conflict can facilitate change through increased communication.

Summary

In our search to understand how an administrator can facilitate changes in organizational processes and employee behavior, Figure 15-1 identifies that (1) communication leads to change; and (2) conflict leads to communication which leads to change.

Figure 15-1 also tells us, of course, that change itself can produce conflict and again set into motion the process to bring about further change, and that communication can produce conflict without change.

Hopefully, the above confirms our statement that change, communication, and conflict are closely and complexly intertwined. We can now attempt to clarify some of this complexity by addressing the three concepts individually.

The administrator as a change agent

In very simple and general terms, the administrator can concentrate his change efforts either at individuals and groups or at structural processes. The first seeks to change the attitudes and behavior of individuals and groups through communication, decision making, and problem solving. The structural process approach to change represents interventions which change the work content and relationships among employees. We discussed these interventions in chapter 12, under the function of organizing. These include: job enrichment, job rotation, work modules, the shorter workweek, and flex-time. Since these have been thoroughly reviewed previously, we will use this section to elaborate on those interventions that change attitudes and behavior.

| Resistance to | Efforts to bring about change will frequently meet resistance. <u>Change both
| change | threatens the "investment" one has already made in the status quo and increases an individual's feelings of ambiguity and uncertainty.</u>

From a contingency perspective, we can see how individual differences affect one's reaction to change. For instance, why do older people tend to resist change more than younger ones? The answer is that older people have generally invested more in the current system and, therefore, have more to lose by adapting to a change. If you have spent twenty years of your adult life as a mail sorter with the post office, you can be expected to resist automatic mail sorters more actively than a recent high school graduate who has been performing the job for only six months. Having invested relatively little time and effort in developing his skills as a mail sorter, the latter has little vested interest in the old system and is less threatened by automation.

Change also increases uncertainty, and the research demonstrates that people dislike uncertainty. Change requires individuals to trade the known for the unknown. Employees want to know how a different work assignment, a transfer, or new co-workers will affect them. Individuals and groups fear that a change may adversely impact on their self-interest. As a result, employees will frequently create significant barriers to block change, even if this change may later prove to be beneficial to them.

Several classic studies have offered insight into how this resistance to change may be managed. A study designed to change food habits among housewives found that 32 percent of housewives exposed to a group-decision method changed to new variety of meats, in contrast to only 3 percent of the women who received information through the lecture method.[1] The researcher concluded that involvement and group pressure reduced the housewives' resistance to change. Similarly, an experiment in a textile factory established three approaches for bringing about a change in work methods.[2] In the first group, the change was made autocratically by management and announced to the employees. The second involved employee participation through elected representatives. These representatives, with management, worked out the details of the change; then tried the new methods and trained others in the new procedures. In the third approach, there was full participation. All employees shared in the designing of new methods with management. The results strongly favored the value of participation. In the first group, output actually dropped from the previous 60 units per hour to 48 units. However, the participation-by-representation group generated 68 units per hour and the total-participation group averaged 73 units per hour.

[1] Kurt Lewin, "Group Decision and Social Change," in *Readings in Social Psychology*, ed. G. E. Swanson, T. M. Newcome, and E. L. Hartlye, 2nd ed. (New York: Holt, 1952), pp. 459–73.
[2] Lester Coch and John R.P. French, Jr., "Overcoming Resistance to Change," *Human Relations*, 1, no. 4 (1948), pp. 512–32.

**MANAGING
CHANGE,
COMMUNICATION,
AND CONFLICT**

As with the study to change food habits, employee involvement again appeared to reduce resistance to change.

Though both of the above studies are nearly thirty years old, their findings have not been overlooked by students of change. As we shall see, the most popular techniques have a generous bias toward participatory methods. For example, the advocates of sensitivity training, nondirective counseling, and group processes believe that changes are more likely to be accepted by individuals who have been given a voice in determining the content and process of the change.

Change interventions The techniques that follow have been offered as ways to bring about change. Some are far more well known than are others. Transactional Analysis and Transcendental Meditation, for instance, have received extensive media exposure during recent years. Some techniques, particularly behavior modification, smack of manipulation and contain obvious ethical dilemmas. The decision to ever utilize any of these interventions is yours. Your author's objective is not to advocate their usage, but rather to familiarize you with their existence.

Sensitivity training It can go by a variety of names—laboratory training, sensitivity training, encounter groups, or T-groups (training groups)—but all refer to a method of changing behavior through unstructured group interaction. Members are brought together in a free and open environment in which participants discuss themselves and their interactive processes, loosely directed by a professional behavioral scientist. The group is process-oriented, which means that individuals learn through observing and participating rather than being told. The professional creates the opportunity for participants to express their ideas, beliefs, and attitudes. He or she does not accept—in fact, overtly rejects—any leadership role.

The objectives of the T-groups are to provide the subjects with increased awareness of their own behavior and how others perceive them, greater sensitivity to the behavior of others, and increased understanding of group processes. Specific results sought include increased ability to empathize with others, improved listening skills, greater openness, increased tolerance of individual differences, and improved conflict resolution skills.

If individuals lack awareness of how others perceive them, then the successful T-group can effect more realistic self-perceptions, greater group cohesiveness, and a reduction in dysfunctional interpersonal conflicts. Further, it will ideally result in a better integration between the individual and the organization.

Research investigations into sensitivity training indicate that it can effectively change individual behavior. However, the impact of these changes on performance is inconclusive,[3] and the technique is not void of psychologi-

---

[3] John P. Campbell and Marvin D. Dunnette, "Effectiveness of T-Group Experience in Managerial Training and Development," *Psychological Bulletin,* August 1968, pp. 73–104.

cal risks. There have been cases reported of personality damage to those who were not adequately screened prior to participation. One study found that 19 percent, almost one out of five, of group participants suffered from negative psychological effects some six to eight months after the group met, and nearly one out of ten had suffered serious psychological harm.[4]

"The evidence, though still limited, is reasonably convincing that T-group training and the laboratory method do induce behavioral changes in the 'back-home' setting."[5] But behavioral change means little unless we know what kind of change will be achieved. It has been argued, for instance, that there is no "typical" pattern of change; rather, there is a unique response for each individual.[6]

> If this is true, the present lack of knowledge about how individual differences variables interact with training program variables makes it nearly impossible for anyone to spell out ahead of time the outcomes to be expected from any given development program. That is, if training outcomes are truly unique and unpredictable, no basis exists for judging the potential worth of T-group training from an institutional or organizational point of view. Instead, its success or failure must be judged by each individual trainee in terms of his own personal goals.[7]

To summarize the results from sensitivity training, we find that the process changes behavior. Just specifically what that change means, however, in terms of on-the-job behavior, is still the subject of considerable debate.

Sensitivity training, probably because it has been around for a number of years, has been operationalized in some organizations, but there is no evidence to suggest that usage is widespread. For instance, a study of over two hundred business firms that employed 1,000 or more employees found that nearly half gave no sensitivity training in their development programs, and only 7 percent spent more than 10 percent of their development time using this technique.[8]

Other group processes In addition to sensitivity training, there are other less well-known group techniques for bringing about individual change. These include survey feedback, team building, and intergroup development.

[4] Morton A. Lieberman, Irvin D. Yalom, and Matthew B. Miles, "Encounter: The Leader Makes a Difference," *Psychology Today,* March 1973, pp. 69–76.

[5] John P. Campbell, et al., *Managerial Behavior, Performance, and Effectiveness* (New York: McGraw-Hill, 1970), p. 323.

[6] D. R. Bunker, "Individual Applications of Laboratory Training," *Journal of Applied Behavioral Science,* no. 1, 1965, pp. 131–47.

[7] Campbell et al., *Managerial Behavior,* p. 323.

[8] William J. Kearney and Desmond D. Martin, "Sensitivity Training: An Established Management Development Tool?" *Academy of Management Journal,* December 1974, pp. 755–60.

Regardless of the specific approach chosen, the commonality among these techniques is that they use groups to bring about ideas for change through interaction and feedback and as a way to reduce resistance and gain acceptance for change.

For example, *survey feedback* makes use of the questionnaire to assess the attitudes of organizational members. A questionnaire is usually completed by all members in the organization or unit. It typically asks members for their perceptions on a broad range of topics—including decision-making practices, communication effectiveness, and satisfaction with the organization, job, peers, and their immediate supervisor. The data from the questionnaires is tabulated, distributed back to the members, and becomes a springboard for group discussion which centers on identifying problems and clarifying issues that may be creating difficulties for people. The survey feedback method has been shown to change attitudes, but any long-term change in behavior depends on whether the discussions initiate follow-up action.

The objective of *team building* is to improve the coordinative efforts of interdependent members in order to increase an organization's performance. This approach uses high interaction between members to increase trust and openness, and typically includes goal setting, development of interpersonal relations among group members, role analysis to clarify each member's job and responsibilities, and analysis of key processes that go on within the group in search of ways to improve them. But is team building an effective change intervention? The evidence indicates that it is successful in increasing member involvement and participation in group activities and in improving the effectiveness of meetings. Team building, like survey feedback, affects attitudes, but its impact on job behavior is less certain.

Still another group process is *intergroup development*. Intergroup development seeks to change the attitudes, stereotypes, and perceptions that groups have of each other. For example, in one company the engineers saw the accounting department as composed of shy and conservative types, and the personnel department as having a bunch of "smiley-types who sit around and plan company picnics." Such stereotypes can have an obvious negative impact on the coordinative efforts between the departments.

Though there are a number of approaches for improving intergroup relations, a popular method emphasizes problem solving. In this method, each group meets independently to develop lists of its perception of themselves, the other group, and how they believe the other group perceives them. The groups then share their lists, after which similarities and differences are discussed. Differences are clearly articulated, and the groups look for the causes of the disparities.

Are the groups' goals at odds? Were perceptions distorted? On what basis were stereotypes formulated? Have some differences been caused by misunderstandings of intentions? Have words and concepts been defined differently by each group? Answers to questions like these clarify the exact nature of the conflict. Once the causes of the difficulty have been identified the groups can move to the integration phase—working to develop solutions that will improve relations between the groups.

Subgroups, with members from each of the conflicting groups, can now be created for further diagnosis and to begin to formulate possible alternative actions that will improve relations.

There is little hard evidence upon which to evaluate the effectiveness of intergroup development methods like the problem-solving approach we have described. Reports of attitudes being positively influenced by the process exist, but little can be concluded as to the effect on individual behaviors or organization performance.

The use of group processes such as survey feedback and intergroup development is not high but apparently it is growing. *Business Week* reports that the total number of employees that participated in 1977 exceeded 100,000.[9]

Nondirective counseling　As an outgrowth of the Hawthorne studies, the 1940s saw counseling grow in popularity. Administrators became increasingly aware of the importance of human relations in dealing with their workers, and counseling was a major way of improving management–worker relations. If "a happy worker is a productive worker," administrators should strive to make the employee's life as pleasant as economically possible. Obviously, listening to employee problems and offering advice, if it made the worker happier, would be a vital segment of a human-relations program.

All administrators have the responsibility of listening to the legitimate job complaints of their subordinates. However, this listening may be either active or passive. Active listening requires the superior not only to absorb what the worker is saying, but to respond. It is a two-way communication process. The administrator's objective is to understand what bothers the employee, demonstrate empathy for the worker, and suggest possible solutions to the problem(s). This is referred to as directive counseling.

Passive listening differs only to the extent of the administrator's response. In this form of counseling, rather than suggesting answers, the administrator acts as a sounding board. This is nondirective counseling.

Nondirective counseling is based on the belief that people can solve their own problems with the aid of a sympathetic listener. The administrator listens, repeats, synthesizes, understands, and gives feedback; but the subordinate determines the alternatives and makes the decision. Most important, the administrator avoids passing judgment.

Successful nondirective counseling allows the subject to release ten-

[9] "A Productive Way to Vent Employee Gripes," *Business Week,* October 16, 1978, pp. 168–71.

sion and develop greater insight into his problems, and creates the opportunity for him to begin formulating new plans and choices.

When a person is frustrated, nondirective counseling can help in two ways: First, he has the opportunity to vent his frustrations; second, when frustrations are not reduced, he can still improve his ability to adjust to the problems when they are stated and listened to, and solutions are formulated.

Nondirective counseling has received its greatest thrust from the works of Carl Rogers.[10] Referring to it as client-centered counseling, Rogers views it as based on the theory that people have the capacity to grow and develop so as to meet conditions found in the real world.

To illustrate client-centered counseling, here are the rules that the Western Electric Company has established for its counselors:

1. The interviewer should listen to the speaker in a patient and friendly, but intelligently critical manner.
2. The interviewer should not display any kind of authority.
3. The interviewer should not give advice or moral admonition.
4. The interviewer should not argue with the speaker.
5. The interviewer should talk or ask questions only under certain conditions:
   a. To help the person talk
   b. To relieve any fears or anxieties on the part of the speaker that may be affecting his relation to the interviewer
   c. To praise the interviewee for reporting his thoughts and feelings accurately
   d. To veer the discussion to some topic that has been omitted or neglected
   e. To discuss implicit assumptions, if this is advisable.

These rules stress that the interview is clearly the client's and places a premium on his right to be psychologically independent. Frequent questions that the interviewer might ask include: "You feel that. . . ?" and "Why?" If the client achieves, through the counseling process, an insight that will enable him to understand his relation to the situation, he will be able to choose the method of adapting to the reality of the situation.

Nondirective counseling seems to improve morale and reduce worker alienation. Unfortunately, there is little substantive evidence either to support or to negate the value of nondirective counseling. In some instances, a person may be fully capable of resolving his own problems with only the help of a good listener; but experience indicates that a number of problems cannot be resolved through this method. Further, the most viable solution may still not effectively reduce the employee's burden, improve his morale, and reduce alienation.

However, to those who have suggested that nondirective counseling might be worthless, one author has responded that "listening does little actual harm and has the possibilities of doing considerable good."[11] If there is harm, it occurs when administrators expand their nondirective counseling

[10] Carl R. Rogers, *Counseling and Psychotherapy* (Boston: Houghton Mifflin, 1942).
[11] Edwin Flippo, *Management: A Behavioral Approach* (Boston: Allyn & Bacon, 1970), p. 489.

roles and become pseudopsychiatrists. Certain employee problems are beyond the scope of counseling and require professionally trained psychological consultation.

Behavior modification   Behavior modification seeks to shape, improve, and direct the behavior of organizational members through concentration on consequences. As the noted Harvard psychologist, B. F. Skinner, has said, "Behavior is a function of its consequences."[12] By creating pleasing consequences to follow specific forms of behavior, we can increase the frequency of that behavior.

Briefly, behavior modification can be explained as follows: People will most likely engage in desired behavior if they are rewarded for doing so; these rewards are most effective if they immediately follow the desired response; and behavior that is not rewarded, or is punished, is less likely to be repeated. We can expand somewhat upon the research base of this argument.

Skinner has assumed behavior to be determined from without rather than from within. Therefore, he believes it can be exactly predicted. Since we repeat behaviors that are positively rewarded and avoid behaviors that are punished, administrators can effectively influence behavior of others by reinforcing favorable behaviors. However, unfavorable behaviors are to be ignored rather than punished, since the emphasis is on positive reinforcement rather than punishment. Even though punishment eliminates undesired behavior more quickly than nonreinforcement does, its effect is often only temporary and may later have unpleasant side effects, such as dysfunctional conflictual behavior, absenteeism, or turnover.

The two major schedules of reinforcement are called *continuous* and *intermittent*. A continuous schedule reinforces the desired behavior each and every time it is demonstrated. For example, in the case of someone who has historically had trouble being at work on time, every time he is *not* tardy, his administrator might compliment him on this desirable behavior. In an intermittent schedule, on the other hand, not every instance of the desirable behavior is reinforced, but reinforcement is given often enough to make the behavior worth repeating. This latter schedule can be compared to the workings of a gambling slot machine, which people will continue to play even when they know that it is adjusted to give a considerable return to the gambling house. The intermittent payoffs occur just often enough to reinforce the behavior of slipping in quarters and pulling the handle. Evidence indicates that the intermittent or varied form of reinforcement tends to promote steadier and stronger behavior than does the continuous form.[13]

For example, most organizations' policy on sick pay and paid holidays tends to reward undesirable behavior. Rather than rewarding people for

[12] B. F. Skinner, *Science and Human Behavior* (New York: Free Press, 1953).
[13] Fred Luthans and Robert Kreitner, *Organizational Behavior Modification* (Glenview, Ill.: Scott, Foresman, 1975), pp. 49–52.

being on the job, reinforcement—in this case money—rewards absenteeism. In organizations where employees are allowed, say, ten days' sick leave with pay each year, it is not surprising that the vast majority of them consume their full allotment of gratis days. If behavior is truly a function of its consequences, our personnel practice should be adjusted to pay employees something every day for being at work and to omit pay during absent periods. This concept was applied at a Mexican division of a large U.S. corporation to deal with chronic tardiness. Workers were given a small cash bonus, equal to approximately 3 percent of their basic wage, each day they reported to work on or before the designated starting time. The result was a clearly lower level of worker tardiness. By only altering the consequences, the researchers, as predicted from behavior modification experiments, similarly altered the behavior.[14]

One of the most widely publicized uses of behavior modification has been with freight packers at Emery Air Freight.[15] The company has reported that over a three-year period, $2 million was saved by identifying performance-related behaviors and strengthening them with positive reinforcement. Emery sought to have freight containers used for shipments whenever possible, because of specific economic savings. When employees were queried as to the percentage of shipments containerized, the standard reply was 90 percent. An analysis by Emery found, however, that the container utilization rate was only 45 percent. In order to encourage employees to use containers, Emery established a program of feedback and positive reinforcements. Each packer kept a checklist of his daily packings, both containerized and noncontainerized. At the end of each day, he computed his container utilization rate. Almost unbelievably, container utilization jumped to more than 90 percent on the first day of the program and held to that level.

Applications of behavior modification have also been reported by such organizations as Addressograph-Multigraph, Collins Foods International, and Dayton Hudson Corp.[16] At Addressograph-Multigraph, they held a series of meetings between administrators and employees to discuss mutual needs and problems and propose solutions. At these meetings, the administrators set standards for job performance and outlined how they were to be met, and employees identified their needs and provided a list of reinforcers to the administration that would help them to achieve the standards. For instance, these meetings identified that what clerk typists wanted most was a sense of belonging, a sense of accomplishment, and a sense of teamwork. In return, the administrators asked for quicker filing of reports with fewer errors.

At Collins Foods, a behavior modification program was introduced for

[14] J. A. Hermann, et al., "Effects of Bonuses for Punctuality on the Tardiness of Industrial Workers," *Journal of Applied Behavioral Analysis,* Winter 1973, pp. 563–70.
[15] "At Emery Air Freight: Positive Reinforcement Boosts Performance," *Organizational Dynamics,* Winter 1973, pp. 41–50.
[16] "Productivity Gains From a Pat on the Back," *Business Week,* January 23, 1978, pp. 56–62.

clerical employees in the accounting department. Supervisors and employees first met to review the department's actual performance in such areas as billing error rates, and based on this data, improvement goals were established. Employees were praised for reports containing fewer errors than the norm, and results were charted on a regular basis. Significant results were achieved; for example, the error rate in accounts payable fell from more than 8 percent to less than 0.2 percent.

Dayton Hudson experimented with behavior modification in the men's department of one of its stores. The goal was to increase the average sale from $19 to $25. Employees were taught how to make extra sales and were congratulated by supervisors each time a sale went above $19. Within two months, department sales averaged $23.

Behavior modification is gaining popularity among practitioners. As noted, several organizations have used behavior modification to reduce employee mistakes and increase productivity. Additionally, the philosophy behind this concept appears to be affecting some administrators in the feedback they give to employees, the design of employee performance appraisals, and the type and allocation of organizational rewards.

Transactional analysis Transactional Analysis (TA) is both an approach for defining and analyzing communication interactions between people and a theory of personality. The fundamental theory underlying T.A. holds that an individual's personality is made up of three ego states—the *parent,* the *child,* and the *adult.* These labels have nothing to do with age, but rather with aspects of the ego. The parent state is made up of one's attitudes and behavior incorporated from external sources. It is an ego state of authority and superiority. A person acting in his or her parent state is usually dominant, scolding, and otherwise authoritative.

The child contains all the impulses that are natural to an infant. Acting in this state, one can be obedient or manipulative; charming at one moment and repulsive the next. Whereas the parent acts as he or she was taught, the child is emotional and acts according to how he or she feels at the moment.

The adult state is objective and rational. It deals with reality and objectively gathers information. Since it reasons and is reasonable, its actions are almost computerlike—processing data, estimating probabilities, and making decisions. It is not prejudiced by the values of the parent or the natural urges of the child.

In T.A. theory, the parent and child ego states feel and react differently, while only the adult state thinks or processes transactional data logically before acting. Therefore, in most situations, the ideal interaction is an adult stimulus, followed by an adult response.

As long as transactions are parallel—that is, parent-parent, child-child, adult-adult, or parent-child followed by child-parent—dialogue or transactions can go on indefinitely. Parallel transactions leave communication channels open for further exploration of the relationship or resolution of the matter being discussed, even if the initial response does not include all the information sought by the initiated transactions. But real communication is short-circuited whenever a cross-transaction occurs.

Central to any consideration of T.A. is the concept of stroking, or a need for recognition, which influences much of our activity in early life and influences our dominant ego states. Strokes may be either positive or negative, but whenever two or more persons are engaged in a transaction, they are, in T.A. language, exchanging strokes. The types of stroking we learn to accept early in life become established as patterns that stay with us throughout our lives. Understanding of these stroking patterns, according to supporters of T.A., is the first step toward changing them.

What opportunities are there for applying the concepts of T.A. to administration? As described in *Born to Win,* the transactional method is a personal method for analyzing and understanding behavior.[17] Although its primary concern is the discovery and fostering of awareness, self-responsibility, self-confidence, and sincerity, it lays the foundations for changing dysfunctional behavior through the development of mutual trust between people. T.A. promotes authentic interpersonal relationships and provides a means of opening up communication channels and of identifying, analyzing, and deciding on ways to eliminate communication barriers.

Although little substantive research has yet been conducted on T.A.'s effectiveness, responses to T.A. programs have generally been favorable. For example, all sixty-eight managers at the Bank of America who participated in a T.A. seminar believed that their adult ego states had been strengthened, and 86 percent believed that they were better able to handle difficult interpersonal problems.[18] The Bank of New York, which has trained about 250 of its first-line managers and about 50 middle and senior divisional managers in T.A. has been generally pleased with the effect of T.A. "Transactional analysis is clearly not the salvation of the organization, so we've never introduced it as such. But we are convinced after nearly three years of experience with T.A. that it can be a useful tool for both personal and organizational growth."[19]

Although much of the support for T.A. is based on intuitive feel rather than on hard evidence, the T.A. experience may help people to understand others better and assist them in altering their responses so as to produce more effective results.

[17] Muriel James and Dorothy Jongeward, *Born to Win* (Reading, Mass.: Addison-Wesley, 1971).
[18] "Business Tries Transactional Analysis," *Business Week,* January 12, 1974, pp. 74–75.
[19] Harold M.F. Rush, and Phyllis S. McGrath, "Transactional Analysis Moves into Corporate Training," *Conference Board Record,* July 1973, p. 42.

Transcendental meditation   Transcendental Meditation (TM) is a process of self-improvement wherein one mentally repeats a *mantra* (a word with sound but no meaning to the meditator) twice a day for approximately fifteen to twenty minutes at each session. Evidence indicates that this technique may be effective in coping with the problems of worker dissatisfaction.[20] It is claimed that with just a few hours of instruction, any person can correctly practice it.

During meditation, physiological changes occur. Some medical evidence finds that breathing and heart rate decrease significantly, skin resistance increases, and brain-wave patterns are altered.[21]

Supporters of TM claim that it releases tension and anxiety, brings about a sense of physical and psychological relaxation, increases creativity, helps one to cope more effectively and efficiently with daily activities, and lessens dependence upon drugs, including such socially acceptable drugs as cigarettes, alcohol, and tranquilizers.

Several research studies that have appeared within recent years indicate that TM may elicit powerful behavioral, psychological, and physiological changes in participants. The results of one study show a positive relationship between TM and productivity, and that this relationship increases as one moves up in the organization.[22] Based on six measures of productivity, it was concluded that TM is positively related to productivity. Meditators report that they experienced more job satisfaction, improved performance, less desire to change jobs, better interpersonal relationships, and a decreased motivation to rise in the organization hierarchy.

The researchers' evidence also suggested that productivity gains are an increasing function of structural level. The higher the level, the greater the gain in productivity. Gains in job satisfaction and performance, reductions in turnover propensity, and improvements in interpersonal relationships reported by meditators at higher levels were significantly more positive than those of meditators who worked at lower levels in organizations.

The lack of systematic research into transcendental meditation, as it might be applied to administration and organizations, precludes any generalizations. However, the technique does indicate a potential for reducing many negative components associated with the work situation and for changing behavior.

Usage of transactional analysis and transcendental meditation in organizations is limited to date but may increase in future years. The popularity of *I'm O.K.—You're O.K., Born To Win,* and the meditation movement

---

[20] David R. Frew, "Transcendental Meditation and Productivity," *Academy of Management Journal,* June 1974, pp. 362–68.

[21] Susan Tasler, "T.M.: A Prescription to Cure Stress," *Canadian Business,* February 1975, p. 40.

[22] Frew, "Transcendental Meditation."

suggests that administrators may be becoming exposed to TA and TM off the job, yet we have little information to assess its impact in the organization. If a 1975 estimate is correct—that as many as 600,000 Americans practice TM[23]—then we should expect it to become more popular in organizations as a way to reduce stress and bring about behavioral change.

The administrator as a communicator

Since it is only through transmitting meaning from one person to another that information and ideas can be conveyed, the administrator who is a poor communicator is certain to have his or her effectiveness curtailed. The speaker who is not heard or the writer who is not read does not communicate. The philosophical question, "If a tree falls in a forest and no one hears it, does it make any noise?" must, in a communicative context, be answered negatively.

However, for communication to be successful, the meaning must not only be imparted, but also be understood. A letter addressed to me, but written in Portuguese, cannot be considered a communication until I have it translated. Therefore, communication is the *transference and understanding* of meaning.

An idea, no matter how great, is nothing until it is transmitted and understood by others. Perfect communication, if there were such a thing, exists when a thought or idea is transmitted so that the mental picture perceived by the receiver is exactly the same as that envisioned by the sender. Although elementary in theory, perfect communication is never achieved in practice, for reasons to be expanded upon later in this section.

Before making too many generalizations concerning communication and problems in communicating effectively, we should construct a model to depict and explain the components in the communication process.

Communication process model

Before communication can take place, a purpose expressed as a message to be conveyed is needed. It passes between a sender and a receiver. The message is encoded (conversion of an idea or thought to symbolic form) and transmitted through a channel. The message is then decoded (retranslated) by the receiver. To insure that the original meaning of the sender has been transmitted accurately, the receiver concludes the process by providing feedback.

Figure 15-2 depicts the communication process. This model is made up of seven parts: (1) the communication source or sender, (2) the message, (3) encoding, (4) the channel, (5) decoding, (6) the receiver, and (7) feedback. Unfortunately, each of these components has the potential to create distortion and therefore impinges upon the goal of communicating properly.

The source initiates a message by encoding a thought. Four conditions

[23] "The TM Craze: Forty Minutes to Bliss," *Time*, October 13, 1975, p. 49.

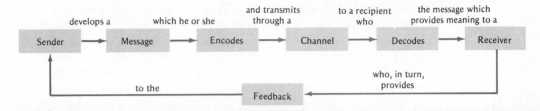

FIGURE 15-2 The communication process

have been described that affect the encoded message: skill, attitudes, knowledge, and the social-cultural system. An author's success in communicating to you is dependent upon his writing skills; his total communicative success includes his speaking, reading, listening, and reasoning skills as well. In the writing of textbooks, if the authors are without the requisite skills, their message will not reach students in the form desired. Each of us is aware that our attitudes greatly influence our behavior. We hold predisposed ideas on numerous topics, and our communications are affected by these attitudes. Further, we are restricted in our communicative activity by the extent of our knowledge on the particular topic. We cannot communicate what we do not know; and should our knowledge be too extensive, it is possible that our receiver will not understand our message. Clearly, the amount of knowledge the source holds about his subject will affect the message he seeks to transfer. And finally, just as attitudes influence our behavior, so does our position in the social-cultural system in which we exist. Your beliefs and values, all part of your culture, act to influence you as a communicative source.

The message itself can cause distortion in the communicative process, regardless of the supporting apparatus used to convey it. Our message is the actual physical product from the source encoding. "When we speak, the speech is the message. When we write, the writing is the message. When we paint, the picture is the message. When we gesture, the movements of our arms, the expressions on our face are the message."[24] Our message is affected by the code or group of symbols we use to transfer meaning, the content of the message itself, and the decisions that the source makes in selecting and arranging both codes and content. Each of these three segments can act to distort the message.

The channel is the medium through which the message travels. It is selected by the source, who must determine which channel will most effectively transfer his message. It is the selection of this mechanism that will bridge the gap between the source and the receiver. The most distinct classification of channels is formal and informal. Formal channels are established by the organization and transmit messages that relate to the professional ac-

[24] David K. Berlo, *The Process of Communication* (New York: Holt, Rinehart & Winston, 1960), p. 54.

tivities of members. They traditionally follow the authority network within the organization. Other forms of messages, such as personal or social, follow the informal channels in the organization.

The receiver is the object to whom the message is directed. But before the message can be received, the symbols in it must be translated into a form that can be understood by the receiver. This is the decoding of the message. Just as the encoder was limited by his skills, attitudes, knowledge, and social-cultural system, so is the receiver equally restricted. Just as the source must be skillful in writing or speaking, the receiver must be skillful in reading or listening, and both must be able to reason. One's level of knowledge influences his ability to receive, just as it does his ability to send. Additionally, the receiver's predisposed attitudes and cultural background can distort the message being transferred.

The final link in the communicative process is a feedback loop. "If a communication source decodes the message that he encodes, if the message is put back into his system, we have feedback."[25] Feedback is the check on how successful we have been in transferring our messages as originally intended. It determines whether understanding has been achieved.

Barriers to effective communication

It was stated previously that perfect communication is an ideal that cannot be achieved. The reason is that there are physical, individual, and semantic barriers to the transference of meaning.

Organizations, because they have formal structures, cannot help but create barriers to effective communication. The existence of excessive hierarchy creates physical distance between people. Additionally, the reliance upon the unity-of-command concept requires that formal communications follow prescribed channels through the organization. As a result, they must frequently pass through many layers of the organization, each offering a potential for distortion. Remember the parlor game of "Telephone," where one person makes up a story that is passed around the group until it reaches the final member, who relates, in his own words, the message that he has received? Anyone who has played that game can see the distortion that can occur as information is passed between levels in an organization.

Human limitations also act as a hindrance to effective communication. Instead of listening in a rational, objective manner to what is being said, we occasionally become emotionally involved. Judgments are imposed in place of rational fact appraisal. People inject their value systems into what they hear or read and, too often, instead of decoding objectively, lose rationality—either because they do not agree with what is being said or, if they have mentally stereotyped the sender, by perceiving the message to be other than the way it was intended. As a result, the receiver hears what he or she expects to hear.

[25] Ibid., p. 103.

March and Simon reported that organizational channeling of information introduces both physical and individual barriers into material that is communicated.[26] They found that when information was passed between levels, it became altered as people interpreted "facts" differently. This phenomenon presents serious problems for executives, who, by definition, work through others and who depend upon their subordinates to interpret information and direct what they perceive to be the main facts upward through the organization's hierarchy.

For example, the mayor of a large city cannot possibly know all the activities going on in the recreation, manpower, or permits and inspections divisions of his city government. He depends on section supervisors, department managers, and division administrators to channel upward key information, so that the decisions he makes that affect these units will be of the highest quality. What the section supervisors deem relevant may determine what is transmitted upward, which in turn will dramatically influence what the division managers receive. All along this chain, facts have been interpreted. Therefore, the information that finally reaches the mayor's office has been substantially filtered. What one manager perceives as superfluous, another may view as critical. Hence, the perceptions of subordinate administrators can restrict an accurate flow of information and create distortions.

Things mean different things to different people. This is particularly true with word connotations. When a person is described as a "real winner," is it to be interpreted literally, or is it being said facetiously? "The meanings of words are *not* in the words; they are in *us*."[27] Semantic problems can impede the communication that is essential for effective organizational performance. A poor choice of symbols, confused meaning of symbols, or the ignoring of nonverbal cues could mean distorted communiques. For example, it has been reported that the differences in the training of purchasing agents and engineers contribute to their difficulty in communicating.[28] As with physicians and professional hospital administrators, their academic training and orientation differ significantly, and the resultant disparate terminology and jargon impede the effective movement of ideas.

Dearborn and Simon performed a perceptual study in which 23 business executives read a comprehensive case describing the organization and activities of a steel company.[29] Six of the executives were in the sales function, five in production, four in accounting, and eight in miscellaneous

[26] James G. March and Herbert A. Simon, *Organizations* (New York: John Wiley, 1958).

[27] S. I. Hayakawa, *Language in Thought and Action* (New York: Harcourt Brace Jovanovich, 1949), p. 292.

[28] George Strauss, "Work-Flow Frictions, Interfunctional Rivalry, and Professionalism: A Case Study of Purchasing Agents," *Human Organization,* Summer 1964, pp. 137–49.

[29] De Witt C. Dearborn and Herbert A. Simon, "Selected Perception: A Note on the Departmental Indentification of Executives," *Sociometry,* June 1958, pp. 140–44.

functions. Each was asked to write down the most important problem he found in the case. Five of the six sales executives, or 83 percent, rated sales important, in contrast to 29 percent of the others. This, along with other results of the study, led the researchers to conclude that the participants perceived aspects in the situation that related specifically to the activities and goals of the unit to which they were attached. Clearly, a group's "selective perception" of organization actions is altered to align with the vested interests they represent.

The response, "I don't understand what you're saying," may result from any of the barriers noted above. Occasionally, an inadequate communication is recognized immediately: "That contradicts what you told me yesterday," or "What you're asking is not clear to me," gives rapid feedback to the sender that there is a problem. More often, there is an absence of feedback, and the sender is unaware of the ineffectiveness of the communication until later, when the behavior of the receiver indicates a lack of communication, or when the receiver states something approximating, "Oh, *that's* what you meant . . . ," or, "I thought you meant . . ."

Techniques for improving communication

As the discussion above demonstrates, one of the key elements to successful communication is feedback. It indicates to the sender whether his ideas have been received as they were originally intended. The feedback concept is as important in the transmission of written communication as it is in oral. Too often in the organizational setting, it is assumed that effective communication has taken place merely by the issuance of a written document: "Of course she must have known about the change in policy; we sent out a memo on it last month!"

The use of feedback improves the communication process and reduces the chance of major disparities between the information or idea received and the one intended. Teachers use examinations for just such a purpose—as feedback to ensure that the messages received by the students were the ones that were originally sent out. An oral technique that administrators often use is to ask, "Would you repeat, in your own words, what you think I said?"

Guetzkow has described feedback, or what he calls verification, as one of two remedies for dealing with distorted communications.[30] His other recommendation is repetition—the repeating of a message over and over again, ideally using various media and different formats. Airport controllers use this technique so that information relayed between the tower and arriving and departing aircraft is as distortion-free as possible. An organization that seeks to promote safety may place "Think Safety" messages on bulletin boards, on operating equipment, and in the organization's newspaper, and

---

[30] Harold Guetzkow, "Communication in Organizations," in *The Handbook of Organizations,* ed. James March (Chicago: Rand McNally, 1965).

also remind employees of the slogan at weekly departmental meetings. Advertisers use repetition in their communications to increase effectiveness. Television, radio, magazines, newspapers, and billboards may all be employed to remind you that, for example, "At McDonald's, we do it all for you."

Listening: the lost art in communication

The problem of ineffective communication is most frequently thought to concern the sender, his encoding, or his selection of the message. However, one of the most necessary communication skills, yet often taken for granted, is listening. Most administrators, unless they have consciously worked to develop this ability, are poor listeners.

The reason for poor listening is easily explained. The average person speaks at the rate of approximately 150 words per minute, whereas we have the capacity to listen at the rate of over 1,000 words per minute. The difference obviously leaves idle brain time, and opportunities for mind wandering. And people who do not have good listening skills are flagrant mind wanderers.

Administrators can improve their ability as empathetic listeners. This ability means listening and not making value judgments. It requires allowing the speaker to express his point or points fully before you react. It means not second-guessing the sender. It requires separating objective from subjective data, and recognizing feelings and emotions in the sender's message. It utilizes feedback to restate the other's position in one's own words. Finally, the empathetic listener uses his idle brain time to review and assimilate what he is hearing.

When these suggestions are put into practice, the result is more efficient communications, more accurate absorbtion of the idea or information the sender has intended, and the setting of an example for others, encouraging them to reciprocate by being empathetic listeners.

Communication and change

Our discussion was meant to demonstrate the importance that communication plays in effective administration. Therefore, at this point in the chapter, it is particularly worth noting two points: (1) successful administrators need to be effective communicators and (2) successful administrators are change agents. The interrelationship between these two roles should not be overlooked.

Effective change interventions require effective communications. Most change interventions rely heavily on interpersonal interactions—between administrators and subordinates, between administrators and other administrators, and among nonadministrative personnel. In fact, sensitivity training, group processes, and transactional analysis specifically seek to create an environment of openness, trust, cooperation and participation. Such an environment can only be achieved where ideas and feelings can be openly expressed and clearly understood.

The administrator as conflict manager

The third role we had attributed to a successful leader is that of conflict manager. By this we mean the responsibility for keeping a conflict at a level that maintains vitality but does not hinder a unit's performance. In the following pages, we will define conflict management, note its importance, and present techniques that administrators can use for managing conflict.

Defining conflict and conflict management

When we use the term "conflict," we refer to all kinds of "opposition or antagonistic interaction. It is based on scarcity of power, resources or social position, and differing value structures."[31] Further, it covers a range that includes the extremes, from subtle, indirect, and highly controlled forms of opposition to overt acts such as strikes, riots, and war.

The noun *conflict,* however, requires a modifier, for there are both functional and dysfunctional forms of conflict. The former, functional, represent confrontation that benefits or supports the goals of the organization. Any conflict that cannot meet this standard is undesirable, and the administrator should seek its eradication. The demarcation between functional and dysfunctional is neither clear nor precise. No level of conflict can be adopted at face value as acceptable or unacceptable. We will find that the level that creates healthy and positive evolvement toward one group's goals may, in another group or in the same group at another time, be highly dysfunctional, requiring immediate conciliatory attention by the administrator.

Thus, functional and dysfunctional conflict is defined in terms of organizational effect. If the conflict supports the goals of the organization and improves the organization's performance, it is by definition a functional or constructive form of conflict. Without functional conflict, there would be few new challenges; there would be no stimulation to think through ideas; organizations would become apathetic and stagnant. In the same vein, those interactions that hinder organizational performance are defined as dysfunctional.

While the above terminology may seem rational and acceptable, it should be pointed out that our use of criteria for defining functional and dysfunctional conflict is not without detractors. Many administrators, for instance, think that the functional or dysfunctional nature of conflict is determined by people's perceptions and response to the conflict, not by its effect on the organization. In our definition, how the participants perceive the conflict is irrelevant. The participants may perceive an action as dysfunctional, in that the outcome is personally dissatisfying to them. In our framework, it would be functional if it furthers the objectives of the organization.

Given our definition of conflict, what then is conflict management? It obviously includes the activities involved in resolving conflicts that are dysfunctional. But it also includes techniques for stimulating conflict when the

---

[31] Stephen P. Robbins, *Managing Organizational Conflict: A Nontraditional Approach* (Englewood Cliffs, N.J.: Prentice-Hall, Inc., 1974), p. 23.

level is insufficient to promote high quality decisions, stimulate creativity and innovation, and foster change. That is, just as the level of conflict may be too high, requiring resolution, it may be too low and in need of stimulation. So, as a conflict manager, the administrator should be concerned with manipulating the tools at his or her disposal, to stimulate or resolve conflict levels as necessary, in order to further the goals of his or her unit. Such actions insure that there is adequate functional conflict to maintain adaptability and promote necessary change, yet prevent conflict from becoming disruptive and destructive.

What are these tools? In the following pages, we will review various methods for reducing conflict and then briefly highlight some ways that conflict may be intensified within the organizational context. You should note, particularly in the review of resolution techniques, how these techniques align with our previous discussion of change interventions. Many of the change interventions use tactics developed for conflict resolution.

Resolution techniques

The two most widely accepted approaches to the resolution of conflict are problem solving and the use of superordinate goals. Additionally, we can note seven other methods that administrators can use to resolve conflicts within their organization: expansion of resources, avoidance, smoothing, compromise, authoritative command, altering of the human variable, and altering of structural variables.

Problem solving   Problem solving, also known as confrontation, seeks resolution of disagreements through face-to-face confrontation of the conflicting parties. Rather than accommodating various points of view, this approach aims at solving the *problem*. It does not determine who is right, who is wrong, who wins, or who loses. Conflict stemming from semantic misunderstanding can be quickly and effectively alleviated in this manner. But problem solving is inherently weak in resolving more sophisticated conflicts, especially those based on different value systems of individuals or groups. The conflict that results when a sales executive must deal with engineers in his day-to-day activities but believes that "engineers cannot work with people" usually cannot be resolved through problem solving.

Superordinate goals   Common goals that two or more conflicting parties each desire and that cannot be reached without the cooperation of those involved are called superordinate goals. These goals must be highly valued, unattainable without the help of all parties involved in the conflict, and commonly sought.

A union-management dispute illustrates the functioning of the superordinate goal. In times of economic plenty, unions are frequently adamant in their demands. But in numerous cases where an organization's survival has been seriously threatened owing to economic pressures, a union has accepted pay reductions to keep the organization in business. Once this crisis is overcome, demands for higher wages return. A compelling and highly valued goal, survival, has preceded other individual objectives and temporarily resolved the labor conflict. Evidence supports the fact, that, when used cumulatively, superordinate goals develop long-term "peacemaking" potential, thereby reinforcing dependency and developing collaboration.

Expansion of resources   A certain college in a university had five departments. Each department was headed by a chairman, who served on a three-year rotating basis. These positions were highly sought because of their status and their incumbents' ability to influence the decision process. As a result, there was a continual struggle within the departments to achieve these chairmanship positions. The dean of the college, after considering what he believed to be dysfunctional consequences from this conflict, decided on a solution: He increased the number of department chairmen to fifteen and redefined the departments as areas. Instead of each chairman having ten to twenty in his department, the new area chairmen would supervise five to seven members.

What the dean had done, in effect, was to expand the scarce resource—in this case, chairmanship positions. By increasing the number from five to fifteen, he reduced the conflict and, hence, its resulting tensions. This technique is extremely successful, because it leaves the conflicting parties satisfied. However, its use is obviously restricted by the nature of its inherent limitation; that is, resources rarely exist in such quantities as to be easily expanded.

Avoidance   One method of dealing with conflict is to avoid it. Avoidance does not offer a permanent way of resolving conflict, but it is an extremely popular short-run solution. In our day-to-day relations, each of us frequently withdraws from the arena of confrontation or suppresses a particular conflict. These are examples of avoidance. The method has obvious limitations, but it has nonetheless been described as "society's chief instrument for handling conflict."[32]

Smoothing   Smoothing can be described as the process of playing down differences that exist between individuals or groups while emphasizing common interests. Differences are suppressed in smoothing, and similarities are accentuated. When we recognize that all conflict situations have within them points of commonality, we further recognize that smoothing represents a way in which one minimizes differences.

Compromise   Compromise techniques make up a major portion of resolution methods. Included here are external or third-party interventions, plus internal compromise between conflicting parties through both total-group and representative negotiation and voting. What differentiates compromise

[32] Herbert Shepard, "Responses to Situations of Competition and Conflict," in *Power and Conflict in Organizations,* eds. Robert L. Kahn and Elise Boulding (New York: Basic Books, Foundation for Research on Human Behavior, 1964).

from the other techniques is that in a compromise decision, each party must give up something of value. While there is no clear winner, there is also no clear loser. In a democratic society, compromise is the classic method in which conflicts can be resolved.

Authoritative command   In an organizational context, probably the most frequently used method for resolving opposing interactions is the use of formal authority. Members of organizations, with rare exception, recognize and accept the authority of their superiors, and even though they may not be in agreement with their decisions, they will almost always abide by them. Thus, authoritative command is highly successful in achieving short-term reduced conflict levels. Its major weakness is the same as that of avoidance, smoothing, and compromise; that is, the cause of the conflict is not treated, but only its effects.

Altering of the human variable   Probably the most difficult method of conflict resolution is to alter the human variable. This specifically means changing the behavior of one or more of the conflict parties. Although such techniques are slow and are frequently quite costly, the results can be substantial. Furthermore, in contrast to smoothing, compromise, or formal authority, changing the behavior of the human variable has the potential to alleviate the source of conflict as well as to end the conflict itself. In other words, even though it takes longer to achieve, it frequently results in long-term and more meaningful harmony.

Potential methods for changing behavior include those techniques previously discussed on pages 346–355.

Altering of structural variables   Our final technique for resolving conflicts is to change the structural variables. Herein lies one of the most manageable of resolution techniques, since we can assume that most administrators have the ability to change their organizational structure, or at least have major input to such changes. In fact, for those scholars who believe that all conflicts result from the structure, techniques such as transferring and exchanging group members, creating coordinating positions, developing an appeals system, and expanding the group's or organization's boundaries are the only realistic methods for dealing with intraorganizational conflicts.

The descriptions above have been brief critiques. I have made no attempt to fully analyze the strengths and weaknesses of each resolution technique; rather, the objective has been only to create awareness of each technique in the minds of students of administration and briefly denote how they differ.

Stimulation techniques   Since our approach to conflict management considers the stimulation of conflict, as well as its resolution, to be a responsibility of the administrator, let us briefly consider some ways in which conflict can be increased when it is in the best interests of the organization to do so.

Communication   Conflict can be increased by manipulation of the communication channels—for instance, by deviation of messages from traditional channels, repression of information, transmission of too much information about other individuals or units, and communication of ambiguous or threatening information.

By deviating formal and informal messages from the traditional communication channels, we can stimulate functional conflict. The division executive, seeking to increase confrontation among his department heads, succeeds by issuing a divisional memo to all heads but one. Similarly, by carefully selecting the messages to be distributed through the grapevine and the individuals to carry them, the administrator can increase conflict.

The administrator who withholds all or part of pertinent communiqués leaves some parties disadvantaged and increases opposition between the haves and the have-nots. On the other hand, the transmission of too much information forces parties to separate important factors from the superfluous. Ambiguity is created, and rethinking and reevaluating are forced. Threatening information also stimulates conflict. Information that a plant will close, that a department is to be eliminated, or that a layoff is imminent will rapidly accelerate conflict intensity and can result in increased unit performance.

Structure   By the way we group activities, we can inject both healthy and unhealthy conflict into the organization. Through redefinition of jobs, altering of tasks, and reforming of departments, sections, or total activities, previously established relationships are broken down. These altered structural forms also redistribute power and, as we might expect, increase conflict. Conflict is increased as a result of fear among participants—of uncertainty, of perhaps having to assume or learn new tasks, or of possible loss of status.

Contingency considerations   The probability of conflict arising and its value to an organization depend on the organization's size, the clarity of the organization's purpose, task technology, and the degree of environmental uncertainty.

As organizations get larger, conflict tends to increase. With increased size, goals become less clear, relationships become more formal, specialization expands, and opportunities for communication distortion occur since information must be passed through a greater number of levels.

The greater the ambiguity over the organization's purpose, the greater the potential for conflict. If the organization's goals are limited in number and complexity, it is easier to direct and coordinate people's efforts. When the goals are ambiguous, the opportunity to interpret them differently increases, and with it an increase in conflict levels.

The more complex and ambiguous the tasks being done in the organization, the less routine is the activity of members. In such cases, decisions surrounding these tasks tend to be nonprogrammed, therefore, conflict should have greater value; that is, it is more likely to be functional. In nonprogrammed decision making, diversity of ideas and difference of opinion will be conducive to innovative alternatives. This is in contrast to routine tasks, involving programmed decisions, where less change is needed and where conflict is more apt to be dysfunctional.

A final consideration affecting conflict is the external environment. Since change is less important in stable environments, conflict is more likely to be functional in uncertain and dynamic environments where adaptation to change is more important.

Administrators, in general, still tend to treat conflict as a universal sin. They see any conflict as bad and try to resolve it. Yet, we do find some evidence of practitioners recognizing the functionality of conflict, and occasional instances where it is purposely stimulated. For example: (1) A sales manager rewards the salesman who, because he has questioned the manager's sales allocation budget, has caused a major error to be uncovered. The environment also becomes reinforcing for challenging that manager on other issues. (2) Promotion of a new city manager is delayed for six months by the mayor, with the intention of letting the five prime candidates "show their stuff." The fittest survives to take the position. (3) An administrator uses the grapevine to pass threatening information and keep his unit "on its toes." (4) Another administrator "shakes up" the department structure within his unit to get some new ideas flowing and reduce apathy. (5) The White House allows the rumor to spread that the president is considering a specific action. Based on the public's response to the rumor, the president gets a reading on public opinion to this action before he takes it.

Administrative practice suggests, however, that the examples above are rarities. For the most part, administrators take an anticonflict posture. Regardless of whether the conflict is functional or dysfunctional, the predominant practice is to attempt to eliminate all conflict. The reasons appear to be, first, that the home, school, and church have historically reinforced anticonflict values; and second, that administrators are frequently appraised and rewarded on the lack of conflict within their units.

> The home has historically reinforced the authority pattern through the parent figure. Parents knew what was right and children complied. Conflict between children or between parents and children has generally been actively discouraged. The traditional school systems in developed countries have reflected the structure of the home. Teachers had *the* answers and were not to be challenged. Disagreements at all levels were viewed negatively. The last major influencing institution, the church also has supported anticonflict values. Church doctrines, for the most part, advocate acceptance without questioning. The religious perspective emphasizes peace, harmony and tranquility.[33]

[33] Robbins, *Managing Organizational Conflict*, p. 17.

Additionally, these anticonflict values carry over into the culture of organizations, whereby tranquility and harmony are praised and rewarded, whereas disequilibrium, confrontation, and dissatisfaction are viewed negatively. As a result, administrators become concerned with eliminating, suppressing, and avoiding conflict.

The effect of anticonflict values on administrative practice is significant. Administrators perceive conflict management to be synonymous with conflict resolution. They attempt to placate any and all disturbances. The value to the organization from functional conflicts is severely curtailed; change is resisted; creativity is stifled; caution is taken to avoid disturbing the status quo; and directives from superiors are accepted without challenge or questioning.

summary of major points

1. The successful leader is responsible for stimulating *change,* promoting effective *communication,* and managing *conflict.*

2. Change brings about adaptation, and only through adapting can an organization survive.

3. Conflict precedes change; communication leads to change; and change itself can stimulate conflict.

4. Change is frequently resisted because it threatens the "investment" one has already made in the status quo; it also increases an individual's feelings of ambiguity and uncertainty.

5. Change interventions include:
   a. Sensitivity training—seeks to provide increased awareness of an individual's behavior and how others perceive him, increased sensitivity to the behavior of others, and increased understanding of group processes.
   b. Other group processes—uses group processes such as survey feedback, team building, and intergroup development to bring about individual change.
   c. Nondirective counseling—provides a "sounding board" through which employees can vent their frustrations.
   d. Behavior modification—seeks to shape, improve, and direct the behavior of organizational members through concentration on consequences.
   e. Transactional analysis—presents a framework for understanding interactions and changing participants' behavior.
   f. Transcendental meditation—a relaxation exercise that releases tension and anxiety.

6. Communication is the transference and understanding of meaning.

7. The communication model is composed of seven parts:
   a. The communication source
   b. The message

      c. Encoding
      d. The channel
      e. Decoding
      f. The receiver
      g. Feedback

8. Barriers to effective communication can develop because of structural limitations or human limitations.

9. Communication effectiveness can be improved through use of feedback and repetition.

10. One of the most important communicative skills, which is often taken for granted, is effective listening.

11. Conflict consists of all kinds of opposition or antagonistic interaction.

12. Organizational conflict has both functional and dysfunctional aspects.

13. Conflict management refers to stimulating or resolving conflict levels, as necessary, toward the end of furthering the goals of an administrator's unit.

14. Nine techniques exist for resolving conflicts:
      a. Problem solving
      b. Superordinate goals
      c. Expansion of resources
      d. Avoidance
      e. Smoothing
      f. Compromise
      g. Authoritative command
      h. Altering of the human variable
      i. Altering of the structural variables

15. Methods of stimulating conflict include:
      a. Deviating messages from traditional channels
      b. Repression of information
      c. Transmission of too much information
      d. Communicating ambiguous or threatening information
      e. Redefinition of jobs
      f. Altering of tasks
      g. Reforming of departments, sections, or total activities.

FOR DISCUSSION

1. Discuss why people resist change and what can be done to lessen this resistance.

2. What is sensitivity training? How effective is it in changing attitudes and job behavior?

3. Contrast survey feedback, team building, and intergroup development.

4. Describe the communication process. How can it facilitate or impede administrators in their change agent role?

5. "Ineffective communication is the fault of the sender." Do you agree or disagree with this statement? Support your position.

6. What can be done to improve one's listening skills?

7. What is the difference between functional and dysfunctional conflict?
8. "Change creates conflict, and conflict creates change." Build an argument to support this statement.

Tip says no way

Marc Lattoni is supervisor of an eight-member cost accounting department in a large metals fabricating plant in Albuquerque, New Mexico. He was promoted about six months ago to his supervisory position after only a year as an accountant, predominantly due to his education—he has an M.B.A., whereas no one else in the department has a college degree. The transition to supervisor went smoothly, and there was little in the way of problems until this morning.

The need for another cost accountant in the office had been obvious to Marc for over a month. Overtime had become commonplace and was putting a strain on department members, as well as the department's budget (overtime was computed at time-and-a-half). Marc had his eye on one particular individual in production control who he thought would fit his needs quite well. He had talked with the production control supervisor and the plant's personnel administrator, and the three had agreed that a young black clerk in production control named Ralph might be a good candidate to move into cost accounting and help with the increased departmental work load. Ralph had been with the company for eight months, shown above average potential, and was only six units shy of his bachelor's degree (with a major in accounting) which he was earning at night at State College.

Marc had discussed the cost accounting position with Ralph earlier in the week, and Ralph had been enthusiastic. Marc had said that, while he could make no promises, he thought that he would recommend Ralph for the job. However, Marc emphasized that it would be a week or so before a final decision was made and the announcement made official.

Well, this morning Marc came into his office and found himself confronted by Tip O'Malley, a 58-year-old cost accountant, who had been at the plant since the opening over 24 years ago. Tip, born and raised in a small town in the deep south, had heard a rumor that Ralph would be coming up and working in the cost department. Tip minced no words: "I've never worked with a black and I never will." Tip's face was red, and it was obvious that this was an emotionally charged issue for him. His short, one-way confrontation closed with the statement: "I have no intention of working in the same department as that fellow."

Questions

1. What is the source of this conflict?
2. What conflict resolution techniques would be relevant in handling this situation?
3. Which do you recommend for Marc and why?

FOR FURTHER READING

Filley, A. C., *Interpersonal Conflict Resolution.* Glenview, Ill.: Scott, Foresman, 1975. Analyzes the conflict process and describes the integrative decision making method of conflict resolution through problem solving.

French, W. L., and C. H. Bell, Jr., *Organizational Development: Behavioral Science Interventions for Organization Improvement,* 2nd ed. Englewood Cliffs, N.J.: Prentice-Hall, Inc., 1978. Popular introductory text that reviews change intervention theory and practice.

Hall, J., "Communication Revisited," *California Management Review,* Spring 1973, pp. 56–67. More often than not, the communication dilemmas cited by people are not communication problems at all, but rather symptoms of difficulties at more fundamental levels of organizational life.

Huseman, R. C., E. R. Alexander III, C. L. Henry, Jr., and F. A. Denson, "Managing Change Through Communication," *Personnel Journal,* January 1978, pp. 20–25. Presents a model for communicating change which can reduce the negative consequences that result from change.

Powell, G., and B. Z. Pozner, "Resistance to Change Reconsidered: Implications for Managers," *Human Resource Management,* Spring 1978, pp. 29–34. Employee resistance to change depends on the information available to them, their influence on decision making, and their past experience with change.

Robbins, S. P., " 'Conflict Management' and 'Conflict Resolution' Are Not Synonymous Terms," *California Management Review,* Winter 1978, pp. 67–75. Discusses functional conflict, conflict stimulation, and reviews the strengths and weaknesses of various conflict resolution techniques.

PART

VI

CONTROLLING

Chapter

16

An Overview of Control

**AFTER
STUDYING
THIS CHAPTER,
YOU SHOULD
BE ABLE TO—**

Measuring
Comparing
Correcting
Personal observation
Statistical reports

Oral reports
Written reports
Significant deviations
Controls by exception
Organizational climate

The relationship between planning and control
The control process
The qualities of an effective control system
Dysfunctional effects of control systems

Most organizations, most of the time, cannot rely on most of their participants to carry out their assignments voluntarily, to have internalized their obligations. The participants need to be supervised, the supervisors themselves need supervision, and so on, all the way to the top of the organization. In this sense, the organizational structure is one of control, and the hierarchy of control is the most central element of the organizational structure.[1]

As the above quote emphasizes, just because planning has been done, an organization structure provided to facilitate achievement of the objectives formulated in planning, and the leading function performed, this does not mean that the organization's goals have in fact been attained. The poor accomplishment of any of the administrative functions increases the importance of making some adjustments, either in the means to the objectives or in the objectives themselves. Control is the final link in the functional chain of administration—checking up on activities to ensure that they are going as planned and, in those instances where there are significant deviations, taking the necessary action to correct the deviations.

Control can be defined as the process of monitoring activities to determine whether individual units and the organization itself are obtaining and utilizing their resources effectively and efficiently so as to accomplish their objectives, and, where this is not being achieved, implementing corrective action. To adjust to changing conditions and to compensate for previous errors, administrators appraise previous and current organizational activities; and they may undertake actions not only to correct actual deviations in performance, but also to prevent deviations before they occur.

The importance of the control function is highlighted when we recall one of the essential elements of administrative activity: the delegation of authority. Delegation requires that the delegator have information and feedback on the performance of his or her subordinates. Since administrators are ultimately responsible, they must know whether or not their subordinates are performing as planned. That, in essence, explains the necessity for control.

The control process

The control process is made up of three separate and distinct steps:

1. *Measure* actual performance.
2. *Compare* it with a standard to determine if there is any difference.
3. *Correct* any significant deviations through remedial action.

[1] Amitai Etzioni, "Organization Control Structures," in *Handbook of Organizations,* ed. James G. March (Chicago: Rand McNally, 1965), p. 650.

Before we consider any of them in detail, note that these steps in the control process assume that standards exist. Without desired performance standards, there is nothing against which to compare actual performance. Therefore, it becomes clear that planning must *precede* control, since it is in the former function that standards are established. However, not only does planning influence control; the process also works the other way, since effective control provides feedback for altering inadequate standards. Therefore, we should view planning and control as being closely linked, each influencing the other.

> The more realistic the standards are, the more meaningful will be the conclusions which can be drawn from comparing results to standards. If those using the standards participate in their creation, the meaning of the deviations from the standards can be uncovered more quickly and easily and the necessity of taking "corrective" action kept to a minimum. Experience has shown that inaccurate standards are found to be the cause of a deviation almost as often as operating deficiencies.[2]

However, since we have discussed standards in the section on planning, we will take that input as given in our consideration of control.

The model in Figure 16-1 depicts the control process, describing the

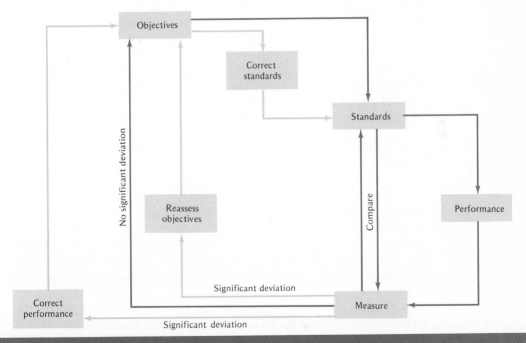

FIGURE 16-1 The control process

[2] Robert J. Mockler, *The Management Control Process* (New York: Appleton-Century-Crofts, 1972), p. 3.

flow from objectives and standards through measuring, comparing, and correction, and back again to objectives.

An example of how this process works can be seen in the activities of the city manager attempting to run his city within his budget. The objectives of the municipality are to provide necessary services to its citizens, at the lowest cost possible. One set of standards that is established to assist in meeting this end is the yearly financial budget. This document provides detailed amounts to be allocated for such diverse activities as personnel salaries, maintenance equipment, utilities, office supplies, and salt for the roads.

On the third working day of each month, the city manager receives a computer printout that categorizes all expenses incurred in the prior month. This printout represents adequate information by which he can compare the actual expenditures during the month against the budgeted standards for that period. Where there are no significant deviations, no action need be taken. However, in those expenditure categories where there is a significant deviation, expenditures either far exceeding or considerably short of the standard, corrective action is necessitated.

Notice from our example that effective administrators do not look only for one-way deviations—that is, in this case, overexpenditures—but for *all* deviations—such as considerable underexpenditures. A significant underexpenditure may mean an inflated and erroneous standard, inadequate performance, or both, and the correction of this deficiency can increase organizational efficiency.

Finally, as Figure 16-1 depicts, when performance has been corrected, we return to our objectives. Additionally, as the figure implies, it is very possible that the standards themselves may need to be altered to accurately reflect changes that have occurred within or outside the organization.

Measure　　To determine what actual performance is, it is necessary to acquire information about it. This first step in control, then, is measuring. Let us consider *how* we measure and *what* we measure.

How we measure　Four common sources of information, frequently used by administrators to measure actual performance, are personal observation, statistical reports, oral reports, and written reports. Each has particular strengths and weaknesses; however, a combination of them increases both the number of input sources and the probability of receiving reliable information.

Personal observation provides firsthand and intimate knowledge of the actual activity, without the filtering of information through others. Also, it permits more intensive coverage, since minor as well as major performance activities can be observed, and since personal observation offers the opportunity to interpret as much from what is not overt as from what is explicit.

Omissions, facial expressions, and tones of voice can inform the administrator greatly on what is actually occurring.

Unfortunately, in a time when quantitative information suggests objectivity, personal observation is often viewed as highly subjective, particularly since it offers little precision. In addition, it does consume a good deal of time. And finally, personal observation is frequently interpreted by employees as the sign of a lack of confidence in them, or of mistrust.

The current wide usage of computers in organizations has resulted in a rapid increase of the use of *statistical reports* for measuring actual performance. This measuring device, however, is not limited to computer outputs. It also includes graphs, bar charts, and numerical displays of any form. Although statistical data are easy to visualize and effective for showing relationships, such reports offer limited feedback and the possibility of inaccurate interpretation of composite figures.

Acquisition of information through conferences, meetings, one-to-one conversations, or over the telephone represents examples of *oral reports*. The advantages and disadvantages of this method of measuring performance are similar to those of personal observation. Although the information is filtered, it is fast, allows for feedback, and permits language expression and tone of voice, as well as the words themselves, to convey meaning. Historically, one of the major drawbacks of oral reports was the problem of recording this information for later reference. But, as was well documented by the Watergate hearings, our technological capabilities to record conversations have progressed, in the last several decades, to the point where oral reports can be as permanent as if they were written.

Actual performance may also be measured by *written reports*. As with statistical reports, they are slower yet more formal than first- or second-hand oral measures. This formality also often means greater comprehensiveness and conciseness than oral reports give. Finally, because they provide a permanent record, they are usually easy to catalogue and reference.

Given the varied advantages and disadvantages of each of these four measurement techniques—personal observation, and oral, statistical, and written reports—comprehensive control efforts by administrators should entail the utilization of all four. Such an approach increases both input sources and reliability.

What we measure *What* we measure is probably more critical to the control process than *how* we measure. The selection of the wrong criteria can result in serious dysfunctional consequences. Besides, what we measure determines, to a great extent, what people in the organization will attempt to excel at.

Obviously, what we measure is determined by those criteria for which standards have been established. Areas commonly controlled include financial efficiency (return on investment, or accounts-receivable turnover), operating efficiency (revenue dollars generated per employee, or salaries as a percentage of gross revenue), administrative performance (efficiency in resource usage, and effectiveness in attaining stated objectives), quantity of output, quality of output, employee absenteeism and turnover, and waste and scrap generation.

A freight-transport company might consider the following criteria for control:

Number of cars per train, compared to standard
Tons carried per car or truck
Ratio of long hauls to short hauls
Cost per ton-mile
Frequency and value of damage per shipment
Frequency and value of lost freight per shipment
Storage charges collected or paid per month
Maintenance cost per unit
Labor cost per ton-mile
Cost of maintenance of buildings, grounds, or trackage per ton-mile[3]

In contrast, a service organization's criteria might include:

Number of words typed per minute (office-clerical)
Number of pages proofread per hour (office-clerical)
Number of forms processed per hour (office-clerical)
Number of transactions posted per hour (accounting-clerical)
Number of orders processed per hour (billing)
Number of services offered versus number offered by competitors
Cost of services as a percentage added to base operating costs
Cost of services per revenue dollar
Frequency of services versus competitor's service
Average length of time required to adjust customer complaints, versus standard
Number of employees trained and encouraged to greet customers cordially
Time required to process service calls, versus standard
Average length of time from order initiation to delivery, versus standard
Percentage of orders shipped on time[4]

In many activities, we find it difficult to measure performance in quantifiable terms. For example, it is far more difficult to measure the effectiveness of a teacher or a research chemist than of a seamstress on a piecework wage plan. As a result, some activities and jobs must be subjectively appraised. However, as we noted in our discussion of management by objectives in chapter 8, using standards against which performance will be compared requires that the standards be verifiable, measurable, and tangible.

[3] Paul M. Stokes, *A Total Systems Approach to Management Control* (New York: American Management Association, 1968).
[4] Ibid.

We should, therefore, attempt to quantify subjective criteria—determine what value a task, job, unit, or department makes to the total organization, and then break down its value in objective segments. So even though a teacher's effectiveness is difficult to measure, it is not impossible. If we assume that the objectives of the teacher's job are stimulating his students to the excitement of continued learning, developing good work habits among them, and transferring basic reading, writing, mathematical, and logic skills, we might include criteria such as the following:

Percentage increase in reading comprehension during school year
Percentage increase in reading speed during school year
Percentage of work assignments turned in on time
Comparison of absenteeism rates with school norms
Average number of outside books read by students during school year
Comparison of scores on standardized grammar tests between beginning and end of school year
Comparison of scores on standardized mathematical computation tests between beginning and end of school year

Compare   Comparison is the determination of the degree of difference between actual performance and the performance that is desired. The comparison step in the control process requires that the standard be known, that actual performance has been measured, and that guidelines exist for determining the extent of allowable tolerances. For example, the sales manager for the Middletown Volkswagen dealership prepares a report during the first week of each month that describes sales for the previous month, classified by model. Figure 16-2 displays both the standard and actual sales figures for the month under review.

Should the sales manager be concerned with the July performance? Business was a bit better than he had originally forecasted, but does that mean that there are no significant deviations? Even though performance in this situation is generally quite favorable, there are several items that de-

---

FIGURE 16-2   Middletown Volkswagen sales performance for July

Model	Goal	Actual	Over (under)
Rabbit	50	57	7
Rabbit Deluxe	35	33	(2)
Beetle Convertible	2	2	—
Dasher	10	16	6
Sirocco	8	8	—
Bus	13	5	(8)
Total units	118	121	
Total sales $	$581,000	$593,000	
Average sales $	$ 4,924	$ 4,901	

serve the sales manager's attention. However, the number of items that deserve attention depend on what the sales manager and his superiors have agreed or believe to be *significant*. How much tolerance should be allowed before corrective action is precipitated?

Obviously, two items can be ignored by the sales manager, since there are no deviations; that is, the goal and actual performance were exactly the same. But is the shortage on Rabbit Deluxe sales significant, or within a reasonable tolerance? Why was the sales goal so far off on the Dasher? It oversold budget by 60 percent, a fact that appears to deserve investigation. Was the goal too low, or were actual sales just particularly high for this one month? What are the implications for orders of this model from the factory?

An item needing obvious attention is Bus sales. The fact that it was off by over 60 percent requires an explanation and specific corrective action. In this case, the sales manager had a quick explanation for the difference; it had been expected that a major local hotel would purchase nine of these vehicles for shuttling guests to and from the airport and downtown. Since that forecast was made, however, the sale of those nine buses had become highly uncertain.

Corrective action

The third and final step in the control process is the action that will correct the deviation. It will be an attempt either to adjust actual performance or to correct the standard, or both.

There are two distinct types of corrective action. One is immediate and deals predominantly with symptoms. The other is basic and delves into the causes. Immediate corrective action is often described as "putting out fires," whereas basic corrective action gets to the source of the deviation and seeks to adjust the differences permanently.

Immediate action corrects something right now and gets things back on track. Basic action asks how and why performance deviated. In many organizations, administrators rationalize that they do not have the time to take basic corrective action and therefore must be content to perpetually "put out fires." Good administrators recognize that they must find the time to analyze deviations and, in situations where the benefits justify such action, permanently correct significant differences between standard and actual performance.

To continue our example of the Volkswagen sales manager, he might take basic corrective action on the positive deviation for Dashers and the negative deviation on Bus sales. If sales of the Dasher have been greater than expected for the past several months, the cause may be a general increased demand for the vehicle. This might justify upgrading the standard for future-month sales of this model. The recognition that the poor showing for Bus sales was attributed to the loss of one anticipated sale may justify an intensive effort to restimulate the hotel prospect, or possibly, a one-month promotion of buses so that inventories of this model will not become too inflated.

Almost every organization has some type of controls. They may be crude, informal, or ineffective, but they are usually there. Where they work, they can significantly reduce opportunities for decision makers to act in ways that allow their self-interest to override the interests of the organization. In other words, the better the control system, the more difficult it is for decision makers to satisfy their own interests at the *expense of the organization*. However observation suggests that controls are frequently designed poorly, thus allowing decision makers to act in their self-interest, often to the detriment of the organization's goals.

Control criteria

We can control four characteristics of performance in an organization: quantity, quality, cost, and time.

Quantity

The easiest type of control device to use are those that appraise measurable outputs. Number of applications processed, cars sold, patients treated, full-time-equivalent students taught, and rounds of ammunition fired are all quantity criteria.

Quality

Quality if often difficult to measure. It is far simpler for the manager of an automobile assembly plant to determine whether the daily output of vehicles is achieved than whether the quality of that output met specific standards. To appraise the quality of a given output, it is necessary to have input on form, dimensions, color, and so on. And determining the quality of a person's performance in a service area is even more complex. An employee may process 200 applications a day, but if the level of skill and judgment he exercises is unsatisfactory, performance suffers and the organization is less effective.

Cost

Organizational inputs and outputs, whether they are human or physical, can be translated into dollar terms. Budgets represent the most frequently used cost-control device.

Items as diverse as absenteeism, hiring efforts, labor activity, capital-equipment usage, and public relations can all be "costed out," thus making it possible to compare apples, oranges, and bananas through a common denominator.

Time

Since time is a scarce resource in any organization, it is a criterion by which administrators can gauge efficiency. The difference in completing a project in six months or in seven, or in meeting or not meeting a bid deadline, may be the difference between outstanding organizational performance and failure. Similarly, if the standard time for performing medical examinations at an army induction center is 35 minutes, performing them in 45 minutes will significantly reduce the output of the administering physician.

Qualities of an effective control system

Effective control systems have certain qualities in common. Following are half a dozen prescriptions for controls.

Timeliness

Controls should call attention to deviations in time to prevent serious infringements on organizational performance. For example, consider a five-step production process in which we can afford only two evaluations, the second of which must be final quality control following the last operation. The probability that an error will be made in any step in the process—that is, the product's becoming out of tolerance—is .01, or 1 in 100. Assume also that the cost of the beginning raw material is 10¢. If the five steps are cutting, cleaning, copper-coating, drying, and polishing, and the cost for these steps is 15¢, 5¢, $1.40, 10¢, and 40¢, respectively, where do we put our first checkpoint?

Answer: After the cleaning process! If necessary, at this time in the process we can scrap the product with only 30¢ worth of labor and material expended. If the product is out of tolerance at this point, we waste $1.40 by copper-coating it.

Flexibility

Effective controls must be flexible enough to adjust to changes in both the internal operations and the external environment that the organization confronts. The recognition that change is a constant, which all organizations must confront, requires that the controls be adjustable. Therefore, in our example above, if a breakthrough were to be made in the coating process so that in the place of copper we could use tin, reducing the cost from $1.40 to 20¢, we might find it expedient to move our control checkpoint from after the cleaning process to after the drying process.

Economy

Although a comprehensive control system is desirable, it must be economically reasonable to operate. Any system of control has to justify the benefit that it gives in relation to the costs it incurs. As a result of some of the positive synergistic results that are possible with comprehensive controls, we find that larger organizations can justify, and therefore impose, more detailed and comprehensive controls than can small organizations.

Understand-ability

If administrators and operatives cannot understand the controls, their value is highly questionable. Therefore, it is sometimes necessary to substitute less complex controls for sophisticated devices in order to attain universal comprehension. People should perceive that the criteria by which they are being evaluated are realistic, valid, and consistent with their understanding of what is expected of them.

Strategic placement

Effective and efficient controls suggest that attention be given to those factors that are strategic to the organization's performance. Controls should cover the critical operations, activities, and events within the organization.

Further, they should be placed only on those factors that administrators can influence.

Peter Drucker suggests, for example, that controls should focus only on internal operations.[5] He believes that you cannot "control" revenues; you can control only those things inside the organization that generate the costs.

In a department where labor costs are $20,000 a month and postage $35 a month, a 5 percent overrun in the former is more critical than a 20 percent overrun in the latter. Hence, we should establish controls for labor, a critical dollar allocation; postage expenses would not appear to be critical.

In most organizations, approximately 90 percent of an administrator's problems come from 10 percent of what he is responsible for. Only a few clients, services offered, products produced, or people he leads are major problem areas, so by establishing strategic controls on the 10 percent, he can make his efforts achieve the highest return.

Ability to stress the exception

Since we cannot control all activities, we place our strategic control devices where they can call attention to the exceptions and omit alerting us when the system is within tolerance. An exception system ensures that not all deviations receive the administrator's attention, but only those outside the acceptable tolerance range.

In complex organizations, there is too much information to pass all data upward through the organization. In fact, the greater the degree to which delegation is utilized, the greater the necessity to use an exception system of control. For example, a supervisor may have authority to give semiannual raises, approve individual expenses up to $500, and make capital expenditures up to $1,000. Any deviations above the activities or amounts within the supervisor's authority require approval from higher levels in the organization. The checkpoints or controls are then in the authority constraints.

The exception view suggests that efficiency in control draws the administrator's attention specifically to significant exceptions. If an activity is within tolerance, it would not get the administrator's attention.

In contrast to the previous discussion of what an effective control system *should* look like, we find that systems tend to control the visible and convenient factors rather than the important ones. And, of course, the measures chosen satisfice rather than optimize.

Controls tend to be placed on activities that are visible and easy to measure. Consistent with decision-making realities, performing well on visible criteria is more likely to lead to personally desirable outcomes. Similarly, because important measures are often difficult to obtain, administrators frequently substitute convenient measures for the more difficult, yet important,

[5] Peter F. Drucker, *Management: Tasks, Responsibilities, Practices* (New York: Harper & Row, 1973), p. 497.

ones. Of course, there is no problem when criteria that are visible and easy to measure are also important. Unfortunately, however, this is not always the case. We might note that the tendency to favor the visible and convenient is enhanced where the unit's objectives are not clear, previously agreed upon, or expressed in measurable terms.

Because different individuals and constituencies use different criteria to define and measure performance, we should expect that administrators resort to satisficing.[6] This is certainly evident when evaluating individuals and departments, and is even applicable when appraising the organization as an entity.

> The hospital is evaluated on one set of grounds by patients, on another set by medical personnel, and on still a third set by third-party payers such as Blue Cross or welfare agencies. Employers of the university's graduates have a different set of criteria for assessing the university than do its alumni, and the faculty employ still different measures. Prisoners, guards, and legislative groups emphasize different aspects when evaluating the prison.[7]

So, what happens? Lacking any clear agreement on what is "good performance," relative measures are used.[8] But relative to what? Administrators use their organizational unit as the reference point, and compare current levels of performance against the unit's past performance. This, too, is consistent with our discussion of incrementation and risk-minimization in chapter 5. By using the past performance of the unit as the standard for defining effectiveness, slow but steady gains can be rewarded, and risks can be kept to their lowest level. This is particularly evident if, for example, the standard were other units in the organization or other similar organizations. It is a lot easier to compete against oneself than it is to confront the uncertainty of external forces.

Dysfunctional effects of control systems

Until now we have ignored the negative impact that control systems can have on an organization's performance. An increasing body of research indicates that, like the tail wagging the dog, controls can dominate the organization.

"Lookin' good" on control criteria

Because any control system has imperfections, problems occur when individuals or organizational units attempt to look good exclusively in terms of the control devices. In actuality, the result is dysfunctional in terms of the organization's goals. More often than not, this is caused by incomplete

[6] James D. Thompson, *Organizations in Action* (New York: McGraw-Hill, 1967), p. 88.
[7] Ibid., p. 88.
[8] Ibid., p. 89.

measures of performance. If the control system evaluates only the quantity of output, don't be surprised when people ignore quality. Similarly, if the system measures activities rather than results, people will spend their time attempting to look good on the activity measures. A few examples will illustrate.

In a public employment agency, which served workers seeking employment and employers seeking workers, employment interviewers were appraised by the number of interviews they conducted. The result should not have been surprising: interviewers emphasized the *number* of interviews conducted rather than the *placements* of clients in jobs.[9]

A management consultant specializing in police research has noted that police departments generally respond as they perceive the community wants them to respond. For example, he tells of one city in which officers rarely stopped their patrol cars: "They kept cruising. Fast. Why? Because the City Council thought it was important to have high mileage—that this indicated police effectiveness." Another city's police force concentrated its efforts on the arresting of drunks, because police administrators were appraising officer efficiency on the total number of arrests. Statistically, a drunk was as good a catch as a cat burglar, and much easier to collar.[10]

Where performance is measured in output and there are choices offering different degrees of difficulty, we find employees taking the easiest, fastest approach to success. The one that makes them look the best will be the one selected. Unfortunately, single criterion controls frequently direct the behavior of the organization's members away from the attainment of organizational objectives.

Publications by university faculty, number of arrests by law-enforcement organizations, number of acquittals in a law firm, or number of books issued by a publisher are all single criteria that, should they become the only criteria for performance, can have a negative effect on the overall performance of the organization.

Similarly, financial and accounting efficiency reports can result in the same dysfunctional effects. When these reports are used alone—since they are easy to interpret and readily applied—people become preoccupied with "looking good" on the single efficiency criterion. For example, if an administrator is appraised on output per man-hour, both operatives and administrators can be expected to act in a manner that makes them look good on this criterion, regardless of the effect on the efficiency of the organization. But why does this occur?

The answer must be found by watching the behavior of people whose efficiency is judged—or misjudged—on the basis of these quick, simple indexes

[9] Peter M. Blau, *The Dynamics of Bureaucracy,* rev. ed. (Chicago: University of Chicago Press, 1963).

[10] "The Cop-Out Cops," *The National Observer,* August 3, 1974.

that never were designed to tell the whole story or reveal the whole picture. People who must pass these rigid tests quickly acquire a pattern of behavior that has but one objective—to make their score look better, even though this may mean the sacrifice of other, less tangible advantages and of longer-run gains for the business as a whole.[11]

When a measure such as return on investment, number of units of output generated per day, or some other single criterion is used to appraise personnel, people give their greatest attention to this criterion and, most often, ignore other important attributes of their job performance. If you tell a plant administrator he will be measured only on profit, do not be surprised to find him depleting the human resources of his organization so that he may look impressive on his financial statement. If you tell workers they will be paid relative to the number of units of output they generate, you can anticipate an increase in rejects. If you evaluate inspection control on the number of rejects the inspectors find, a number of marginally acceptable units are bound to be rejected.

Manipulation and "covering your behind"
In order to protect themselves from being reprimanded by the control system, people can engage in behaviors solely designed to influence the information system's data output during a given control period. Rather than actually performing well, employees can manipulate measures to give the appearance that they are performing well.

Budgets, for example, are not infrequently manipulated so as to defer bad news. Sales made on October 1st are recorded as of September 30th to make September's figures look better. Major expenses that occur in December of 1980 are charged against January 1981 operations, causing the 1980 figures to look better than they actually are. Of course, this can work two ways: good results can be prolonged over longer periods. It is not unheard of, for instance, for retail store managers to cut off the day's sales in the midafternoon, after a particularly busy morning, changing the dates on the cash registers, and running the rest of the day's sales as if they were made the following day. While contrived, it protects the manager should "tomorrow's" sales prove to be low. Of course, this can be carried on to manipulate revenues and expenses on weekly, monthly, or yearly reports.

Protecting one's "behind" was recently evident at a large New England manufacturing plant. The plant had had a history of dramatic ups and downs in the receipt of orders, the down part of the cycles ultimately culminating in major lay-offs. When the plant manager told *all* staff administrators to cut their personnel by one-third, regardless of the lay-off's impact on their workload, one new supervisor quickly learned her lesson. When

[11] Frank J. Jasinski, "Use and Misuse of Efficiency Controls," *Harvard Business Review,* July–August 1956, pp. 105–12.

business picked up, she overstaffed her department so when the next "cut your department by one-third" dictum came, she would have enough fat to cut without hurting her department's output. In other words, the lesson she learned, dysfunctional as it was, was that if lay-offs are going to be dictated across the board, ignoring individual department needs, there was no incentive to run a lean and efficient department. To do so would only hurt her department at some future time.

Where future budgets are allocated on the basis of past expenditures, this protective behavior often leads to spending sprees at the end of the budget period. Where money not spent is not allocated again, there is little incentive to cut costs. This occurs in military units where fuel allocations are based on the previous year's expense. For instance, when an Air Force unit is consuming less than its allocation, usage levels are raised to ensure the budget is spent. It is not unusual to see a significant increase in flight-time during the last month or two of a fiscal year.

It has recently been reported that the federal government "plays the game" by manipulating its figures for federal civilian employment, which is figured as of the last day of the fiscal year, September 30. In order to keep the figures within predetermined bounds, "departments and agencies often 'discharge' their temporary employees—about 160,000—on September 29 and 'rehire' them on October 1."[12]

Observations of practice indicate the importance of an activity will influence the probability that its evaluation will be manipulated. Organizationally important activities are more likely to make a difference in a person's rewards; therefore, there is a greater incentive to look good on these particular measures.[13] Individuals are motivated to manipulate data in favorable ways—distorting actual data, emphasizing successes, suppressing evidence of failures—when it is likely to influence rewards; on the other hand, "we would not expect other than random errors on matters which do not affect the distribution of rewards."[14]

In addition, it has been observed that, in practice, employees are very much aware that: "bosses are not always right, but they *are* the bosses." The boss, in most cases, is the person who determines rewards. Employees, including administrators, look to see what their superior gives the greatest attention to and checks the most. Regardless of its relevance to actual job performance, employees will attempt to please their boss by looking good on the measures that he or she has defined as important. As we are often reminded in the classroom, if instructors evaluate class participation by re-

[12] "The Inflationary Federal Pay Ripoff," *Business Week,* October 23, 1978, p. 132.
[13] Edward E. Lawler III and John Grant Rhode, *Information and Control in Organizations* (Pacific Palisades, Cal.: Goodyear Publishing Co., 1976), p. 108.
[14] Thompson, *Organizations in Action,* p. 124.

AN OVERVIEW
OF CONTROL

warding not what is said, but rather how it is said, don't be surprised that students pay a lot more attention to style than substance.

One remedy for dysfunctional controls: multiple measures

Since incomplete measures of performance are the basic cause of the dysfunctions reported above, we suggest that one remedy, in addition to those discussed in our description of the qualities of an effective control system, is the use of multiple measures of performance. Multiple measures have a dual effect. Since they are more difficult to manipulate than a single measure, they can discourage efforts to merely, "look good." And, since performance can rarely be objectively appraised by looking at a single indicator, multiple measures can offer a more accurate assessment of performance.

Just as football quarterbacks have to be rated on more criteria than merely the percentage of passes completed, so must all organizational members be rated on more than one criterion. If a professional quarterback were judged only on this, he would concern himself with (1) passing only, (2) doing it only when the probability of completion was quite high, and (3) emphasizing the short passes, which are easiest to complete. Such behavior would make his percentage high, yet probably at the expense of the final performance criteria—such as whether his team outscored its opponents. (Or, possibly, whether all tickets to the game were sold out.) Completing the key pass at the right time, completion of the long, unexpected touchdown pass, and reasonable risk taking may be necessary to win games. Even though there is probably a positive correlation between high pass-completion percentages and team standings, the relationship is far from perfect. Therefore, a quarterback must be judged on other criteria also. In reality, almost every starting quarterback in the National Football League has an incentive clause in his contract that stipulates a bonus for his team's winning the division, conference, or Super Bowl championships.

In the same way, consistent with our analogy, all organizational members must be judged on composite criteria.

> To adequately balance the stress on the contradictory objectives or criteria by which performances of a particular individual or organization are appraised, there must be an implied or explicit weighting of these criteria. When such a weighting system is available, it is an easy task to combine the measures of the various subgoals into a composite score for overall performance.[15]

Were such a multiple-criteria system of ratings employed by an organization and found acceptable by administrators, it would presumably serve as a balanced guide that would stress desired objectives.

[15] V.F. Ridgway, "Dysfunctional Consequences of Performance Measurements," *Administrative Science Quarterly*, September 1956, p. 246.

Some organizations are considerably more difficult to appraise than others, but it can be done. For instance, appraising the performance of a city like New York is indeed ambitious, yet a comprehensive productivity evaluation system has been employed by New York City since 1972, with impressive results.[16] In 1974, for example, the administration realized a savings of $80 million through measuring and correcting below-target productivity in sixteen departments, including Parks and Recreation, Parking Violations, Fire, Police, Corrections, Vital Records, Social Services, and Consumer Affairs. The prime objectives of this control system are to achieve budgetary gains and to give the public tangible evidence that the city is concerned with performance.

New York has established 336 measures of productivity performance in the sixteen departments. Some of the factors measured are quite interesting—for example, pothole filling, felony and misdemeanor arrests, correctional-facility population, playground bench repairs, and noise levels. Such a composite control system discourages employees from emphasizing and "looking good" on any one or two criteria.

Contingency factors in the control process

The amount and extent of control exercised is contingent upon the degree to which it is necessary for the organization to achieve its objectives. All administrators control *in kind,* but deviate *in degree;* that is, they all perform the control function, but the time and effort devoted to the function vary. Given the organization's objectives, we need to know what the critical or strategic points are in the organization's operation, and the benefits versus the cost of control.

More specifically, we should be looking at three variables to ascertain the amount of controlling that is necessary:

1. Degree of decentralization
2. Organizational climate
3. Cost-benefit of control data

The greater the degree of decentralization, the more important it is that top administrators have feedback on the performance of subordinate decision makers. Since the top executives hold ultimate responsibility for the actions of those decision makers down through the organization, they must be properly assured that their subordinates' decisions are both effective and efficient.

The organizational climate may be one of trust and confidence, or one of fear and reprisal. In the former, we can expect to find considerably more

---

[16] Fred Ferreti, "Greater Productivity Cited by Beame Administration," *New York Times,* March 9, 1975, pp. 1 and 43.

self-control, and in the latter, externally imposed control systems to ensure that performance is within standards. As with leadership styles, motivation techniques, degree of structuring, and the extent to which organization members participate in decision making, the type and extent of controls should be consistent with the organizational climate.

The importance of an activity influences the matter of whether, and how, it will be controlled. Importance is interpreted in terms of the benefit that accrues from appraising, compared to the cost incurred in making the appraisal. Critical activities are obviously more important than superfluous activities and provide greater benefits.

For example, assume that we work in an electronics firm that wants to know the strength of vacuum tubes it manufactures. Ideally, we would like to know the strength of each, but the test destroys the tube. Therefore, we cannot test the strength of every vacuum tube. We sample a number of them sufficient to tell us statistically the effectiveness of our vacuum-tube manufacturing operation. We have inherently valued the benefits derived from evaluating a given number of tubes versus the costs incurred.

Similarly, in some organizations, the ramifications from the failure of an activity can be so high that a disproportionate amount of resources may be expended to ensure that standards are met. This would certainly have been the case with the NASA program. Each item aboard the space ships had to be of the highest quality and within the tightest of tolerances. Extensive controls can be justified in these cases, since the benefits from success are high and the costs of failure enormous.

summary of major points

1. Control is the process of monitoring activities to determine whether individual units and the organization itself are obtaining and utilizing their resources effectively and efficiently so as to accomplish their objectives and, where this is not being achieved, implementing corrective action.

2. The control process comprises three activities:
   a. Measuring
   b. Comparing
   c. Correcting

3. Four common sources of performance measurement are:
   a. Personal observation
   b. Statistical reports
   c. Oral reports
   d. Written reports

4. Comparing is the determination of the degree of difference between actual performance and what is desired.
5. Corrective action can adjust actual performance, correct the standard, or both.
6. There are four criteria by which performance can be controlled:
   a. Quantity
   b. Quality
   c. Cost
   d. Time
7. Effective control systems have certain qualities in common. They are:
   a. Timely
   b. Flexible
   c. Economical
   d. Understandable
   e. Strategically placed
   f. Designed to stress the exception
8. Controls can create dysfunctional effects:
   a. Emphasis is placed upon looking good in terms of the control devices rather than in terms of the organization's goals.
   b. Information is manipulated to distort, to emphasize successes, or to suppress evidence of failures.
9. One remedy for dysfunctional effects is to overcome incomplete measures of performance by using multiple criteria.
10. Contingency factors in the control process include:
    a. Degree of decentralization
    b. Organizational climate
    c. Cost-benefit of control data

FOR DISCUSSION

1. Describe the control process.
2. How do administrators measure performance?
3. "Basic corrective action is always superior to immediate corrective action." Do you agree or disagree with this statement? Support your position.
4. "Control systems are not necessarily objective or effective." Discuss the validity of this statement.
5. Elaborate on the human problems in controlling any criterion.
6. Discuss the variables that effect the degree of control necessary.
7. Since an administrator cannot control everything, what should guide his or her decision as to what should be controlled?
8. "Multiple measures of performance can significantly reduce the dysfunctional impact of controls." Build an argument to support this statement. Now build an argument against this statement.

Would someone please tell me what's going on here?

"I took office six weeks ago," the new mayor began, "and I'll be honest—I haven't the slightest idea of what is going on in this city. The thing that surprises me the most, I guess, is that things *are* as bad as I'd been saying in my campaign speeches!"

The mayor of this community of 200,000 people continued, "I was a business executive for nearly thirty years. I know how things are supposed to be! And one thing I know for sure is that if you're gonna run an organization properly, you've got to have decent information on what's happening. That information just isn't here. For instance, I don't know how much of this year's budget each department has spent, and neither do they. Monthly expense reports are issued at least six months *after* the month ends! Can you believe it—getting a report on February's expenses in August? What can you do about it *then?* But that's the good news! The bad news is that there are no mechanisms in the system to tell me how well departments are performing. I don't know if waste collection is being done, never mind if it's being done effectively and efficiently. The same goes for police and fire protection, snow removal, health care, recreational facilities, and so on. The only feedback I get is nasty phone calls when someone has a complaint. The problem is immense. I really don't know where to begin."

Questions

1. If you were the mayor, what questions would you be asking?
2. Describe the type of controls you would install if you were mayor.

FOR FURTHER READING

Argyris, C., *The Impact of Budgets on People.* New York: Controllership Foundation, 1971. A now classic review of the dysfunctional effects that budgets can have on people.

Cammann, C., and D.A. Nadler, "Fit Control Systems to your Managerial Style," *Harvard Business Review,* January–February 1976, pp. 65–72. Managers should choose the control strategy that is appropriate for his or her particular situation and managerial style.

Giglioni, G.B., and A.G. Bedeian, "A Conspectus of Management Control Theory: 1900–1972," *Academy of Management Journal,* June 1974, pp. 292–305. A comprehensive review of the literature on control theory.

Hofstede, G., "The Poverty of Management Control Philosophy," *Academy of Management Review,* July 1978, pp. 450–61. The traditional control process is applicable only when there is a single powerholder whose objectives count as the organization's, or when there is a dominant coalition of powerful individuals who hold a consensus on objectives.

CONTROLLING

Holloway, D.C., "Subjective Quantification of Performance in Hospitals," *Hospital Administration*, Summer 1972, pp. 54–63. Presents various types of performance measures, their validity, and why performance measures have not been used.

Tannenbaum, A.S., *Control in Organizations*. New York: McGraw-Hill, 1968. Demonstrates the relationship between control, coordination, and information.

Chapter 17

Control Techniques

**AFTER
STUDYING
THIS CHAPTER,
YOU SHOULD
BE ABLE TO—**

Cost-benefit analysis
Cost-benefit planning
Cost-benefit evaluation
Planning-programming-
budgeting-system

Zero-base budgeting
Sunset legislation
Management audit
Human resource accounting

How cost-benefit evaluation facilitates control
Measures of effectiveness and efficiency
The steps in the PPB System
How PPBS improves the public sector budgeting process
The role of decision packages in ZBB
Criteria that the management audit considers
The logic behind using human resource accounting

In the following pages, we will introduce a number of techniques by which administrators can evaluate and control the performance of organizational programs and units. While these techniques are applicable to all sizes of organizations, their sophistication and cost of implementation may make them inappropriate for smaller organizations. In fact, in very small organizations, the most popular control technique is far from sophisticated—it is direct observation by the administrator. It's a walk through the office or plant to identify those activities that are not going as planned. But personal observation may not result in a correct interpretation—as is so evident when everyone "looks busy" when the boss is around. And, of course, as organizations become larger and more complex, there is a need for more sophisticated control techniques. It is the purpose of this chapter to introduce some of these more sophisticated techniques. We can begin by advocating the control potential in looking at activities in cost-benefit terms.

Cost-benefit analysis

An interesting overall approach for appraising and controlling performance is through cost-benefit analysis. Developed during World War II, it is both a way of thinking and a control device. In the former role, it forces us to look at all activities as having strengths (benefits) and weaknesses (costs). The goal is to minimize efforts where benefits do not equal or exceed the accompanying costs. As a technique, cost-benefit analysis lends itself to situations in which it is difficult to measure the benefits from a given program or objective and determine its relevant costs. Its usage grew rapidly during the 1960s as administrators in public-sector organizations became increasingly concerned with evaluating defense, welfare, education, and other high-cost programs. The value of these programs was intuitively believed to be high, but little had been done to objectively support this belief. We will consider how cost-benefit analysis can appraise performance of projects and organizations, particularly in the public sector, but in profit-making firms as well. Cost-benefit analysis requires organizational units to clearly define their major objectives or programs, systematically analyze the alternative ways these objectives can be reached, and evaluate whether the objectives have been effectively and efficiently achieved.

In the administrative process, the statement of objectives and the alternative approaches to their achievement are considered to lie within the function of planning. It would be entirely appropriate, therefore, to consider cost-benefit analysis under planning. However, the topic is included here under controlling to emphasize that the approach is particularly valuable when one seeks to assess the impact and effectiveness of existing activities in achieving a unit's objectives, in contrast to the actions of problem definition or alternative development, which are properly part of planning.

Cost-benefit *planning* is used in appraising alternatives, as shown in Figure 17-1. This example shows comparative estimates, in a typical year for a valley community, of the costs of flood damage without protection and costs of progressively sophisticated protection alternatives. Plans A through D all have benefits that exceed their costs, but Plan C offers the greatest marginal advantage. From Plan B to Plan C, costs increase $8,000 and benefits $9,000, but from Plan C to Plan D, costs increase $12,000 while benefits are expanded by only $7,000. The progressive marginal benefits from C to D do not offset the marginal costs incurred.

Figure 17-1 demonstrates the value of cost-benefit planning. However, we want to look at cost-benefit *evaluating,* which assumes that the alternatives have already been appraised and that the activity is ongoing. Therefore, we desire to appraise ongoing performance by determining the degree to which organizational units are achieving the goals to which they have addressed themselves, and how successful the units are in achieving their goals with the minimum usage of resources. We can review past results and compare these against standards and objectives to determine our relative success—in other words, consider the benefits derived against the costs incurred.

Why cost-benefit evaluation?

In formulating appropriation needs, an organization's administrators attempt to expand their domain by seeking greater resources for the same objectives or by expanding their objectives. If dollars exist, needs will be found. For, like individuals, organizations traditionally find ways to spend what is available. What is needed, therefore, is to assess the objectives of a unit and its efficiency and effectiveness in achieving these objectives.

Given our understanding of the political realities in decision making, it is not unreasonable to expect administrators to exceed their budgets, "pad" their objectives, and take whatever action is necessary to increase

FIGURE 17-1 Comparative estimates of flood-protection programs, using cost-benefit planning

Plan	Annual cost of project	Average annual Damage	Total benefit (Reduction of Damage)	Incremental Benefit
Without protection	0	$38,000	0	0
A. Levies	$ 3,000	$32,000	$ 6,000	$ 6,000
B. Small reservoir	$10,000	$22,000	$16,000	$10,000
C. Medium reservoir	$18,000	$13,000	$25,000	$ 9,000
D. Large reservoir	$30,000	$ 6,000	$32,000	$ 7,000

Source: Adapted from Otto Eckstein, *Public Finance*, 3rd ed. (Englewood Cliffs, N.J.: Prentice-Hall, 1973), P. 23. With permission.

their appropriations. If dollars govern size, if size is a base from which power can be built, and if power is the key to political influence, it is only natural that administrators actively covet higher budgets and relatively greater dollar inflows for their units. As a result, it is necessary that some form of evaluation compare the benefits that are derived from a unit's performance against the costs that are incurred in achieving its goals.

Evaluation by cost-benefit analysis

To evaluate the cost-benefit performance of the organization as a whole, an organizational unit, or a specific program, we must review the objectives, the activities undertaken to achieve the objectives, and the cost of the resources consumed in attaining them. Moreover, we must be sure that we determine not only whether the objectives were accomplished, but to what extent the achievement of the objectives is directly attributed to the activities of the program or unit. For instance, to appraise the benefits resulting from a high school education, one must be sure that the changes a youngster undergoes between, say, ages 15 and 18, regardless of whether high school is attended or not, are corrected for. Similarly, to attribute the success of the film *Star Wars* to the millions of dollars that 20th Century-Fox spent in promoting it is to assume that the film's box-office success was due only to the marketing. To accurately determine the impact of a promotion, it is necessary to consider the performance that would have occurred if the promotion had not taken place, the performance after the promotion is conducted, and the difference. It is this difference that is attributable to the promotion.

If cost-benefit evaluation is closely interrelated to the concept of performance, we should ensure that we understand what performance is and how it can be measured. What we find is that performance consists of two parts: effectiveness and efficiency.

Effectiveness   A program or unit's effectiveness is defined in terms of the degree to which it attains its objectives. The effect on objectives can be measured by criteria such as number of clients enrolled, percentage of a target population reached by the program, or decrease in crime rate. For appraising the performance of faculty members in higher education institutions, one writer has suggested the objectives of (1) student development, (2) expansion of knowledge through research, and (3) public service. He says that these objectives might be measured by, respectively, (1) student evaluation, standardized test scores, and average beginning salaries of graduates; (2) patents secured, funded grants obtained, and publications; and (3) consultations provided and workshops given.[1] Similarly, the effectiveness of a department of justice might be measured in terms of reduction and prevention of crime, protection of internal security, and maintenance of competition in the business community.

[1] James S. Dyer,"The Use of PPBS in a Public System of Higher Education: Is It Cost-Effective?" *Academy of Management Journal,* September 1970, pp. 285–99.

It has been suggested that ratios can be used as ways to measure the effectiveness of objectives, resources, and activities.[2] Let us review some of the more popular of these ratios.

The ratio RC/PR represents the relationship between actual resources consumed (RC) and the planned use of resources (PR). The higher the ratio of actual to planned, the greater the effectiveness of resource utilization. AP/PA represents the ratio of actual program activities performed (AP) to planned activities (PA). Again, effective activities will be evident by a high ratio of actual to planned. Finally, the ratio AO/PR represents the relationship between the net attainment of the objective attributable to the program activity (AO) and the attainment desired, less the status that would have existed in the absence of the program (PR). This last factor is either estimated or based on prior performance data or performance by a control group, if such is available.

A community agency established to reduce air pollution, for instance, can measure its effectiveness by utilizing these ratios. If $1.5 million was allocated to the agency and it spent only $1.2 million, its resource-utilization ratio (RC/PR) would equal 0.8. In this case, the agency has failed to consume its full allocation; and since this is an effectiveness ratio, a higher figure is desirable. In contrast, if we were concerned with efficiency, then the lower this ratio, the more efficient the program would have proved to be. This example illustrates how effectiveness and efficiency can work against each other. By giving up efficiency, it is often easier to be effective, and vice versa. To continue the example of a pollution-reduction agency, the effectiveness of its activities can be made evident in its AP/PA ratio. Assume that the agency used for its planned activities (PA) the number of companies that generated air-pollution waste in excess of federal standards, and the number of actual contacts it made as AP. If all known violators were contacted, this ratio would be equal to 1.0 indicating 100 percent effectiveness.

The final effectiveness ratio, AO/PR, is the agency's determination of how much of the reduction in air pollution was attributable to the agency's direct efforts. This is computed by monitoring actual toxic airborne gases and acid vapors generated in the city, and then estimating how much greater that figure would have been had the agency not been in existence.

As pointed out previously, particular emphasis should be put on the net or incremental performance that can be attributed to the activities performed. One method of comparing the net accomplishment attributable to the program with the accomplishment intended for the program is to:

> . . . determine the status of the objective at the time of evaluation and then to subtract from it an estimate of what the status would have been had the program not been undertaken. For example, if a program operator finds that

[2] O.L. Deniston, et al., "Evaluation of Program Effectiveness and Program Efficiency," in *Planning, Programming, Budgeting: A Systems Approach to Management,* 2nd ed, ed. Fremont J. Lyden and Ernest G. Miller (Chicago: Markham, 1973), p. 157.

ninety percent of a group of clients are immune to a disease following the conduct of a program, he cannot properly take credit for all ninety percent, but only for those who would not be immune had this program not been undertaken.

What is true for the actual status of the objective, the numerator, is also true for planned attainment, the denominator. One must subtract from planned attainment that portion of the desired status that would have occurred in the absence of the program. For example, suppose it was desired that ninety percent of the population be immune to a disease. Evaluation shows that eighty percent actually became immune but that half, forty percent, became immune through activities outside the program (visits to physicians and so forth). Program effectiveness would then be

$$\frac{80 - 40}{90 - 40} = \frac{40}{50} = 80\%^3$$

In the absence of a program, how is it possible to estimate the status of objectives? Three approaches have been suggested:

1. Use a control group, unexposed to the program.
2. A control group can be approximated by comparing community status before and after the program with information about nearby communities not exposed to the program.
3. If no comparison group can be derived, one can formulate alternative explanations for the outcome of the program and then seek facts to support or negate each alternative explanation.[4]

Suppose, for example, one wishes to determine whether a decline in the incidence of tuberculosis in a community can properly be attributed to an ongoing tuberculosis control program, as the community in question cannot be compared to another.

The operator might examine other possible explanations for the following incidence. He might consider improved nutrition and improved housing as two possible alternative explanations and investigate whether nutrition and housing indeed improved over the period being considered. If neither improved substantially, he could with greater confidence attribute the reduced incidence of tuberculosis to his program. If one or both alternative hypotheses were borne out by evidence, he could not attribute the outcome to his program.[5]

Efficiency   Since resources are not unlimited and their costs not irrelevant, we must be concerned with efficiency. Let us consider some efficiency ratios that might be used by administrators.

In terms of analysis, the ratio AO/RC explains efficiency as attained objectives (AO) related to resources consumed (RC). Depending on the organization and its objectives, efficiency might be the number of murders committed divided by the number of policemen on the force, deaths per

[3] Ibid., p. 157.
[4] Ibid., pp. 159–61.
[5] Ibid., p. 159.

CONTROL
TECHNIQUES

401

doctor, subordinates per supervisor, or miles per gallon of gasoline. Our example of an institution of higher education might include the following efficiency measures: cost per full-time-equivalent student, student–faculty ratio, or percentage of classroom time utilized. Our community air-pollution agency could compare the reduction in pollution attributed to the agency's efforts against the funds it has expended.

In addition to using the major efficiency ratio of AO/RC, we may also measure efficiency in terms of activities and objectives. Deniston recommends AP/RC, which represents actual activities performed (AP) compared to resources expended (RC), and AO/AP, attained objectives (AO) to activities performed (AP), as additional measures of program efficiency.[6] Utilization of all three ratios, in combination with the effectiveness ratios mentioned above, can accurately evaluate the overall performance of a program.

An example: evaluating police performance To illustrate how cost-benefit evaluation can be used, let us take a look at the performance of the Saratoga Park Police Department, which is responsible for a suburban community of 25,000 citizens that is within commuting distance of a major metropolitan city. The police force includes 105 police officers and approximately 15 administrative and staff personnel. Last year's budget for the department was $2.87 million.

If we limit our evaluation of the police department's performance to its success in solving crimes, we can show how a cost-benefit perspective can provide some interesting information. However, let us first make some assumptions. For our illustration, we will restrict the definition of police performance to crime solving, and we will identify only seven categories. We know that police perform many more functions in addition to crime solving and that there are more than seven categories of crime, but this will make our discussion and analysis much easier. Further, we will arbitrarily define police effectiveness as those crimes in which a suspect was not only charged but also found guilty. This latter constraint obviously also means that we are indirectly measuring the performance of the legal prosecutor, but it will reduce any tendency for police officers merely to make arrests. Finally, not all the crimes solved in Saratoga Park are due to the efforts of the police. We will assume that if there were no police department, 4 percent of the crimes would be solved anyway, and the suspect would be convicted.

In analyzing the Saratoga Park's police performance, we find that the department spent $2.96 million. Their crime-solving effectiveness is shown in Figure 17-2.

In terms of crime-solving effectiveness (AP/PA) we find that the department gets a 58 percent rating. Interestingly, we might also note that if one of the department's goals was to insure that it spent its budget, it would

[6] Ibid., pp. 159–61.

FIGURE 17-2   Saratoga Park's police performance (prior 12 month period)

Category of Crime	No. reported	No. solved and found guilty	Effectiveness
Murder	5	4	.80
Rape	23	5	.22
Assault	152	90	.59
Robbery	648	155	.24
Larceny	2130	1210	.57
Burglary	1455	1085	.75
Auto theft	92	78	.85
Totals	4505	2627	.58

have achieved a 103.1 percent rating (RC/PR = $2.96/$2.87 mil.). While this may appear to be an absurd measure, if the police administrators believe it is important that the department spend its full budget allocation so as to insure that its allocation in the following year is not decreased and hopefully increased, the concern for reaching at least 100 percent on this effectiveness measure makes sense.

When we look at efficiency (AO), we have to look only at the impact attributable to police effort. That turns out to be 58% − 4%/100% − 4% = 56 percent. If we divide this by the amount of money spent (AO/RC), we find that each $100,000 spent results in a little less than two percentage points of effectiveness. In other words, each percentage point of crime effectiveness costs the community about $52,860.

It is now possible to appraise the department's performance in a tangible way. For instance, community officials can compare their police department's crime efficiency against other similarly sized communities. The figures obtained from the above evaluation can be used as a rough guide as to how well the dollars they are committing to crime-fighting are being used. Additionally, within a narrow range, they can be used to determine how much more the police department's budget would have to be increased to solve and get convictions, for instance, on 65 percent of the crimes committed. The answer is about $370,000 ($52,860 × 7 additional effectiveness points). Note, however, that this is only valid within a narrow range. If the city administrators wanted 90 percent of all reported crimes to be successfully solved, it might take a budget ten or twenty times as large. Why? Because the additional crimes are more difficult to solve and will require considerably more manpower. The cost of improving crime-solving effectiveness by 10 percentage points when the department's total effectiveness is only 25 percent is significantly less expensive than when that department's total effectiveness is 75 percent.

CONTROL TECHNIQUES

Cost-benefit evaluation is probably more applicable and effective as an informal measuring concept than as a formal control technique. The reason is that it is difficult to objectively quantify subjective qualitative factors. For instance, one researcher noted that "in practice, we have not found it possible to use benefit/cost ratios to compare programs except for the most general terms. . . . The fact is that no benefit/cost model yet devised measures precisely what it purports to measure because of the need to use proxies on (in many cases) both the benefits and cost side of the model."[7]

Cost-benefit evaluation, it should also be remembered, gives no final answers as to whether a program or activity is "justified" or "good," or whether it should be expanded or contracted. It merely suggests how well an activity is operating when viewed in a specific manner.

The above leads us to the major reason why cost-benefit evaluation will not be an important technique in practice—it assumes, incorrectly, that administrators consider efficiency the primary criterion in decision making. We know this is not the case. This was made quite evident in two large-scale public investments: the $2.8 billion California Water Project and the U.S. supersonic transport (SST). Cost-benefit analysis was undertaken in each of these projects, yet only minimally influenced public policy.[8] The emphasis in these two projects was on cost-benefit planning rather than evaluation, but it is significant that even though both projects were evaluated several times from several points of view, efficiency criteria were largely ignored in the decisions to proceed.

In the California Water Project, it has been claimed that costs were grossly understated, benefits overstated, and inappropriate discount rates chosen. Some of the project's programs that were approved had benefit-cost ratios considerably lower than ones that were permanently scuttled. Political interests and difficult-to-measure "other criteria" eventually played a major part in the final decision.

Research on the SST project began as early as 1956. Federal funds for exploratory research were first appropriated in 1961. A report in 1963 by the Stanford Research Institute found no economic justification for an SST program. The Institute for Defense Analyses found the project viable only if the ridiculous interest rate of 1.33 percent were assumed. From the sizable number of reports commissioned by the Federal Aviation Agency, which came to a wide range of conclusions, it is interesting that this agency selected "only those that favored the aircraft's development."[9]

> Major decision points on the SST came in 1963, 1967, 1969 and 1971. In the first, President Kennedy decided to go ahead despite SRI's negative report, primarily in order to gain international prestige. Further, it was argued that

[7] William R. Dymond, "The Role of Benefit/Cost Analysis in Formulating Manpower Policy," in *Cost-Benefit Analysis of Manpower Policies* ed. G.G. Somers and W.D. Wood (Kingston, Ontario: Hanson & Edgar Ltd., 1969), pp. 50 and 53.
[8] Leonard Merewitz and Stephen H. Sosnick, *The Budget's New Clothes: A Critique of Planning-Programming-Budgeting and Benefit-Cost Analysis* (Chicago: Markham, 1971), pp. 239–71.
[9] Ibid., p. 256.

business would not pursue a goal involving such uncertainty; therefore, government must. Both these motivations, prestige and uncertainty, are sufficiently nebulous that benefit-cost arguments are unlikely to be persuasive.[10]

Our discussion in chapter 5 on the use of quantitative techniques is particularly relevant here. It suggests that cost-benefit evaluation, like any technique that quantitatively appraises organizational activity and performance, can be manipulated to objectively support decisions that are made subjectively. The effect a given decision will have on the decision maker and his or her self-interests is the predominant influence upon which choice is made.

Where cost-benefit evaluation is used, it is predominantly in the public sector, where no profit and loss statement is available by which economic performance can easily be evaluated. Government activities in such varied areas as outdoor recreation, drug prevention, highway investment, urban renewal, and Head Start programs can be appraised by this method. It is used in U.S. state and local governments, school districts, and institutions of higher education. It has also been implemented in federal government units, including the Department of Health, Education and Welfare, the Office of Equal Opportunity, and the Atomic Energy Commission.

Budgets

The most well-known form of formal control used by administrators is the common budget, which is simply a numerical plan. While we traditionally think of budgets in terms of money, they can also be expressed in physical units, as when a department talks about budgeting 1,500 man-hours to complete a given project. But if a budget is a plan, why do we call it a control technique?

Budgets are control devices in that they are designed to guide the actions of a unit and to provide feedback if the budget is exceeded. They are the standard by which actual expenditures are compared.

Budgets are the most popular formal planning and control device used by administrators. Almost all organizations make extensive use of revenue and expense budgets, and many also prepare budgets for manpower and capital expenditures.

Planning-programming-budgeting-system

The most important development in the area of control of public organizations took place in the 1960s. This new development was called the planning-programming-budgeting-system (PPBS). Originally developed for the Air Force by the Rand Corporation, it was implemented in

[10] Ibid., p. 261.

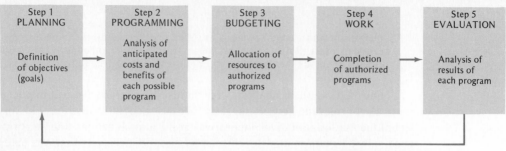

Step 1 PLANNING	Step 2 PROGRAMMING	Step 3 BUDGETING	Step 4 WORK	Step 5 EVALUATION
Definition of objectives (goals)	Analysis of anticipated costs and benefits of each possible program	Allocation of resources to authorized programs	Completion of authorized programs	Analysis of results of each program

From Martin J. Gannon, *Management: An Organizational Perspective*, p. 127. Copyright © 1977 by Little, Brown and Company, Inc. Reprinted by permission.

FIGURE 17-3   Steps in the planning-programming-budgeting-system

the Department of Defense in 1961. Its success prompted then President Johnson to announce in 1965 that the PPBS concept was to be used by every department and agency of the federal government. PPBS was being hailed by some experts as potentially the most significant administrative improvement in the history of American government.[11] What could PPBS offer that elicited so much enthusiasm?

PPBS combines elements of cost-benefit analysis, budgeting, and management by objectives. As shown in Figure 17-3, it forces administrators to define their goals in terms of activities or programs, ascertain costs and benefits, formulate a budget to achieve the goal, and evaluate the program against its goals.

The important difference between PPBS and the common budget is the central unit around which the budget allocation is made. In the traditional budgeting process, funds are allocated to departments, and the administrators within the departments allocate these resources to departmental projects as they see fit. With PPBS, the focus of the budget is on program goals. Funds are allocated for the attainment of specific program goals. Similarly, an administrator's effectiveness is measured in terms of the degree of success in reaching these goals. In public organizations where there is no profit-and-loss statement and goals (services that can be provided) always exist to a far greater extent than do resources to achieve them PPBS provides a mechanism for choosing among goals and determining that a dollar's worth of service is obtained for each dollar spent. In summary, PPBS makes the following improvements in the public sector budgeting process:

1. Planning is primary, with budgets derived from the planning process.
2. Objectives are set so as to reflect the major missions of the department.
3. Programs are determined, including possible alternatives, to achieve the stated objectives.
4. Budgeting is on a program basis rather than funding overall departmental needs.

[11] Bertram M. Gross and Michael Springer, "A New Orientation in American Government," *The Annals of the American Academy of Political and Social Science,* May 1967, p. 9.

CONTROLLING

5. Budgets reflect the alternatives available to achieve a given objective, rather than a single alternative that is scaled either up or down.
6. Planning, programming, and budgeting steps are completed on an annual cycle.
7. The planning horizon is extended for five years beyond the budget, or through the total cycle of the program if it exceeds five years.
8. Program results are continuously re-examined, contrasted against anticipated costs and outcomes, allowing for identification of the need for revisions or terminations of programs.

In spite of the early enthusiasm behind PPBS, much of its glitter has vanished. In the U.S. federal government, for instance, PPBS quietly faded from the federal budget process in 1971. This may be substantially explained by the short-term time horizon used by administrators, which is reinforced if they must come up for election every two or four years, and the changing power structure as applied to the priority of programs.

Zero-base budgeting

Zero-base budgeting (ZBB) may be to the 1970s what PPBS was to the 1960s. Originally developed at the Texas Instrument Company in the late 1960s and applied by Jimmy Carter during his tenure as governor of Georgia, ZBB is now being touted as a revolutionary approach to establishing program priorities and reducing inefficiencies.

As the name implies, ZBB requires administrators to justify their budget request in detail from scratch, without any reference to the level of previous appropriations. They must state why any money should be allocated for each activity. This forces all activities to be identified, evaluated, and ranked in order of importance. Traditional budgets are made incrementally; that is, the cost levels of the previous year are assumed, and budget decisions focus on whether to increase the present budget or continue it at its current level. As a result, prior inefficiencies are carried forward, budgets increase every year, it becomes very difficult to discern the impact of reducing or eliminating programs, and there is little encouragement for administrators to identify and evaluate alternative means of accomplishing tasks. ZBB seeks to overcome these problems by considering what would happen if the activity were eliminated.

ZBB can be viewed as made up of three steps: (1) describing each discrete departmental activity in a "decision package," (2) evaluating and ranking all these packages using cost-benefit analysis, and (3) allocating resources accordingly.[12] The decision package is a document that identifies and describes a specific activity. Usually prepared by the operating administrators, it includes a statement of the expected result or purpose of the ac-

[12] Peter A. Pyhrr, "Zero-Base Budgeting," *Harvard Business Review,* November–December 1970, pp. 111–18.

tivity, its costs, personnel required, measures of performance, alternative courses of action, and an evaluation from an organization-wide perspective of the benefits of performance and consequences of nonperformance. In more specific terms, each package will list a number of alternative methods of performing the activity, recommendation of one of these alternatives, and delineation of effort levels. These effort levels identify spending targets; for instance, how the activity would be completed at 50, 70, and 90 percent of the current budget level. Any large organization that adopts ZBB will have literally thousands of these packages. For instance, the state of Georgia identified approximately 11,000 packages for its 1972–1973 fiscal year.[13]

Once the decision packages have been completed by departmental administrators, they are forwarded to the top executive group which will determine how much to spend and where to spend it. This is done by ascertaining the total amount to be spent by the organization and then ranking all packages in order of decreasing benefits to the organization. Packages are accepted down to the spending level. When properly executed, the zero-base budgeting process should have provided for a careful evaluation and prioritizing of every organizational activity and resulted in either a continuance, modification, or termination of the activity.

Zero-base budgeting is difficult and expensive to implement. Therefore, it is not recommended for every organization. It is most valuable for public and nonprofit organizations, as well as for staff units in business firms where tasks and resources required are not related to the firm's output, yet tend to increase in cost every year. In these instances, it is difficult to determine whether a budget is realistic and reflective of efficient operations, so ZBB becomes an appropriate technique for increasing control.

A recent survey indicated that ZBB is used by 54 of the 1,000 largest companies in the U.S., by eleven state governments, and by many municipalities.[14] Jimmy Carter has also given it the highest priority in his effort to bring modern and sophisticated administrative techniques to the federal government. In the spring of 1977, Carter issued instructions to all agencies that they were to implement ZBB. The fiscal 1979 budget was supposedly developed on ZBB concepts, though one scholar states that this budget "hardly terminates or curtails anything of significance, continues most spending at inflation-adjusted levels, and offers few program initiatives. . . . The fiscal 1979 budget comes out just about where disembodied incrementalism would tend to."[15]

---

[13] George S. Minmier and R.H. Hermanson, "A Look at Zero-Base Budgeting—The Georgia Experience," *Atlanta Economic Review,* July–August 1976, p. 5.
[14] Graeme M. Taylor, "Introduction to Zero-Base Budgeting," *Bureaucrat,* Spring 1977, p. 33.
[15] Allen Schick, "The Road From ZBB," *Public Administration Review,* March–April, 1978, p. 177.

Sunset legislation

Government legislative bodies have the power to terminate programs, laws, or agencies, but the evidence indicates that they rarely utilize their powers. Government programs and agencies have a tendency to proliferate and perpetuate.[16] Sunset legislation has been proposed as a control device to rectify this tendency toward immortality.

Sunset laws attempt to do the same thing as ZBB, except they extend the time frame. A typical Sunset law establishes a timetable—usually between three and eight years—for review of a given activity. Unless it is affirmatively recreated by statute, the activity would automatically be abolished at the end of the specified period. To be resurrected, the activity would have to pass the same type of review and scrutiny given to a new proposal.

If a legislature takes no action, under Sunset laws, the decision to terminate is automatically made. This is in direct contrast to the traditional procedure, where no action becomes a decision to continue. Therefore, it is a Sunset law's threat of termination that is designed to force evaluation. Sunset legislation can provide a commitment of resources for some multiple year period, yet has a built-in mechanism that allows for the identification and modification or termination of outdated, redundant, or low-priority activities.

Sunset legislation is a new idea, but it is rapidly gaining supporters. In 1976, the Colorado legislature passed a law requiring state regulatory agencies to be examined every six years to determine whether they should be spared from automatic termination. By 1978, every U.S. state legislature had at least considered bills embodying this concept. Twenty-four states have enacted Sunset laws; four are engaging in further study; and in ten other states, Sunset legislation had passed one house.[17] At the federal level, pilot legislation has been introduced to require periodic Congressional review of evaluations of agencies prepared by the General Accounting Office, Office of Management and Budget, and Congressional Budget Office.[18]

Management audit

Auditing is an accounting term that has historically meant the checking or review of an organization's financial performance. More recently, it has been expanded to include the performance review of any organizational activity. An interesting adaptation of the audit concept to the eval-

[16] H. Kaufman, *Are Government Organizations Immortal?* (Washington, D.C.: Brookings Institute, 1976).

[17] Bruce Adams and Betsy Sherman, "Sunset Legislation: A Positive Partnership to Make Government Work," *Public Administration Review,* January–February 1977, p. 79.

[18] Michael A. Hitt, R. Dennis Middlemist, and Charles R. Greer, "Sunset Legislation and the Measurement of Effectiveness," *Public Personnel Management,* May–June 1977, p. 188.

uation of the overall performance of an organization is the management audit.

First fully developed by Jackson Martindell and his American Institute of Management, it analyzes all organizational activities, past, present, and future, to ensure that the organization is getting the maximum effort out of its resources. Using a 10,000-point analysis sheet, Martindell appraises performance in ten areas: economic function, organizational structure, health of earnings, service to stockholders, research and development, board of directors, fiscal policies, production efficiency, sales vigor, and executive evaluation.[19] Although a number of these criteria are relevant to profit-making organizations alone, the concept is important and could be modified for use in the nonprofit sector.

By the use of a multiple set of criteria by which an organization can measure its *overall* performance, significant progress can be made toward eliminating behavior that keys on only one or two evaluation criteria. Single-performance evaluative criteria are dangerous when used to appraise an organization's overall effectiveness. The business firm that seeks to increase its return on sales, the hospital that is trying to improve its bed-occupancy rate, or the tax-collecting agency that strives to increase its net collections can be hindering long-term effectiveness by appraising short-term performance.

Another way to look at the value of the management audit is through a systems perspective. We recognize that no organization can reach its performance potential if one or more of its sub-units is performing inadequately. Similarly, if any important organizational activity is not performing well, the entire organization suffers.

Consistent with this overall-performance evaluation, the General Electric Corporation has highlighted eight areas for evaluation as part of its overall-performance appraisal: profitability, market position, productivity, product leadership, personnel development, employee attitudes, public responsibility, and the balance between short- and long-term goals. GE strives to attain balanced performance in these key areas, which is believed to be in the best long-term interests of the firm.

The management audit studies the present and looks to the future. It considers policies, organization, operating methods, financial procedures, personnel practice, physical facilities, and reports on the organization's overall condition. The information generated from a management audit assists top executives in ensuring that current policies and procedures relate to the overall objectives of the organization. It highlights major areas needing attention and improves communication by informing all employees of the state of the organization. Finally, management audits act as a test of the effectiveness of the current management control system.

[19] Jackson Martindell, *The Scientific Appraisal of Management* (New York: Harper & Row, 1962).

Human resource accounting

Another control device developing out of the auditing area has been the technique of human resource accounting (HRA).[20] Its goal is to enhance the accuracy of financial statements by adding the human assets to the physical and financial assets traditionally included on them.

Traditional balance sheets and income statements tend to distort the reality of the organization's past performance and current status, because of their inability to include the value of the human assets in the performance and value of that organization. For example, there are currently about 600 million shares of International Business Machines (IBM) stock outstanding. At a recent market price of $75 a share, the marketplace values the corporation at approximately $45 billion. Now, part of that value includes the knowledge, skills, abilities, and commitment of the more than 250,000 employees of IBM; but the company's financial statements do not reflect the value of these quarter-million employees. Actually, if every one of these employees—or even a large proportion—were to quit, the value of IBM stock would undoubtedly tumble, because investors know that even though financial statements do not include the value of the human factor, an organization, which is made up of people, will succeed or fail based on the skills, abilities, motivations, and commitment of these people. What HRA attempts to do, therefore, is to value the human resource in the organization.

Advocates of HRA propose that its value lies in better long-term decisions. For example, the dollars spent on sending an employee to a one-month skills school, the cost of which may be $1,000 plus another $800 for replacing the employee during his absence, would, under normal financial costing, be charged against the current operation of the operating unit to which he belonged. However, the value of this schooling will not be consumed in the month during which he is gone. Rather, it will provide benefits over several years if he remains within the organization. The value to the organization, therefore, is long term, but the normal accounting method treats it as an immediate operating expense. Utilizing HRA, if the organization will benefit from this $1,800 expense for, say, four years, we would charge $450 of the $1,800 against the current year's operations, and capitalize—that is, consider as an investment—the remaining $1,350. In each succeeding year, $450 would be charged to the employee's unit until the entire $1,800 had been written off.

There are two popular approaches to appraising the human assets of an organization. The simplest method is that used in the example above—the calculation of direct human-asset costs, such as in the recruiting and training of organizational members. This method avoids the difficulty of estimating a person's future value, yet deals effectively with problems such as hiring new college graduates at $15,000 a year. Such employees are, in actu-

[20] Eric Flamholtz, *Human Resource Accounting* (Encino, Cal.: Dickenson Publishing Co., 1974).

**CONTROL
TECHNIQUES**

411

ality, overpriced for the first several years they are with the organization. The practicing administrator, as you would expect, is often reluctant to have people in his department who are earning considerably more than the value they are adding to the operation of the unit. But if, during the first year, $5,000 of the $10,000 salary is charged to operations, with the remainder being capitalized, administrators would be more willing to hire new employees who have high organizational potential, but whose salary at the beginning exceeds their marginal productivity.

The second method for appraising human assets is a replacement-cost approach, which, unfortunately, is considerably more difficult to calculate. It requires that the organization estimate the value that each employee contributes or will contribute. Basically, this is done by taking the discounted value of the person's future earnings. Although this approach more accurately reflects the true value the organization receives from the employee, the subjectivity in estimating future value detracts considerably from its achieving wide acceptance.

HRA, like the management audit, developed in the profit sector. However, its value for improving decisions in the nonprofit sector appears encouraging. As long as organizations appraise their performance in dollar terms, the use of HRA can be valuable in improving the quality of decisions and directing the administrator's perspective at the long-term period.

The management audit and HRA appear to be sparsely used in practice. Both these techniques have been around for over a decade, yet there is no evidence that they are either widely practiced or gaining in popularity.

summary of major points

1. Cost-benefit analysis defines an organizational unit's major objectives or programs, systematically analyzes the alternative ways these objectives can be reached, and evaluates whether the objectives have been effectively and efficiently achieved.
2. Cost-benefit evaluation appraises ongoing performance by determining the degree of success organizational units have in achieving the needs to which they have addressed themselves.
3. Effectiveness is the degree to which a program attains its objectives.
4. Efficiency refers to the relationship between inputs and outputs.
5. The common budget is simply a numerical plan.
6. The planning-programming-budgeting-system requires administrators to define their goals in terms of activities or programs, ascertain costs and

benefits, formulate a budget to achieve the goal, and evaluate the program against the goals.

7. Zero-base budgeting requires administrators to justify their budget request in detail, from scratch, without any reference to the level of previous appropriations.

8. Sunset legislation creates a definite timetable for review of a given activity. Unless affirmatively recreated by statute, the activity would automatically be abolished on a given date.

9. The management audit provides a method for appraising total organizational performance.

10. Human resource accounting adds the human factor to the physical and financial criteria traditionally included on organizational financial statements.

FOR DISCUSSION

1. Contrast cost-benefit analysis, planning, and evaluating.

2. How can an administrator determine a program's effectiveness? Its efficiency?

3. "PPBS combines elements of cost-benefit analysis, budgeting, and MBO." Build an argument to support this statement.

4. Identify the similarities between ZBB and Sunset legislation.

5. Contrast the assumptions and methods of traditional accounting with those of HRA.

6. What factors in this chapter's Saratoga Park Police Department example can you identify that would question the validity of the cost-benefit data generated for decision-making purposes?

7. Using Figure 17-3, give an example of how PPBS might be used in a business firm with which you are familiar.

8. What problems could you foresee as a result of implementing ZBB?

case exercise

I know you're there—I can hear you breathing

The Rocky Mountain Air Quality Control Agency (RMAQCA) was established in 1972 for the purpose of monitoring and reducing air pollution levels in a four-state region of the western U.S. The Agency is presently involved in preparing a report on the costs and benefits of air pollution abatement in the region during the prior year (1979).

CONTROL
TECHNIQUES

The Agency operates on the assumption that costs of abating air pollution are immense, whether measured in higher prices, lower corporate profits, unemployment, obsolete capital equipment, or greater use of scarce resources. These costs are too high for a casual conclusion that an affluent society can afford a clean environment. It is easy to say that we should have clean air. It is another to inquire: How clean? So the Agency prepares an annual report on the benefits and costs of air pollution abatement efforts.

There are direct benefits to human health, plants and crops, animals, cleaning expenditures, life of materials, odor reduction, visibility, and general psychic conditions. The indirect benefits include a better quality of life.

Direct costs include the expense of new capital equipment, increased operating costs, and the costs associated with impaired and less efficient design. Indirect costs must consider temporary unemployment, migration, and private and social capital losses.

The Agency knows that any analysis they do will include significant estimates, yet they desire to evaluate the efficiency of dollars spent. Table 17-1 presents dollars spent in four major categories and the resulting percentage decrease in emission level. Table 17-2 provides estimates of benefits measured in terms of reduction of damage costs.

Questions

1. How should the Agency interpret its findings?
2. What recommendations might they make based on these findings?
3. What caveats should be provided with these recommendations?

TABLE 17-1

Costs of air pollution control (1979):

Mobile sources	$419 millions
Solid waste	11
Stationary fuel combustion	124
Industrial processes	67
	$621 millions

Percentage decrease in emission level (1979):

	Suspended particles	SC$_x$	CO	HC	NO$_x$
Mobile sources	—	—	66	72	44
Solid waste	96	0	92	86	0
Stationary fuel combustion	72	88	0	0	—
Industrial processes	86	89	98	80	89
Total	39	81	57	17	60

TABLE 17-2   1979 Benefits (in millions of dollars)

	Benefit class			Total benefit	Control cost
	Health	Residential property	Materials & vegetation		
Mobile	$DNA	$DNA	$ 47	$ 47	$419
Solid waste	9	7	6	22	11
Stationary fuel combustion	192 (UNE)	164	119	475	124
Industrial processes	72	65	37	174	67
Totals	$273	$236	$209	$718	$621

DNA: Value of benefits not available due to lack of data.
UNE: Figure is underestimated since data not available on health damage cost due to No, from stationary fuel combustion.

FOR FURTHER READING

Cowen, S.S., B.V. Dean, and A. Lohrasbi, "Zero Base Budgeting As a Management Tool," *MSU Business Topics,* Spring 1978, pp. 29–39. The success of ZBB depends on implementation procedures and on appropriate evaluation.

Craft, J.A., and J.G. Birnberg, "Human Resource Accounting: Perspective and Prospects," *Industrial Relations,* February 1976, pp. 2–25. Reviews HRA movement, alternative uses to which HRA can be put, and the movement's progress to date.

Lave, L.B., and E.P. Seskin, "Air Pollution and Human Health," *Science,* August 21, 1970, pp. 723–33. Interesting cost-benefit analysis of pollution abatement.

Novick, D., "Cost-Benefit Analysis and Social Responsibility," *Business Horizons,* October 1973, pp. 63–70. Uses cost-benefit analysis to decide how and where to use funds earmarked for a "socially responsible" plan.

Schick, A., "Zero-Base Budgeting and Sunset: Redundancy or Symbiosis?" *The Bureaucrat,* Spring 1977, pp. 12–32. Reviews both concepts in the public sector, their measures of effectiveness in several state governments, and how they compare as different paths to the same objective.

Suver, J.D., and R.L. Brown, "Where Does Zero-Base Budgeting Work?" *Harvard Business Review,* November–December 1977, pp. 76–84. Answers the how, when, and where for implementing ZBB.

CONTROL
TECHNIQUES

VII

CONCLUSIONS

Chapter 18

A Look Back and a Look Ahead

**AFTER
STUDYING
THIS CHAPTER,
YOU SHOULD
BE ABLE TO—**

**Define and
explain the
following
key terms
and
concepts:**

Government intervention   Lifetime employment
Economic stagnation   Efficiency value system

Describe:

The objectives of this book
Why administrators cannot achieve perfection
How the four administrative functions interrelate
The major differences between the normative and descriptive views of
    the administrative process
The actions that can bring practice closer to theory
How the administrative process may change during the next decade

As we near the end of our discussion of the administrative process, it would be valuable to summarize what it is that administrators do and how the picture we presented in this book might be different in the year 1990. In the following pages, we will review what we have attempted to accomplish and then forecast some potential changes that may affect the job of an administrator a decade from now.

Summary

This book has sought to give you (1) an awareness and understanding of the administrative process and (2) an indication of the differences, where they are relevant, between idealized presentations of how administrators should act and the realities of administrative practice. Toward achieving these ends, I have presented administrators as decision makers and the administrative process as composed of planning, organizing, leading, and controlling. However, because of the political realities in decision making, administrators cannot and do not follow the idealized prescriptions offered by administrative theory, and the deviations in many cases are significant.

Figure 18-1 represents all administrative practice as existing somewhere between two extremes—that of the idealized "perfect" administrator and that of the complete incompetent (A to Z). Whereas most textbooks in administration and management argue that a student can operate to the extreme left along this continuum, we propose that there are human and organizationally imposed limitations that make it impossible for any administator to reach this perfect state. Point A on the continuum is consistent with economic-man assumptions, while point B is the best that can be achieved given the realities of modern administrative man. Realistically, then, administrators can operate only in the B to Z range along the continuum. Our approach, therefore, has been, without entirely eliminating the goal of point A, to assist in the path from Z toward B.

The message of Figure 18-1 is particularly relevant to those readers who plan to embark in the near future on a career in administration. All the novice administrator, gaining his or her first administrative position, can basically attempt to do is move toward point B. By being aware of the realistic environment in which decisions are made and in which actions occur, the conscientious supervisor or low-level administrator can perform quite well,

FIGURE 18-1   Ranges of administrative practice

420

while at the same time acting in his or her self-interest. It is naive, however, to believe that one person in the lower echelons of an organization can single-handedly overcome the political constraints so as to *optimize* his or her unit's resources and *maximize* objective attainment. To make the attempt, ironically, can only result in some level of administrative performance to the right of point B in Figure 18-1.

Integrating the administrative functions

One of the frustrations of a book is that it is a static object and therefore creates a simple and discrete entity out of a dynamic subject. Administration is a lively and dynamic subject, with its components highly interrelated. The result is that no book or lecture can fully do justice to the field. It is therefore necessary to remind you that planning, organizing, leading, and controlling are interrelated.

Planning is deciding in advance what to do, how to do it, when to do it, and who is to do it. *Organizing* is the means or process by which administrators coordinate their input resources through a formal structure of tasks and authority relationships to achieve common objectives. *Leading* is actuating people to perform their required activities. The function requires the motivation and direction of subordinates, effective communication, and the management of change and conflict. *Controlling* is the process of measuring actual performance, comparing it with preestablished standards, noting deviations, and initiating corrective action in those cases where deviations are significant.

In spite of their being presented in a specific order—beginning with planning and ending with controlling—administrators engage in all four functions simultaneously. Also, no one function is more important than any other. If any one function is performed poorly, it impacts adversely on the effectiveness of the administrator and the performance of his unit. Although there may be differences in the degree of importance attached to each function at various levels in the organization, *all administrators plan, organize, lead, and control.*

Integrating administrative theory and practice

In chapter 5 we presented a description of how administrative decisions are made in practice. We found that actual decision making was to a considerable degree different from the normative decision process outlined in chapter 4. The section on decision making concluded with the statement that it was the political realities in decision making that caused administrative practice to deviate from administrative theory. As we then reviewed the administrative process, we were constantly reminded throughout each chapter that practitioners often behaved considerably different from what one would have expected based on the theory. It was emphasized that the difference between theory and practice in administration was not due to lack of knowledge or bad intentions on the part of practitioners. Rather, it merely recognized that many of the assumptions upon which administrative theory was built are not consistent with the realities of organizational life. Our descriptive approach to administration, therefore, offers some interesting insights into the practice of administration.

Planning   Planning, in the normative view, assumes rationality, optimization, organizational loyalty over individual self-interest, and anticipatory perceptions. In contrast, the descriptive view acknowledges satisficing and self-serving behaviors, as well as reactionary rather than anticipatory responses to change.

Objectives set within the organization, whether overall, unit, or individual objectives, reflect the seeking of satisfactory rather than optimum levels of performance. Rewards for optimum performance do not justify the risk. Peer pressures, organizational norms, and cost-benefit appraisals do not favor high-risk decision making, which optimization would require. It is no more in an individual administrator's best interest to maximize than to satisfice. As a result, maximizing performance is the exception rather than the rule. This of course, undermines much of the logic behind MBO, which emphasizes the attainment of organizational goals. The compatability of individual and organizational goals tends to be overstated. Planning theory overlooks the fact that when there is a conflict between these goals, the individual's will tend to predominate.

Consistent with decision-making realities, we also find that planning emphasizes the short term rather than the long range. Reliable forecasting is difficult beyond the very short term; therefore, consistent with the risk aversion orientation of modern administrative man, administrators give minimal attention to long term strategic planning and react to change rather than attempt to anticipate it.

Organizing   Organizing, in the normative view, assumes that optimum performance criteria determine structures; that an organization's structure is a premeditated attempt to reduce technological and environmental uncertainties; that jobs are altered to meet the individual differences of employees; and that clear lines of authority and responsibility have been articulated to provide accountability. In contrast, the descriptive view finds that an organization's structure is often unplanned and merely a response to varying interests' attempts for control; that selection and job design in practice reaffirm that jobs are relatively fixed commodities, requiring individuals to do the adapting, rather than the reverse; and that authority lines are rarely delineated clearly, responsibility is difficult to place, and accountability is a highly political process. More specifically, when decisions prove to have been well conceived, credit is allocated to allies who were associated with the action, whereas poor decisions can be "pinned" on those whom it is in one's best self-interest to have carry the blame.

Leading   Leading, in the normative view, assumes that the organizational environment and leadership style are directed toward optimizing worker performance; that leaders are chosen to reflect the situational differences they may confront; that performance feedback is continually flowing from administrator to subordinate; that rewards are allocated on the basis of performance; and that these rewards reflect the individual needs of employees. Further, the normative view acknowledges the functional dimension of conflict within the organization.

In contrast to the above, the descriptive view indicates that the selection of administrative leaders is based on traits, not contingency elements. Money and extrinsic rewards are still given the primary role in motivating workers; performance feedback to employees is weak; rewards are not differentiated to reflect differences in performance, they do not reflect the individual needs of employees, nor is performance the dominant determinant of reward allocations. A worker who cooperates in helping his superior look good in the eyes of his boss will be taken care of. It is politically intelligent to reward those who support you; hence, rewards are allocated on the basis of self-serving criteria. Finally, administrators seek to keep the peace, even at the expense of unit performance. Most administrators attempt to minimize all conflicts, even when they may be functional.

Controlling   The normative view assumes that controlling is performed at key or strategic points within the organization, and that all equally significant deviations will be equally treated and corrected. In contrast, the descriptive view acknowledges that events and activities to be monitored are selected more on their ease of measurement and visibility than on their importance to the attainment of organizational objectives. Not all equal deviations are given equal treatment. Deviations that attract attention and are corrected are those that it is in the best interest of the administrator to bring attention to, and may have nothing at all to do with the best interests of the organization.

Can we make practice more like theory?   The answer to the question in the left margin is a definite yes, but it is no easy task. Those top executives who are sincerely interested in improving the performance of their organization will need to undertake some unpopular and unique actions, but it can be done! Let me briefly suggest a few ideas which, if implemented by senior administrators, will go a long way toward encouraging administrative personnel to perform more as theory would suggest.

State clear objectives   The organization's objectives should be communicated clearly to all administrators, so that dysfunctional forms of behavior are more obvious. The objectives need not be specific; however, they should be clear. An MBO-type program, instituted in an environment that fully supports the philosophy behind MBO, can identify standards of performance and create the control mechanisms to determine if objectives are achieved. Importantly, when an individual's objectives are clear, there are fewer opportunities to engage in actions which may be personally gratifying

but not consistent with the objectives of the organization.

Align individual and organizational objectives If individuals are going to act in their own self-interest, it is logical to structure their jobs so that when they act for themselves they also act for the benefit of the organization. In other words, we should attempt to merge individual and organizational interests. The alignment of individual and organizational interests requires an evaluation and reward system that clearly makes it worthwhile for an individual to exert maximum effort. A well-designed incentive pay system for salespersons is an example of turning an individual's self-interest into effective performance for the organization.

Hold all administrators accountable Every administrator must be held accountable for his or her decisions. Buck-passing and other actions which are specifically engaged in to avoid or spread the risks in a decision can be effective only if responsibility is unclear and the obligation to perform is nebulous. Top administrators should ensure that every decision can be attributed to someone. If people are allowed to take credit for their successes but are not held accountable for failures, it becomes impossible to pinpoint sources of problems. Additionally, those "in the know" can utilize this loophole in the system to further their own best interest, often at the organization's expense.

Identify reward paths It is desirable to clarify for each administrator the path from effective performance to the rewards he or she values. Consistent with the expectancy model of motivation, an individual's effort to produce will be a function of his particular goals and his perception of the relative worth of a specific behavior as a means of attaining these goals. By linking rewards to performance criteria beneficial to the organization, opportunities for dysfunctional behavior are reduced.

Individualize rewards Not every administrator desires more money, a promotion, or a write-up in the organization's monthly newspaper. What turns me on may not turn you on! It is necessary, therefore, if we are to get the most out of an organization's reward system, to move away from homogeneous rewards toward individualized reward allocations. As noted in our discussion of motivation, the ability to identify rewards that an administrator may find attractive is only constrained by the creativity of top-level decision makers.

Reward those who perform It may appear obvious to say that senior administrators should ensure that rewards are allocated to those who perform, but many organizations fail to do so. The reason for this failure usually lies not with the lower-level administrators but rather the "system"—the personnel policies that determine how rewards are to be allocated. Such policies have traditionally been developed for the average performer and rarely provide for the adequate treatment of superior performance.

Generally, organizations do not provide a wide enough differential in rewards to parallel differences in contributions to the organization's objectives. Senior executives should strive to increase the parameters for distribution of formal rewards and use informal rewards to reinforce behaviors that significantly contribute to the organization's purpose.

Don't reward nonperformance　The statement that nonperformers should *not* be rewarded appears even more obvious than the preceding suggestion, but it is not. One of the easiest ways to resolve conflicts at reward time is to avoid recognizing differences in performance. It is assumed that if everyone is rewarded equally, no feelings are hurt. Of course, this ignores the hurt we impose on the organization and upon outstanding employees by reinforcing mediocre performance. Performance, after all, follows a normal distribution; that is, a few excel, a few perform poorly, and the vast majority cluster about the middle. Rewards should reflect this reality.

Reward creative decisions　Top executives should encourage and reward the efforts involved in making unique and creative decisions, where such decisions are desirable. It must be worthwhile for middle- and lower-level administrators to take risks, consider unique and creative decisions, restructure jobs, and tolerate functional conflicts. If rewards are allocated on performance rather than poor substitutes for performance, we can provide the type of environment which supports and encourages reasonable risk-taking.

Set favorable examples　Our final suggestion is for top administrators to set favorable examples for others to imitate. Highly dysfunctional forms of self-serving behavior can flourish only when directly or indirectly supported by senior executives. The behavior of the chief operating officer sets the tone for what can be gotten away with. Middle-level administrators look to their superiors for standards of acceptable conduct. Similarly, lower-level administrators look to their superiors for direction. When top executives abuse the system, exploit opportunities for their own benefit, or reward on the basis of nonperformance criteria, they encourage middle- and lower-level administrators to do the same.

The future

Attempts to forecast the future are fraught with dangers. Prediction is an exercise that reasonably intelligent people have learned, through experience, to avoid. Unfortunately, at least for authors of textbooks on administration, it is necessary to confront the future and consider its implications for administrators and their organizations. Our approach will be to look at the future through the dimension of change.

To the inevitability of death and taxes, we can add that of change. It may be difficult to predict its direction and intensity, but change itself is a fact of life and we can always predict it with certainty.

Because there are too many forces at work to enable us to make prediction relatively simple and accurate, in this section we will confine our

A LOOK BACK AND A LOOK AHEAD

425

prediction to the expansion of current trends and our time frame to the period through the 1980s. The approach, therefore, will be to describe some of the major changes going on in our society and then to attempt to interpret, with the knowledge that this is surely a risky endeavor, the possible implications of these changes on future administrators and their organizations.

The future reflects the recent past

The last quarter century has seen significant changes in our society brought about by technological advancements, social alterations, economic influences, and political pressures. A short list of the more obvious would include:

Technological:
Polio and measles vaccines
Capability to place men on the moon
Mass use of Xerographic reproduction printing
Introduction of microcomputers

Social:
Mass acceptance of "the pill" and concurrent reduction in sexual taboos
Women's movement
Unprecedented growth in higher education enrollments
Growth of suburban shopping centers and concurrent death of downtown commercial areas in the U.S.

Economic:
Dramatic rise in the average North American's living standard
Rapid expansion of the checkless society (i.e., credit cards)
Skyrocketing rise in interest rates
Unprecedented escalation of oil prices

Political:
Medicare for the aged
End of the military draft
Equal rights amendment
Civil rights laws

Current trends and their implications for administrative practice

The above changes, however, reflect only the past. Our concern is with the future. Therefore, let us extend some current trends to predict some changes that are likely to occur within the next decade; and further, let us consider the impact of these changes on administrative practice.

High inflation *The Trend.* The 1980s will see a continuation of inflationary levels, very probably in excess of 7 to 8 percent per year. This will mean the average price of goods and services will be over double the price they were at the beginning of the decade.

The Implications. Administrators will be under increased pressure to increase wages and salaries to keep up with inflation. At a 10 percent compounded rate, a department with a $250,000 budget in 1979 will require $648,000 in 1989 to do exactly the same thing. Unless productivity is increased commensurately, the prices of organizational products and services will have to be raised. High pay increases to reflect the cost of living will also

CONCLUSIONS

426

leave less to allocate for merit. For public administrators, inflation may mean reluctance on the part of taxpayers to accept tax increases. Stagnant revenues and increased costs of inputs may mean significant cutbacks in services. Taxpayer concern with high taxes and high inflation may result in increased attention to efficiency measures and accountability.

On a more positive note, administrators should find an increase in the labor force. More wives and teen-agers will be entering the work force, creating a broadened pool from which job candidates can be selected. Additionally, many of these new entrants will prefer part-time employment, offering administrators greater flexibility in aligning personnel with organizational needs.

Increased government intervention *The Trend.* Since the early 1930s, there has been a significant increase each decade in the government's influence on the personal lives of people in North America. This activity accelerated with the "Great Society" programs of the 1960s, and there appears no evidence that the trend will subside during the 1980s. During the past decade, government has been the fastest-growing sector in the North American economy.

Given the rapid changes taking place as a result of the rethinking of society's priorities, the influence of local, state, and federal governments on each of our lives can be expected to accelerate further during the next decade. Immediately evident is the federal government's influence on banking and finance, competition and trade, employment and discrimination, energy and the environment, and safety and health.

The Implications. With the expansion of government activities, administrators will find themselves increasingly burdened by more laws and regulations that constrain decision-making alternatives.

Automobile companies, for instance, are finding their freedom to determine styles and performance capabilities reduced. Regulations on bumpers, roof strengths, emissions, and mileage standards decrease their freedom to choose what they will produce. Similarly, laws on hiring procedures no longer permit administrators to hire arbitrarily whom they want. In many industries, government pressures to maintain price structures reduce the administrator's ability to raise prices to reflect market or cost changes. In the future, building regulations, taxing bodies, health requirements, and other government activities will expand, resulting in even greater constraints on administrative decision making.

Even government bodies themselves will find restrictions on their freedom. States will become more dependent on the federal government, cities more dependent on state government.

We can predict two distinct effects on future administrators: They will have less discretion or freedom to decide; and they will, of necessity, have to become more familiar with the legal implications of their administrative actions. Administrators who have little knowledge of the law, or inaccessability to continual legal advice, will become rare.

Economic Stagnation   *The Trend.* The greatest shift of wealth in world history quietly took place in October 1973 when the thirteen members of the Organization of Petroleum Exporting Countries boosted the price of oil from $2.25 to $11 per barrel. In addition to its inflationary implications, this action highlighted the fact that the North American economy may have peaked in the early 1970s. We may have begun a trend of economic stagnation. The North American ideology which has been built on the assumptions of growth and abundance may be replaced by decline and scarcity.

The Implications. A lack of growth has serious implications for administrators. First, "organization growth creates organizational abundance, or surplus, which is used by management to buy off internal consensus from the potentially conflicting interest group segments that compete for resources in organizations."[1] Secondly, under conditions of abundance, habit, intuition, snap judgments and other forms of informal analysis will suffice for most decisions because the cost of making mistakes can be easily absorbed without threatening the organization's survival.[2] And thirdly, the lack of growth creates a number of serious personnel problems as promotions all but disappear and the organization no longer has a constant infusion of new young talent.[3]

Rising educational levels   *The Trend.* Since the end of World War II, there has been a rising level of education among the population and, with it, a significant alteration in work values. In the early 1950s, less than 26 percent of the work force had high school diplomas. Currently, nearly 45 percent hold them, and by the end of the 1980s, this figure will approach 60 percent. The proportion of the work force that has attended four or more years of college has also increased substantially. In the early 1950s, it was approximately 8 percent; it is currently 15 percent, and we can expect that by the end of the 1980s, the figure will approach 20 percent.

With changing levels of education, we will also see an increase in the ratio of white-collar to blue-collar workers. This ratio, which was 1.3:1 in the late 1960s, increased to 1.7:1 by the end of the 1970s, and should approach 2.0:1 by the late 1980s. These changes in the work force will manifest themselves in a different type of worker—one who is seeking more interesting work, greater challenges to his abilities, and opportunities for growth and promotion.

The Implications. Rising educational levels and changing values among younger workers will result in an increased desire by workers for jobs that provide challenge, autonomy, and self-fulfillment. Life aspirations of

---

[1] William G. Scott, "Organization Theory: A Reassessment." *Academy of Management Journal,* June 1974, p. 245.

[2] Naomi Caiden and Aaron Wildavsky, *Planning Budgeting in Poor Countries* (New York: John Wiley & Sons, 1974).

[3] Charles H. Levine, "Organizational Decline and Cutback Management," *Public Administration Review,* July–August 1978, p. 317.

CONCLUSIONS

new entrants to the work force are considerably higher than those of their parents, a generation earlier. In addition to providing them with means of survival, workers will increasingly be seeking jobs that are themselves intrinsically rewarding. We can, therefore, expect administrators to be faced with the challenge of designing jobs that can be perceived as personally gratifying and capable of stimulating high performance. Those administrators who fail will find a dwindling of their labor supply, difficulty in acquiring the services of those talents that are least available, and the necessity of hiring marginal performers.

In general, people will seek more interesting work, challenges to their abilities, and opportunities for growth and promotion. Additionally, operative employees will demand a greater say in decisions that affect them.

Those with skills will be in high demand, and it will be necessary to provide jobs that they perceive as personally gratifying in order to acquire their services. On the other hand, increasing educational levels will make more better-qualified people available, possibly for fewer job opportunities. Therefore, paradoxically, administrators may find reduced job mobility among their subordinates in forthcoming years.

Increased participation of women in the work force *The Trend.* The stereotyped image of a woman as passive, unambitious, low in achievement need, noncompetitive, and one whose primary functions are those of wife and mother is rapidly disintegrating. Women are increasingly seeking freedom and financial independence, whether they marry or not. A career is the most obvious solution toward this end.

In the 1970s, 14 million new jobs were created in the U.S. and women filled 10 million of them. In late 1978, the percentage of American women who held or were looking for work reached 50 percent. In 1947, this percentage was less than 32 percent, and as recently as 1963, it stood at only 38 percent.

The Implications. Women will be moving rapidly into administrative careers. In the late 1970s, in spite of women's representing 50.4 percent of the population, only one out of every eight administrators was female. Organizations will be hiring, developing, and promoting a proportionally larger number of females for administrative positions during the 1980s.

Search for lifetime employment *The Trend.* Legislation regarding the evaluating and terminating of employees has increasingly placed the burden of proving inadequate performance on the employer. This trend, coupled with increased demands by unions for guaranteed lifetime employment, should find more employees permanently attached to organizations.

The Implications. Lifetime employment, whether controlled by legislation or contract, will reduce the flexibility of administrators to pursue new opportunities requiring personnel with different skills and will reduce the administrator's power to enact compliance through the threat of termination. There will be a greater need for the organization to get actively involved in career and life planning with its employees.

Extension of employment beyond age 65   *The Trend.* Effective in 1979, mandatory retirement before the age of 70 was banned by an amendment by President Carter to the Age Discrimination in Employment Act of 1967. It is possible that, by the end of the 1980s, forced retirement at any age will be eliminated for all workers.

The Implications. Administrators will face "growing demands to cater to the needs of elderly workers by changing job structures, rewriting pension and benefit plans, developing phased retirement programs, and finding ways to accommodate the less productive older workers with less demanding jobs."[4] The elimination of forced retirement should have varying implications for different labor groups. Extensions will be predominantly taken by employees whose jobs offer more than monetary satisfaction. This includes administrative and professional personnel, and excludes many blue-collar and unskilled white-collar jobs. This trend can be expected to particularly reduce promotion opportunities for younger employees in skilled and professional positions. However, this trend should have little impact on productivity. If it is true that, "except in manual work, age has little to do with productivity,"[5] as the evidence indicates, then these jobs will be where regular and early retirements will tend to predominate.

Challenge to the "efficiency" value system   *The Trend.* Administrators are evaluated on whether they are effective and efficient in carrying out their missions. These criteria for determining good or bad performance have historically been accepted by students and practitioners of administration without much criticism. When criticism was forthcoming, it tended to be packaged in socialistic dress, and was traditionally discarded with comments such as "inconsistent with the American way of life," or "inappropriate in a competitive environment, where the strong survive."

There appears to be growing concern as to whether efficiency and organizational performance criteria are primary measures any more. Further, the concern is no longer being articulated by only small minority factions or by those outside the "mainstream."

Government has indicated that it will no longer allow the weak firm, when it employs tens of thousands of workers, to fail. Capitalism and the profit motive are undergoing increasing attack. All members of organizations, regardless of level, are showing greater interest in participating in decisions that affect them. Even though resources are becoming more scarce and thus more expensive, there appears paradoxically to be growing senti-

---

[4] "When Retirement Doesn't Happen," *Business Week,* June 19, 1978, pp. 72–73.
[5] Ibid., p. 82.

ment for placing human values before economic values. Some even suggest that we may be undergoing a moral revolution.

Former Canadian Prime Minister Trudeau confronted this issue and questioned our traditional measures of performance:

> The twentieth-century devotion to material gain has created an imbalance in the human condition that infects the attitudes of all too many men and women and the policies of most governments. . . . The Gross National Product is no measurement of social justice, or human dignity, or cultural attainment. . . .
>
> Are we here, in our lands of apparent—though limited—plenty, unable to expand our consciousness and our attitude, to reexamine our value system, to discount the worth of purely economic factors as an evaluation of the human condition? Are we unable to replace these with standards which will measure not Gross National Product, but Net Human Benefit?[6]

The Economic Council of Canada responded to Trudeau's challenge by proposing a series of social indicators to eventually replace the gross national product, to measure progress in such areas as housing, health, and the natural environment.

The Implications. There will be continued pressures on administrators to subordinate efficiency and performance criteria to human considerations. This may truly be one of the most revolutionary of those trends that we are considering, and its implications for administrators are even more dramatic.

There may be a necessity to completely replace the value system that administrators have traditionally espoused and by which an organization's success or failure has been evaluated. In a society where no major organizations can fail because government will not allow it, a "survival of the fittest" value system may no longer be appropriate. Administrators may find that performance appraisals using economic criteria alone may be preempted by those that place human values first. It is possible that organizations will be evaluated not on how effectively they attain their goals, but how satisfied their employees are with the activities that go on within the organizations.

Declining trust in organizational spokesmen *The Trend.* Much of the population has become discouraged by the difficulty of obtaining open and truthful comments from organizational spokesmen. The environment created in recent years among government officials has destroyed much of the public trust. American planes were bombing Cambodia while government officials denied it. The Watergate break-in and the subsequent investigation found few administrators consistently telling the "facts." President Carter, elected in 1976 on the promise to balance the federal budget by 1980,

[6] Pierre Trudeau, quoted in "New Values PM Priority," *Montreal Gazette*, February 7, 1975, p. A-3.

431

admitted in the fall of 1977 the impossibility of the task. Corporate executives vocally affirm their organizations' commitment to socially responsible action in statements that are later contradicted by administrative behavior.

"Fact-twisting" prevails in business, educational, and medical organizations, as well as public organizations. In response to organizational spokesmen giving the public what it wants to hear, the public has become weary of their statements and, in some cases, cynical. For instance, a study by Cambridge Survey Research found that 69 percent of the U.S. public believe that their country's leaders have consistently lied to them over the past ten years.[7]

The Implications. All administrators must play numerous roles, but members of society are finding it increasingly difficult to reconcile these roles. Although they recognize that it is often necessary for administrators to say different things to different publics, there is a growing disillusionment with this practice. We can expect, therefore, that what administrators say to the public will be less likely to be taken at face value in the future. As a result, it will be more difficult for top administrators to gain support from many of their constituencies for their actions.

A qualifying note	I have attempted to describe briefly those societal trends that have a high probability of occurring through the 1980s, and the resulting implications for administrative practice. For my own protection, however, let one thing be clear: Times change rapidly. What seemed evident in the late 1970s may not be so evident later. As we noted in chapter 6, attempts to forecast beyond the very short term are highly speculative.

Some of the trends articulated here may have been understated or overstated, so an interesting exercise for all students of administration is to discuss the trends they currently see in society and to draw from them the potential implications for administrators and their organizations.

A closing remark

Our journey through the administrative process has come to an end. I have attempted to give you an accurate description of administrative functions, how administrators act, why they act as they do, and what can be done to improve their performance.

Whether or not we seek careers in administration, we are all consumers of organizational goods and services. Hence, each of us has a vested interest in improving administrative performance. Our future and the future of all of those who follow us will be significantly influenced by the efficiency and effectiveness of today's and tomorrow's administrators.

[7] "Ground Rules for Telling Lies," *Time,* April 3, 1978, p. 67.

CONCLUSIONS

summary of major points

1. This book sought to:
   a. Give the reader an awareness and understanding of the administrative process.
   b. Indicate the differences, where they are relevant, between administrative theory and practice.
2. The four functions of planning, organizing, leading, and controlling are interrelated; all are engaged in simultaneously by the administrator.
3. Practice can be more like theory if senior administrators would:
   a. State clear objectives.
   b. Align individual and organizational objectives.
   c. Hold all administrators accountable.
   d. Identify reward paths.
   e. Individualize rewards.
   f. Reward those who perform.
   g. Not reward nonperformers.
   h. Reward creative decisions.
   i. Set favorable examples.
4. Predicting the future has a high risk of error, but the following trends have implications for administrators:
   a. High inflation
   b. Increased government intervention
   c. Economic stagnation
   d. Rising educational levels
   e. Increased participation of women in the work force
   f. Search for lifetime employment
   g. Extension of employment beyond age 65
   h. Challenge to the "efficiency" value system
   i. Declining trust in organizational spokesmen

FOR DISCUSSION

1. Explain the constraints that deter administrators from optimizing their organization's resources.
2. Contrast major discrepancies between the normative and descriptive views of the administrative process.
3. Is the future an extension of the present? Discuss.
4. Is there a conflict between judging organizational performance on economic criteria and judging it on human criteria? Explain.
5. Why have computers been excluded from our list of major changes having a significant impact on administrative practice? Why have minorities, such as blacks and Chicanos, been excluded?
6. Will operatives in 1989 be different from operatives in 1979? Explain.

A LOOK BACK AND
A LOOK AHEAD

7. Will administrators in 1989 be different from administrators in 1979? Explain.

8. You are a consultant who has been hired by the chief executive officer of a large corporation to offer *general* suggestions on what he might do to improve his firm's effectiveness. Using the information learned in this book, identify and very briefly discuss the *six* most important suggestions you could offer.

case exercise

The big fish in the small pond

Bill Graham received his B.A. from Princeton in 1966 and his M.B.A. from Harvard in 1968. Upon graduating from Harvard, he spent five years as an investment broker with Bache & Co., followed by three years as an account supervisor at E.F. Hutton, and then a few years as coordinator of property investments for the Ford Foundation. When Bill heard that the newly formed Anstey Foundation was looking for a director, he applied. To his pleasant surprise, he was selected over a reported three dozen candidates.

John R. Anstey was a prosperous midwestern business executive. He was establishing the Anstey Foundation with a cash donation of $40 million and the stipulation that the income from the foundation's assets be used "to improve the practice of administration, at all levels, in organizations throughout North America."

As Bill walked into his temporary office, on this first day on the job, he knew he had a challenging task ahead. He would need, among other things, to establish an operating budget, hire a support staff, and identify specific areas for foundation funding. Here was the opportunity Bill had worked so hard for. He now had his own foundation to run. Sure, it wasn't the Ford Foundation, but he would be the big fish in this pond. Undoubtedly Bill's greatest excitement flowed from the chance to build an organization from scratch.

Questions

1. If you were Bill, where would you begin and what would you do?
2. If you were Bill, what types of projects would you want to fund; that is, in what activities do you think his dollars would have the best chance of "improving the practice of administration?"

FOR FURTHER READING

Gordon, F.E., and M.H. Strober, *Women in Management.* New York: McGraw-Hill, 1975. Discusses the attitudes toward women that have perpetuated their exclusion from the top ranks of management; impact of legal decisions

CONCLUSIONS

on corporate obligations and attitudes; problems of role identification for female managers; and the likely influence of female managers on organizations.

"Government Intervention," *Business Week,* April 4, 1977, pp. 42–90. Special issue discusses how the Carter administration would speed up and shape the rising trend toward big government.

Lazer, W., "The 1980's and Beyond: A Perspective," *MSU Business Topics,* Spring 1977, pp. 21–35. Projections of some of the fundamental population and income statistics suggest that the longer run business climate is a cautiously optimistic one.

McFarland, D.E., "Whatever Happened to the Efficiency Movement?" *Conference Board Record,* June 1976, pp. 50–55. Considers the views of those who are against efficiency or who wish to redefine it. Argues that efficiency alone is an inadequate objective today.

Martin, W.F., and G.C. Lodge, "Our Society in 1985—Business May Not Like It," *Harvard Business Review,* November–December 1975, pp. 143–52. Responses from *HBR* readers reflect a fear that the individualistic ideology is giving way to communitarianism.

Yankelovich, D., "The New Psychological Contracts at Work," *Psychology Today,* May 1978, pp. 46–50. No issue will dominate the workplace in the 1980s more than how to revamp incentives to match the new motivations of workers.

A LOOK BACK AND
A LOOK AHEAD

CASES

DANDY DIAPER SERVICE COMPANY

Bob Harris founded the Dandy Diaper Service Company (DDSC) in Flint, Michigan, sixteen years ago. It was incorporated two years later, though Bob controls all the outstanding stock.

Bob began the business after serving two years in the Army, and although he was only 21 years old at the time, he borrowed $6,500 from the bank to get the business started. DDSC was an immediate success. There was little competition for Dandy's service of providing diapers, delivered twice weekly to the home, washed and sanitized, for the busy mother. Dandy's competition could not compete with Bob's aggressive marketing tactics and quality service. Sales accelerated from $65,000 in the first full year of operation, to $180,000 in three years. More recently, total revenue and profits have been:

Year	Revenues	Profit (Loss)
1978	$157,300	$(16,800)
1977	178,800	(2,500)
1976	204,800	14,200
1975	222,700	17,500
1974	235,000	39,700
1973	240,600	47,500
1972	238,000	47,000
1971	235,500	43,500

Bob attributes the downturn "primarily to the introduction and rapid acceptance of disposable diapers, and secondarily to the decline in the birth rate." The decline in home delivered diaper business apparently is real. When Bob began the business there were three other competitors in Flint. A recent screening of the Flint Yellow Pages found DDSC to be the only home-delivered diaper service listed.

DDSC currently has eighteen employees, in addition to Bob. This is down from a high of twenty-three in 1973. The layoffs have been viewed as a threat by many of the employees, creating what some employee's described as a "hostile environment." Bob volunteered that five years ago, "the organization was very efficient and employee morale was quite high." With the decline in morale has come increased activity by the Teamsters Union to organize the laundry plant personnel and the company's truck drivers. Bob

Harris and his plant manager admit to fighting vigorously to keep the union out.

When King was asked about the unionization issue. He stated, "We have everything under control. Anybody we catch supporting the union will be fired on the spot. But if you quote me on that, I'll deny it!" Gibson, in response to the case writer's question of whether he was concerned about the drop in revenues and the two consecutive losses, replied, "Look, we're currently in a bind. Disposables are competitively priced and more convenient. We're charging $5.75 a week for six dozen diapers, compared with a package of 30 Pampers that sell from between $2.29 and $2.49 at markets and discount stores. It's difficult for us to do much. But things will get better. I think we've seen the end of the decline. Mothers will be returning to cloth diapers again."

When the case writer asked Bob Harris whether he was concerned with the decline in business, his voice rose. "Sure I'm concerned. But what can I do? I'm a little guy with a small business. The union is breathing down my neck, production efficiency has gone down the drain, and billion dollar corporations are putting me to the wall by marketing disposables. Do you know anyone who might be interested in buying me out?"

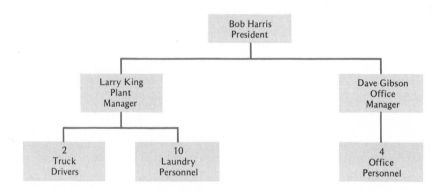

THE BUDGET DILEMMA

Denise Fortier has been director of the Windsor, Ontario, office of the Planned Parenthood Association (PPA) for four years. She operates with a small staff—two full-time counselors, a receptionist-secretary, and a varying number of women who volunteer a few hours a week to help Denise out. The office's 1979 budget—which covered staff salaries, rent, office supplies, and travel—was $67,000.

Approximately ten weeks ago, Denise submitted her 1980 budget request to her superior, Mary McKenzie, in Ottawa. In contrast to last year's budget, the budget request asked for an amount to cover inflation and also reflected Denise's objective to expand PPA's efforts at reaching Windsor's 12 to 16-year-old girls. To achieve this end, she had requested an additional lump sum of $4,000. In all, her 1980 budget request totaled $78,000.

In today's mail, Denise received the following letter from Mary McKenzie:

Dear Denise:

I have been very impressed with the way you have been operating our Windsor office. You have shown consistently good judgment in your development of programs and you have done an excellent job of promoting PPA in the Windsor-Detroit area. Please be assured that your efforts have not gone unnoticed. I have spoken favorably about you with the Canadian Executive Director on numerous occasions. I am pleased to tell you that your achievements are about to be rewarded.

We decided this year to review each regional office's budget from scratch. It was felt that in this way we could redistribute our funds in order to achieve a greater impact for each dollar spent. As a result of this review, we have budgeted your office in 1980 for $192,000.

I am sure you will be pleased by this dramatic increase in your office's budget. I look forward to receiving a detailed outline of how you expect to utilize these funds.

Sincerely,

Mary McKenzie
Assistant Exec. Director

A PRICE-FIXING SCANDAL

Harry Yettkin is president and chief executive officer of Amalgamated Electric Co., one of America's largest manufacturers of consumer appliances and industrial electrical components. Its 1979 sales exceeded $5 billion.

Harry has just been through a day he could only describe as a nightmare. He received a call in the morning from an investigator with the Federal Trade Commission asking him if he was aware of an impending indictment against his corporation for allegedly colluding with two other major manufacturers of electrical generating equipment to set bid prices on at least twenty multi-million dollar projects. Harry told the investigator the truth—he had no knowledge of his company's involvement in a price collusion, but if the investigator could give him the details he "sure as hell would look into it immediately." In brief, the investigator related the following scenario.

In the summer of 1976, David Murray, a vice-president at Amalgamated and head of the corporation's electrical equipment division, met with a senior executive from both Weltric Industries and Americo Electric in a New York hotel. At that meeting, the three men agreed to a strategy whereby they would divide up and predetermine bids for the major electrical projects coming up in 1977. For instance, they agreed to let Americo win the bid on generating equipment for a large dam in northern California. Americo would bid $4,235,300. Weltrix and Amalgamated would both place higher bids. Using this sharing strategy, they spread the business between themselves, and since the three firms dominated the industry, they were in a position to determine what the winning bid would be. Additionally, they inflated all their bids so the "low" bidder was still significantly higher than if there had been no collusion. These same executives also met again in 1977, 1978, and 1979 for the purpose of colluding and price-fixing.

Yettkin listened to the investigator carefully document the evidence. There appeared to be little question that Amalgamated Electric, along with its two competitors, were in violation of the antitrust laws. It was now clear to Yettkin how Murray's division had recorded such impressive profit increases over the last several years.

It took Harry Yettkin only a few hours to reach Murray by phone, a thousand miles away at a national convention of electrical suppliers. Yettkin related the conversation he had just had with the FTC investigator, and then began with the question: "Is the investigator's report factual?" Murray said it was.

UNBALANCED BOOKKEEPERS

The Central City Bank is the largest state chartered bank in the state. CCB boasts over forty-nine million dollars in deposits. It draws most of its customers from the upper-lower to upper-middle-class working groups. The bank itself is located in a predominately residential area with its main bank located in a shopping center. The main bank houses the installment, commercial, and mortgage loan departments, the personnel department, the auditing department, teller lines, safe deposit vault, and new accounts. CCB also has an Auto-Drive-in-Walk-in bank located five blocks from the main bank. The Drive-in Bank houses teller lines, safe deposit vault, new accounts, and the bookkeeping and customer service departments.

Whereas the Central City Bank opened about fifteen years ago, the Drive-in Bank has been in operation for only two years. The Drive-in Bank is managed by Dennis Oliver, an operations officer. Dennis is the only officer permanently based at the Drive-in Bank. Dennis has two supervisors working under him: Bernie Smith looks after the tellers and new accounts and Tom Stetson manages the bookkeeping and customer service departments.

Dennis Oliver was formerly in charge of the bookkeeping department before he was promoted to operations officer. Tom Stetson has been in charge of the bookkeeping department for ten months. Prior to his promotion to bookkeeping manager, Tom worked nights supervising proof operators. Tom attended college but did not graduate. He is friendly with most bank employees, but is known to be rather nervous and high strung.

The bookkeeping department is historically the bottom of the ladder in banking. Most bank employees start in this department. When you are a check filer, there is no way to go but up or out.

Tom supervises about twenty employees in all areas of bookkeeping. His subordinates are proof operators, check filers, customer service clerks, a return desk clerk, a messenger, and a central file clerk.

The operators who run proof machines must rerun each teller's work to check accuracy and then the operator routes the work through clearings. There are three proof machines in the department and the average tenure of each proof operator is two years.

Check filers are responsible for filing thousands of checks and deposits in the proper file, checking signatures for accuracy, and preparing the cancelled checks for monthly bank statements. The average tenure here is three to six months. These people must also answer phone calls from tellers who need to verify balances before cashing a check or processing a savings withdrawal. These people spend close to 50 percent of their time on the phone.

There are three women working in customer service helping customers with problems. These women have worked in the bank for at least a year and most have been in the community longer. The woman at the return desk has been in bookkeeping for nine months but is new at the desk. She is responsible for returning checks that are insufficient or not cashable for some reason. She works closely with Tom Stetson in deciding which checks are to be paid or returned to bank customers.

The woman in central file is responsible for keeping files in order. She changes addresses and cleans closed accounts out of the files and other similar tasks. She has been in central file for six months.

For the last six months Dennis Oliver has spent most of his time helping Tom in the bookkeeping department. This is because of a crack-down by top management on the large amount of write-offs and checks written with insufficient funds (N.S.F.). In the past, the bank has had a policy to pay an N.S.F. check rather than return it, except in cases where the account has a bad history. Tom has been under great pressure lately because N.S.F. checks have increased to nearly $1,500 per day.

The bookkeeping and customer service departments close at 5:00 P.M., whereas the operations areas of the bank remain open until 8:00 P.M. The night crew handles the greatest percentage of the bank's customers because most of the customers stop at the bank after work. Thus, the personnel in the new accounts area have to deal with many customers whose accounts have errors or discrepancies. Lately, many customers have complained that they are receiving the wrong checks in their bank statements. Additionally, some are complaining that they are not even receiving their monthly bank statements.

Another serious problem has arisen lately: established customers, with good accounts, are getting notices that their accounts are overdrawn. This is due to deposits not being posted. The result, needless to say, has been a growing desertion by good customers to other banks.

The personnel in the new accounts area are complaining to their supervisors about the number of unhappy customers with whom they are having to deal. Specifically, they are upset because the women in bookkeeping make the errors, but they are the ones the customers see and at whom they take out their anger.

The tellers have started to complain to their supervisors because they must wait on the phone an excessively long time when calling bookkeeping for a balance. Tellers have had to wait as long as ten minutes to cash a customer's check. This makes the teller unhappy, but more important, it inconveniences the customers.

Mrs. Carr, the personnel director, has been plagued with complaints from employees in the bookkeeping department. They have expressed displeasure with the supervision they are receiving.

Most of the jobs in the bookkeeping department require little training or background in general banking and the workers find their jobs boring and monotonous. They also complain about the workload because the department is perpetually short of help.

The employees in bookkeeping are also complaining about harassment from their supervisors. They believe they are being punished for any mistake. They perceive their supervisor's behavior to indicate that he views them as unimportant. Tom Stetson is known to have a quick temper and the workers complain about his foul language. Most of the employees in the bookkeeping department have asked to be transferred, and a few have quit.

CHANGE IN DEPARTMENT THREE

Arco, Incorporated is a computer parts company located in the middle west United States. It handles over 20 percent of the region's parts contracts. Its present plant facilities utilize an assembly area involving twenty separate departments and a highly technical area that handles the heavy construction material.

Arco is in the process of installing new plant equipment capable of cutting production time by 5 percent and increasing finished product lines by 10 percent every six months. The new facilities will revamp three of the assembly areas. Each of these three areas were notified six months ago of the new change. The members of each department were sent preliminary material on how the equipment functioned and each was instructed to attend a short meeting to be held one department at a time.

Department Three consists of one general foreman, three grade II operators, and three grade III operators. Bill is the youngest in his department, a 22-year-old grade III operator. He is married and has one child. He is liked by most, well-mannered, seldom tardy, and has missed only two days in the four years he has been with Arco. Bill has worked hard to garner a working knowledge of his department, which is one of the more complex units in the company.

The men of Department Three are on a higher pay scale than most of the other departments, and the thought of an even more complex job made things look quite promising to the department's members—a higher pay scale, more job security, and a new and interesting approach to their tasks.

But while the men of the department were anxious, they were also fearful of what was going to happen. They knew they all worked well together under the present system and the new, more complex, untried system made them eager but uneasy.

The plant supervisor and the department foreman presided over the meeting to discuss the change. They passed out up-to-date material on the equipment and explained the procedure that would be used to start production in the new department. While the starting date was six months away, full cooperation and interaction was asked. To work in Department Three, it would be necessary to attend a four week in-depth school and to complete an oral and written exam. Half of this class time would be spent actually working with the new equipment. It was explained that the department would be staffed with one foreman, two grade II operators, and two grade III operators. According to management, the two individuals who did not qualify for the department would be transferred to another unit, not necessarily requiring the same grade skill, but as close to the present pay scale as possible. Further, it was stated that seniority would make no difference, for the operation was much too complex to use it as a criterion. The most qualified would be assigned the job. It was also explained that no other departments would be qualified, for it was believed that the skills in Department Three's operation were the closest to those required in the new tasks. Each man would be given the opportunity to achieve any of the grade II or III jobs. The supervisor stated that they did not want to eliminate these jobs, but the new system was operable only with five men, and there were no other feasible alternatives.

The hot topic for the two weeks prior to the beginning of school was how the school would be run and the degree of difficulty for qualifying in the new job areas.

Bill usually eats lunch with the other men. Recently, during lunch, he opened the conversation with some angered comments concerning the breaking up of the unit and then began talking about how a change in positions might make it necessary for him to take on a part-time job. He volunteered that his wife was expecting, which put an additional financial burden on his family. His co-workers and friends followed Bill's remarks with some of their own comments on how a change to another job would affect them and their families.

The workers were becoming very conscious of each other and short quarrels and criticisms developed. The men were obviously tense. The supervisor and foreman asked the men separately what was bothering them. When Bill was asked, he replied that he was very concerned about his future and his family, especially with the new change coming. He expressed his concern over not having as much experience as the other men at his level, and his belief that he would not have a fair chance at getting assigned to one of the jobs. He felt the present unit worked effectively together and breaking up their team would affect the new group's cohesiveness and performance.

The school began on schedule and right from the beginning Bill exhibited considerable enthusiasm. His goal was clearly to pass all the qualifications and get into the new unit. He attended classes regularly, participated actively in all the sessions, and often led the discussions. He asked and answered many questions. It surprised many of his co-workers that he was so intelligent, energetic, and alert to all the ramifications caused by the change. During lunch sessions Bill always talked favorably about how the unit could still work together well as a team.

But Bill still expressed reservations concerning his chances of being accepted. The men in his department did not share his view, although they did concur that seniority could not be totally ignored.

Bill soon realized from the apprehension of his co-workers that he had been mistaken in feeling he had little chance to get a position in the new department. In fact, he recognized he was doing extremely well relative to his classmates. But the once close ties between Bill and his co-workers seemed to be slowly deteriorating.

Department members grew increasingly vocal in expressing their desire to not be the one shifted to another department, yet at the same time they did not feel good about someone having to step out of their unit, just because of some "new fangled" equipment. The discussions eventually led to the subject of Bill. The departmental consensus was that Bill might even have a chance for one of the Grade II operator slots. They began to overtly show their concern that a younger department member, with fewer years in the company, might be moving ahead and taking one of their slots. The more the subject was pursued, the deeper their resentments became.

Halfway through the schooling period, one could discern a noticeable difference in the attitude of the entire group. Almost as if there were an inner pressure retarding progress, the members of the class worked hard to make each other look good at Bill's expense. The group seemed to be more concerned with attacking Bill than pursuing the subject matter.

When the time came for the oral and written examinations and for the trial run on the equipment, all of the members of the group scored below average, except Bill. The men obviously were considerably interested in who would be let go and who would stay. The group generally reconciled their low performance to pressures in class that impeded their study. They were unable to explain Bill's superior performance.

After conducting individual discussions with each of the men, the supervisor discovered that Bill had a just reason for his exceptional work. His young daughter of two years was undergoing necessary physical therapy to correct weak muscle tone from birth. It was extremely expensive and treatment was necessary every other week for the next year or so. If he were to be demoted to another department with a reduction in his current pay scale, he would be unable to meet the bills that had already accumulated or afford future treatments for his daughter.

Management decided to extend the schooling for an additional two weeks, in order that test performance might improve. After only a day or two into the extended period, it became obvious that the participants were not responding. The result was increased pressure from the foreman and supervisor. It was made clear to the men that if they were going to take a passive role in getting into the new department, other alternatives would be used to get the area started into production. For example, other departments could be screened for approximate skills, or the tests could be eliminated and past performance used as the selection criteria. Whatever action is taken, the new equipment would have to be in full production within ninety days. At the moment, only Bill met the standards to operate the new equipment.

SIX PLANT MANAGERS IN THREE YEARS

The case writer was plant manager for Maiden Industrial Service in Omaha, Nebraska, for one year while attending night classes at the local university. Maiden Industrial is an industrial laundry, supplying towels, walk-off mats, uniforms, dust cloths, windshield cloths, and other cleaning items to customers within a 260 mile radius of Omaha.

Maiden Industrial Service is a company of four industrial laundry plants; one located in Omaha, one in Grand Island, Nebraska, and two in Texas. The company is owned exclusively by Mr. G. Temple Dexter who maintains his office at the Omaha plant. Mr. Dexter is from a wealthy Chicago family. He never finished college but was left with a sizable inheritance when his father died. Mr. Dexter took his inheritance, entered the industrial laundry business, and built the present company completely on his own.

Every plant has the same formal organization as the Omaha plant. The lines of authority run from the owner, Mr. Dexter, to the district general manager, departmental coordinator, plant manager, and section foremen. The plant manager, sales and service manager, and office manager report directly to the departmental coordinator.

The plant manager is held directly responsible for coordination of plant activities, production schedules, training of plant personnel, supplies, maintenance, record keeping, payroll, and security. The plant is divided into six sections: cotton uniform wash section, pressing section, synthetic uniform dry clean section, grease and ink towel wash aisle, regular industrial wash aisle, and packaging and assembly. Seventeen route trucks unload incoming laundry at the east docks. The articles are sorted and cleaned while they are moved through the plant and assembled for delivery at the west docks.

Five plant managers had preceded the case writer during the last two years in Omaha. The immediate predecessor had said during the writer's three week training period that there was "too much for any one man to do." He advised on concentrating in just two areas: "meet production schedules on time and correctly calculate the weekly gross pay of each plant employee for the Saturday afternoon payroll reports."

It soon became clear that the plant management problems were seriously exacerbated by three important factors: the quality of the plant employees, the routemen, and Mr. Dexter himself. The plant was intentionally located in a ghetto area for the purpose of having a ready supply of inexpensive labor. The plant manager had fifty-six employees under him. Seven employees were high school graduates. These seven were section foremen and boiler room workers whose duties included planning, section supervision, and the actual operation of the more sophisticated equipment both in their respective sections and in the boiler room. These seven men were fairly well paid and responsible in their duties. The forty-nine remaining employees were paid the minimum wage regardless of responsibilities. Thirty-eight of the forty-nine minimum wage employees were women.

A yearly turnover rate of 60 percent for plant personnel was not unusual. Many of the women would work only two or three weeks to earn pocket money and then quit. Over a third of the plant manager's time was spent training new employees and updating records because of this extremely high turnover rate.

At times, to maintain the production schedules, any warm body that walked through the front door would be hired. Even employees that had been fired only a month before had been rehired when they reapplied for employment. The employees knew that management was in desperate straits, so they took advantage of the situation. The absenteeism rate reached 25 percent on some work days that, when added to fighting, stealing, goofing-off, drinking, and drug abuse during working hours, created quite a chaotic organization. Mr. Dexter believed that the only solution to the employee problem was the increased use of automation. He would not listen to or consider other suggestions or possible solutions.

The work environment and quality of the minimum wage employees perpetuated endless related problems. So much of the plant manager's time was spent training new employees that the fulfillment of his other duties began to deteriorate. Finally, he placed more training responsibility of new employees on the section foremen who reluctantly agreed to do the best they could. However, they allowed the training to deteriorate to the level of turning loose a trainee with the other section employees and hoping the trainees would learn enough from them. This method kept the trainees out of the foreman's way, so he could concentrate on other duties, but this so-called training produced increased inefficiency and higher accident rates.

The plant manager found he now had more time to concentrate on his other duties and to scrutinize the problem areas more closely. The biggest problems were trying to meet production schedules and attempting to sort all materials according to route so that everything would be placed on the correct trucks. The routemen were always short of uniforms, towels, or some other item, and they would come directly to the plant manager for a solution. The assembly department felt they were doing fairly well if they got 90 percent to 95 percent of the routes sorted and completed; but 100 percent completion was necessary in this highly competitive service industry in order to keep customer complaints to a minimum. No route was ever completely assembled and ready for delivery on time during the one year that the case writer was with the company.

The routemen were paid a good salary plus a commission on their service contracts. This correctly motivated them to give their customers good service. The routemen wanted all of their materials clean and ready for delivery on time. Since this was rarely the case, occasional cancellation of customer contracts occurred.

The routemen felt the plant manager was responsible for any shortcomings they discovered in the assembled laundry so they came to him with their complaints. He would go through the entire plant with one routeman after another searching for missing uniforms or other material. Occasionally one would find some of the missing items, but not very often. The paperwork would be reviewed to check for repair orders, replacement orders, or cancellation orders, and occasionally in the orders would be found the reason for the missing items. A copy of these orders could have been sent to the routemen, through the sales office, but this was never done.

The only reasonable conclusion that could be reached for the constantly disappearing material was employee theft. The routemen did not seem to care why the necessary items were missing. They wanted the missing material, usually shirts and trousers, on the truck and ready for morning delivery. The routemen knew this demand was impossible for two reasons. First, the assembly department finished work every day at 3:00 P.M., and the routemen never returned to the plant before 4:30 P.M. Secondly, new stock and replacement stock could not be issued from the storeroom without signed forms from the office. The office always took two days to issue the forms authorizing replacement stock for the routes. The routemen knew of this arrangement but they frequently sought out the plant manager to avoid the procedure and be able to complete their next day route deliveries. Many of the routemen believed that if they yelled loud enough and long enough that what they needed would somehow be produced.

The antagonism increased greatly between the routemen and the plant manager when the manager accidentally discovered one of the routemen stealing uniforms and towels from the plant. He was reported and promptly fired by Mr. Dexter after a very brief investigation. From that moment on, this case writer was regarded by the routemen collectively as an enemy.

The quality and attitudes of the minimum wage employees in the plant and the demands made by the routemen created many problems for the foremen, but these problem areas were of minor significance when compared to the policies and practices of Mr. Dexter. The company was organized along formal lines of authority and responsibility, which the managers and foremen followed efficiently. Orders would come down the line and be executed promptly. But in almost every instance, the order would be revoked or corrected by Mr. Dexter personally. He rarely went through his managers in order to do this. Instead, he would storm into the plant, stand nose to nose with his object of wrath, and scream his correction or new decision at his victim. His victim could be anybody: plant manager, section foreman, or hapless employee. These almost daily scenes created such confusion and frustration that the foremen decided to ignore all office directives until they had an opportunity to talk with Mr. Dexter and receive his personal blessing.

On several occasions when Mr. Dexter was out of town, the case writer noticed that the plant functioned more smoothly and efficiently. There appeared a definite lifting of spirits among supervisors and operators alike. The case writer tried several times to make Mr. Dexter aware of the damaging effects of his random outbursts, but to no avail. Every suggestion, comment, or opinion relayed to Mr. Dexter was invariably met with his crisp stock speech. "Look, I'm paying you to be plant manager. Do the job. You got problems with employees and routemen? Take care of them. And when I see something wrong I'll handle it myself. So I'm actually helping you do your job. So don't complain."

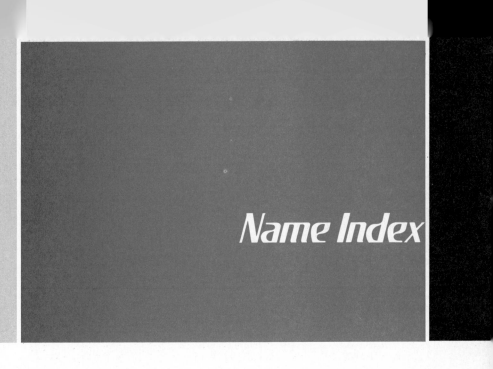

Name Index

455

Subject Index

Standards, 72, 377
Star Wars, 399
State of New York's Commerce Department, 283
Statistics, 51
Strategic plans, 131-32
Strategy:
defined, 158-60
as nonprogrammed decision guides, 78
in practice, 160
types of, 161-67
Structural change, 150-51
Structural variable, altering the, 365
Style vs. substance, 115
Sunset legislation, 409
Superordinate goals, 363-64
Supersonic transport (SST), 404-5
Supervision, 332-38
Survey feedback, 347-48
Survival, objective of, 138
Synectics, 81
Synergy, 158
Systems movement, 44-45

Tall structures, 200-201
Task approach, 43
Task forces, 273-74
Task structure, 327-28
Task technology, 47-48

Tavistock group, 209-10
Team building, 347-48
Technological conditions, forecasting, 148
Technology, 208-14, 217-18
Temporary help services, as recruiting source, 257
Tests in selection, 261-62
Texas Instruments, 162
Theories "X" and "Y", 296-97
Theory vs. practice, 18-19, 119-20
Third Wave study, 238-39
Time:
control of, 383
dimension in forecasts, 151-53
Traditional view of authority, 224
Training, 27-29
Trait theories of leadership, 320-21
Transactional analysis (TA), 353-54
Transcendental meditation (TM), 355
Transferability of administrators, 19-23
Type I error, 260
Type II error, 260

Uncertainty conditions, 90-92, 207-8

U.S. Office of Management and Budget (OMB), 183-84
Unity of command, 206-7
Unsolicited applicants, 258
Up the Organization, 99-100

Valance, 301
Values:
anti-conflict, 366-67
in decision-making, 26-27
efficiency, 430-31
Volkswagen of America, 13
Volvo experiment, 277-78

Waiting-line theory, 82
Wealth of Nations, 196
Westinghouse Electric Corporation, 12, 164
Weyerhauser Company, 177-78
Winning by Intimidation, 100-102
Women in administration, 429
Work modules, 272-73

Zero-base budgeting (ZBB), 407-8
Zone of indifference, 225